Teaching Self-Det...
to Students with Disabilities

Teaching Self-Determination to Students with Disabilities

Basic Skills for Successful Transition

by

Michael L. Wehmeyer, Ph.D.
The Arc National Headquarters
Arlington, Texas

and

Martin Agran, Ph.D.
Utah State University
Logan

and

Carolyn Hughes, Ph.D.
Vanderbilt University
Nashville, Tennessee

·P A U L·H·
BROOKES
PUBLISHING Co

Baltimore • London • Toronto • Sydney

Paul H. Brookes Publishing Co.
Post Office Box 10624
Baltimore, Maryland 21285-0624

www.brookespublishing.com

Second printing, October 1999.
Third printing, March 2001.
Typeset by PRO-Image Corporation, Techna-Type Division, York, Pennsylvania.
Manufactured in the United States of America by
Versa Press, East Peoria, Illinois.

All cases in this book are completely fictional. Any similarity to actual individuals or circumstances is coincidental, and no implications should be inferred. The one exception is the case study of Bill Crane, who has given permission for release of his real name and story.

Permission to reprint the following material is gratefully acknowledged:
Pages 25–47: Allen, J. (1996). A conversation with cerebral palsy. In L.E. Powers, G.H.S. Singer, and J. Sowers (Eds.), *On the road to autonomy: Promoting Self-competence in children and youth with disabilities.* Baltimore: Paul H. Brookes Publishing Co.; reprinted by permission.

Library of Congress Cataloging-in-Publication Data

Wehmeyer, Michael L.
    Teaching self-determination to students with disabilities : basic skills for successful transition / Michael L. Wehmeyer, Martin Agran & Carolyn Hughes.
      p.   cm.
    Includes bibliographical references and index.
    ISBN 1-55766-302-5
    1. Handicapped students—Education—United States.   2. Autonomy (Psychology)—United States.   3. Self-culture—United States.   4. Handicapped youth—Services for—United States.   5. School-to-work transition—United States.
I. Agran, Martin.   II. Hughes, Carolyn.   III. Title.
LC4031.W438   1998
371.91—dc21   97-22271
                                                       CIP

British Library Cataloguing in Publication data are available from the British Library.

Contents

About the Authors

Michael L. Wehmeyer, Ph.D., is an assistant director in the Department of Research and Program Services at The Arc National Headquarters in Arlington, Texas. Dr. Wehmeyer received his Ph.D. in human development and communication sciences from The University of Texas at Dallas and holds undergraduate and graduate degrees in special education. In 1987, Dr. Wehmeyer was a Rotary Foundation Teacher of the Handicapped Fellow to the University of Sussex, England, where he received an M.Sc. in experimental psychology. Prior to joining The Arc, Dr. Wehmeyer taught adolescents with severe, multiple disabilities in several public and private schools and was a behavioral psychologist for the Texas Department of Mental Health and Mental Retardation. Dr. Wehmeyer has conducted numerous federally funded projects related to self-determination and has published widely in the area of self-determination for individuals with cognitive disabilities. He is the co-editor of *Self-Determination Across the Life Span: Independence and Choice for People with Disabilities* (Paul H. Brookes Publishing Co., 1996) and is on the editorial board for the journal, *Career Development for Exceptional Individuals.*

Martin Agran, Ph.D., is a professor in the Department of Special Education and Rehabilitation and Chair of the Severe Disabilities Personnel Preparation Program at Utah State University in Logan. Dr. Agran received his Ph.D. in special education in 1984 from the University of Illinois at Urbana-Champaign, with areas of emphasis in the education of students with moderate and severe disabilities, transition and employment preparation, and applied behavior analysis. Dr. Agran was a 1991 Fulbright Scholar to Czechoslovakia. He has conducted research in the areas of self-management, student-directed learning, and promotion of health and safety. He has published extensively in professional journals in these areas and was co-editor of the book, *Promoting Health and Safety: Skills for Independent Living* (Paul H. Brookes Publishing Co., 1994). He has served on the editorial boards of several journals, including *Education and Training in Mental Retardation and Development Disabilities, Research in Developmental Disabilities,* and the *Journal of The Association for Persons with Severe Handicaps.*

Carolyn Hughes, Ph.D., is an associate professor in the Department of Special Education at Vanderbilt University in Nashville, Tennessee. In 1990, she received her Ph.D. in special education from the University of Illinois at Urbana-Champaign, specializing in the areas of secondary transition, supported employment, and severe disabilities. At Vanderbilt, Dr. Hughes teaches courses on severe disabilities, behavior management, and community and employment integration for individuals with disabilities. She has published widely in the areas of self-instruction; support management for the transition from school to adult life; and the social integration of youth and adults with disabilities into school, work, and the community. Dr. Hughes serves as an associate editor for the *Journal of The Association for Persons with Severe Handicaps* and is a consulting editor for the journals *Education and Training in Mental Retardation and Developmental Disabilities, Career Development for Exceptional Individuals,* and the *American Journal on Mental Retardation.*

Foreword

We live in an era in which individual freedom, choice, and control over one's life are more valuable than ever. The power that comes with individual choices is perceived by most to be among the most important values in American society. Although this belief has always been a trademark of American life, it does seem that in the 1990s there has been an even greater emphasis placed on choices by both the public and private sectors of our society. These values permeate the mass media, coming to us from business and industry in efforts to persuade consumers to purchase products. Wide selections among product lines are seen by many people as more valuable than 1) product quality, 2) speed of service, 3) price, and even 4) availability of the product or the service. One of the reasons for the large upsurge in mail-order companies and discount warehouse outlets is the increased emphasis on breadth of choice.

The issues of choice and individual control have been manifested more than ever within varying political philosophies in the United States. Some people believe that government at all levels, especially the federal government, should provide only minimal help and intervention and that anything further is an intrusion. Choice, individual control, and government intervention will continue to be debated issues. Regulatory control over airlines, eligibility for holding a driver's license, health standards for food cleanliness, as well as literally hundreds of other areas, all require some form of protection and control for the unsuspecting public, despite the call from many people for limited government involvement in their lives.

The movement to greater individual control and choice has not gone unnoticed by people with disabilities, who historically have been among the most disenfranchised and devalued populations in the world. Most people with disabilities, especially those with any level of significant disability, have been at the "back of the bus" for much of their lives. One very distinguishing characteristic between people with and without disabilities is the difference in offered choices. Historically, the number of choices available to most people with disabilities has been very limited, and their ability to exercise self-determination with any level of integrity certainly has been minimal. It is difficult for people with disabilities to choose a career, decide on apprenticeship training in an unfamiliar industry, or pick a work shift if the only work-related choices they have been exposed to are an adult activity center or a sheltered workshop. It is difficult for people with disabilities to determine whether they want to take community college courses, join the school photography club, or participate in general education class lessons if they have been assigned to a segregated school that enrolls only children with disabilities. It is difficult for people with disabilities to choose a form of transportation to get around the community, pick a theater to see the latest movie, or decide on a mall to go shopping if they live in an institution 60 miles away from town. It is difficult for people with disabilities to develop friendships with people without disabilities and to get involved in community activities if their only recreational outlet is Special Olympics. These are examples of restrictions in the lives of thousands of people with disabilities, and they do not know how to break out of these shackles or even become aware that another world is available.

With the passage of the Americans with Disabilities Act (ADA) of 1990 (PL 101-336), the 1990s ushered in a new spirit of hope for the self-determination of America's children, teenagers, and adults with disabilities. The ADA provides a statutory framework and an implicit moral call for every citizen with a disability to exercise his or her rights of self-determination and individual choice. For people with disabilities, there is little doubt that the 1990s will become known as a decade characterized by self-determination, much like the 1980s were characterized by community living and community-based employment and the 1970s were characterized by deinstitutionalization and rights to special education.

There was a time that self-determination was, in many ways, nothing more than a loosely consolidated set of well-meaning philosophies that were used to undergird person-centered planning and other more consumer-oriented approaches to educational and adult services planning. However, with the leadership of writers such as Michael L. Wehmeyer, Martin Agran, and Carolyn Hughes, there has been a pronounced shift from self-determination as a philosophical concept to, in fact, an instructional strategy associated with specific curriculum targets. An increasing number of transition plans for youth with disabilities are reflecting self-determination needs. An increasing number of writers, as well as direct services practitioners who are "in the trenches" and able to see firsthand the positive results of teaching self-determination skills, are finally paying attention to self-determination as not only a philosophical theme but also a viable curriculum and instructional area for individuals with disabilities.

It is important to note that the three authors of this book have helped pave the way toward the acceptance and use of self-determination with a long and distinguished history of self-determination and self-instruction research. This book is an outstanding culmination of the authors' earlier articles, curricula, and books that have been written since the mid-1980s. This book is a required reading for all those who are interested in how to implement self-determination programs and how best to teach self-determination skills to individuals with disabilities. The book goes far beyond a philosophical discussion of choice and control and goes well beyond efforts at assessment; instead, it brings the whole self-determination instructional package together into a very easy-to-read and easy-to-understand model for direct service practitioners.

In the 1960s and 1970s, Albert Bandura was prominent in social learning; in the 1970s and 1980s, researchers such as Thoresen and Mahoney, as well as Meichenbaum, wrote eloquently on the positive attributes of social learning, such as modeling, cognitive reinforcement, and imitation. This line of research led to many studies in the areas of self-instruction and self-management, which are often confused with the concept of self-determination. It is important to note that self-determination takes this field of study to a higher level. The foundations of modeling, social learning, cognitive training, and self-management are important stepping stones for a truly self-determined individual; but without capturing the full spirit and philosophy developed by Wehmeyer and his colleagues, one is missing the entire contribution of this area.

Self-determination—control over one's life and choices—is the critical difference separating people with disabilities from those without disabilities. People with disabilities are frequently the objects of discrimination and often have not been made aware of their options or choices within the community. The community, of course, involves school, work, leisure, personal relationships, financial situations, and so forth. This book has utility for *all* students with disabilities, from those individuals with the most severe disabilities to individuals with mild disabilities. The approach taken is comprehensive; the use of chapter objectives at the beginning of each chapter, followed by a number of helpful tables and charts, helps make this a very user-friendly book. Perhaps one of the strongest features of this book is the support given from high-quality empirical research that the authors have compiled over the years. The authors have translated their research findings, as well as the findings of others who have been engaged in the social learning and self-instructional area for several decades, into a highly valuable compendium of knowledge on self-determination. This is the only book of which I am aware that looks specifically at teaching self-determination skills to students with disabilities and leaves ample room for expanding into greater depth and detail in the years ahead.

Teaching self-determination in schools to children at an early age and following through with a longitudinal pattern of instruction as they grow into adults is very important to people with disabilities because once they are older, it will be more difficult to develop self-determination skills and strategies. This book does a wonderful job of delineating types of self-determination strategies and explaining how effective they can be. It is a required reading for all special educators.

Paul Wehman, B.B.A., M.S., Ph.D.
Director
Virginia Commonwealth University
Rehabilitation Research and Training Center on Supported Employment
Richmond

REFERENCES

Americans with Disabilities Act (ADA) of 1990, PL 101-336, 42 U.S.C. §§ 12101 *et seq.*

Preface

You've just arrived at JFK airport in New York City for your first visit to the "Big Apple!" You've rented a compact car, and you're ready to drive to your hotel. The problem confronting you at the moment is that you know basically where your hotel is, but you don't know how to get there. What you need are strategies to resolve your problem. So, you dig in the glove compartment, find a map of the city of New York, look up the address, and chart your course. Or, you pull up alongside a taxi driver waiting in line for his next fare and ask him because all the cabbies have to know where the hotels are located. Strategies. Fortunately for you, you have two of them to get you to your hotel—use a map or ask directions. Strategies. This text is a book of strategies, instructional methods, and materials that will enable you to teach self-determination skills to youth with disabilities.

There is a growing recognition that teaching students to become self-determined young adults is an important transition-related objective. Much of this recognition was spurred by a series of U.S. Department of Education grants that funded model demonstration projects to promote self-determination (Ward, 1996; Ward & Kohler, 1996). These projects developed a wide array of instructional materials and methods that could be used to promote self-determination. In addition, however, these model demonstration projects and federally funded research and assessment-development projects documented the complexity of promoting self-determination. This complexity is evident when one examines a list of characteristics of self-determined individuals that have been proposed across multiple models or frameworks of self-determination. Self-determined people

- Initiate events in their lives and take action when needed
- Are aware of personal preferences and interests
- Are aware of and can differentiate between their wants and needs
- Make choices based on preferences, interests, wants, and needs
- Consider multiple options and consequences for decisions
- Make decisions based on these considerations
- Evaluate the efficacy of their decisions based on the outcomes of previous decisions and revise future decisions accordingly
- Set and strive for personal goals
- Define and approach problems in a systematic, if not always successful, manner

- Strive for independence, while recognizing their interdependence with others in their world
- Advocate on their own behalf when deemed appropriate
- Possess a knowledge and understanding of their own personal strengths and weaknesses
- Apply this knowledge and understanding to maximize their quality of life
- Self-regulate their behavior
- Are persistent toward the achievement of preferred goals and objectives and can use negotiation, compromise, and persuasion to reach these goals
- Hold positive beliefs about their ability to act in a situation and believe that if they do act, preferred outcomes will occur
- Are self-confident and proud of their achievements
- Can communicate wants and needs to others
- Are creative in their response to situations

Developing a single curriculum that deals with all these issues seems like a daunting task. Most such efforts make no attempt to teach each self-determination skill to mastery, but instead introduce the skills, stress their importance, and rely on teachers to augment instruction in areas that need attention. Fortunately, there are a significant number of educational strategies, materials, and approaches that have been developed, validated, and applied to promote individual self-determination skills, such as goal setting or decision making, which lead to self-determination and can either augment a specific curriculum or, in conjunction with other skills-development efforts, become the curriculum. Some of these strategies have been developed for use with students with disabilities, whereas others represent recommended practices in general education that have not been applied to students with special learning needs, although there is no theoretical reason these strategies should not be useful with this population. This book provides a comprehensive, practice-oriented overview and description of these practices. To this extent, it is part textbook and part curriculum.

The text is consciously organized around a framework of self-determination as an educational outcome, which is described in the first chapter. This framework proposes that self-determined behavior reflects four essential characteristics (i.e., autonomy, self-regulation, psychological empowerment, and self-realization), which emerge as students develop or acquire specific skills and beliefs, referred to as the component elements of self-determined behavior. Each section of the book focuses on one specific essential characteristic, and each chapter of the book identifies strategies, methods, and materials to promote one or more of the component elements.

SECTION I: INTRODUCTION

The first section provides an introduction to self-determination and transition. This section consists of three chapters introducing self-determination as an educational outcome that is critical for students with disabilities if they are to leave school as capable and self-sufficient young adults. The first and second chapters in this section introduce self-determination as an educational outcome, describe essential characteristics of self-determined behavior and component elements critical to the development of self-determination, discuss the historical roots of self-determination, and examine the impetus for the educational focus on self-determination. The third chapter in this section overviews transition services, the federal transition requirements, and recommended practices in transition for youth with disabilities; it also discusses the relationship between self-determination and transition.

SECTION II: PROMOTING AUTONOMOUS BEHAVIOR

One essential characteristic of self-determined behavior is acting autonomously. This implies that self-determined people act in an independent manner, free from undue interference or influence from other people and on the basis of personal beliefs, values, interests, and abilities. Independent functioning refers to 1) actions that involve self and family-care activities, such as assuming household chores, fulfilling work and other responsibilities, or maintaining personal grooming activities; and 2) managing one's interactions with the environment, such as using community resources (e.g., library, post office) or interacting with service providers (e.g., store clerks, disability service providers). Acting on the basis of personal beliefs, values, and preferences encompasses the skills of identifying preferences and making choices and applying these skills in areas such as leisure and recreational time, postsecondary education, career decision making, or social interactions. The chapters in the second section, Promoting Autonomous Behavior, provide hands-on instructional strategies to promote independence skills, teach students important risk-taking and safety skills, and enable learners to be more effective choice and decision makers and identify preferences, interests, and abilities.

SECTION III: PROMOTING SELF-REGULATED BEHAVIOR

Another characteristic of self-determined behavior is that it is self-regulated. That is, self-determined people act on their environment based on an evaluation of the need for action (i.e., an examination of the individual's response repertoire to identify an appropriate action); use information in that environment to evaluate the efficacy of their action, maintain the action, or correct the action; and, eventually, decide on the utility of the action. Three other topics contribute to the individual's capacity to act in a self-regulated manner: their problem-solving capacities, their ability to identify and set goals, and their ability to act based on these goals. The chapters in the third section, Promoting Self-Regulated Behavior, introduce strategies to teach students with disabilities self-observation, self-evaluation, and self-reinforcement skills; problem solving in applied settings and social problem solving; and goal setting and attainment skills.

SECTION IV: PROMOTING SELF-ADVOCACY AND LEADERSHIP SKILLS

One component of self-regulated behavior that is very important for people with disabilities is the development and use of self-advocacy and leadership skills. In a very real sense, in order for people with disabilities to move into the mainstream of community life, they must possess the skills to stand up for their rights, communicate effectively and assertively, learn to negotiate and compromise, and become effective leaders. The fourth section, Promoting Self-Advocacy and Leadership Skills, overviews the teaching strategies that can be employed to enable learners with disabilities to reach these outcomes and take greater control of and responsibility for their lives. This section includes a chapter discussing student involvement in transition planning as a means of promoting self-advocacy.

SECTION V: PROMOTING SELF-REALIZATION AND PSYCHOLOGICAL EMPOWERMENT

The final two characteristics of self-determined behavior involve students' beliefs about themselves (i.e., their capacities), and their interactions with the environment. Although these characteristics reflect student beliefs about themselves, these perceptions are enhanced by the acquisition of a number of skills. For students to become self-aware, they need to learn about physical and psychological needs, how to meet these needs, how their behavior affects other people, and other skill development areas. The fifth section, Promoting Self-Realization and Psychological Empowerment, addresses how teachers can provide instruction that leads to students acquiring self-realization and psychological empowerment.

SECTION VI: SUMMARY AND CONCLUSIONS

The final section returns to the topic of the transition period, which is an important time to address self-determination skill areas for students with disabilities. This section provides a description of strategies and methods that will enable teachers to promote self-determination through all phases of the transition process.

REFERENCES

Ward, M.J. (1996). Coming of age in the age of self-determination: A historical and personal perspective. In D.J. Sands & M.L. Wehmeyer (Eds.), *Self-determination across the life span: Independence and choice for people with disabilities* (pp. 3–16). Baltimore: Paul H. Brookes Publishing Co.

Ward, M.J., & Kohler, P.D. (1996). Teaching self-determination: Content and process. In L.E. Powers, G.H.S. Singer, & J. Sowers (Eds.), *On the road to autonomy: Promoting self-competence in children and youth with disabilities* (pp. 275–290). Baltimore: Paul H. Brookes Publishing Co.

Acknowledgments

We would like to acknowledge the editorial and production staff at Paul H. Brookes Publishing Co., particularly Theresa Donnelly, editorial director, and Scott Beeler, our editor on this text. We appreciate their hard work, support, assistance, and, perhaps most important, their patience and forbearance! We are also deeply appreciative to Dr. Paul Wehman for contributing the foreword to the book. Our research and programmatic efforts in the area of self-determination have benefited from our interactions with many colleagues, and we would like to acknowledge the contributions of the following individuals: Sue Eades, Kathy Kelchner, Dr. Susan Palmer, Michelle Schwartz, and Margaret Lawrence (MW); Kimberly Snow, Jayne Swaner, and Susan Nash (MA); Beth Clark, Joy Godshall, Bogseon Hwang, Jin-Ho Kim, and McGavock High School (CH).

Teaching Self-Determination to Students with Disabilities

SECTION I

Introduction

CHAPTER 1

Self-Determination as an Education and Transition Outcome

After reading this chapter, you will be able to

1. Identify the four essential characteristics of self-determined behavior

2. Identify component elements of self-determined behavior and discuss specific learning experiences to foster the acquisition of each component element

3. Cite seven ways to effectively incorporate choice making (elementary level) and decision making (secondary level) into instructional activities

4. Discuss the importance of student participation in the decision-making process, especially as related to educational planning

KEY TERMS

1. Behavioral autonomy
2. Choice making
3. Decision making
4. Goal attainment
5. Goal setting
6. Independence
7. Internal locus of control
8. Outcome expectations
9. Problem solving
10. Psychological empowerment
11. Self-advocacy
12. Self-determination
13. Self-efficacy
14. Self-realization
15. Self-regulated behavior
16. Transition services

Robert could hardly believe that in 2 weeks he would be graduating from Nathan Hale Senior High School. Sure, he was excited...who wouldn't be! No more classes...no more having to get up early...no more teachers bossing him around! It all sounded pretty good. All of his friends were busy making plans—plans to celebrate their graduation, plans to get a job, or plans to go on to college or the local technical school. Robert didn't even want to think about all that! In fact his mom was planning his graduation party, and she was going to get the invitations all addressed and sent out.

One reason he didn't like to think about all these plans was that when he did, it only made him worried. Oh, he didn't have to worry about a place to live in 2 weeks. His parents were remodeling and redecorating his room as a graduation present so he would feel more like an adult—you know, take out the kid stuff and add adult stuff like a desk. He wasn't too keen on living at home, but he didn't really know where else to live.

The thing is, even with a new desk and a new room, he didn't really feel like an adult. Sure, he was a registered voter—someone had come out to his class during the year when they were studying elections and politics and had registered everyone. He would probably vote when his parents did. He had thought about getting a job. His parents had heard there would be an opening at the convenience store right down the block, sweeping and straightening the shelves. His teacher, who thinks Robert enjoys being outdoors, told him about a job in her neighborhood delivering fliers door to door. Robert thinks he might like to try working in the auto body shop a block over, but he's not sure how to go about getting a job there or even what types of jobs they have. In the meantime, his parents had picked up an application from the convenience store and said they would fill it out and take him to talk to the store manager. It would be easy enough to have them take him back and forth to work all the time, and it would give him something to do. It's just that...well, he thought stocking shelves sounded boring.

Only 2 weeks...Robert had liked school, really. He kind of hated to see it end if the truth were to be told. At least he liked hanging around with his friends and going to ball games. That was another reason he didn't like to think about the future...it seemed pretty empty.

Rebecca could hardly believe that in 2 weeks she would be graduating from Nathan Hale Senior High School. Those 2 weeks might be the busiest 2 weeks of her life! First, there were all the decisions about the graduation party she was hosting—who to invite, where to have it, and what to eat? On top of that, she had a second interview with the senior data entry manager at Greenbelt Technologies. Rebecca had been working part time at the convenience store for the last year, stocking shelves and performing general maintenance. The hours had fit her schedule and she could earn some extra cash, so that job had been fine for then. However, she knew that she didn't want to spend much more time stocking shelves! Too boring! She had been talking with some of her teachers and counselors as well as a person from the career guidance office at the community college; and she had decided that a job working with computers would be something she would be good at, that she would like, and at which she could make enough money to live on her own. The data entry job for which she was interviewing would be a good way to get some experience in the field while she took some courses at the community college.

It was important to Rebecca to get a good job for a lot of reasons. First, she wanted to be independent. She didn't like relying on others, like her parents, to take care of her. Second, she wanted to move away from home as soon as she could. Rebecca and her friend Liz had been planning to share an apartment together as soon as they had enough for the deposit and could afford the monthly payment. Rebecca figured that would be in about 6 months. It seemed like a long time, but Rebecca knew that she needed to save some money for a deposit, pay for some of her school (her folks were going to lend a hand there!), and find some inexpensive furniture before she could move out. The data entry job would help with that too because it paid a lot more than the convenience store.

Only 2 weeks...Rebecca had liked school...all her friends, the different sports activities, and the clubs to which she belonged. She would hate to see that end. But, there were a lot of exciting things happening in her life now! Somehow, she didn't think she was going to miss high school all that much!

In every school in this country, a few children succeed regardless of the instruction they receive. Teachers identify these students early, because they have purpose in their lives. They know what they like, what they can do, what they want and how to get it. They are self-determined. (Mithaug, 1991, p. 1)

What are the purpose and goal of education? Why do children spend at least 12 years in school? Although there may be no single answer to these questions that would gain universal support, there are some outcomes that most people would agree are part of the purpose of the educational process. Sarason (1990) suggested that one such outcome is that education should "produce responsible, self-sufficient citizens who possess the self-esteem, initiative, skills and wisdom to continue individual growth and pursue knowledge" (p. 163).

Unfortunately, far too many students with disabilities do not become self-sufficient citizens. Instead, like Robert, they drift along without a purpose and without direction. Studies show conclusively that important adult outcomes, such as employment, independent living, and community integration, are much less positive for youth with disabilities than families, educators, and students themselves would desire (Chadsey-Rusch, Rusch, & O'Reilly, 1991). Why have students with disabilities not succeeded once they leave school? Why are there not more graduates like Rebecca instead of like Robert? Many reasons are possible. One of these reasons, however, is that the educational process has not adequately prepared students with special learning needs to become self-sufficient citizens. Students have not been taught to be self-determined young people. Martin, Marshall, Maxson, and Jerman put it this way:

If students floated in life jackets for 12 years, would they be expected to swim if the jackets were suddenly jerked away? Probably not. The situation is similar for students receiving special education services. All too often these students are not taught how to self-manage their own lives before they are thrust into the cold water of post-school reality. (1993, p. 4)

Educators are beginning to understand that self-determination is an important educational outcome for learners with and without disabilities. Also, they are recognizing that many students do not become self-determined unless they receive direct instruction in self-determination skills and experience repeated opportunities to practice these skills. This instructional emphasis is particularly important for transition-age students because the purpose of transition services is to prepare youth for adulthood. Wehman (1993) identified one short-coming of the earliest transition models as their lack of focus on student choice, family choice, and self-determination.

Halloran (1993) identified self-determination as the "ultimate goal of education" (p. 214). If students with disabilities are to become more self-sufficient and better able to manage their own lives and if they are to succeed as adults, promoting self-determination skills must become a critical part of transition services. As such, educators need to determine what is "teachable" about self-determination and to identify what they can do to foster self-determination for young people.

WHAT IS SELF-DETERMINATION?

Martin and Marshall summarized the "evolving definition of self-determination in the special education literature" as describing individuals who

> know how to choose—they know what they want and how to get it. From an aware-ness of personal needs, self-determined individuals choose goals, then doggedly pursue them. This involves asserting an individual's presence, making his or her needs known, evaluating progress toward meeting goals, adjusting performance and creating unique approaches to solve problems. (1995, p. 147)

As illustrated by this description, the actions of self-determined people enable them to fulfill roles typically associated with adulthood. Wehmeyer (1992, 1996) described self-determination as an educational outcome, defining it as "acting as the primary causal agent in one's life and making choices and decisions regarding one's quality of life free from undue external influence or interference" (1996, p. 24). A *causal agent* is someone who makes or causes things to happen in his or her life. Self-determined people, therefore, act as the causal agents in their lives.

A mistaken belief is that being self-determined is the same as having complete control over all of one's choices and decisions. Deci and Ryan (1985) pointed out that what is important to self-determination is not absolute control but being the causal agent in decisions and choices that have an impact on one's life. One may choose to give up actual control to others who are better able or more qualified to act, but it remains the individual's decision to grant that control. Thus, a self-determined person can choose a personal care attendant to perform daily care activities, an accountant to complete his or her annual tax form, or a surgeon to be in charge of his or her knee operation! Although in many cases control over decisions and choices is exactly what is called for, absolute control is not a prerequisite for self-determined behavior.

People who consistently engage in self-determined actions can be described as self-determined, where "self-determined" refers to a *dispositional characteristic.* Dispositional characteristics are used to describe people whose actions and behaviors are consistent across time and settings. Within this definitional framework, self-determined behavior refers to actions that are identified by four essential characteristics: 1) the person acted *autonomously,* 2) the behavior(s) are *self-regulated,* 3) the person initiated and responded to the event(s) in a *psychologically empowered* manner, and 4) the person acted in a *self-realizing* manner. Figure 1 illustrates the relationship among these four essential characteristics.

Self-determination emerges across the life span as children and adolescents learn skills and develop attitudes that enable them to become causal agents in their own lives. These attitudes and abilities are the *component elements* of self-determination, and it is at this level of the definitional framework that instructional emphasis should occur.

Essential Characteristics of Self-Determined Behavior

People who are self-determined act autonomously, self-regulate their behavior, and are psychologically empowered and self-realizing. The term *essential characteristics* means that an individual's actions must reflect, to some degree, each of the four characteristics. Age, opportunity, capacity, and circumstances may have an impact on the degree to which any of the essential characteristics are present; and, as such, the relative self-determination expressed by an individual will likely vary, sometimes over time and other times across environments. Nonetheless, each of these essential elements must be present; each characteristic is necessary to the whole but insufficient by itself to represent self-determined behavior.

Behavioral Autonomy   Sigafoos, Feinstein, Damond, and Reiss (1988) stated that "human development involves a progression from dependence on others for care and guidance to self-care and self-direction" (p. 432). The outcome of this progression is autonomous functioning or, when describing the actions of individuals achieving this outcome, behavioral autonomy. Lewis and Taymans defined autonomy as

a complex concept which involves emotional separation from parents, the development of a sense of personal control over one's life, the establishment of a personal value system and the ability to execute behavioral tasks which are needed in the adult world. (1992, p. 37)

Within the definitional framework for self-determined behavior, a behavior is autonomous if the person acts according to his or her own preferences, in-

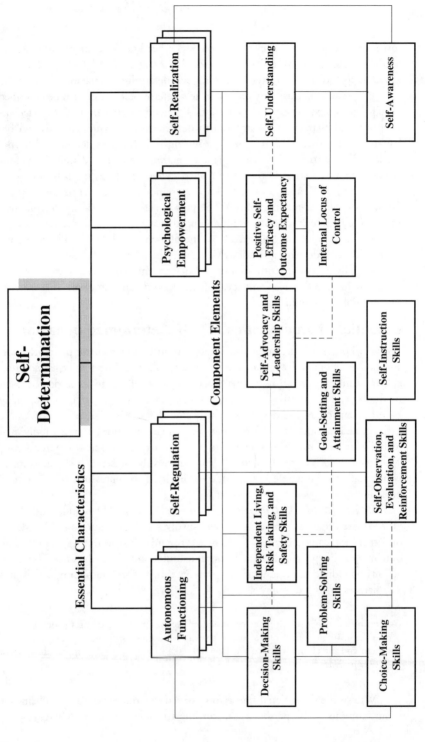

Figure 1.   Essential characteristics of self-determination and their component elements. (———— = direct relationship; -------- = indirect relationship.)

terests, and/or abilities and in an independent manner, free from undue external influence or interference.

Sigafoos and colleagues (1988) identified four behavioral categories contributing to autonomous functioning: self-care/family-care activities, management activities, recreational/leisure activities, and social/vocational activities. Self-care/family-care activities include routine personal care and family-oriented functions, such as preparing meals, caring for possessions, performing household chores, shopping, doing home repairs, and performing other activities of daily living. Management activities refer to the degree to which a person handles interactions with the environment independently. These activities involve the use of community resources and the fulfillment of personal obligations and responsibilities. Recreational activities reflecting behavioral autonomy are not specific actions per se but rather the degree to which an individual uses personal preferences and interests to choose to engage in such activities. Likewise, social and vocational activities include social involvement, vocational activities, and the degree to which personal preferences and interests are applied in these areas.

Autonomous behavior should not be confused with self-centered or selfish behavior. Although people often act according to personal interests, occasions arise when one must act in ways that do not reflect specific interests. In such cases one's preference may be to act in a manner that does not directly reflect a specific interest if that is prudent or useful. Likewise, most people cannot be viewed as strictly independent, acting alone and with no external influences. The field of disability has moved toward recognizing interdependence as a desirable outcome because all people are influenced by others, from family members to strangers, on a daily basis. Contextual and social variables will define for each person an "acceptable" level of interference and influence.

Self-Regulated Behavior   Whitman defined self-regulation as

> a complex response system that enables individuals to examine their environments and their repertoires of responses for coping with those environments to make decisions about how to act, to act, to evaluate the desirability of the outcomes of the action, and to revise their plans as necessary. (1990, p. 373)

Self-regulated behaviors include self-management strategies (including self-monitoring, self-instruction, self-evaluation, and self-reinforcement), goal setting and attainment behaviors, problem-solving behaviors, and observational learning strategies, all of which students need to learn to become the causal agent in their lives (Agran, 1997).

Acting in a Psychologically Empowered Manner   Psychological empowerment is a term referring to the multiple dimensions of perceived control, including the domains of personality (locus of control), cognition (personal efficacy), and motivation (outcome expectations) (Zimmerman, 1990). Essentially, people acting in a psychologically empowered manner do so on the basis of a belief that 1) they have control over circumstances that are important to them (internal locus of control); 2) they possess the skills necessary to achieve desired outcomes (self-efficacy); and 3) if they choose to apply those skills, the identified outcomes will result (outcome expectations).

Researchers in self-determination have stressed that acting in a self-determined manner requires a combination of abilities and attitudes (Ward, 1988; Wehmeyer, 1992). Most people can readily identify someone who possesses some of these skills but not others. A person who knows an effective decision-making strategy (ability) but who does not believe that if he or she applies that strategy he or she will achieve the desired outcomes (attitude) is not likely to make decisions. Likewise, someone who believes that he or she is effective and can influence outcomes by acting but who lacks the requisite decision-making skills may be more likely to act but no more likely to come to a satisfactory outcome from that action.

The inclusion of psychological empowerment and self-realization as essential elements for self-determined behavior illustrates the importance of both cognitive and behavioral contributions to this definitional framework. Bandura (1977b) argued that a "theory of human behavior cannot afford to neglect symbolic activities" (p. 13). Agran (1997) noted the importance of cognitive behaviors in achieving self-regulation, including the use of metacognitive, self-instructional, self-reinforcement, and observational learning strategies. Such cognitive aspects of self-determined behavior are not easily observed, but they are essential if someone is to become self-determined.

Self-Realization   Self-determined people are self-realizing in that they use a comprehensive, and reasonably accurate, knowledge of themselves and their strengths and limitations to act in such a manner as to capitalize on this knowledge. This self-knowledge and self-understanding is formed through experience with and interpretation of one's environment and is influenced by evaluations of significant others, reinforcement, and attributions of one's own behavior.

Validating the Definitional Framework

To test the validity of the definitional framework of self-determination just presented, Wehmeyer and colleagues interviewed more than 400 adults with mental retardation and developmental disabilities, using self-report measures of self-determined behavior and each of the essential characteristics (Wehmeyer, Kelchner, & Richards, 1995, 1996). The sample was divided into two groups: people who scored high on the self-determination measure and those who scored low. These groups were then compared based on their self-determination scores on measures of each essential characteristic. Measures used included assessments of behavioral autonomy and life choices (autonomy); social problem solving and goal setting (self-regulation); locus of control, self-efficacy, and outcome expectancy (psychological empowerment); and self-awareness/self-knowledge (self-realization). As Figure 2 illustrates, scores from measures of each of the four essential characteristics differed significantly based on the self-determination grouping. In each case, individuals who were in the high self-determination group held more positive beliefs or exhibited more adaptive behaviors. Measures of behavioral autonomy and self-regulation were particularly potent predictors of self-determination status.

Component Elements of Self-Determined Behavior

The essential characteristics that define self-determined behavior emerge through the development and acquisition of multiple, interrelated component elements. Table 1 lists these elements and identifies chapters in this text that describe instructional strategies to promote their development and acquisition. Although not intended as an exhaustive list, these component elements are particularly important to the emergence of self-determined behavior. The remainder of this chapter provides an introduction to each of the component elements so that subsequent chapters can focus on effective practices to promote each outcome.

Each of these component elements has a unique developmental course or is acquired through specific learning experiences (Doll, Sands, Wehmeyer, & Palmer, 1996). The development and acquisition of these component elements is lifelong and begins when children are very young. Some elements have greater applicability to secondary education and transition, whereas others focus more on the elementary years. As such, promoting self-determination as an educational outcome requires not only a purposeful instructional program but also one that coordinates learning experiences across the span of a student's educational experience.

Choice Making   Perhaps more emphasis has been placed on the choice-making component element as critical to a positive quality of life for people with disabilities than most of the other elements combined, particularly for

Table 1.   Component elements of self-determined behavior

Component element	Instructional methods
Choice-making skills	Chapter 5
Decision-making skills	Chapter 6
Problem-solving skills	Chapter 8
Goal-setting and Attainment skills	Chapter 9
Independence, risk taking, and safety skills	Chapter 4
Self-observation, evaluation, and reinforcement skills	Chapter 7
Self-instruction skills	Chapter 8
Self-advocacy and leadership skills	Chapters 10, 11, and 12
Internal locus of control	Chapter 14
Positive attributions of efficacy and outcome expectancy	Chapter 15
Self-awareness	Chapter 13
Self-knowledge	Chapter 13

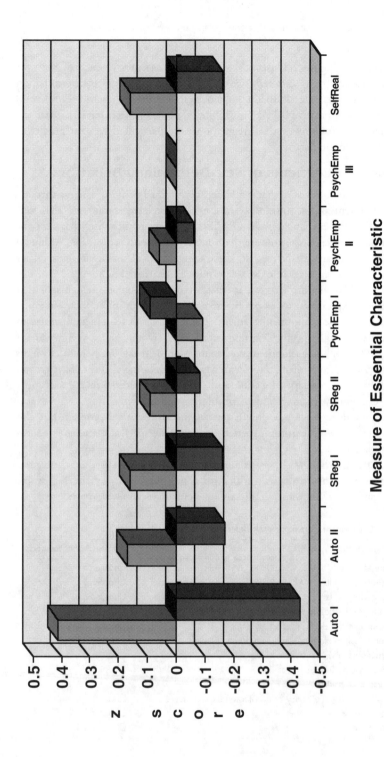

Measure of Essential Characteristic

Figure 2. Empirical validation of definitional framework. (Auto I and Auto II = measures of behavioral autonomy; SReg I and SReg II = measures of self-regulation; PsychEmp I, II, and III = measures of psychological empowerment; SelfReal = measure of self-realization.) (▨ = high self-determination; ▧ = low self-determination.)

individuals with significant disabilities. Training programs have been developed to teach choice making and increase choice-making behaviors (Gothelf, Crimmins, Mercer, & Finocchiaro, 1994; Parsons, McCarn, & Reid, 1993; Reid, Parsons, & Green, 1991; Warren, 1993), efforts have been made to increase the diversity of choices for people with disabilities (Brown, Belz, Corsi, & Wenig, 1993), discussions have been offered about the importance of making choices to people with disabilities (Ficker-Terrill & Rowitz, 1991; Guess, Benson, & Siegel-Causey, 1985; Shevin & Klein, 1984; West & Parent, 1992), procedures have been developed to assess individual preferences and choices (Mithaug & Hanawalt, 1978; Stancliffe, 1995), and research efforts have been undertaken to determine the degree to which people with disabilities express choices and preferences (Houghton, Bronicki, & Guess, 1987; Kishi, Teelucksingh, Zollers, Park-Lee, & Meyer, 1988; Stancliffe & Wehmeyer, 1995; Wehmeyer et al., 1995; Wehmeyer & Metzler, 1995).

Guess et al. (1985) proposed three levels of choice making: 1) choice as indicating preferences, 2) choice as a decision-making process, and 3) choice as an expression of autonomy and dignity. Reid and colleagues (1991) identified the instruction of choice making as consisting of two basic components: the act of choosing and the identification of a preference. The first component involves "emitting specific behaviors necessary to select one item or event from two or more alternatives" (Reid et al., 1991, p. 3), whereas the second directs that action toward the selection of preferred outcomes.

The limited body of research on choice making suggests that, too frequently, the preferences of individuals with disabilities are ignored or not acknowledged (Houghton et al., 1987; Kishi et al., 1988; Stancliffe & Wehmeyer, 1995; Wehmeyer et al., 1995; Wehmeyer & Metzler, 1995). This finding is ironic because increased opportunities and capacities to express preferences and make choices have been linked to reductions in problem behaviors exhibited by individuals with severe disabilities (Gardner, Cole, Berry, & Nowinski, 1983; Grace, Cowart, & Matson, 1988; Munk & Repp, 1994), increased participation in appropriate or adaptive tasks (Koestner, Ryan, Bernieri, & Holt, 1984; Realon, Favell, & Lowerre, 1990; Swann & Pittman, 1977), and more positive educational or achievement outcomes (Koenigs, Fielder, & deCharmes, 1977).

Kohn described another benefit of involving students in choice making in the classroom...it is beneficial to the teacher. He quotes one educator who stated,

I've been teaching for more than 30 years and I would have been burned out long ago but for the fact that I involve my kids in designing the curriculum. I'll say to them, "What's the most exciting way we could study this next unit?" If we decide their first suggestion isn't feasible, I'll say, "Okay, what's the next most exciting way we could study this?" They always come up with good proposals, they're motivated because I'm using their ideas, and I never do the unit in the same way twice. (1993, p. 12)

Shevin and Klein (1984) identified three essential components to a choice-fostering curriculum: 1) the cognitive/discrimination skills cluster, 2) the affective skills cluster, and 3) the generalization of skills to real-life experiences cluster. Under the first of these clusters, Shevin and Klein identified "those skills which enable the learner to understand and discriminate from among alternatives as a prerequisite to acting" (p. 162). They included in this cluster visual, auditory, and tactile discrimination skills and an understanding of such concepts as "choose" and "more." Affective skills in the second cluster involve student identifications of likes; dislikes; interests; abilities; wants; needs; and, ultimately, preferences. Shevin and Klein defined real-life experiences as "activities, both inside and outside of the classroom, which form the content of choices to be made" (p. 162) and identified choices of food, clothing, toys, or activities as examples of these. Learned cognitive/discriminative and affective skills should be generalized to these experiences.

Decision Making   Considerable overlap exists in theory and in practice between choice making and decision making. Further overlap is involved with the third essential element, problem solving. All three are important to becoming autonomous and self-regulating. Choice making refers to a process of selecting between alternatives based on individual preferences. Decision-making skills refer to a broader set of skills that incorporate choice making as but one component. Beyth-Marom, Fischhoff, Jacobs Quadrel, and Furby suggested that most models of decision making incorporate the following steps:

a)   listing relevant action alternatives;
b)   identifying possible consequences of those actions;
c)   assessing the probability of each consequence occurring (if the action were undertaken);
d)   establishing the relative importance (value or utility) of each consequence; and
e)   integrating these values and probabilities to identify the most attractive course of action. (1991, p. 21)

Baron and Brown (1991) proposed that "deficient decision-making is a serious problem throughout society at large and [this] problem needs addressing in childhood or adolescence" (p. 8). Students need to learn how to define the issue or problem about which a specific decision is to be made, collect information about their specific situation, and use this information to identify options for consideration. Once these options are clarified, students need to learn to be able to identify and evaluate the consequences and outcomes of actions based on the various options. When those consequences have been detailed, choice-making skills can be applied to select a specific alternative. Last, students must implement this plan of action.

Many people with disabilities are prohibited from making decisions, due primarily to an assumption of incompetence; this is particularly true if the individual has a cognitive disability. Wehmeyer and Metzler (1995) found that youth and adults with mental retardation were largely uninvolved in major decisions that had an impact on their lives. For example, only 33% of a sample of 4,500 adults indicated they had a voice in deciding where they lived, 44% indicated they had a role in the decision about where they work, and 44% reported that they had provided consent (either unassisted or with assistance) for their most recent medical procedure.

An underlying assumption held by many educators and parents is that minors do not have the capacity to make informed choices and decisions. The same assumption is also frequently made about individuals with disabilities; so the overwhelming assumption about adolescents with disabilities is that they are incapable of participating in the decision-making process. A number of researchers have suggested, however, that minors are competent at making important decisions.

Adelman and colleagues showed that students with and without disabilities demonstrate the ability to make competent decisions. Taylor, Adelman, and Kaser-Boyd (1983) found that the majority of adolescents referred for special support services wanted to participate in a decision-making meeting regarding those services, knew what outcomes they wanted, believed they were capable of participating in the meeting, followed through on actions agreed to at the meeting, and subsequently rated their involvement in the meeting as effective. Taylor, Adelman, and Kaser-Boyd (1985) replicated these findings with students identified as having a learning disability or severe emotional disorder and also found that these students were interested in improving the skills they would need to participate more effectively. Adelman, Lusk, Alvarez, and Acosta (1985) found that youth with school-related problems were competent to understand, evaluate, and communicate their psychoeducational problems.

Other researchers have determined that when provided the opportunity to participate in educational decision-making meetings, students with disabilities do as well as other team members. Salend (1983) found considerable congruence between student self-selected individualized education program (IEP) objectives and those selected by the interdisciplinary team. Phillips (1990) and Van Reusen and Bos (1994) found that students with learning disabilities were able to participate in the decision-making process, a finding duplicated by Wehmeyer and Lawrence (1995) with students with mental retardation.

The belief that minors are incapable of making competent decisions results, in part, from the perception that minors and students with disabilities cannot take into account the degree of risk involved with various options. This assumption is not supported, however, by research in developmental psychology. Grisso and Vierling (1978) reviewed the cognitive and behavioral characteristics of minors in relation to the question of competence to consent to treatment. They concluded that "there is no psychological grounds for maintaining the general legal assumption that minors age 15 and above cannot provide competent consent, taking into account risk-related factors" (p. 423). In fact, these authors contended that there are "circumstances that would justify the sanction of independent consent" (p. 424) by minors between the ages of 11 and 14.

Kaser-Boyd, Adelman, and Taylor (1985) asked students, ages 10–20, who were identified as having a learning or behavior problem, to list potential risks and benefits of entering psychoeducational therapy. As expected, there was a relationship between age and effectiveness in this task. Even the younger students, however, were able to identify relevant concerns that were appropriate to their situation and their developmental needs.

Although emphasis on choice making should occur early in a student's educational career, specific decision-making skills are probably better addressed at the secondary level. Beyth-Marom and colleagues (1991) suggested that to achieve generalization, decision making and problem solving must be taught in terms of familiar knowledge domains. By this, they refer to the effectiveness of teaching such skills in the context of a life-skills or functional education curriculum, with decision-making skills learned by applying the process to real-world issues, such as deciding where to work and live or how to spend leisure time.

Problem Solving   The third component element is problem-solving skills. Decision making is a process of weighing the adequacy of various solutions. A problem, in contrast, is "a task whose solution is not immediately perceived" (Beyth-Marom et al., 1991, p. 20). More specifically, however, a problem "is a specific situation or set of situations to which a person must respond in order to function effectively in his environment" (D'Zurilla & Goldfried, 1971, p. 108).

People are presented with problems that require resolution on a day-to-day basis. Problem-solving skills have typically focused on problem resolution in two primary contextual domains: impersonal problem solving and interpersonal or social problem solving. The former has received the most attention from researchers in studies that have focused on an individual's ability to complete puzzles and anagrams or solve mathematical problems. Such problems typically have only one correct solution with answers remaining the same over time (Wheeler, 1991).

In contrast, problems involving interactions between people are complex, with multiple processing demands and decision points, and have numerous possible solutions that may vary according to time or setting (Wehmeyer & Kelchner, 1994). Although both types of problem-solving skills are important for self-determination, social problem-solving skills are critically important for the emergence of self-determined behavior.

Social problem solving, alternatively referred to as interpersonal cognitive problem solving, emphasizes cognitive and behavioral strategies that enable individuals to interact with one another and to cope in an increasingly social world. Much of the focus for intervention in special education has been strictly on social-skills training. Although such instruction is important, in the absence of similar emphasis on social problem-solving skills, social-skills training alone is not enough to address deficits in social interactions exhibited by youth and adults with disabilities (Chadsey-Rusch, 1986; Park & Gaylord-Ross, 1989; Wehmeyer & Kelchner, 1994).

As in the choice-making process, problem-solving skills are embedded into virtually all decision-making procedures. The first step in most interventions to promote decision-making skills is to identify the issue or the problem at hand. As it is conceptualized by most researchers, however, the decision-making process begins with the listing of *already identified* options. Practically, one must first engage in problem solving before decision making can occur! Thus, the instructional emphasis for problem solving overlaps considerably with that for decision making and choice making.

Such instructional emphasis typically includes three focal points: problem identification, problem explication and analysis, and problem resolution. Instruction should occur within environments that emphasize the student's capability to solve problems, promote open inquiry and exploration, and encourage generalization. Teachers should serve as role models by verbalizing the problem-solving steps used on a day-to-day basis and should make sure that students are provided adequate support and accommodations.

Goal Setting and Attainment   To become the causal agent in his or her life, a person needs to learn the skills necessary to plan, set, and achieve goals. Goal-setting theory is built on the underlying assumption that goals are regulators of human action. This is true for educational motivation and achievement. For example, Schunk (1985) found that student involvement in goal setting improved performance on math activities for students with learning disabilities. The effects of goal setting on behavior are a function of goal difficulty and specificity as well as previous experiences with the activity or action. Goal attainment is typically a function of two related aspects of goals: content and intensity. Goal content refers to the topic of the goal whereas goal intensity reflects that goal's priority in the person's hierarchy of goals. Considerable differences in these aspects exist among individuals, and goal attainment or achievement will be affected by the salience and importance of the topic and the intensity of the individual's desire to achieve the goal.

Although self-determined behaviors are goal directed, it is incorrect to assume that self-determined and goal-directed behaviors are always successful or reach the intended goal! Self-determined behavior cannot be judged by the relative success of the action, just as goal-directed action cannot be determined by the achievement of the specific target or objective.

Educational efforts to promote goal-setting and attainment skills should focus on the identification and enunciation of specific goals, the development of objectives and tasks to achieve these goals, and the actions necessary to achieve a desired outcome. Martino (1993) identified several important considerations in goal identification and enunciation:

1. Goals should be specific and measurable.
2. Goals should be attainable.

3. Goals should reflect something on which the student wants to improve.
4. Goals should have specific, practical starting and finishing dates.
5. Goals should be written.
6. Goals should be stated in terms of anticipated outcomes.
7. Students should be able to visually track their progress on the goal.

The educational planning and decision-making process is an enterprise that revolves around goal setting, implementation, and evaluation. The involvement of students in this process, from elementary school through graduation, is a good way to promote effective goal-setting and attainment skills. Teachers and parents can model effective skills, such as identifying short- and long-term goals, describing objectives, implementing plans based on these goals and objectives, and reevaluating and refining these plans.

Independence, Risk Taking, and Safety Skills   One of the frequently cited goals of special education is to enable students to become as independent as possible. What is meant by this is that students should become able to perform a wide range of tasks on their own. Becoming independent means not being dependent on others for one's support, care, or funds. Turnbull and Turnbull (1985) emphasized the importance of independence, calling it a "fundamental value in our society" (p. 108). They pointed out that there are two prerequisites to independence for a person with a disability: access to the same opportunities of life as are available to people without disabilities and the capacity to participate in those activities. One of the barriers to this outcome is that, because of caregiver fears about safety, students (and adults) with disabilities are not allowed to perform many activities. It is obvious that some students with disabilities, particularly students with more significant disabilities, will never be completely "independent" because they may need ongoing support. It is also apparent, however, that many people with disabilities are not as independent as they could be because others limit their opportunities to take risks.

Concerns about risk taking and safety also limit the degree to which others allow individuals with disabilities to make choices and decisions. Schloss, Alper, and Jayne discussed four levels of risk associated with various choices:

1. The choice involves some potential for immediate risk, but little possibility of long-term harm to the individual or others.
2. The decision involves mild risk with minimal possibility of long-lasting harm to the individual or others.
3. The choice results in a moderate probability for long-lasting harm to the individual or others.
4. The decision involves an almost certain outcome that includes personal injury. (1993, p. 218)

Be it choice making or engaging in independent living behaviors, the real barrier for many people with disabilities is that the needs of the caregiver for absolute assurance of safety tend to lead to the prohibition of activities that have very low-level risks. Certainly behaviors that lead to a certain injury or those that have a moderate probability for harm should be cause for concern. Most behaviors, however, do not involve that level of risk and students with disabilities can be taught to assess the level of risk and weigh the consequences of action, using an effective decision-making process. In addition, students can be taught safety and health promotion skills that they need to achieve independent living. These skills can include teaching students basic first-aid and job-safety skills, nutrition, diet and medication facts, and skills to prevent abuse and disease (Agran, Marchand-Martella, & Martella, 1994).

Self-Observation, Self-Evaluation, and Self-Reinforcement Skills   The definitional framework of self-determined behavior identified such actions as self-regulated. Self-regulated behavior includes, at the very least, the essential skills of self-observation or self-monitoring, self-evaluation, and self-reinforcement.

Self-monitoring strategies involve teaching students to assess, observe, and record their own behavior. Self-monitoring strategies are most frequently used to improve work-related activities, such as attention to task, task completion, and task accuracy (Hughes, Korinek, & Gorman, 1991), and are thus important for transition-related programs. Agran and Martin (1987) pointed out that in addition to the benefits of self-monitoring to increase the efficacy of educational interventions, asking a student to monitor a target behavior may produce a desired change, in and of itself, without any further intervention. Agran (1997) suggested that this is because self-monitoring activities function as a discriminative stimulus to cue appropriate or desired responses.

Self-evaluation activities include the use of systematic strategies to enable students to track and evaluate their progress on educational activities, including goals and objectives. This frequently involves the use of self-recording procedures in which the student graphs, charts, or otherwise documents progress on a goal or objective. Such progress is typically determined through some form of self-observation, during which the student discriminates and records that a given target behavior has occurred, then compares that behavior with a previously determined standard or expected outcome (Agran, 1997). Students can be taught to score worksheets; identify the occurrence of a target behavior; track time intervals for the occurrence or nonoccurrence of a target behavior; and record this information in a graphic or chart format or using some other means of tracking, including the use of tokens.

A third aspect of self-regulation is the use of self-reinforcement strategies. Agran (1997) defined self-reinforcement as the self-administration of consequences, either positive or negative, contingent on the occurrence of a target behavior; and he suggested that self-reinforcement should have two functions: self-identification of reinforcers and delivery of the identified reinforcer. Student involvement in the former, identification of reinforcers, can enhance the efficacy of the latter. Self-reinforcement can be more effective than having another person deliver the reinforcer, not the least because self-reinforcement can almost always be immediate.

Self-Instruction Skills   Linked closely to the previous three elements, and discussed in Chapter 8, are self-instruction strategies. Self-instruction strategies involve teaching students to "provide their own verbal prompts for solving an academic or social problem" (Hughes et al., 1991, p. 272). This technique has been used successfully to solve job- and work-related problems (Agran, Fodor-Davis, & Moore, 1986; Hughes & Rusch, 1989) and to teach social skills critical to independence (Agran, Salzberg, & Stowitschek, 1987; Hughes & Agran, 1993). In essence, self-instruction strategies move the responsibility for providing verbal prompts and cues from an external source, typically the teacher, to the student.

Self-Advocacy and Leadership Skills   Self-advocacy skills are those skills individuals need to, quite literally, advocate on their own behalf. To advocate means to speak up or defend a cause or a person. By definition, then, instruction to promote self-advocacy focuses on two common threads: how to advocate and what to advocate. Elementary-age students can begin to learn basic self-advocacy skills, but most instructional emphasis in this area will apply to secondary education. Obviously, it is not feasible to teach students everything for which they could possibly advocate. One particularly important area in which students with disabilities should receive instruction, however, involves the education and transition process itself and their rights (and responsibilities) within that system. For many students with disabilities, school is a place where they are forced to go to do things that someone else decides on. It is little wonder that motivation becomes a problem!

Students who are approaching transition age can be taught about their rights under the Individuals with Disabilities Education Act Amendments of 1997 (PL 105-17) and, more specifically, about the purpose and process involved in transition decision making. As discussed in Chapter 12, the IEP and transition planning meetings provide an ideal vehicle for teaching self-advocacy skills in a meaningful manner. Other topics that could become the "cause" for which students will need to advocate on their own behalf include the adult services system (disability and general), basic civil and legal rights of citizenship, and specific civil and legal protections available to people with disabilities (e.g., those provided by the Americans with Disabilities Act [ADA] of 1990 [PL 101-336]). Such instructional efforts will necessarily deal with both rights and responsibilities.

The curricular strategies for the "how to advocate" side of self-advocacy include instructional emphasis on being assertive but not aggressive; how to communicate effectively in one-to-one, small-group, and large-group situations; how to negotiate, compromise, and use persuasion; how to be an effective listener; and how to navigate through systems and bureaucracies. It is evident that each of these is closely tied to the acquisition and emergence of other self-determination skills. For example, a reliable understanding of one's strengths and weaknesses is an important component if one is to actually use strategies such as negotiation and compromise to achieve an outcome. Likewise, students need to be able to link such advocacy to specific goals and incorporate it into the problem-solving or decision-making process.

Internal Locus of Control   The final four component elements of self-determined behavior focus not on skill development but on the attitudes that enable individuals to act in a psychologically empowered or self-realizing manner. If a person is to act in or upon a given situation, it is important for that person to believe that he or she has control over outcomes that are important to his or her life. People who hold such beliefs have been described as having an internal locus of control. Rotter (1966) defined locus of control as the degree to which a person perceives contingency relationships between his or her actions and outcomes. Mercer and Snell described the construct as follows:

> When a person is characterized as having an internal locus of control, he views reinforcement as primarily the consequences of one's own actions; whereas, if a person is characterized as having an external locus of control, reinforcement is viewed as the result of outside forces, e.g., luck, fate, chance and/or powerful others. (1977, p. 183)

The locus of control construct has proven to be a powerful tool for explaining, at least partially, individual and group differences in motivation, personality, and learning. Internal locus of control has been linked to adaptive outcomes, including positive educational and achievement outcomes and increased time and attention to school-related tasks (Lefcourt, 1976). External orientations have, conversely, been linked to increased impulsivity in decision making, distractibility, and sociometric ratings of rejection from peers (Ollendick, Greene, Francis, & Baum, 1991; Ollendick & Schmidt, 1987). In other words, students who feel in control of their lives and their destiny perform better than students who feel that other people or circumstances dictate everything that is happening to them.

Limited exploration has been done into the locus of control construct for individuals with disabilities. The available data do suggest that people with disabilities hold perceptions of control that are more external, and thus more maladaptive, than their peers without disabilities (see Wehmeyer, 1994).

The role of educators in promoting internal perceptions of control, as well as adaptive efficacy and outcome expectations, a positive self-awareness, and a realistic self-knowledge, is more complex than just providing adequate instructional experiences. An internal locus of control emerges as children make choices about things that they do every day, such as selecting clothing, and as these choices are honored and supported. To understand contingency relations between their actions and positive outcomes, children have to learn to distinguish between outcomes due to ability, effort, and chance. This progression takes place within a typical developmental course. Very young children attribute positive outcomes solely to effort and do not take into account ability or chance. As they get older children begin to distinguish between chance or luck and effort or ability, and in early adolescence, begin to differentiate between effort and ability. Children with disabilities may need specific instruction at these critical time periods to ensure that they can realistically assign causality to their actions.

It is particularly important to consider the learning environment and to evaluate its effect on student perceptions of control. Teachers who use an overly controlling style or whose classrooms are rigidly structured limit the development of positive perceptions of control. This does not mean that classrooms must become chaotic; allowing greater control is not the same as relinquishing all control and abolishing all rules and regulations (Deci & Chandler, 1986). Instead, classrooms can be structured such that students can perform more actions for themselves such as obtaining their own instructional materials. In addition, an educational program that emphasizes problem-solving, choice- and decision-making, and goal-setting and attainment skills by using student-directed learning activities will provide ample opportunities for students to learn that they have control over reinforcers and outcomes that are important to them.

Positive Attributions of Self-Efficacy and Efficacy Expectations   Self-efficacy and efficacy expectations are two related constructs, introduced by Bandura (1977a). Self-efficacy refers to the "conviction that one can successfully execute the behavior required to produce a given outcome" (Bandura, 1977a, p. 193). Efficacy expectations refer to the individual's belief that if a specific behavior is performed, it will lead to the anticipated outcome.

It should be evident that the two are individually necessary, but not sufficient, for behavior such as goal-directed and self-determined actions. Simply put, a person has to believe that 1) he or she can perform a specific behavior needed to achieve a desired outcome and 2) if that behavior is performed, it will result in the desired outcome. If a person does not believe that he or she can perform a given behavior (independent of the validity of that belief), then consequently he or she will not perform that action. A person may believe that he or she is capable of performing a given behavior; but due to past experience, however, the person may not believe that a desired outcome will occur even if that behavior is exhibited and, subsequently, will not perform the action. For example, a student with a disability may not believe that she has the social skills necessary to initiate a conversation with peers without disabilities and will refrain from initiating such actions. Conversely, that same student may believe that she has the requisite skills, but having been ignored in the past, she may believe that she will be ignored again and will, likewise, refrain from initiating the action.

Like perceptions of control, perceptions of efficacy and expectancy have been linked to academic achievement and persistence at academic activities

(Lent, Bron, & Larken, 1984; Ollendick & Schmidt, 1987). Very little research has examined the self-efficacy and efficacy expectations of individuals with disabilities. Most of the extant literature in the area of learning disabilities focuses on changing self-efficacy and efficacy expectations through environmental or instructional modifications (Schunk, 1989). Wehmeyer (1994) found that individuals with mental retardation held less adaptive attributions of efficacy and expectancy than did peers without disabilities and that such attributions became even less adaptive as the student got older, a trend not consistent with typical developmental functions for these attributes.

Attributions of efficacy and expectancy emerge as children and adolescents interact with the world around them. One holds positive beliefs of self-efficacy and efficacy expectations because one has acquired specific skills, exercised such skills, and experienced the outcomes anticipated by such activities. Several factors limit the acquisition of these perceptions by people with disabilities. As Kennedy (1996) highlighted, overprotection by well-intentioned others frequently limits opportunities for children and youth with disabilities to engage in actions that would enable them to establish a sense of self-efficacy and efficacy expectations.

Overly structured environments, including many special education classrooms, limit the opportunities to acquire skills related to choice and decision making, hinder the development of an internal locus of control, and prohibit students from learning that they are effective and that their behaviors can have beneficial outcomes. Again, an educational program that focuses on promoting self-determined behavior through the means detailed above will provide the opportunities students need to develop adaptive perceptions of self-efficacy and efficacy expectations.

Self-Awareness and Self-Knowledge   In order for one to act in a self-realizing manner, one must possess a basic understanding of one's strengths, weaknesses, abilities, and limitations as well as knowledge about how to utilize these unique attributions to beneficially influence one's quality of life. Students do not learn what they can or cannot do from lectures, role playing, social skills simulations, or any other more traditional teacher-directed instructional activities. They learn, as do all people, through their own interpretation of events and experiences. At any given time, *The New York Times* Bestseller List for nonfiction contains one or more books that are classified as "popular psychology," and it provides interested readers the chance to learn more about themselves and, if necessary, change this or that aspect of their personality; intelligence; or, often as not, self-image. Most adults who want to improve some aspect of their lives do so in a self-directed manner.

This process is not one of pure introspection, however, and does not focus exclusively or even primarily on an understanding of limitations. In many cases, students with disabilities are quite able and more willing to identify what they do poorly than those things they do well. The specter of having a disability, as pictured in disease or deficit models, hovers over any given circumstance; and students dwell more on what they are unable to accomplish than on what they can achieve. Because special education is essentially remediative in nature, this is hardly surprising. It is particularly important for adolescents to focus on developing their strengths so that they can accomplish more in these areas. Lipsky and Gartner (1989) pointed out that if universities adopted the same structure that the special education process uses, college students would enter universities and spend 4 years trying to improve, even slightly, on the activities and subjects they have the most trouble doing while basically ignoring areas of strengths and interests. Secondary special education programs should adopt, instead, the model used in postgraduate education, in which students focus almost exclusively on their strengths and interests and attempt to utilize these skills to their benefit.

CONCLUSION

Ensuring that students with and without disabilities are self-determined will be as complex and difficult a process as comparable efforts to ensure that students with disabilities attain gainful employment or community involvement. An educational program to promote self-determination will not consist of only instructional activities; but it will also include efforts to create peer and adult mentor programs, structure learning environments and incorporate community-based learning, introduce functionally derived curricula, increase interactions with peers without disabilities, provide experiences with success, and involve students in educational planning and decision making.

Skills development in the component elements of self-determined behavior is one key to success; and many proven, effective practices are available that teachers can use to achieve this outcome. The purpose of this text is to enable teachers and other educational professionals to teach students with disabilities the skills they need to be self-determined young people and to look forward to their future with anticipation and excitement, like Rebecca, instead of drifting along aimlessly, like Robert. The chapters in Section II of this text identify and describe such practices and enable teachers to provide their students with the learning experiences they need to become self-determined young people.

QUESTIONS FOR REVIEW

1. Discuss some of the shortcomings of early transition models.
2. What is self-determination?
3. What is meant by the term *causal agent?*
4. Identify and discuss the four essential characteristics of self-determined behavior.
5. Identify component elements of self-determined behavior and discuss their relevance to the lives of people with disabilities.

6. Too frequently the preferences of individuals with disabilities are ignored or not acknowledged. What factors have contributed to this situation?
7. A frequent argument against allowing students to make decisions is that they are not capable of doing so. Discuss whether this argument is based in fact or based on stereotypes.

REFERENCES

Adelman, H.S., Lusk, R., Alvarez, V., & Acosta, N.K. (1985). Competence of minors to understand, evaluate and communicate about their psychoeducational problems. *Professional Psychology: Research and Practice, 16,* 426–434.

Agran, M. (1997). *Student-directed learning: A handbook on self-management.* Pacific Grove, CA: Brooks/Cole.

Agran, M., Fodor-Davis, J., & Moore, S. (1986). The effects of self-instructional training on job-task sequencing: Suggesting a problem-solving strategy. *Education and Training in Mental Retardation, 21,* 273–281.

Agran, M., Marchand-Martella, N.E., & Martella, R.C. (Eds.). (1994). *Promoting health and safety: Skills for independent living.* Baltimore: Paul H. Brookes Publishing Co.

Agran, M., & Martin, J.E. (1987). Applying a technology of self-control in community environments for individuals who are mentally retarded. In M. Hersen, R.M. Eisler, & P.M. Miller (Eds.), *Progress in behavior modification* (pp. 108–151). Newbury Park, CA: Sage Publications.

Agran, M., Salzberg, C.L., & Stowitschek, J.J. (1987). An analysis of the effects of a social skills training program using self-instructions on the acquisition and generalization of two social behaviors in a work setting. *Journal of The Association for Persons with Severe Handicaps, 12,* 131–139.

Americans with Disabilities Act (ADA) of 1990, PL 101-336, 42 U.S.C. §§ 12101 *et seq.*

Bandura, A.B. (1977a). Self-efficacy: Toward a unifying theory of behavioral change. *Psychological Review, 84,* 191–215.

Bandura, A.B. (1977b). *Social learning theory.* Englewood Cliffs, NJ: Prentice Hall.

Baron, J., & Brown, R.V. (1991). Introduction. In J. Baron & R.V. Brown (Eds.), *Teaching decision making to adolescents* (pp. 7–18). Hillsdale, NJ: Lawrence Erlbaum Associates.

Beyth-Marom, R., Fischhoff, B., Jacobs Quadrel, M., & Furby, L. (1991). Teaching decision-making to adolescents: A critical review. In J. Baron & R.V. Brown (Eds.), *Teaching decision making to adolescents* (pp. 19–59). Hillsdale, NJ: Lawrence Erlbaum Associates.

Brown, F., Belz, P., Corsi, L., & Wenig, B. (1993). Choice diversity for people with severe disabilities. *Education and Training in Mental Retardation, 28,* 318–326.

Chadsey-Rusch, J. (1986). Identifying and teaching valued social behaviors. In F.R. Rusch (Ed.), *Competitive employment issues and strategies* (pp. 273–287). Baltimore: Paul H. Brookes Publishing Co.

Chadsey-Rusch, J., Rusch, F., & O'Reilly, M.F. (1991). Transition from school to integrated communities. *Remedial and Special Education, 12,* 23–33.

Deci, E.L., & Chandler, C.L. (1986). The importance of motivation for the future of the LD field. *Journal of Learning Disabilities, 19,* 587–594.

Deci, E.L., & Ryan, R.M. (1985). *Intrinsic motivation and self-determination in human behavior.* New York: Plenum.

Doll, B., Sands, D.J., Wehmeyer, M.L., & Palmer, S. (1996). Promoting the development and acquisition of self-determined behavior. In D.J. Sands & M.L. Wehmeyer

(Eds.), *Self-determination across the life span: Independence and choice for people with disabilities* (pp. 65–90). Baltimore: Paul H. Brookes Publishing Co.

D'Zurilla, T.J., & Goldfried, M.R. (1971). Problem-solving and behavior modification. *Journal of Abnormal Psychology, 78,* 107–126.

Ficker-Terrill, C., & Rowitz, L. (1991). Choices. *Mental Retardation, 29,* 63–64.

Gardner, W.I., Cole, C.L., Berry, D.L., & Nowinski, J.M. (1983). Reduction of disruptive behaviors in mentally retarded adults: A self-management approach. *Behavior Modification, 7,* 76–96.

Gothelf, C.R., Crimmins, D.B., Mercer, C.A., & Finocchiaro, P.A. (1994). Teaching choice-making skills to students who are deaf-blind. *Teaching Exceptional Children, 26,* 13–15.

Grace, N., Cowart, C., & Matson, J.L. (1988). Reinforcement and self-control for treating a chronic case of self-injury in Lesch-Nyhan syndrome. *Journal of the Multihandicapped Person, 1,* 53–59.

Grisso, T., & Vierling, L. (1978). Minors' consent to treatment: A developmental perspective. *Professional Psychology, 9,* 412–427.

Guess, D., Benson, H.A., & Siegel-Causey, E. (1985). Concepts and issues related to choice-making and autonomy among persons with severe disabilities. *Journal of The Association for Persons with Severe Handicaps, 10,* 79–86.

Halloran, W.D. (1993). Transition services requirement: Issues, implications, challenge. In R.C. Eaves & P.J. McLaughlin (Eds.), *Recent advances in special education and rehabilitation* (pp. 210–224). Boston: Andover Medical.

Houghton, J., Bronicki, G.J.B., & Guess, D. (1987). Opportunities to express preferences and make choices among students with severe disabilities in classroom settings. *Journal of The Association for Persons with Severe Handicaps, 10,* 79–86.

Hughes, C., & Agran, M. (1993). Teaching persons with severe disabilities to use self-instruction in community settings: An analysis of applications. *Journal of The Association for Persons with Severe Handicaps, 18,* 261–274.

Hughes, C., & Rusch, F.R. (1989). Teaching supported employees with severe mental retardation to solve problems. *Journal of Applied Behavior Analysis, 22,* 365–372.

Hughes, C.A., Korinek, L., & Gorman, J. (1991). Self-management for students with mental retardation in public school settings: A research review. *Education and Training in Mental Retardation, 26,* 271–291.

Individuals with Disabilities Education Act Amendments of 1997, PL 105-17, 20 U.S.C. §§ 1400 *et seq.*

Kaser-Boyd, N., Adelman, H.S., & Taylor, L. (1985). Minors' ability to identify risks and benefits of therapy. *Professional Psychology: Research and Practice, 16,* 411–417.

Kennedy, M.J. (1996). Self-determination and trust: My experiences and thoughts. In D.J. Sands & M.L. Wehmeyer (Eds.), *Self-determination across the life span: Independence and choice for people with disabilities* (pp. 37–49). Baltimore: Paul H. Brookes Publishing Co.

Kishi, G., Teelucksingh, B., Zollers, N., Park-Lee, S., & Meyer, L. (1988). Daily decision-making in community residences: A social comparison of adults with and without mental retardation. *American Journal on Mental Retardation, 92,* 430–435.

Koenigs, S., Fielder, M., & deCharmes, R. (1977). Teacher beliefs, classroom interaction and personal control. *Journal of Applied Social Psychology, 7,* 95–114.

Koestner, R., Ryan, R.M., Bernieri, F., & Holt, K. (1984). The effects of controlling versus informational limit-setting styles on children's intrinsic motivation and creativity. *Journal of Personality, 52,* 233–248.

Kohn, A. (1993). Choices for children: Why and how to let students decide. *Phi Delta Kappan, 75*(1), 8–20.

Lefcourt, H.M. (1976). *Locus of control.* Hillsdale, NJ: Lawrence Erlbaum Associates.

Lent, R.W., Bron, S.D., & Larkin, K.C. (1984). Relationship of self-efficacy expectations to academic achievement and persistence. *Journal of Counseling Psychology, 31,* 356–362.

Lewis, K., & Taymans, J.M. (1992). An examination of autonomous functioning skills of adolescents with learning disabilities. *Career Development for Exceptional Individuals, 15,* 37–46.

Lipsky, D.K., & Gartner, A. (Eds.). (1989). *Beyond separate education: Quality education for all.* Baltimore: Paul H. Brookes Publishing Co.

Martin, J.E., & Marshall, L.H. (1995). ChoiceMaker: A comprehensive self-determination transition program. *Intervention in School and Clinic, 30,* 147–156.

Martin, J.E., Marshall, L.H., Maxson, L., & Jerman, P. (1993). *Self-directed IEP: Teacher's manual.* Colorado Springs: University of Colorado, Center for Educational Research.

Martino, L.R. (1993). A goal-setting model for young adolescent at risk students. *Middle School Journal, 24,* 19–22.

Mercer, C.D., & Snell, M.E. (1977). *Learning theory research in mental retardation: Implications for teaching.* Columbus, Ohio: Charles E. Merrill.

Mithaug, D.E. (1991). *Self-determined kids: Raising satisfied and successful children.* Lexington, MA: Lexington Books.

Mithaug, D.E., & Hanawalt, D.A. (1978). The validation of procedures to assess prevocational task preferences in retarded adults. *Journal of Applied Behavior Analysis, 11,* 153–162.

Munk, D.D., & Repp, A.C. (1994). The relationship between instructional variables and problem behavior: A review. *Exceptional Children, 60,* 390–401.

Ollendick, T.H., Greene, R.W., Francis, G., & Baum, C.G. (1991). Sociometric status: Its stability and validity among neglected, rejected and popular children. *Journal of Child Psychology and Psychiatry, 32,* 525–534.

Ollendick, T.H., & Schmidt, C.R. (1987). Social learning constructs in the prediction of peer interaction. *Journal of Clinical Child Psychology, 16,* 80–87.

Park, H.-S., & Gaylord-Ross, R. (1989). A problem-solving approach to social skills training in employment settings with mentally retarded youth. *Journal of Applied Behavior Analysis, 22,* 373–380.

Parsons, M.B., McCarn, J.E., & Reid, D.H. (1993). Evaluating and increasing meal-related choices throughout a service setting for people with severe disabilities. *Journal of The Association for Persons with Severe Handicaps, 18,* 253–260.

Phillips, P. (1990). A self-advocacy plan for high school students with learning disabilities: A comparative case study analysis of students', teachers', and parents' perceptions of program effects. *Journal of Learning Disabilities, 23,* 466–471.

Realon, R.E., Favell, J.E., & Lowerre, A. (1990). The effects of making choices on engagement levels with persons who are profoundly mentally handicapped. *Education and Training in Mental Retardation, 25,* 248–254.

Reid, D.H., Parsons, M.B., & Green, C.W. (1991). *Providing choices and preferences for persons who have severe handicaps.* Morganton, NC: Habilitative Management Consultants.

Rotter, J.B. (1966). Generalized expectancies for internal versus external control of reinforcement [Entire issue]. *Psychological Monographs, 80*(609).

Salend, S.J. (1983). Self-assessment: A model for involving students in the formulation of their IEPs. *Journal of School Psychology, 21,* 65–70.

Sarason, S.B. (1990). *The predictable failure of educational reform: Can we change course before it's too late?* San Francisco: Jossey-Bass.

Schloss, P.J., Alper, S., & Jayne, D. (1994). Self-determination for persons with disabilities: Choice, risk, and dignity. *Exceptional Children, 60,* 215–225.

Schunk, D.H. (1985). Participation in goal setting: Effects on self-efficacy and skills of learning-disabled children. *Journal of Special Education, 19,* 307–316.

Schunk, D.H. (1989). Self-efficacy and cognitive achievement: Implications for students with learning problems. *Journal of Learning Disabilities, 22,* 14–22.

Shevin, M., & Klein, N.K. (1984). The importance of choice-making skills for students with severe disabilities. *Journal of The Association for Persons with Severe Handicaps, 9,* 159–166.

Sigafoos, A.D., Feinstein, C.B., Damond, M., & Reiss, D. (1988). The measurement of behavioral autonomy in adolescence: The Autonomous Functioning Checklist. In C.B. Feinstein, A. Esman, J. Looney, G. Orvin, J. Schimel, A. Schwartzberg, A. Sorsky, & M. Sugar (Eds.), *Adolescent psychiatry* (Vol. 15, pp. 432–462). Chicago: University of Chicago Press.

Stancliffe, R. (1995). Assessing opportunities for choice making: A comparison of self-report and staff reports. *American Journal on Mental Retardation, 99,* 418–429.

Stancliffe, R., & Wehmeyer, M.L. (1995). Variability in the availability of choice to adults with mental retardation. *Journal of Vocational Rehabilitation, 5,* 319–328.

Swann, W.B., & Pittman, T.S. (1977). Initiating play activity of children: The moderating influence of verbal cues on intrinsic motivation. *Child Development, 48,* 1128–1132.

Taylor, L., Adelman, H.S., & Kaser-Boyd, N. (1983). Perspectives of children regarding their participation in psychoeducational decisions. *Professional Psychology: Research and Practice, 14,* 882–894.

Taylor, L., Adelman, H.S., & Kaser-Boyd, N. (1985). Minors' attitudes and competence toward participation in psychoeducational decisions. *Professional Psychology: Research and Practice, 16,* 226–235.

Turnbull, A.P., & Turnbull, H.R. (1985). Developing independence. *Journal of Adolescent Health Care, 6,* 108–119.

Van Reusen, A.K., & Bos, C.S. (1994). Facilitating student participation in individualized education programs through motivation strategy instruction. *Exceptional Children, 60,* 466–475.

Ward, M.J. (1988). The many facets of self-determination. *NICHCY Transition Summary: National Information Center for Children and Youth with Disabilities, 5,* 2–3.

Warren, B. (1993). *The right to choose: A training curriculum.* New York: New York State Office of Mental Retardation and Developmental Disabilities.

Wehman, P. (1993). Transition from school to adulthood for young people with disabilities: Critical issues and policies. In R.C. Eaves & P.J. McLaughlin (Eds.), *Recent advances in special education and rehabilitation* (pp. 178–192). Boston: Andover Medical.

Wehmeyer, M.L. (1992). Self-determination and the education of students with mental retardation. *Education and Training in Mental Retardation, 27,* 302–314.

Wehmeyer, M.L. (1994). Perceptions of self-determination and psychological empowerment of adolescents with mental retardation. *Education and Training in Mental Retardation and Developmental Disability, 29,* 9–21.

Wehmeyer, M.L. (1996). Self-determination as an educational outcome: Why is it important to children, youth, and adults with disabilities? In D.J. Sands & M.L. Wehmeyer (Eds.), *Self-determination across the life span: Independence and choice for people with disabilities* (pp. 17–36). Baltimore: Paul H. Brookes Publishing Co.

Wehmeyer, M.L., & Kelchner, K. (1994). Interpersonal cognitive problem-solving skills of individuals with mental retardation. *Education and Training in Mental Retardation, 29,* 265–278.

Wehmeyer, M.L., Kelchner, K., & Richards, S. (1995). Individual and environmental factors related to the self-determination of adults with mental retardation. *Journal of Vocational Rehabilitation, 5,* 291–305.

Wehmeyer, M.L., Kelchner, K., & Richards. S. (1996). Essential characteristics of self-determined behaviors of adults with mental retardation and developmental disabilities. *American Journal on Mental Retardation, 100,* 632–642.

Wehmeyer, M.L., & Lawrence, M. (1995). Whose future is it anyway? Promoting student involvement in transition planning. *Career Development for Exceptional Individuals, 18,* 69–83.

Wehmeyer, M.L., & Metzler, C.A. (1995). How self-determined are people with mental retardation? The National Consumer Survey. *Mental Retardation, 33,* 111–119.

West, M.D., & Parent, W.S. (1992). Consumer choice and empowerment in supported employment services: Issues and strategies. *Journal of The Association for Persons with Severe Handicaps, 17,* 47–52.

Wheeler, D. (1991). Metaphors for effective thinking. In J. Baron & R. Brown (Eds.), *Teaching decision making to adolescents* (pp. 309–327). Hillsdale, NJ: Lawerence Erlbaum Associates.

Whitman, T.L. (1990). Self-regulation and mental retardation. *American Journal on Mental Retardation, 94,* 373–376.

Zimmerman, M.A. (1990). Toward a theory of learned hopefulness: A structural model analysis of participation and empowerment. *Journal of Research in Personality, 24,* 71–86.

CHAPTER 2

Impetus for an Educational Focus on Self-Determination

After reading this chapter, you will be able to

1. Discuss historical and current conceptualizations of disability

2. Identify the contributions of the independent living movement, the normalization principle, and the self-advocacy movement to the emergence of self-determination as an educational outcome

3. Describe 1) three types of organizations composed of people with disabilities that emerged to provide consumer monitoring and self-advocacy and 2) two examples of civil rights legislation that guarantee and safeguard the rights of people with disabilities

4. Discuss the strategies and outcomes of students in the transition process from school to the adult world, especially as related to self-determination

KEY TERMS

1. ADA
2. Deinstitutionalization
3. "Holy innocents"
4. IDEA
5. Independent living
6. Normalization

7. Quality of life
8. Section 504
9. Self-advocacy
10. Self-directed learning
11. Self-fulfilling prophecy
12. Social role valorization

In January of 1989, the U.S. Department of Education, Office of Special Education and Rehabilitative Services (OSERS), convened a 2-day conference to discuss the direction the agency should take to promote self-determination. Invited to participate in this event were 60 people who represented key stakeholders in the educational process. Over half of the participants were people with disabilities; the remainder were parents and siblings of people with disabilities and disability advocates. The conference provided the impetus needed to move self-determination from a disability rights issue to an accepted educational practice. In a relatively short period of time, self-determination has gained wide acceptance as a critical outcome for youth with disabilities.

Federal funding initiatives that emerged from the National Conference on Self-Determination have had considerable impact on the ability of practitioners in the field to promote self-determination. Since 1990 OSERS has funded numerous model demonstration, research, and dissemination projects focused on self-determination and student involvement (Ward, 1996; Ward & Kohler, 1996). These projects have developed curricular and assessment materials and instructional strategies to promote self-determination and provided research findings to drive practice and policy in this area (Field, 1996; Wehmeyer, Martin, & Sands, 1997).

The National Conference on Self-Determination was not the only factor contributing to the emergence of self-determination as an educational outcome, however. In addition, the receptiveness of the education and disability communities to the topic of self-determination is due to changes in the way disability has been conceptualized in U.S. society, changes in the philosophy driving disability-related services, and the contributions of the disability-rights movements of previous decades. This chapter discusses the historical antecedents to the self-determination movement and more recent factors that spurred its emergence.

HISTORICAL ROOTS OF SELF-DETERMINATION

The movement to promote self-determination reflects the culmination of a process that began several decades ago. In 1972, Nirje argued that

> One major facet of the normalization principle is to create conditions through which a...person [with disabilities] experiences the normal respect to which any human is entitled. Thus, the choices, wishes, desires and aspirations of a...person [with disabilities] have to be taken into consideration as much as possible in actions affecting him. To assert oneself with one's family, friends, neighbors, co-workers, other people, or vis-à-vis an agency is difficult for many people. It is especially difficult for someone who has a disability or is otherwise perceived as devalued. Thus, the road to self-determination is indeed both difficult and all-important for a person who is impaired. (p. 177)

Sixteen years later Michael Ward, branch chief of the Office of Special Education Programs (OSEP), Secondary Education and Transition Services branch, and a person with a significant disability, wrote

> While acquiring the personal characteristics which lead to self-determination is important for all people, it is a critical and often more difficult goal for people with disabilities. They must shatter the pervasive stereotypes which imply that they cannot, or perhaps should not, practice self-determination. (1988, p. 2)

Although separated by almost 2 decades, these writers make virtually the same point—although self-determination is critically important for people with disabilities, they do not, and sometimes cannot, attain this outcome. In the 2 decades between Nirje's call for self-determination and that of Ward, too little had changed in the lives of people with disabilities. Much had changed, however, in the field of disability services and in the way people with disabilities were perceived in these services and in society; so that although Nirje's call for self-determination remained largely unheeded, the demands of Ward and his peers have been attended to and are coming to fruition.

This section examines some of these societal and service-related changes. With few exceptions, these influences occurred outside of the realm of education; yet they still had a profound effect on the education of learners with disabilities.

Conceptualizations of Disability

The way disability is conceptualized in a society directly influences, in fact basically circumscribes, the opportunities available to individuals with disabilities within that society. Such conceptualizations influence how other members of society perceive people with disabilities and what they expect from people with disabilities, and they influence how people with disabilities perceive themselves and what they expect from themselves. One significant change that prepared the way for the self-determination movement has been the way in which disability has been conceptualized within our society.

Historical conceptualizations of disability can be described in many ways, including descriptions based on the theoretical approach within which treatment or intervention is delivered (e.g., a behavioral conceptualization of disability, a psychoanalytical conceptualization); certain religious and cultural belief systems (e.g., a folk religion conceptualization); or the general discipline within which theory, practice, and research has been conducted (e.g., medicine, education, psychology, social work). Using the latter, the conceptualization of disability has differed among various disciplines. A medical model of disability focuses on disability as equated with disease. People with disabilities are seen as patients with a disease. Intervention within this model rests in curing, or at least halting the progress of, the disease. An educational model assumes a "fix-it" approach to disability, focusing not on cure, but on remediation. A social work model focuses on disability as dysfunction.

The medical model has dominated service delivery to people with disabilities over the 20th century, and its influence is clearly seen in other models, including the educational model. Independent of how disability has been conceptualized, however, the common theme shared by these disciplines has been that disability is outside the norm for typical or accepted human behavior and functioning. Disability has been seen as pathological, aberrant, atypical, and dysfunctional. The stereotypes of people with disabilities built from these conceptualizations, and subsequent expectations of people with disabilities based on stereotypes, are often as debilitating as the disabling condition itself. This is evident from an overview of the way in which people with disabilities have been seen by the general public in the last 100 years.

Late 19th and Early 20th Century View of Disability   In the late part of the 19th century and the early part of the 20th century, people with disabilities were viewed as menaces and linked with crime, poverty, promiscuity, and the decline of civilization. They were seen as subhuman (i.e., as a vegetable, animal-like) or as objects to be feared or dreaded. Goddard summarized his study of the Kallikak family, using these devaluing concepts of disability:

> We find on the good side of the family prominent people in all walks of life and nearly all of the 496 descendants owners of land or proprietors. On the bad side we find paupers, criminals, prostitutes, drunkards, and examples of all forms of social pest with which modern society is burdened.
>
> From this we conclude that feeble-mindedness is largely responsible for these social sores. (1912, p. 116)

Goddard concluded that "feeble-mindedness" should be combatted with a program of segregation and sterilization. He stopped short of recommending eugenics (i.e., controlling a race or breed through selective breeding), recommending instead further study of the mechanisms of heredity. By 1926, Goddard had dropped his hesitation to the implementation of eugenics, which he defined as a science and equated with race betterment, recommending a program of segregation and sterilization to control the spread of feeble-mindedness and concluding that

> feeble-mindedness is sufficiently prevalent to arouse the interest and attract the attention of all thotful [sic] people who are interested in social welfare; that it is mostly hereditary; that it underlies all our social problems; that because of these facts it is worth the attention of our most thotful [sic] statesmen and social leaders; that much of the time and money and energy now devoted to other things may be more wisely spent in investigating the problem of feeble-mindedness; and that because feeble-mindedness is in all probability transmitted in accordance with the Mendelian Law of

heredity, the way is open for eugenic procedure which shall mean much for the future welfare of the race. (Goddard, 1926, pp. 589–590)

Post–World War II Conceptualizations of Disability   After the Depression and World War II, advances in science and medicine changed the way disability was perceived and greatly increased the life span of people with disabilities. Influenced by the large number of veterans disabled in the second World War, which spurred an emphasis on rehabilitation and training, and successes in developing vaccines for diseases such as polio, giving hope to greater cures for disabling conditions, the earlier stereotypes of disability were replaced with more humane, though still in many ways debilitating, stereotypes. People with disabilities were viewed as objects to be fixed; cured; rehabilitated; and, at the same time, pitied. People with disabilities came to be viewed as "victims" worthy of charity. Shapiro described this phenomenon when discussing the emergence of the poster child as a fund-raising tool:

> The poster child is a surefire tug at our hearts. The children picked to represent charity fund-raising drives are brave, determined, and inspirations, the most innocent victims of the cruelest whims of life and health. Yet they smile through their unlucky fates...no other symbol of disability is more beloved by Americans than the cute and courageous poster child. (1993, p. 12)

Within this stereotype, people with disabilities were viewed as "holy innocents" (i.e., special messengers, children of God) and thus incapable of sin and not responsible for their own actions. Based at least partially on the prevalent use of mental age calculated from intelligence scores, people with disabilities came to be perceived as "eternal children." Although no longer feared and blamed for all social ills, people with disabilities were perceived as children for whom to care, protect, and pity. It was within this general perception of disability that Nirje (1972) first called for self-determination. Obviously, such perceptions were antithetical to the portrayal of people with disabilities as self-determined, self-sufficient, and competent human beings. Adults with "the mind of a 3-year-old" are not expected to hold a job, make decisions, or live independently. "Holy innocents" are not expected to learn about sexuality and human relationships. Recipients of pity and charity are to be helped but not accepted as colleagues, friends, or neighbors (Wehmeyer & Davis, 1995).

Changing Stereotypes of People with Disabilities Since the 1960s   Since the early 1960s, a different perception of disability has emerged, first within the disability rights and advocacy movement; then within the disability services field; and, increasingly, within the general public. Many factors contributed to this shift, including 1) the introduction of the normalization principle; 2) the rise of the independent living, self-help, and self-advocacy movements; 3) the shift from institutional to community-based services; 4) civil rights legislation and protections, such as Section 504 of the Rehabilitation Act of 1973 (PL 93-112), the Individuals with Disabilities Education Act (IDEA) of 1990 (PL 101-476) and its amendments, and the Americans with Disabilities Act (ADA) of 1990 (PL 101-336); and 5) resulting access to education and community life. As a result of these forces, there has been a significant change in the way in which disability is defined or described and, consequently, in the way in which people with disabilities are viewed. This change is perhaps best represented in language from the 1992 reauthorization of the Rehabilitation Act. The findings of Congress from that act read as follows:

1. millions of Americans have one or more physical or mental disability and the number of Americans with disabilities is increasing;
2. individuals with disabilities constitute one of the most disadvantaged groups in society;
3. disability is a natural part of the human experience and in no way diminishes the right of individuals to:
   a. live independently;
   b. enjoy self-determination;
   c. make choices;
   d. contribute to society;
   e. pursue meaningful careers; and
   f. enjoy full inclusion and integration in the economic, political, social, cultural and educational mainstream of American society; and
6. the goals of the nation properly include the goal of providing individuals with disabilities the tools necessary to:
   a. make informed choices and decisions; and
   b. achieve equality of opportunity, full inclusion and integration into society, employment, independent living and economic and social self-sufficiency, for such individuals. (Section 2 [29 U.S.C. § 701])

The significant change that is reflected in this conceptualization is that disability is no longer seen as aberrant, outside the norm, or pathological but instead as a part of being human. Within this conceptualization all human abilities and experiences exist on a continuum; and disability is a part of, rather than outside, that continuum. Whereas Nirje's (1972) call to self-determination came before such a conceptualization of disability was in place, the demands of people with disabilities today for more control and choice come at a time when changing stereotypes of disability, coupled with progress in education, rehabilitation, and legislative protections, ensure that people with disabilities, including the most significant disabilities, can with adequate support work competitively, live independently, and become a contributing member of the community.

The history of education and the stereotypes held within educational settings share a similar historical path. Even a cursory review of articles related to the education of students with disabilities even since the 1970s shows that expectations for students with disabilities have changed substantially in a relatively short time. Although most educators do not retain perceptions about disability that reflect beliefs held early in the century, vestiges of later perceptions remain and continue to have an impact on the educational setting. The well-known "self-fulfilling prophecy" is still alive and well. Cutler (1993) listed several myths about children with disabilities that are still found in schools, including the belief that a child's disability is the source of all that student's problems, that children with disabilities can learn only by rote, or that students with disabilities cannot handle a full school day and would be better off if placed simply in a caregiving situation. In addition, the language still used by too many educators reflects long-held assumptions of pathology and dysfunction. One hardly expects a "trainable" student to hold adult roles, such as spouse or employee.

Addressing self-determination as an educational outcome is one action that reflects the historical shift of viewing disability as pathology to viewing disability as a part of the continuum of human experiences. Such instructional emphasis has the reciprocal impact of improving the capacity of people with disabilities to live, work, play, and learn as independently as possible and of recognizing that people with disabilities have the basic right to the opportunity to live self-determined lives.

Normalization Principle

Scheerenberger (1987) suggested that "no single categorical principle has ever had a greater impact on services [for people with mental retardation] than that of normalization" (p. 116). The influence of the normalization principle went beyond the field of mental retardation, changing the way in which services have been delivered to people with developmental and other disabilities. In conjunction with the independent living movement, which had an influence that was felt most heavily by people with physical and sensory impairments, the normalization principle paved the way for self-determination. Indeed, self-determination is but one outgrowth of the normalization principle; other movements resulting from this principle include the deinstitutionalization and community living movements (Braddock, 1977).

Nirje (1969) explained that the normalization principle had its basis in Scandinavian experiences from the field and had emerged, in essence, from a Swedish law on mental retardation that was passed on July 1, 1968. In its original conceptualization, the normalization principle provided guidance for creating services that "let the mentally retarded obtain an existence as close to the normal as possible" (p. 227). Nirje stated, "As I see it, the normalization principle means making available to the mentally retarded patterns and conditions of everyday life which are as close as possible to the norms and patterns of the mainstream of society" (p. 227).

Nirje (1969) identified the following facets and implications of the normalization principle:

1. Normalization means a normal rhythm of day.
2. Normalization implies a normal routine of life.
3. Normalization means to experience the normal rhythm of the year.
4. Normalization means the opportunity to undergo normal developmental experiences of the life cycle.
5. Normalization means that the choices, wishes, and desires of people with mental retardation have to be taken into consideration as nearly as possible, and respected.
6. Normalization means living in a bisexual world.
7. Normalization means normal economic standards for people with mental retardation.
8. Normalization means that the standards of the physical facility should be the same as those regularly applied in society to the same kind of facilities for ordinary citizens.

Scheerenberger (1987) noted that "at this stage in its development, the normalization principle basically reflected a lifestyle, one diametrically opposed to many prevailing institutional practices" (p. 117). Burton Blatt's exposé of the conditions of institutions in the United States, *Christmas in Purgatory* (Blatt & Kaplan, 1966), illustrated the degree to which the ideas and lifestyle forwarded by the normalization principle differed from the practice of the day. In fact, the ideas forwarded by Nirje in 1969 remain, to a significant extent, the philosophical basis on which exemplary services are based almost 30 years after their original presentation.

Nirje (1969) expanded on these ideas, explaining that a "normal rhythm of the day" means that people with disabilities should go about their day in much the same way most people do: getting out of bed, getting dressed, eating under normal circumstances within typical settings (e.g., with their families), going to bed at times comparable with peers, and having opportunities for personal time and relaxation. A "normal routine of life" means that people with disabilities should live in one place, work or attend school in another, and have leisure activities in various places. A "normal rhythm of the year" means that people with disabilities should experience holidays and family days of personal significance, including vacations.

Much of the emphasis in the normalization principle relates to the importance for people with disabilities to experience the rich stimulation of being involved in one's community, living with family members, and experiencing friendships. The normalization principle stresses that contact with people without disabilities and people from both genders is critically important for people with disabilities of all ages. The importance of economic self sufficiency is also highlighted. Finally, it is evident that self-determination is critical to the normalization principle, as Nirje (1972) went on to describe in subsequent writings. At a time when most service providers to people with disabilities viewed them as patients, when public education was not available, and when public opinion viewed them as charity cases and eternal children, Nirje stressed the importance of choice and the need to respect the preferences and dreams of people with mental retardation. In many ways the self-determination movement is not new; it simply took almost 30 years before others recognized its importance.

Over the years, the normalization principle has had several reconceptualizations. In 1972, Wolfensberger, who more than anyone else is responsible for bringing the normalization principle to the attention of Americans, redefined the normalization principle as the "utilization of means which are as culturally normal as possible in order to establish and maintain personal behaviors and characteristics which are as culturally normative as possible" (p. 28). As Scheerenberger (1987) noted, Wolfensberger's redefinition shifted the definition of the normalization principle from "what previously had been a means or a process" to a goal, focusing on the behavior of people with mental retardation as well as their lifestyle and physical environment. In 1983, Wolfensberger again redefined normalization, adopting the term *social role valorization* in its stead and focusing on the issues of valuing or devaluing people who fall out of the traditional norms of society (Scheerenberger, 1987).

The application of the normalization principle has had a significant impact on the lives of people with disabilities. For the first time, issues such as choice and the dignity of risk surfaced and became part of the discussion. Eventually, through civil and legal protections, people with disabilities themselves came to the table to join that discussion and stressed the primacy of choice and control in their lives. Self-determination is considered a critical educational outcome at least partially because the normalization principle provided fuel for the fire, particularly the earliest, and in many ways most radical, conceptualization of normalization as a way of living for people with disabilities that was very different from the reality of the late 1960s and 1970s.

Independent Living, Self-Help, and Self-Advocacy Movements

Driedger (1989) pointed out that "many disabled people view their rights movement as the last in a long series of movements for rights—labor, blacks, colonized people, poor people, women—and now people with disabilities" (p. 1). Critical to this rights movement has been the emergence of organizations composed of people with specific disabilities. Driedger suggested that three branches of the people with disabilities movement have emerged since 1970: the independent living movement, consumer organizations, and self-help groups. The independent living movement, which emerged almost in parallel with the normalization principle, focused on enabling people with disabilities to live as independently as possible in their communities. The movement was given considerable impetus when the Rehabilitation Act of 1973 allocated money to establish Independent Living Centers (ILCs), consumer-controlled, cross-disability, nonresidential, private, nonprofit organizations that provide services that promote independence, productivity, and an enhanced quality of life for people with disabilities. The key to the success of ILCs was the fact that they were consumer controlled, that is, run by people with disabilities providing assistance to other people with disabilities. The Centers for Independent Living program supports approximately 250 centers nationally, providing services to more than 100,000 people with significant physical and mental disabilities. Consumer organizations are similar to ILCs, but they do not provide services and instead serve a monitoring and advocacy role.

Self-help groups are also consumer organized and run entities that have been formed around the world to lobby and advocate for government funding of disability services and legislative protections to combat discrimination and achieve equal access to housing, employment, education, and other basic civil rights. The international organization that includes most consumer and self-help groups is called Disabled People's International. In the 1980s, groups for people with mental retardation began to emerge that emulated the structure and intent of existing self-help groups and also provided a vehicle for personal advocacy and socialization. These groups became known as self-advocacy groups, and currently there are more than 500 self-advocacy groups around the nation, organized and run by people with mental retardation (Dybwad & Bersani, 1996).

The importance of these consumer organized and controlled organizations in the emergence of the self-determination movement cannot be underestimated. Not only did such organizations provide opportunities for greater independence and expand the desire for increased choice and control, they also provided the opportunity for people with disabilities to become informed, active advocates. Such advocacy eventually led to the passage of civil rights legislation that has been equally important in the emergence of self-determination.

Civil Rights Protections

One of the most visible outcomes of the disability rights movement since the 1970s has been the emergence of civil rights legislation protecting the rights of people with disabilities. Turnbull suggested that

> A major legal development in this decade has been the extension of the principle of egalitarianism to people with disabilities. [This principle] says that all persons, however unequal they may be in terms of their abilities, should be treated equally by being granted equal opportunities. (1986, p. 11)

Among the most visible of these protections is the ADA, which was signed into law in 1990. The ADA bans discrimination based on disability and gives individuals with disabilities civil rights protections equivalent to those provided to individuals in previous civil rights legislation on the basis of race, sex, national origin, and religion. The ADA guarantees equal opportunity for individuals with disabilities in employment, public accommodations, transportation, state and local government services, and telecommunication relay services. The ADA provides civil rights protections to individuals with disabilities in areas that are important to transition programming, such as employment, transportation, and public accommodations; and along with other federal initiatives affecting transition (e.g., the Carl D. Perkins Vocational and Applied Technology Education Act of 1990 [PL 101-392], the School-to-Work Opportunities Act of 1994 [PL 103-239]), the ADA provides both more opportunity for students with disabilities to achieve positive adult outcomes and more impetus to the field to focus on transition and self-determination.

The latter is true because these protections guarantee equal rights and access but not success. To maximize the opportunities of the ADA and other protections, people with disabilities

> must become qualified through career education and vocational training and learn how to make employers aware that they are qualified. Students must leave school better able to advocate on their own behalf and use existing resources to network and locate employment. (Wehmeyer & Ward, 1995, p. 108)

This further confirms the importance of the transition requirements of IDEA (see Chapter 3).

The Individuals with Disabilities Education Act has been characterized at its most basic level as a civil rights act. As discussed in Chapter 3, IDEA guarantees students with disabilities access to a free, appropriate public education, and it provides procedural guidelines and safeguards for the education of students with disabilities. The addition of the student involvement requirements in the 1991 reauthorization of IDEA have focused considerable attention on the importance of self-determination. The IDEA Amendments of 1997 kept these student involvement requirements and also required that at age 14 a student's individualized education program include a statement of transition service needs.

FACTORS PROVIDING
IMPETUS TO SELF-DETERMINATION

The changing perspective of disability in U.S. society, coupled with (and brought about by) changes in service delivery driven by the normalization principle and the independent living and self-help/self-advocacy movements and supported by civil rights legislation, provided impetus for self-determination to emerge as an important educational outcome. Once these antecedents were in place, the acceptance of self-determination as a critical educational outcome was propelled by a series of factors, including 1) the emerging voices of people with disabilities demanding greater control and choice, 2) disappointing findings from studies examining current adult outcomes for youth with disabilities exiting the school system, 3) evidence supporting the link between self-determination and more positive adult outcomes, 4) evidence indicating the lack of self-determination for many adults with disabilities, 5) the emergence of self-directed learning as an effective educational practice, and 6) the increased emphasis on creating a successful school-to-work transition. The latter, an increased focus on transition, is considered independently in the next chapter. The remainder are described in greater detail in the following sections.

Voices of People with Disabilities

Bersani (1996) described three "waves" of leadership in the field of developmental disabilities. The first wave, that of professionals as leaders, spanned from as early as 1850 to as late as 1950. Bersani noted that this era of professionalism was a time during which the field we now conceptualize as developmental disabilities was, in essence, an academic discipline. Within this discipline, professionals in the fields of medicine, psychology, social work, and education who "developed test procedures, reached clinical insights, identified new disabilities, described various impairments and started new programs" (p. 259) were the unquestioned leaders. The most visible names from this era, such as Itard, Howe, Seguin, Binet, and Doll, illustrate the overwhelming influence of medical professionals in the field. Not surprisingly, decisions during this era were made almost exclusively by professionals.

The second wave introduced a significant shift in the balance of power. In the late 1940s and early 1950s, parents of children with disabilities began to organize and to demand increased services for their children and a voice in the decisions concerning those services. Parents began to learn the jargon of professionals and, slowly, began to assume visible roles of leadership in the emerging field of developmental disabilities. Parents such as Elizabeth Boggs from the National Association for Retarded Citizens and Elsie Helsel of the United Cerebral Palsy Associations became key players in making policy and decisions (Bersani, 1996). Parents and professionals formed sometimes uneasy alliances and, with the advent of legislative and judicial protections, the types and availability of services expanded dramatically. Although there was an emerging call for self-determination for people with disabilities during this era (Nirje, 1972), control over decisions rested almost exclusively in the hands of professionals and parents.

The third wave described by Bersani (1996), the consumer or self-advocacy wave, brought people with disabilities to the negotiating table. Enabled by legislative protections and emboldened by prior civil rights movements, people with disabilities began to demand that they be involved in decisions that had an impact on their lives. Control, choice, and self-determination emerged as issues critically important to people with disabilities, topics that too rarely had been at the forefront of decisions in previous eras. At the 1989 National Self-Determination Conference, Robert Williams clearly articulated this emphasis:

We do not have to be told what self-determination means. We already know what self-determination means. We already know that it is just a ten dollar word for choice. That it is another word for describing a life filled with rising expectations, dignity, responsibility and opportunity.

But, without being afforded the right and opportunity to make choices in our lives, we will never obtain full, first class American citizenship. This is why we are here today: to reassert these fundamental rights and lay claim to them as ours. (p. 16)

Irving Martin, a member of the Achieving Change Together (ACT) self-advocacy organization in Minnesota, put it this way:

What it all comes down to is choice, and the right to chase our dreams. What I mean is this—the power to direct our lives the way we want, not the way others expect us; the ability to use the control we have as citizens to vote, to choose where and with whom we want to live, to decide where we want to work; and to make decisions that are right for us. Most importantly, self-determination means respecting our right to pursue our own goals and dreams. I don't think that is asking too much, do you? (personal communication, 1988)

The message from people with disabilities was loud and unequivocal. Control, choice, and self-determination were critical to their quality of life; and they had the same right to experience these as any other citizen. Because of the groundwork laid by the disability rights, independent living, normalization, and self-advocacy/self-help movements (see Chapter 3), people with disabilities were ready to speak up and provide leadership when they were given the opportunity.

Adult Outcomes of Graduates with Disabilities

A second factor that provided considerable impetus to the emergence of self-determination as an important educational outcome were findings that students with disabilities were experiencing less positive outcomes after leaving school than would be preferred. As the first generation of students with disabilities who received educational programming under the Education for All Handicapped Children Act of 1975 (PL 94-142) began to graduate and leave school, a number of follow-up and follow-along studies were funded to track graduates and school leavers and to examine adult outcomes for these young people, including employment status, living arrangements, postsecondary educational access, and social/community integration. Chadsey-Rusch, Rusch, and O'Reilly (1991) reviewed these studies, examining the research on employment, residential, and social/interpersonal relationship outcomes for youth with disabilities who made the transition from school to adulthood; they concluded that

The outcomes experienced by youth with disabilities for employment, residential status, and social and interpersonal relationships are disappointing. Although rates vary from state to state, most youths with disabilities are either not employed or under-employed. Few youths live independently, many are not well integrated into their communities, and some appear to be lonely. Overall, youths with disabilities face a very uncertain future that holds little promise of improving as they age. (p. 28)

The National Longitudinal Transition Study of Special Education Students (NLTS), sponsored by OSEP, provided data regarding the adult outcomes of more than 8,000 youth with disabilities (Blackorby & Wagner, 1996). The NLTS used a weighted sample that generalizes to youth with disabilities across the nation. The findings from this comprehensive study (listed next) reinforced the need to continue to focus on transition-related outcomes and to identify practices that will better enable students with disabilities to become self-sufficient young people.

- The rate of competitive employment for youth with disabilities lagged significantly behind the employment rate of youth in the general population both 2 years after high school (46%–59%) and 3–5 years out of school (57%–69%).
- Gender, type of disability, and ethnic background all affected the probability that students would be competitively employed.
- Only 9% of competitively employed youth with disabilities 2 years out of school earned greater than $6 per hour, and that percentage grew to only 40% by 3–5 years.
- Only 14% of youth with disabilities who had been out of school for 2 years reported that they attended some type of postsecondary school compared with 53% of youth in the general population. At 3–5 years, 27% of youth with disabilities reported having been involved in postsecondary education at some time after leaving secondary school, compared with 68% of peers in the general population.
- Thirty-three percent of youth in the general population were living independently less than 2 years after graduation, compared with 13% of youth with disabilities. By 3–5 years, 60% of youth without disabilities lived independently, compared with 37% of youth with disabilities.

Findings from the NLTS, along with results from numerous follow-up and follow-along studies, suggest that, although youth with disabilities have made considerable gains in achieving positive adult outcomes over time, if self-sufficiency is to be realized as a goal of the educational process a great deal more needs to be done. The NLTS and other studies provide a "pulse-check" for educators working with children and youth with disabilities, a chance to examine what has worked and to identify what might be done to reach the next plateau.

Link Between Self-Determination and Positive Adult Outcomes

The proposition that self-determination is an important educational goal if youth with disabilities are to achieve more positive adult outcomes presumes that self-determination and positive adult outcomes are causally linked. Although such a link seems intuitively obvious, until the early 1990s, empirical evidence supporting this assumption has been limited. Instead, the link between self-determination and positive adult outcomes for youths with disabilities was established by examining the contributions of the component elements to an enhanced quality of life and favorable adult outcomes.

Increased opportunities and capacities to express preferences and make choices have been linked to reductions in problem behaviors exhibited by individuals with severe disabilities (Gardner, Cole, Berry, & Nowinski, 1983; Grace, Cowart, & Matson, 1988; Munk & Repp, 1994); increased participation of children, youths, and adults with and without disabilities in appropriate or adaptive tasks (Koestner, Ryan, Bernieri, & Holt, 1984; Realon, Favell, & Lowerre, 1990; Swann & Pittman, 1977); and more positive educational or achievement outcomes (Koenigs, Fielder, & deCharmes, 1977). Teaching effective decision-making and problem-solving skills has been shown to improve the adaptability skills (Mithaug, Martin, & Agran, 1987), employment outcomes (Park & Gaylord-Ross, 1989), parenting skills (Tymchuk, Andron, & Rahbar, 1988), and community living outcomes (Foxx & Bittle, 1989) of youths with disabilities.

Numerous research studies have been done linking self-management techniques to positive adult outcomes. Self-monitoring strategies are frequently used to improve work-related activities, such as attention to task, task completion, and task accuracy (Hughes, Korinek, & Gorman, 1991; McCarl, Svobodny, & Beare, 1991). Lovett and Haring (1989) showed that self-recording activities enabled adults with mental retardation to improve task completion of daily living activities. Self-instruction techniques have been used to solve job- and work-related problems successfully (Agran, Fodor-Davis, & Moore, 1986; Hughes & Petersen, 1989; Rusch, McKee, Chadsey-Rusch, & Renzaglia, 1988; Salend, Ellis, & Reynolds, 1989) and to teach social skills that are critical to independence (Agran, Salzberg, & Stowitschek, 1987; Hughes & Agran, 1993). Agran et al. (1987) found that self-instructional strategies increased the percentages of initiations with a work supervisor when employees, five individuals with mental retardation requiring limited to extensive supports, ran out of work materials or needed assistance. Lagomarcino and Rusch (1989) used a combination of self-reinforcement and self-monitoring procedures to improve the work performance of a student with mental retardation in a community setting. Moore, Agran, and Fodor-Davis (1989) applied a combination of student-directed activities, including self-instruction, goal setting, and self-reinforcement, to improve the production rate of workers with mental retardation who required extensive supports.

Internal locus of control has been linked to adaptive outcomes, including positive educational and achievement outcomes and increased time and attention to school-related tasks (Lefcourt, 1976). External orientations have, conversely, been linked to increased impulsivity in decision making, distractibility, and sociometric ratings of rejection from peers (Ollendick, Greene, Francis, & Baum, 1991; Ollendick & Schmidt, 1987).

Research on the component elements of self-determined behavior provide strong, though not direct, evidence that youth who are self-determined achieve more positive adult outcomes. Wehmeyer and Schwartz (1997) measured the self-determination status of 80 youth with cognitive disabilities (mental retardation or learning disability) using *The Arc's Self-Determination Scale* (Wehmeyer & Kelchner, 1995b), a student self-report measure of self-determined behavior and the essential characteristics of self-determination. One year after these students left high school, they and their families were contacted to determine their status in several areas, including living arrangements, current and past employment situations, postsecondary education status, and community integration outcomes.

These data were then analyzed, controlling for level of intelligence and type of disability. The data suggested a consistent trend in which self-determined youth appeared to do better than their peers 1 year out of school. Members of the high self-determination group were more likely to have expressed a preference to live outside the family home, have a savings or checking account, and be employed for pay. Students who earned the most had significantly higher self-determination scores, and individual subdomains of self-determination contributed significantly to the students' wage per hour. For example, Figure 1 shows the percentage of students in low and high self-determination groups (determined by a frequency distribution analysis) who paid their own telephone bill, maintained a checking and/or savings account, did their own grocery shopping, and arranged for their own transportation. Eighty percent of the high self-determination group worked for pay 1 year after graduation, whereas only 43%

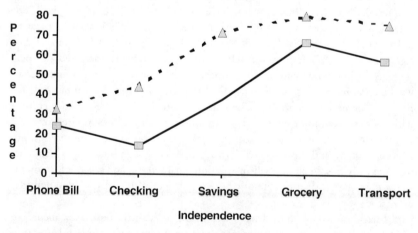

Figure 1. Percentage of students with low or high self-determination scores who controlled independent living activities. (— ▢ — = low self-determination; – –△– – = high self-determination.)

of the low self-determination group did likewise. Among school leavers who were employed, youth who were in the self-determined group earned significantly more per hour (mean = $4.26) than their peers in the low self-determination group (mean = $1.93).

An enhanced quality of life is another important transition-related outcome, one that is emerging as an "overarching principle that is applicable to the betterment of society as a whole" (Schalock, 1996, p. 123), and, specifically, is critically important to achieve significant improvements in the lives of people with disabilities. Schalock went on to state that

> the current paradigm shift in mental retardation and closely related disabilities, with its emphasis on self-determination, inclusion, equity, empowerment, community-based supports and quality outcome has forced service providers to focus on an enhanced quality of life for persons with disabilities. (p. 123)

Schalock suggested that quality of life is best viewed as an organizing concept to guide policy and practice to improve the life conditions of all people. Such a conceptualization recognizes that quality of life is composed of a number of core principles and dimensions. The core dimensions of quality of life include 1) emotional well-being, 2) interpersonal relations, 3) material well-being, 4) personal development, 5) physical well-being, 6) self-determination, 7) social inclusion, and 8) rights.

Like self-determination, quality of life focuses attention on both subjective and objective indicators. Dalkey (1972) stated that

> quality of life is related not just to the environment and to the external circumstances of an individual's life, but whether these factors constitute a major share of an individual's well-being, or whether they are dominated by factors such as a sense of achievement, love and affection, perceived freedom and so on.

An individual's quality of life is determined across settings, environments, and opportunities; and virtually all choices and decisions, at some level, contribute to an individual's quality of life. Conceptualizing self-determination as contributing to an enhanced quality of life reflects the importance of both major decisions that occur infrequently (e.g., buying a house, medical decisions) and daily choices that are less consequential but more frequent, such as what to wear or eat or how to spend one's free time.

Wehmeyer and Schwartz (in press) empirically examined the link between self-determination and quality of life for 50 adults with mental retardation living in group homes, using multiple discriminant function analysis and controlling for level of intelligence and environmental factors. They found that the level of self-determination could be predicted by examining a person's quality of life. That is, a person's relative self-determination was a strong predictor of his or her quality of life; people who were highly self-determined experienced a higher quality of life, whereas people who lacked self-determination appeared to experience a less positive quality of life.

How Self-Determined Are People with Disabilities

An assumption inherent in the need to promote self-determination as an educational outcome for youths with disabilities is that, given the causal relationship between self-determination and positive adult outcomes, individuals with disabilities are not currently achieving this outcome. Obviously, if they were there would be no reason to provide targeted, intensive instruction in these areas. A growing body of research, however, suggests that adults with cognitive and developmental disabilities are not self-determined and that such intervention is warranted.

Wehmeyer and Metzler (1995) examined the self-determination of almost 5,000 adults with mental retardation and developmental disabilities. Findings from this study illustrate the degree to which most adults with cognitive disabilities lack self-determination. From this group, only 33% of respondents indicated that they had a choice regarding where they currently lived; 12% had a voice in hiring the staff or attendant who worked with them; 21% chose, either with or without assistance, their roommate; 44% chose their job or day activity; 26% indicated that they had the opportunity to pay their own bills; and 42% indicated that they did any banking.

Stancliffe and Wehmeyer (1995) reviewed the literature related to choice making by people with mental retardation and developmental disabilities and concluded that individuals had few opportunities to make meaningful decisions about their lives. Similarly, Wehmeyer, Kelchner, and Richards (1995) found that in a sample of more than 400 members of self-advocacy groups, a large percentage made few choices in their lives. Although 30% of the group indicated they did not choose where they live, only 15% indicated they had selected where they live unassisted. Comparatively, Kozleski and Sands (1992) used the same survey with adults without disabilities and found that only 10% indicated they had no choice in where they lived and 13% had no choice in their roommates.

If one examines the essential characteristics and component elements of self-determination, the findings are much the same. Murtaugh and Zettin (1990), in a longitudinal study of the level of autonomy afforded adolescents with learning disabilities, concluded that these students lagged well behind their peers without disabilities on measures that looked at responsibility for actions. Likewise, Wehmeyer and Kelchner (1995a) found that adults and adolescents with mental retardation had limited autonomy. Participants in this research ($n =$ 408) were less likely to perform daily living or caregiving tasks or interact with others in the community than peers without disabilities. Wehmeyer (1994) found that students with mental retardation and learning disabilities held perceptions of psychological empowerment that were significantly less adaptive than peers without disabilities, even when those peers had experienced educational failure. In addition, maladaptive perceptions of self-determination were barriers to career decision making for youth with cognitive disabilities (Wehmeyer, 1993). Wehmeyer and Kelchner (1996) confirmed that students with mental retardation and learning disabilities held less adaptive locus of control orientations than peers without disabilities and perceived their teachers to be more control oriented. For all students, with and without disabilities, perceptions of controlling classroom environments were predictive of less adaptive, more externalized perceptions of locus of control.

Although we have focused most of our research efforts toward examining self-determination of people with mental retardation, these experiences are not unique to this population. Jaskulski, Metzler, and Zierman (1990) surveyed more than 13,000 people with developmental disabilities to determine the degree to which they were integrated into their communities, functioned independently, and led productive lives. Forty-one percent of this sample had a physical disability, 10% experienced a sensory disability, 6% an emotional disability, and 42% were identified as having mental retardation. Thus, 57% of the sample did not have a cognitive disability. From this group (respondents without mental retardation), 41% indicated they had no choice in their current living arrangement. Sands and Kozleski (1994) analyzed differences between adults with disabilities and adults without disabilities on multiple indicators of quality of life. They concluded that

> most importantly, the degree of choice which individuals with disabilities were able to exercise was significantly limited when compared to adults without disabilities. This lack of opportunity to make choices extended from relatively innocuous activities such as decorating a bedroom to such fundamental choices as to who shares that bedroom. (p. 98)

In all, research that has examined adult outcomes for individuals with disabilities suggests that people with disabilities continue to experience limited self-determination and a less positive quality of life. Given the apparent relationship between self-determination and positive adult outcomes, the need to provide more self-determination instruction is compelling.

Emergence of Self-Directed Learning

A final factor in the emergence of self-determination as an important educational outcome has been the development of self-directed learning strategies. As discussed in detail in Chapter 12, student-directed learning refers to instructional activities in which students have control over their learning, experience opportunities to set goals, define actions based on those goals, implement those actions, evaluate their outcomes, and adjust their performances. Several chapters in the text describe various self-management strategies, including self-instruction and self-monitoring. The success of self-management strategies has contributed to the shift from teacher-directed to student-directed learning and has led to emphasis on self-determination and student involvement.

CONCLUSION

The current emphasis on self-determination has been fueled by several factors that, considered together, emphasize the importance of devoting instructional time to promoting self-determination for youth with disabilities. It may well be that, as Halloran (1993) suggested, self-determination is the "ultimate goal of education" (p. 214). It is certainly an outcome that is attainable for many youth with disabilities because, as documented in subsequent chapters, effective practices are available to enable learners with disabilities to acquire or develop the skills and attitudes that comprise the component elements of self-determination and that lead one to be self-determined.

QUESTIONS FOR REVIEW

1. Discuss the impact of stereotypes about disabilities on the self-determination of people with disabilities.
2. List and discuss five rights of individuals with disabilities.
3. The Rehabilitation Act Amendments of 1992 state that all human abilities and experiences exist on a continuum and disability is a part of that continuum. Discuss how this differs from other conceptualizations of disability.
4. Discuss the normalization principle and its impact on the lives of people with disabilities.
5. Briefly describe the three "waves" of leadership in the field of developmental disabilities.
6. Discuss the impact of self-help and self-advocacy organizations on the self-determination movement.
7. How might the self-determination movement have an impact on school reform and educational services? How might it affect disability services outside of education?

REFERENCES

Agran, M., Fodor-Davis, J., & Moore, S. (1986). The effects of self-instructional training on job-task sequencing: Suggesting a problem-solving strategy. *Education and Training of the Mentally Retarded, 21,* 273–281.

Agran, M., Salzberg, C.L., & Stowitschek, J.J. (1987). An analysis of the effects of a social skills training program using self-instructions on the acquisition and generalization of two social behaviors in a work setting. *Journal of The Association for Persons with Severe Handicaps, 12,* 131–139.

Americans with Disabilities Act (ADA) of 1990, PL 101-336, 42 U.S.C §§ 201 *et seq.*

Bersani, H. (1996). Leadership in developmental disabilities: Where we've been, where we are, and where we are going. In G. Dybwad & H. Bersani (Eds.), *New voices: Self-advocacy by people with disabilities* (pp. 258–269). Cambridge, MA: Brookline Books.

Blackorby, J., & Wagner, M. (1996). Longitudinal postschool outcomes of youth with disabilities: Findings from the National Longitudinal Transition Study. *Exceptional Children, 62*, 399–414.

Blatt, B., & Kaplan, F. (1966). *Christmas in purgatory.* Needham Heights, MA: Allyn & Bacon.

Braddock, D. (1977). *Opening closed doors: The deinstitutionalization of disabled individuals.* Reston, VA: Council for Exceptional Children.

Carl D. Perkins Vocational and Applied Technology Education Act of 1990, PL 101-392, 104 Statutes at Large 753–804, 806–834.

Chadsey-Rusch, J., Rusch, F., & O'Reilly, M.F. (1991). Transition from school to integrated communities. *Remedial and Special Education, 12*, 23–33.

Cutler, B.C. (1993). *You, your child, and special education: A guide to making the system work.* Baltimore: Paul H. Brookes Publishing Co.

Dalkey, N.C. (1972). *Studies in the quality of life: Delphi and decision-making.* Lexington, MA: Lexington Books.

Driedger, D. (1989). *The last civil rights movement: Disabled Peoples' International.* New York: St. Martin's Press.

Dybwad, G., & Bersani, H. (1996). *New voices: Self-advocacy by people with disabilities.* Cambridge, MA: Brookline Books.

Education for All Handicapped Children Act of 1975, PL 94-142, 20 U.S.C. §§ 1400 *et seq.*

Education of the Handicapped Act (EHA) of 1970, PL 91-230, 20 U.S.C. §§ 1400 *et seq.*

Field, S. (1996). Self-determination instructional strategies for youth with learning disabilities. *Journal of Learning Disabilities, 29*, 40–52.

Foxx, R.M., & Bittle, R.G. (1989). *Thinking it through: Teaching a problem-solving strategy for community living.* Champaign, IL: Research Press.

Gardner, W.I., Cole, C.L., Berry, D.L., & Nowinski, J.M. (1983). Reduction of disruptive behaviors in mentally retarded adults: A self-management approach. *Behavior Modification, 7*, 76–96.

Goddard, H.H. (1912). *The Kallikak family: A study in the heredity of feeble-mindedness.* New York: Macmillan.

Goddard, H.H. (1926). *Feeble-mindedness: Its causes and consequences.* New York: Macmillan.

Grace, N., Cowart, C., & Matson, J.L. (1988). Reinforcement and self-control for treating a chronic case of self-injury in Lesch-Nyhan syndrome. *Journal of the Multihandicapped Person, 1*, 53–59.

Halloran, W.D. (1993). Transition services requirement: Issues, implications, challenge. In R.C. Eaves & P.J. McLaughlin (Eds.), *Recent advances in special education and rehabilitation* (pp. 210–224). Boston: Andover Medical.

Hughes, C., & Agran, M. (1993). Teaching persons with severe disabilities to use self-instruction in community settings: An analysis of applications. *Journal of The Association for Persons with Severe Handicaps, 18*, 261–274.

Hughes, C.A., Korinek, L., & Gorman, J. (1991). Self-management for students with mental retardation in public school settings: A research review. *Education and Training in Mental Retardation, 26*, 271–291.

Hughes, C.A., & Petersen, D.L. (1989). Utilizing a self-instructional training package to increase on-task behavior and work performance. *Education and Training in Mental Retardation, 24*, 114–120.

Individuals with Disabilities Education Act (IDEA) of 1990, PL 101-476, 20 U.S.C. §§ 1400 *et seq.*

Individuals with Disabilities Education Act Amendments of 1991, PL 102-119, 20 U.S.C. §§ 1400 *et seq.*

Individuals with Disabilities Education Act Amendments of 1997, PL 105-17, 20 U.S.C. §§ 1400 *et seq.*

Jaskulski, T., Metzler, C., & Zierman, S.A. (1990). *Forging a new era: The 1990 reports on people with developmental disabilities.* Washington, DC: National Association of Developmental Disabilities Councils.

Koenigs, S., Fielder, M., & deCharmes, R. (1977). Teacher beliefs, classroom interaction and personal control. *Journal of Applied Social Psychology, 7,* 95–114.

Koestner, R., Ryan, R.M., Bernieri, F., & Holt, K. (1984). The effects of controlling versus informational limit-setting styles on children's intrinsic motivation and creativity. *Journal of Personality, 52,* 233–248.

Kozleski, E.B., & Sands, D.J. (1992). The yardstick of social validity: Evaluating quality of life as perceived by adults without disabilities. *Education and Training in Mental Retardation, 27,* 119–131.

Lagomarcino, T.R., & Rusch, F.R. (1989). Utilizing self-management procedures to teach independent performance. *Education and Training in Mental Retardation, 24,* 297–305.

Lefcourt, H.M. (1976). *Locus of control.* Hillsdale, NJ: Lawrence Erlbaum Associates.

Lovett, D.L., & Haring, K.A. (1989). The effects of self-management training on the daily living of adults with mental retardation. *Education and Training in Mental Retardation, 24,* 306–307.

McCarl, J.J., Svobodny, L., & Beare, P.L. (1991). Self-recording in a classroom for students with mild to moderate mental handicaps: Effects on productivity and on-task behavior. *Education and Training in Mental Retardation, 26,* 79–88.

Mithaug, D.E., Martin, J.E., & Agran, M. (1987). Adaptability instruction: The goal of transitional programming. *Exceptional Children, 53,* 500–505.

Moore, S.C., Agran, M., & Fodor-Davis, J. (1989). Using self-management strategies to increase the production rates of workers with severe handicaps. *Education and Training in Mental Retardation, 24,* 324–332.

Munk, D.D., & Repp, A.C. (1994). The relationship between instructional variables and problem behavior: A review. *Exceptional Children, 60,* 390–401.

Murtaugh, M., & Zettin, A.G. (1990). The development of autonomy among learning handicapped and non-handicapped adolescents: A longitudinal perspective. *Journal of Youth and Adolescence, 19,* 245–255.

Nirje, B. (1969). The normalization principle and its human management implications. In R.B. Kugel & W. Wolfensberger (Eds.), *Changing residential patterns for the mentally retarded* (pp. 227–254). Washington, DC: President's Committee on Mental Retardation.

Nirje, B. (1972). The right to self-determination. In W. Wolfensberger (Ed.), *Normalization: The principle of normalization* (pp. 176–200). Toronto, Ontario, Canada: National Institute on Mental Retardation.

Ollendick, T.H., Greene, R.W., Francis, G., & Baum, C.G. (1991). Sociometric status: Its stability and validity among neglected, rejected and popular children. *Journal of Child Psychology and Psychiatry, 32,* 525–534.

Ollendick, T.H., & Schmidt, C.R. (1987). Social learning constructs in the prediction of peer interaction. *Journal of Clinical Child Psychology, 16,* 80–87.

Park, H.-S., & Gaylord-Ross, R. (1989). A problem-solving approach to social skills training in employment settings with mentally retarded youth. *Journal of Applied Behavior Analysis, 22,* 273–380.

Realon, R.E., Favell, J.E., & Lowerre, A. (1990). The effects of making choices on engagement levels with persons who are profoundly mentally handicapped. *Education and Training in Mental Retardation, 25,* 248–254.

Rehabilitation Act of 1973, PL 93-112, 29 U.S.C. §§ 701 *et seq.*

Rehabilitation Act Amendments of 1992, PL 102-569, 29 U.S.C. §§ 701 *et seq.*

Rusch, F.R., McKee, M., Chadsey-Rusch, J., & Renzaglia, A. (1988). Teaching a student with severe handicaps to self-instruct: A brief report. *Education and Training in Mental Retardation, 23,* 51–58.

Salend, S.J., Ellis, L.L., & Reynolds, C.J. (1989). Using self-instruction to teach vocational skills to individuals who are severely retarded. *Education and Training in Mental Retardation, 24,* 248–254.

Sands, D.J., & Kozleski, E.B. (1994). Quality of life differences between adults with and without disabilities. *Education and Training in Mental Retardation and Developmental Disabilities, 29,* 90–101.

Schalock, R.L. (1996). Reconsidering the conceptualization and measurement of quality of life. In R. Schalock (Ed.), *Quality of life: Conceptualization and measurement* (Vol. I, pp. 123–139). Washington, DC: American Association on Mental Retardation.

Scheerenberger, R.C. (1987). *A history of mental retardation: A quarter century of promise.* Baltimore: Paul H. Brookes Publishing Co.

School-to-Work Opportunities Act of 1994, PL 103-239, 20 U.S.C. §§ 6101 *et seq.*

Shapiro, J.P. (1993). *No pity: People with disabilities forging a new civil rights movement.* New York: Times Books.

Stancliffe, R., & Wehmeyer, M.L. (1995). Variability in the availability of choice to adults with mental retardation. *Journal of Vocational Rehabilitation, 5,* 319–328.

Swann, W.B., & Pittman, T.S. (1977). Initiating play activity of children: The moderating influence of verbal cues on intrinsic motivation. *Child Development, 48,* 1128–1132.

Turnbull, H.R. (1986). *Free appropriate public education: The law and children with disabilities.* Denver, CO: Love.

Tymchuk, A.J., Andron, I., & Rahbar, B., (1988). Effective decision-making/problem-solving training with mothers who have mental retardation. *American Journal on Mental Retardation, 92,* 302–314.

Ward, M.J. (1988). The many facets of self-determination. *NICHCY transition summary: National Information Center for Children and Youth with Disabilities, 5,* 2–3.

Ward, M.J. (1996). Coming of age in the age of self-determination: A historical and personal perspective. In D.J. Sands & M.L. Wehmeyer (Eds.), *Self-determination across the life span: Independence and choice for people with disabilities* (pp. 3–16). Baltimore: Paul H. Brookes Publishing Co.

Ward, M.J., & Kohler, P.D. (1996). Teaching self-determination: Content and process. In L.E. Powers, G.H.S. Singer, & J. Sowers (Eds.), *On the road to autonomy: Promoting self-competence in children and youth with disabilities* (pp. 275–290). Baltimore: Paul H. Brookes Publishing Co.

Wehmeyer, M.L. (1993). Perceptual and psychological factors in career decision-making of adolescents with and without cognitive disabilities. *Career Development of Exceptional Individuals, 16,* 135–146.

Wehmeyer, M.L. (1994). Perceptions of self-determination and psychological empowerment of adolescents with mental retardation. *Education and Training in Mental Retardation and Developmental Disability, 29,* 9–21.

Wehmeyer, M.L., & Davis, S. (1995). Family involvement. In D. Brolin (Ed.), *Career education: A functional life skills approach.* Columbus, OH: Charles E. Merrill/Prentice Hall.

Wehmeyer, M.L., & Kelchner, K. (1995a). Measuring the autonomy of adults with mental retardation: A self-report version of the Autonomous Functioning Checklist. *Career Development of Exceptional Individuals, 18,* 3–20.

Wehmeyer, M.L., & Kelchner, K. (1995b). *The Arc's Self-Determination Scale.* Arlington, TX: The Arc National Headquarters.

Wehmeyer, M.L., & Kelchner, K. (1996). Perceptions of classroom environment, locus of control and academic attributions of adolescents with and without cognitive disabilities. *Career Development for Exceptional Individuals, 19,* 15–29.

Wehmeyer, M.L., Kelchner, K., & Richards, S. (1995). Individual and environmental factors related to the self-determination of adults with mental retardation. *Journal of Vocational Rehabilitation, 5,* 291–305.

Wehmeyer, M.L., Martin, J.E., & Sands, D.J. (1997). Self-determination for children and youth with developmental disabilities. In A. Hilton & R. Ringlaben (Eds.), *Best practices in educating students with developmental disabilities* (pp. 549–569). Austin, TX: PRO-ED.

Wehmeyer, M.L., & Metzler, C.A. (1995). How self-determined are people with mental retardation? The National Consumer Survey. *Mental Retardation, 33,* 111–119.

Wehmeyer, M.L., & Schwartz, M. (1997). Self-determination and positive adult outcomes: A follow-up study of youth with mental retardation or learning disabilities. *Exceptional Children, 63,* 245–255.

Wehmeyer, M.L., & Schwartz, M. (in press). The relationship between self-determination and quality of life for adults with mental retardation. *Education and Training in Mental Retardation and Developmental Disabilities.*

Wehmeyer, M.L., & Ward, M.J. (1995). The spirit of the IDEA mandate: Student involvement in transition planning. *Journal of the Association for Vocational Special Needs Education, 17,* 108–111.

Williams, R.R. (1989). Creating a new world of opportunity: Expanding choice and self-determination in the lives of Americans with severe disability by 1992 and beyond. In R. Perske (Ed.), *Proceedings from the National Conference on Self-Determination* (pp. 16–17). Minneapolis, MN: Institute on Community Integration.

Wolfensberger, W. (1972). *Normalization: The principle of normalization.* Toronto, Ontario, Canada: National Institute on Mental Retardation.

CHAPTER 3

Transition Services
and Self-Determination

After reading this chapter, you will be able to

1. Define transition services and identify the historical antecedents to the transition movement

2. Discuss the link between self-determination and transition

3. Identify ways in which traditional transition models have limited self-determination

4. Describe strategies that support both an effective transition and self-determination

KEY TERMS

1.	Adolescence	7.	Social acceptance
2.	Adult outcomes	8.	Social skills
3.	Career education	9.	Student involvement
4.	Independence objectives	10.	Transition services
5.	IDEA	11.	Transition support services
6.	Outcome-based services	12.	Work-study programs

As discussed in Chapter 2, among the most important factors in the emergence of self-determination as a critical educational outcome for youth with disabilities has been the transition mandates in the Individuals with Disabilities Education Act (IDEA) of 1990 (PL 101-476). Indeed, the increasingly visible role that the transition movement is playing in the education of all learners with disabilities has promoted interest in self-determination. This chapter outlines the history of the transition movement and its link to self-determination and examines the relationship between recommended practices in transition services and self-determination.

TRANSITION SERVICES

The transition movement has its historical roots in the work-study programs of the 1960s and the career education movement of the 1970s (Halpern, 1992). In 1984 Madeleine Will, assistant secretary of the Office of Special Education and Rehabilitative Services (OSERS), released a position paper that emphasized the importance of educational services to students with disabilities in order to facilitate their transition from school to work. The service delivery model described in that paper was the foundation for the transition movement. Subsequent refinements of the OSERS transition model recognized the importance of supporting the movement of students from secondary education settings to a variety of nonemployment environments such as living, recreation, and post-secondary education settings.

The 1990 amendments to the Education for All Handicapped Children Act of 1975 (PL 94-142), which guaranteed a free, appropriate public education for all students with disabilities (renamed IDEA in the 1990 legislation), first mandated that transition services be provided to students 16 years and older or students 14 years and older if appropriate. In this act, transition services were defined as

> a coordinated set of activities for a student, designed within an outcome-oriented process, that promotes movement from school to postschool activities, including post-secondary education, vocational training, integrated employment (including supported employment), continuing and adult education, adult services, independent living, or community participation. (IDEA, Sec. 602[a][19])

This definition illustrates the degree to which transition services have been broadened to focus on more than just employment outcomes. The intent of transition services is to promote movement from school to postschool activities, and the list of such postschool activities covers all domains in students' lives (e.g., social interaction, community involvement, leisure time). In addition, IDEA requires that transition services be designed within an outcome-oriented process. An outcome-oriented process is one that bases current services on students' desired future outcomes and results.

IDEA also mandated student involvement in transition planning by stating that needed transition services *must* be based on students' *preferences* and *interests.* Although IDEA leaves the statutory language regarding student involvement in educational planning meetings somewhat ambivalent (e.g., "when appropriate"), the regulations regarding student involvement in transition planning are clear and unambiguous. The regulations state that if one of the purposes of the meeting is to consider transition services, then the school *must* invite the student (Sec. 300.344[c]). The regulations then rightly point out that "for all students who are 16 years or older, one of the purposes of the annual meeting will always be the planning of transition services, because transition services are a required component of the IEP [individualized education program] for these students" (Sec. 300.344, Note 2). In other words, schools must invite all students ages 16 and older to planning meetings, and decisions made about students' transition services must be based on students' preferences and interests. Amendments to IDEA in 1997 kept the student involvement requirements of 1990, but the age requirement was changed; at age 14 a student's IEP must address needed transition services.

The transition requirements in IDEA basically make two demands related to student involvement: 1) that students be involved in their IEP meetings and 2) that transition programs be based on students' preferences and interests. Mithaug, Wolman, and Campeau (1992) suggested that the requirements in the IDEA transition services language "comprise a logical sequence or causal flow beginning with student-determined and defined needs, which lead to plans for coordinated services, which, in turn, result in community-based experiences that culminate in postschool adjustments" (p. 7). This causal flow is depicted in Figure 1. As Mithaug and colleagues pointed out, "for the first time, the mandated condition is for student preferences to drive service delivery" (p. 7).

In order to achieve both student involvement aspects of the transition mandate, students need to become self-determined. Although a student's physical presence at the IEP meeting may meet the statutory requirements of IDEA, his or her presence alone fails to meet the spirit or intent of IDEA mandate (Wehmeyer & Ward, 1995). Instead, the intent of IDEA is that students become, to the greatest degree possible, equal partners in transition planning and decision making. To accomplish this, students need to learn to solve problems and make decisions, provide informed consent, identify and evaluate goals and objectives and be able to advocate on their own behalf, negotiate and compromise, and provide some leadership. In order for transition programs to be based on students' preferences and interests, students need to be able to identify and communicate wants, preferences, needs, and interests and to identify their own instructional strengths and limitations. Subsequent chapters in this text provide materials and strategies to teach in these areas.

This student-centered model is very different from transition models in place prior to the passage of the transition mandates in IDEA. Although inde-

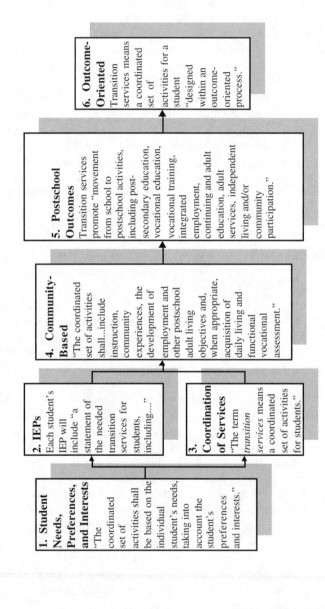

Figure 1. Causal sequence implied by IDEA, PL 101-476. (Adapted from Mithaug, Wolman, & Campeau, 1992.)

pendence and productivity have, historically, been outcomes that advocates of the transition movement and its antecedents (e.g., work-study programs and career education) sought to promote, some transition practices actually limited the degree to which students can achieve these outcomes. Ianacone and Stodden (1987) identified several such practices as follows:

- *Structuring dependence*—Classrooms for secondary-age students with disabilities are typically highly structured, limiting opportunities for students to make choices and decisions and restricting the chance to learn critical independent-living and autonomy skills.
- *Decision taking instead of decision making*—Despite the fact that the transition process presents an ideal situation in which to learn and practice goal-setting, decision-making, communication, group interaction, and other skills important for a successful transition to adulthood, most decisions are made by teachers or parents without any student involvement.
- *Postsecondary irrelevance*—Activities in which students with disabilities spend the bulk of their time are unrelated to vocational or other important post-secondary outcomes.
- *Misguided reinforcement*—Students are reinforced for behaviors such as compliance, staying in line, not talking, and other behaviors that place emphasis on dependence, rather than independence.
- *Self-fulfilling expectations*—Too many educators hold low expectations for students with disabilities that limit positive outcomes.
- *Focus on disability*—The transition process has too frequently followed the path of the general special education process and focused on disability and deficits instead of identifying strengths and weaknesses.

In short, although the increased emphasis on transition services brought about by the transition services mandates in IDEA, including student involvement in transition planning, has stimulated interest in self-determination, too many circumstances remain in which current transition practices stifle self-determination. As is discussed in the next section, more recent conceptualizations of transition services both recognize and seek to redress this situation.

WHY SHOULD SELF-DETERMINATION BE A FOCAL POINT FOR TRANSITION SERVICES?

Adolescence is a critical period for the emergence of self-determination. According to many developmental psychologists, "the major psychosocial task of adolescence is the formation of a coherent personal identity" (Damon, 1983, p. 307). Ward (1988) argued that for many adolescents this process is hindered by the presence of a disability. He indicated that many adolescents with disabilities find it difficult to achieve individuation while they rely on parents and others for meeting basic physical needs. Even when this barrier has been over-come, young people are still often faced with overprotectiveness and tendencies to overstructure environments by those around them.

A focus on self-determination can have an impact on many of the problems with existing transition programs, including those identified by Ianacone and Stodden (1987). Wehman (1993) identified several areas in which positive de-velopments have occurred in the area of transition. These include

- *Increased awareness of post–age-21 outcomes for youth with disabilities—* Numerous follow-up studies from the mid-1980s on document outcomes for youth with disabilities and provide a foundation for future changes.
- *Positive legislative advances—*As discussed previously, transition services are now mandated by IDEA and other legislative protections, particularly the Americans with Disabilities Act (ADA) of 1990, which provides considerable legislative impetus to transition and self-determination.
- *Advances in behavioral and rehabilitation technology—*Wehman (1993) pointed out that the field, as a whole, has made significant advances, albeit sometimes slowly, in identifying the most effective ways to provide vocational and behavioral intervention for individuals with disabilities.
- *Family and student attitudes—*Family and student expectations for the future have changed dramatically as students with disabilities have gained access to a free, appropriate public education. Families now see outcomes such as employment and independent living as options for their son or daughter.

Wehman also identified critical transition issues for the 21st century, the first of which was the issue of student choice. He stated,

> The transition models advanced in the early to mid-1980s...did not focus nearly enough on student choice, family choice and self-determination. Choices of school, type of job, type of work arrangement, and nature of instruction were all assumed to be controlled unilaterally by the special education teacher and school system. (1993, p. 189)

Wehman concluded by explaining the implications of self-determination for a student- and family-oriented approach to transition planning:

> These implications are significant indeed and involve students being directly involved in writing IEPs and individualized transition plans, going out to workplaces and iden-tifying the jobs they want, and vetoing unfair vocational evaluation practices. They further involve students directly picking the type of skills that they believe will be useful. (1993, pp. 189–190)

Other leaders in the area of transition have also emphasized the importance of self-determination as a cornerstone for transition services of the future (see, e.g., Browning, Dunn, & Brown, 1993; Halloran, 1993; Halpern, 1994; Johnson & Rusch, 1993). Halloran (1993), while discussing the impact of the transition mandates in IDEA, referred to self-determination as education's ultimate goal. Halpern (1994), in a position statement on transition for the Council for Exceptional Children's Division on Career Development and Transition, emphasized the importance of empowerment and self-determination to transition, stating that "If the transition process is to be successful, it must begin with helping students to gain a sense of empowerment with respect to their own transition planning" (p. 118).

It seems self-evident that enabling students with disabilities to assume greater control over and responsibility for their transition process should be a focal point for instruction. As highlighted in Chapter 2, far too many students with disabilities do not succeed as young adults. At least one reason they do not succeed is because they lack the skills to be self-determined.

Perhaps the best reason to focus educational attention on self-determination, however, is because it represents educational recommended practice in the area of transition, rather than just in the area of self-determination. In many ways, it is a false dichotomy to talk about recommended practice in transition and self-determination as separate entities. As illustrated throughout this text, strategies to promote self-determination are critical to promoting positive transition outcomes. The following section provides an overview of support strategies that have been shown to promote successful transitions between school and adulthood and that illustrate the close link between effective practice in transition and promoting self-determination.

STRATEGIES THAT SUPPORT THE TRANSITION FROM SCHOOL TO ADULT LIFE

For many students, high school is not a positive experience resulting in a successful transition to adult life. Some students may need additional support that is typically provided by a traditional secondary school curriculum to achieve adult outcomes that many people may take for granted (e.g., having a job, owning a car or home). Providing support for students as they make the transition from school to adult life has been advocated since the mid-1980s (Halpern, 1985, 1992; Rusch & Mithaug, 1985; Rusch & Phelps, 1987; Will, 1984). Support strategies that have received considerable attention in the literature include Will's (1984) "bridges" model of school to employment proposed by the Office of Special Education and Rehabilitative Services (OSERS); Halpern's (1985) model of school to community adjustment; and IDEA legislation, which mandated support for the transition from school to a range of postschool adult outcomes (*Federal Register,* 1992).

Although the scope of these support strategies differs in comprehensiveness, an element common to all is a commitment to match the level and intensity of support to students' individual needs. An assumption on which these support strategies are based is that students require varying degrees and duration of support to experience full community participation as they make the transition from school to adult life (Halpern, 1985; Rusch, DeStefano, Chadsey-Rusch, Phelps, & Szymanski, 1992; Will, 1984). For example, support strategies for a student might include vocational rehabilitation services or supported employment (Will, 1984), support from family members and friends (Halpern, 1985), and instructional support or community experiences (*Federal Register*, 1992). For discussion purposes, *support strategies* are defined as any assistance or help provided directly to a student to facilitate a successful transition from school to adult life.

Unfortunately, little consensus exists regarding recommended practices that comprise strategies that support the transition from school to adult life (Greene & Albright, 1995; Halpern, 1992; Johnson & Rusch, 1993; Kohler, 1993; Rusch, 1992). Kohler (1993) reviewed recommended practices in transition and suggested that there is limited empirical evidence to support a relationship between current transition practices and favorable postschool outcomes. Because practice constitutes the process by which desired outcomes are achieved, it is imperative to identify and validate support strategies that functionally relate to favorable student outcomes (DeStefano & Wagner, 1992; Haring & Breen, 1989). Without knowledge of effective practices, the field cannot expect that schooling will systematically improve the adult outcomes of secondary special education students (Rusch, 1992). Although the type and level of support needed to facilitate a smooth transition to adult life will differ according to students' individual needs, we contend that several critical strategies must be considered when developing any model of student support.

Ten Critical Transition Support Strategies

The applied research offers some insight into critical factors that have been demonstrated empirically to support successful student outcomes, such as paid work experiences during high school (Hasazi, Gorden, & Roe, 1985; Scuccimarra & Speece, 1990), a network of family and friends (Hasazi et al., 1985), and community-based instruction (McDonnell, Hardman, Hightower, Keifer-O'Donnell, & Drew, 1993). In addition, the field is beginning to establish a consensus among stakeholders regarding the essential components of transition support. For example, parents and practitioners concurred that parental involvement, community-based instruction, and social and employment skills training are critical student support strategy components (Benz & Halpern, 1987; Halpern, 1985).

Hughes and colleagues (in press) conducted research to identify and socially validate critical components common to effective strategies to support the transition from school to adult life. They conducted a comprehensive review of the educational literature, searching for articles that met five criteria: 1) the target population comprised individuals with an identified disability (e.g., mental retardation, behavior disorder, physical impairment); 2) the target population was either adolescents or adults, rather than children; 3) if empirical, a reported study was conducted in an integrated versus a segregated setting (e.g., general education high school versus separate school or community employment versus sheltered workshop); 4) the article described or investigated component(s) of a model of support for the transition from school to adult life; and 5) the article was published in a refereed journal.

Hughes and colleagues (in press) then analyzed the articles to locate all student support strategies investigated or discussed in each article (e.g., social skills training, identifying students' preferences and choices, increasing a student's social network) and, subsequently, identified 10 critical support strategies that were identified in the literature and supported empirically as effective ways to promote transition. The link between effective transition practices and promoting self-determination is evident throughout this list; and, as such, each strategy is briefly identified, defined, and discussed next. Table 1 summarizes these practices and provides examples of each.

Teach Social Skills   Hughes and colleagues (in press) identified a clear link between students' acquisition of social skills and positive adult outcomes. Teaching social skills involves teaching students social behaviors that facilitate interactions with significant others in a manner that is considered socially appropriate. The importance of social skills instruction and the use of social skills programs to promote self-advocacy skills are discussed in Chapters 10 and 11. However, as is discussed in Chapter 6, social skills instruction has limited efficacy without parallel instruction in social problem-solving skills. It is, therefore, important to approach social skills instruction with a mind toward promoting self-determination.

Teach Self-Management and Independence   The second critical support strategy identified as linked to successful adult outcomes was the use of self-management skills. Self-management skills are those skills that will enable a student to perform expected behaviors with greater independence. These skills are critical to the emergence of self-determination; the conceptual framework of self-determination as an educational outcome presented in Chapter 1 identified self-management skills as component elements of self-determined behavior. Chapters 7–9 describe strategies to promote self-management skills.

Identify Independence Objectives   The third effective support strategy to promote transition was to identify areas of independence in which a student's performance is not consistent with expectations. This includes observations of students' environments (i.e., home, community, school, work) and interviews with the student and significant others. It is important to include perspectives from all stakeholders in the transition process, including professionals, students, employers, and family members. It is the student's perspective that is, perhaps, most frequently overlooked, and that could potentially be the

Table 1.   Empirically validated transition support strategies

Support strategy	Definition	Example
Teach social skills.	Teach students social behaviors that facilitate interactions with significant others in a manner considered socially appropriate.	A student initiates conversation with peers without disabilities while at lunch or between classes.
Teach self-management and independence.	Teach students self-management skills to enable them to perform expected behaviors more independently.	Using pictures of household tasks while cleaning her home, a young woman looks at a picture, performs the task, records completion of the task, and moves on to the next task.
Identify independence objectives.	Survey students' environments (e.g., home, community, school, work) through observation and by interviewing students and significant others to identify areas in which performance is not consistent with expectations.	In a restaurant in which a student works, ask the supervisor to identify specific tasks that the student is not performing consistently when serving food.
Assess social acceptance.	Assess students' acceptance of everyday performance via evaluations completed by students, teachers, employers, and others and by comparing students' performance to that of peers.	A student compares her evaluation of her attendance at school with her teacher's evaluation.
Identify co-worker, peer, and family support.	Identify individuals who may provide supports for a student at home, school, work, or in the community.	Co-workers are identified who may assist a new employee in learning required job skills and who may interact socially with the employee during breaks or lunch.
Identify students' preferences and choices.	Identify students' expectations and preferences with respect to daily living, and support choice making by observations and interviews with students and other stakeholders. In addition, assess students' choice-making and decision-making skills.	Observe a graduating senior's participation in his or her chosen recreation activity during free time over a 2-week period.
Monitor social acceptance across time.	Establish a continuous schedule by which the student, teachers, employers, co-workers, and significant others evaluate acceptance of student's performance. Use evaluations to identify and discuss discrepancies between observed and expected performance.	A schedule is established in which an employee's job supervisor completes evaluation of employee's social behavior on a weekly basis. Supervisor discusses each evaluation with the employee, including areas that differ from the supervisor's expectations.

(continued)

Table 1.   (*continued*)

Support strategy	Definition	Example
Identify environmental support.	Identify naturally occurring cues in the student's workplace and other environments that will support him or her in initiating and completing expected and desired behavior.	A man employed in housekeeping in a motel learns to empty wastebaskets when they are overflowing with trash.
Match support to student's needs.	Match existing support identified to those areas in which student needs support.	An employee fails to take breaks or return back to his or her work station on time. The employee is taught to go on break when co-workers leave their job stations and return to work when co-workers do.
Teach choice making and decision making.	Teach the student skills that are necessary to make choices and decisions and to express preferences, and provide opportunities to exercise choice.	A high school sophomore chooses to work in a child care center rather than a fast-food restaurant.

most important source of information about performance. Teaching students to self-evaluate and self-monitor behavior, as described in Chapter 9, as well as teaching students to become more involved in educational planning and decision making, as discussed in Chapter 12, are important ways to improve and extend student identification of independence objectives. In addition, Chapter 4 provides strategies to enable learners to become more independent and more effective risk takers.

Assess Social Acceptance   Positive transition outcomes were also linked to teachers' efforts to assess the acceptance of students' everyday social performance (e.g., attendance, personal satisfaction, social interaction) and by observing and comparing a student's performance to that of his or her co-workers or peers (Hughes et al., in press). Once again, the student's capacity to contribute to this process is reliant upon his or her self-determination skills. The development of the capacity to self-evaluate and compare task performances, as well as strategies to achieve this outcome, is an important part of self-determination instruction (see Chapter 14) as are strategies to promote student self-evaluation (see Chapter 9).

Identify Co-worker, Peer, and Family Support   Hughes and colleagues (in press) concluded that one factor critical to a successful transition is that teachers identify others, including co-workers, peers, or family members, who might provide support to the student at home, school, work, and in the community. The use of natural supports is one that has gained popularity in the late 1980s and early 1990s. The importance of these supports cannot be underestimated; however, it is equally important that teachers and other transition stakeholders not overlook the most natural support...the individual him-

or herself! Students need to learn how to be as independent as possible, but they also need to learn how to gain access to resources that are available in their community that provide supports, instead of waiting on someone else to gain access to that resource for them. This involves teaching students to seek out financial or programmatic supports such as vocational rehabilitation or Social Security Income. It also involves teaching students when to ask for help from friends, colleagues, and co-workers. Chapters 12 and 13 discuss several programs that teach students when and how to ask for help, based on their understanding of their own abilities and limitations.

Identify Student's Preferences and Choices   Bearing in mind that Hughes and colleagues (in press) reviewed the literature to determine strategies that best provide supports for successful transitions to adulthood (and not to determine recommended practices for self-determination, per se), it is noteworthy that 2 of the 10 strategies involved choice making. The educational literature clearly shows that if teachers effectively identify students' expectations, choices, and preferences with respect to daily living (e.g., recreational activities, friends, type of employment) by conducting observations, interviews, and assessments with students and significant others, they will be more successful at promoting a positive transition to adulthood. This text provides strategies to achieve this, including strategies for assessing and teaching choice (see Chapter 5).

Monitor Social Acceptance Across Time   Once again, issues of social acceptance showed up as important for successful transition outcomes. In this case, the emphasis is on assessing social acceptance and discrepancies between performance and expectations over time. For example, a teacher could establish a schedule in which a student's work supervisor completes an evaluation of the student's social behavior on a weekly basis and discusses each evaluation with the student, including areas that differ from the supervisor's expectations. Such a strategy not only ensures that problems in the workplace do not build up to become insurmountable; but it also provides a vehicle for all stakeholders (e.g., teacher, student, employer) to discuss student performance, as well as a model for students to learn how to evaluate their behavior and compare their performance, as discussed in Chapter 7. As students become more effective social problem solvers (see Chapter 6), they should be able to close the gap between expectations and performance.

Identify Environmental Support   Just as it is important to identify people to serve as supports, so too is it critical to successful transitions for teachers and families to identify supports in the environment. Again, a missing feature in many support models is the student him- or herself. Teachers can teach students to both learn how to use supports that are naturally occurring in the environment (e.g., clocks, signs) and how to identify what types of supports they should look for in any given circumstance. By enabling students to take responsibility for the identification of supports, teachers can ensure that students will succeed even if no one else is available to locate supports.

Match Support to Student's Needs   The penultimate strategy linked by Hughes and colleagues (in press) to successful transitions was matching supports to student needs. An important aspect of this strategy is that teachers need to be able to assess student interests and preferences (see Chapter 5) and to work collaboratively with students to identify needs (see Chapters 11 and 12).

Teach Choice Making and Decision Making   Hughes and colleagues (in press) identified teaching choice and decision making as critical to successful transitions. As highlighted throughout this text, issues of choice and decision making form much of the core of self-determination instruction. Providing students with both the opportunities and the skills needed to make choices and decisions is the key to success as an adult.

CONCLUSION

The remaining chapters provide strategies, methods, and materials to promote self-determination as a critical transition outcome. Each chapter addresses one or more component elements of self-determination, the development or acquisition of which enable a person to become self-determined. Whenever feasible, we have identified specific transition-related applications. We concur with Halloran (1993) that self-determination is, indeed, education's ultimate goal and suggest that enabling a student to become self-determined may be the most important transition outcome teachers can achieve.

QUESTIONS FOR REVIEW

1.   Describe some of the transition-related factors that have contributed to the emergence of self-determination as a critical educational outcome.
2.   Discuss IDEA and describe its impact on the transition movement and self-determination.
3.   What are transition services?
4.   What demands do the transition requirements in IDEA make regarding student involvement?
5.   How might early transition models have inhibited self-determination?
6.   Why should self-determination be a focal point for transition services?
7.   Discuss how future transition models might differ from early models.
8.   Describe strategies that support the transition from school to adult life.
9.   How are transition support strategies and self-determination linked?
10.   Discuss the importance of choice and decision making to transition and self-determination.

REFERENCES

Americans with Disabilities Act (ADA) of 1990, PL 101-336, 42 U.S.C. §§ 201 *et seq.*

Benz, M.R., & Halpern, A.S. (1987). Transition services for secondary students with mild disabilities: A statewide perspective. *Exceptional Children, 53,* 507–514.

Browning, P., Dunn, C., & Brown, C. (1993). School to community transition for youth with disabilities. In R.C. Eaves & P.J. McLaughlin (Eds.), *Recent advances in special education and rehabilitation* (pp. 193–209). Boston: Andover Medical.

Damon, W. (1983). *Social and personality development: Infancy through adolescence.* New York: Norton.

DeStefano, L., & Wagner, M. (1992). Outcome assessment in special education: What lessons have we learned? In F.R. Rusch, L. DeStefano, J. Chadsey-Rusch, L.A. Phelps, & E. Szymanski (Eds.), *Transition from school to adult life: Models, linkages, and policy* (pp. 173–207). Sycamore, IL: Sycamore.

Education for All Handicapped Children Act of 1975, PL 94-142, 20 U.S.C. § 1400 *et seq.*

Federal Register. (1992, September 29). 57(189), 44794-44852. Washington, DC: U.S. Government Printing Office.

Greene, G., & Albright, L. (1995). "Best practices" in transition services: Do they exist? *Career Development for Exceptional Individuals, 18,* 1–2.

Halloran, W.D. (1993). Transition services requirement: Issues, implications, challenge. In R.C. Eaves & P.J. McLaughlin (Eds.), *Recent advances in special education and rehabilitation* (pp. 210–224). Boston: Andover Medical.

Halpern, A.S. (1985). Transition: A look at the foundations. *Exceptional Children, 51,* 479–502.

Halpern, A.S. (1992). Transition: Old wine in new bottles. *Exceptional Children, 58,* 202–211.

Halpern, A.S. (1994). The transition of youth with disabilities to adult life: A position statement of the Divisions on Career Development and Transition. *Career Development for Exceptional Individuals, 17,* 115–124.

Haring, T.G., & Breen, C. (1989). Units of analysis of social interaction outcomes in supported education. *Journal of The Association for Persons with Severe Handicaps, 14,* 255–262.

Hasazi, S.B., Gordon, L.R., & Roe, C.A. (1985). Factors associated with the employment status of handicapped youth exiting high school from 1979 to 1983. *Exceptional Children, 51,* 455–469.

Hughes, C., Hwang, B., Kim, J., Killian, D.J., Harmer, M.L., & Alcantara, P.R. (in press). A preliminary validation of strategies that support the transition from school to adult life. *Career Development for Exceptional Individuals.*

Ianacone, R.N., & Stodden, R.A. (1987). Transition issues and directions for individuals who are mentally retarded. In R.N. Ianacone & R.A. Stodden (Eds.), *Transition issues and directions* (pp. 1–7). Reston, VA: Council for Exceptional Children, Division on Mental Retardation.

Individuals with Disabilities Education Act (IDEA) of 1990, PL 101-476, 20 U.S.C. §§ 1400 *et seq.*

Johnson, J.R., & Rusch, F.R. (1993). Secondary special education and transition services: Identification and recommendations for future research and demonstration. *Career Development for Exceptional Individuals, 16,* 1–18.

Kohler, P.D. (1993). Best practices in transition: Substantiated or implied? *Career Development for Exceptional Individuals, 16,* 107–121.

McDonnell, J., Hardman, M.L., Hightower, J., Keifer-O'Donnell, R., & Drew, C. (1993). Impact of community-based instruction on the development of adaptive behavior of secondary-level students with mental retardation. *American Journal on Mental Retardation, 97,* 575–584.

Mithaug, D.E., Wolman, J., & Campeau, P. (1992). *Research in self-determination in individuals with disabilities: Technical proposal.* Palo Alto, CA: American Institutes for Research.

Rusch, F.R. (1992). Identifying special education outcomes: Response to Ysseldyke, Thurlow, and Bruininks. *Remedial and Special Education, 13,* 31–32.

Rusch, F.R., DeStefano, L., Chadsey-Rusch, J., Phelps, L.A., & Szymanski, E. (Eds.). (1992). *Transition from school to adult life: Models, linkages, and policy.* Sycamore, IL: Sycamore.

Rusch, F.R., & Mithaug, D.E. (1985). Competitive employment education: A systems-analytic approach to transitional programming for the student with severe handicaps. In K.C. Lakin & R.H. Bruininks (Eds.), *Strategies for achieving community integration of developmentally disabled citizens* (pp. 177–192). Baltimore: Paul H. Brookes Publishing Co.

Rusch, F.R., & Phelps, L.A. (1987). Secondary special education and transition from school to work: A national priority. *Exceptional Children, 53,* 487–492.

Scuccimarra, D.J., & Speece, D.L. (1990). Employment outcomes and social integration of students with mild handicaps: The quality of life two years after high school. *Journal of Learning Disabilities, 23,* 213–219.

Ward, M.J. (1988). The many facets of self-determination. *National Information Center for Children and Youth with Handicaps Transition Summary, 5,* 2–3.

Wehman, P. (1993). Transition from school to adulthood for young people with disabilities: Critical issues and policies. In R.C. Eaves & P.J. McLaughlin (Eds.), *Recent advances in special education and rehabilitation* (pp. 178–192). Boston: Andover Medical.

Wehmeyer, M.L., & Ward, M.J. (1995). The spirit of the IDEA mandate: Student involvement in transition planning. *Journal of the Association for Vocational Special Needs Education, 17,* 108–111.

Will, M. (1984). *OSERS programming for the transition of youth with disabilities: Bridges from school to working life.* Washington, DC: U.S. Department of Education, Office of Special Education and Rehabilitative Services.

SECTION II

Promoting
Autonomous Behavior

C H A P T E R 4

Teaching Independence, Risk Taking, and Safety Skills

After reading this chapter, you will be able to

1. Discuss the importance of teaching students how to respond adaptively to risks present in the community

2. Discuss the reasons safety skills instruction has been ignored as a curricular domain

3. Describe how self-management and problem solving can be used to provide safety skills instruction

4. Identify critical safety skills in the following curricular areas: home and community living, work, fire prevention, crime prevention, HIV/AIDS prevention, self-medication and health care, and substance use

5. Teach a repertoire of safety skills to students with disabilities by having them utilize various self-management and problem-solving strategies

KEY TERMS

1. Crime prevention
2. Dignity of risk
3. Fire prevention
4. Health and safety
5. HIV/AIDS prevention
6. Home and community living safety
7. Problem solving
8. Risks
9. Safety skills
10. Self-evaluation
11. Self-instruction
12. Self-medication and health care
13. Self-reinforcement
14. Substance use
15. Work safety

In 1972 Robert Perske wrote a classic article on the issue of risk and safety for people with disabilities. He suggested that professionals are "overzealous" in their efforts to protect, comfort, and keep safe the people with whom they work and serve. Although professionals behave this way out of the best intentions, Perske suggested that such overprotection compromises individuals' independence and dignity and tends to keep them from experiencing the risks of ordinary life. Perske noted,

> The world in which we live is not always safe, secure and predictable....Every day that we wake up and live in the hours of that day, there is a possibility of being thrown up against a situation where we may have to risk everything, even our lives. This is the way the real world is. We must work to develop every human resource within us in order to prepare for these days. To deny any person their fair share of risk experiences is to further cripple them for healthy living. (1972, p. 199)

To ensure that their dignity is fully respected, Perske suggested we make certain that people with disabilities be exposed to the normal risks all individuals face, rather than to totally avoid them. "We have learned: there can be such a thing as human dignity in risk. And there can be a dehumanizing indignity in safety!" (Perske, 1972, p. 200).

In our efforts to facilitate learning and promote the quality of life-enhancing experiences for people with disabilities, we ensure that their experiences are safe, certain, predictable, and rich with reinforcement. If we are committed, however, to asserting the equality of all people and to actively encouraging their full participation across all aspects of living, shouldn't they be exposed also to situations that are less desirable, including ones that are potentially risky and harmful? This does not mean that students with disabilities should be exposed brazenly to wanton or unnecessary risk or harm. But it does mean that their learning experiences should at least include some exposure to stimuli that are associated with risk or potential danger and that students, regardless of the significance of their disabilities, should be taught to respond adaptively to potential risks.

As more students receive instruction in community settings, they may be exposed to a variety of risks not present in school or sheltered training settings. Likewise, as we design transition and personal futures plans with students, their parents, and significant others, it becomes increasingly clear that students with disabilities may be exposed in the future to a number of potentially unsafe situations with which they have little or no experience. Traditionally, our approach has been to ensure safety by providing instruction in settings in which there are minimal risks and to make sure that there are always staff available to intervene if a potential problem arises (Agran, Marchand-Martella, & Martella, 1994). Such an approach, however, has been largely reactive. It placed the emphasis on what a student shouldn't do, rather than on how to handle such risks adaptively. Failure to teach students how to deal with potential risks may lead parents and administrators to restrict a student's access to community experiences. It denies students, as Perske (1972) suggested, the dignity of risk.

Given the potentially serious consequences of accidents, injuries, or assaults, the curricular domain of health and safety—strategies to promote a student's physical well-being and to teach him or her to identify and respond appropriately to risks that may cause harm—should be paramount in a transition or personal futures plan. Teaching students safety skills, however, has been largely ignored as a curriculum domain (Agran et al., 1994; Gast, Wellons, & Collins, 1994; Juracek, 1994). When they are taught, it is often done in a fragmented and unsystematic way. Virtually any community setting can be dangerous (Agran, 1977; Haller, 1970; Peterson, 1984), and safety skills represent a repertoire of skills many students with disabilities do not have (Pelland & Falvey, 1986).

NEED FOR INSTRUCTION IN INDEPENDENCE AND SAFETY SKILLS

The lack of safety skills instruction is particularly distressing in light of evidence that suggests that individuals with disabilities may be at particular risk for injuries and accidents. Because of such characteristics as "poor judgment; lack of awareness of danger; impulsiveness and restlessness; inability or difficulties in communicating; low pain threshold; abnormal muscle functioning causing difficulties in chewing, swallowing, standing, walking; and impaired vision and/or hearing" (Bryan, Warden, Berg, & Hauck, 1978, p. 88), individuals with disabilities may be particularly vulnerable to injury. Regrettably, the available data may support the above observations. For example, West, Richardson, LeConte, Crimi, and Stuart (1992) determined that 68% of children who were abused had confirmed, likely, or suspected developmental disabilities; and in 1991 it was found that 90% of children who were sexually exploited had developmental disabilities (Muccigrosso, 1991). In addition, Agran and Madison (1995) indicated that out of a sample of 11,000 supported employees, 4,000 injuries were reported. These figures compare with, if not exceed, victimization data for people without disabilities and underscore the seriousness of the issue.

Lack of Instruction

Several reasons are responsible for the lack of instruction in the area of health and safety. First, many parents and teachers may assume that students already possess basic safety skills. Associated with this belief is the feeling that safety is a state of mind or an attitude, and an awareness of potential risks comes with having a positive attitude. Also, it is assumed that safety skills will be acquired coincidentally over time. Second, although injuries may be serious, the likelihood of sustaining one remains small. Instructional time is valuable and could be better served addressing more immediate needs. Third, given the significant learning needs of many students with disabilities, teachers and parents may have low expectations and may think it is unrealistic to provide such instruction. Safety skills instruction may involve teaching students to make complex discriminations. It requires students to attend to a set of stimuli that may be ambiguous. For example, in the case of a fire, how hot must the door be to alert one to either stay in or leave the room? Or which situations are serious enough to warrant calling 911? Last, safety skills instruction represents a domain that, by its nature, can be particularly difficult to teach. The following section describes this challenge.

Challenges of Teaching Safety Skills

Two aspects of safety skills instruction distinguish it from teaching other routines or discrete skills. The first and the most obvious aspect is that such instruction may expose a student to a potential risk. Instruction in community settings may be neither practical nor safe (Gast et al., 1994). Even if the prospect of sustaining an injury is remote, just having such a possibility may cause parents and teachers to have strong objections. In addition, even if the student is not injured, the mere appearance of danger may still produce emotional or psychological harm. For example, to teach a student how to respond to a stranger, a teacher may want to enlist the help of an unknown confederate, who is asked to behave in a suspicious or menacing manner. Even though no harm will come to the student, the interaction may produce fear or alarm. Although this feeling may be the desired response, many parents and teachers may have grave concerns about instilling such feelings in students.

Second, when teaching most skills, there are typically clear cues or consequences. The student learns that when a specified discriminative stimulus is present, performance of a desired response will produce a predictable consequence. The difficulty in teaching health and safety skills is that the consequences may be delayed (e.g., not eating fats will produce long-term cardiovascular benefits, rather than an immediate weight loss) or not easily discernible (e.g., learning a martial art will make one less vulnerable to crime). As a result, the natural consequences are not immediately accessible or obvious. Even more problematic is the fact that most often, good health or safety behavior is measured in terms of what doesn't happen. If the individual doesn't get sick or doesn't get hurt or injured, we say he or she is healthy or acting in a safe manner. This, of course, raises two important issues. First, it is possible that the individual did nothing to promote his or her health or safety. As the saying goes, he or she may have just been lucky enough not to be in the wrong place at the wrong time. Second, we typically reinforce behaviors based on their frequency of occurrence. How do you reinforce someone for an event that one hopes will never occur (e.g., leave a burning building, walk away from a suspicious stranger)? Fortunately, although many accidents or assaults can be serious or even life threatening, their rate of occurrence is always unacceptable but still relatively low. As a result, natural consequences occur infrequently.

To address this reality and to prevent the student from being exposed to unnecessary risk, the use of simulations is recommended when teaching safety skills. Unlike the limited number of instructional opportunities present in community settings to practice safety skills, simulations allow for frequent, repeated trials. They provide students with opportunities to practice the target skills without exposing them to danger or harm. But simulations by nature can only approximate actual situations, and we can only hope that the simulated experience will be close enough to an actual situation to cue correct responding.

Self-Directed Instruction

How, then, can safety skills instruction be delivered effectively? As indicated previously, given the fact that cues and consequences associated with safety behaviors are infrequent and often subtle, a method needs to be used that provides salient and obvious cues and immediate and reinforcing outcomes. It is precisely for this reason that the use of self-management and student-directed strategies is most appropriate.

As indicated in Chapter 1, self-determined behavior emerges based on the development or acquisition of numerous component elements. These include self-management strategies (e.g., self-observation, problem solving) that allow students to present their own cues and consequences in settings in which they are otherwise not available. Such strategies shift instructional responsibility from a teacher to the student so he or she can achieve a level of independent responding under conditions not associated with instructional support (Hughes & Agran, 1994). A student is often in the best position to manage his or her own behavior (Kazdin, 1977). He or she is always available to observe his or her own behavior and provide the appropriate consequence for desired responding.

Because many safety skills are preventive in function (i.e., avoiding an accident by learning what *not* to do) and are performed in nonschool settings in which students may receive little or no supervision (and there may be no one present to observe them), students need to be taught to deliver their own instructional support. Specifically, students should be taught to provide their own cues (e.g., "When walking into a public restroom, I need to remember...") (see Chapter 8), monitor their own performance (e.g., check off on a list whether he or she demonstrated specified safe behaviors) (see Chapter 7), and reinforce his or her correct responding (e.g., verbally praise themselves) (see Chapter 7).

The responsibility for modifying a student's behavior is most often assumed by a teacher, transition specialist, or related services provider (Ferretti, Cavalier, Murphy, & Murphy, 1993). Because of the high degree of external supervision provided to them, students with significant disabilities have limited experience with acquiring skills that will allow them to regulate or manage their own behavior (Westling & Fox, 1995). The individual not prepared to take care of his or her own health and well-being, however, is an individual ill-prepared for contemporary living. Self-management allows students to assume this vital responsibility.

Problem Solving

As mentioned previously, appropriate responding to a potential risk stimulus requires some degree of problem solving, and teachers and parents may believe that problem solving is not feasible for many students with disabilities, particularly with regard to safety skills. Ample evidence, however, shows that individuals with mental retardation or cognitive impairments can solve problems effectively across a variety of problematic situations involving safety. For example, Martella, Agran, and Marchand-Martella (1992) taught nine supported employees to respond appropriately to 24 risk situations across training and natural work conditions. Both constant and novel problem situations were presented. Results indicated that the participants' safety problem-solving skills improved dramatically with skills generalizing to both similar and dissimilar situations. In addition, the participants' performance was maintained and continued to improve up to 12 weeks after training ended.

Martella, Marchand-Martella, Agran, and Allen (in press) also taught nine participants with mental retardation requiring intermittent to extensive support, who were being prepared for supported employment to prevent accidents due to behavioral causes (e.g., throwing objects, not wearing protective clothing, fighting). Again, increases in appropriate responding in both training and natural work environments were reported for all participants.

Agran, Madison, and Bown (1995) evaluated the effects of a problem-solving strategy to teach safe work behaviors to five supported employees with mental retardation who required intermittent to extensive support. The participants were employed at either a community recreational center or a food processing plant. After training was introduced, all participants made dramatic improvements in their performance of the target behaviors, with behavior changes maintaining for up to 4 weeks. The dependent measures included percentages of correct responses to potentially hazardous environmental stimuli.

Last, Hughes and Rusch (1989) combined self-instructions with multiple exemplars or targeted responses to teach two people with mental retardation who required extensive support and were employed in a soap-packaging company to solve work-related problems. First, the work supervisor identified problems that were likely to occur during the workday (e.g., a puddle of soap on a table, a paper towel plugging the drain of a sink). Then, the employees were taught to verbalize a set of self-instructions in response to five of the identified problem situations. After training, acquisition of the problem-solving strategy and generalized use of the strategy to untrained problem situations were demonstrated by both employees.

Powers and colleagues (1996) suggested that adolescents have difficulty with problem solving because of their limited life experiences and difficulty in determining the requirements of different activities and feasible solutions to make completion of these activities easier. It is evident that problem solving is a critical self-determination skill for adolescents, particularly for students with significant challenges. With the many changes that occur in life and the fact that only a limited number of exemplars can be used to teach specific skills, a student with limited problem-solving experience will be at a great loss as he or she faces life experiences. On the positive side is the fact that problem solving can be learned with systematic instruction (Agran & Hughes, 1997; Hughes & Rusch, 1989) (see also Chapter 6). Given the fact that all community and home environments are potentially dangerous, teaching students problem-solving strategies allows them to retrieve information about potential risks and, based on available information, determine appropriate courses of action.

In effect, all self-management strategies serve, in part, to help students problem-solve. Functionally, self-management and problem solving essentially serve the same functions (Mithaug, 1993). As Litrownik (1982) indicated, any situation that places adaptive demands on a student can be thought of as a problem. The value of problem solving is to provide students with information so they can make appropriate decisions. Based on this information, students can set goals, follow through with a proposed action, determine the adequacy of the response by determining if the problem is resolved, and make necessary modifications in goals or actions to achieve desired outcomes. Brigham (1989) indicated, "Self-management...is not a collection of techniques to be used in piecemeal fashion. Instead, the person who has learned self-management can analyze problems, select and implement appropriate interventions, and evaluate the results" (p. 49).

HEALTH AND SAFETY CURRICULAR DOMAINS

As mentioned previously, expanding the environments in which students participate will expose them to various risks. Given this range of potential risks, there is a large number of skills to teach. Ultimately, target skills depend on the student's instructional needs and circumstances (i.e., the settings in which he or she participates, student or parent preferences). However, we suggest that critical safety skills areas include the following: home and community living, work, fire prevention, crime prevention, human immunodeficiency virus (HIV)/acquired immunodeficiency syndrome (AIDS) prevention, self-medication and health care, and substance use. In each of these areas, students need to identify potentially dangerous conditions and to execute actions to correct or modify (or, if necessary, exit from) the situation. This knowledge will lessen their vulnerability to the many dangers of contemporary living (Agran, 1997).

The following sections discuss each of these safety concerns and identify critical skills. Following these descriptions, recommendations for teaching safety skills are provided.

Home and Community Living Safety

The number of accidents that occur in home and community settings is high, and parents and educators are certainly justified in being concerned about health and safety issues, as is illustrated in the following case study.

> Kirsten is 17 years old and attends North Park High School. She is assigned to a regular class and has a general education teacher for homeroom. She has a special education teacher for one period a day. Kirsten has mental retardation and requires limited to extensive supports. She performs most personal and home living skills independently as well as most routines at school (e.g., movement from one classroom to another, following the activity sequence in a particular class). Kirsten is well liked by her peers and works 2 hours a week at a local fast-food restaurant, cleaning tables and helping with miscellaneous stocking responsibilities. After graduation, she would like to be employed at this restaurant on a full-time basis and live in an apartment with her friend, Jan.
>
> Kirsten's parents strongly support her future wishes and are committed to doing everything they can to ensure that these wishes are realized. Recently, there were two events reported in their local newspaper that caught their attention. First, there was an article about the steady increase in crime in the community. Kirsten's parents reflected that, although they were fortunate enough to live in an area that had few crimes, Kirsten might not be so lucky when she has an apartment. Second, a recent fire had destroyed a condominium complex. Although no lives were lost, there was extensive property damage and several occupants were injured. These two stories caused them to acknowledge that, all things considered, their daughter had little or no formal instruction in what to do in the event of an emergency. They had always been available to intervene if a potential risk situation existed. They recalled that, although Kirsten was taught a variety of functional community skills, none had anything to do with safety. They reflected that Kirsten probably knew what to do if there were some kind of crisis, but they realized that they didn't know this for certain. What if there was a fire in an apartment next to hers—would she know what to do? What if she was approached by a stranger who asked her if she wanted a ride home—would she know what to say? What if there were a heavy box to move at her job—would she know the best way to move it? They concurred that at her next individualized education program (IEP) meeting they were going to make sure that safety skills instruction be provided.

One person in 11 has incurred an injury at home that has required professional medical care (National Safety Council, 1988). In addition, one of three Americans sustains some kind of injury at home (Foege, 1988). Risks are present in practically every home setting, and individuals unaware of these risks are potentially in grave danger. Physical dangers within natural environments present an element of risk throughout everyday activities (Gast et al., 1994).

Table 1 presents a list of home and community safety skills identified by Collins, Wolery, and Gast (1991), based on input provided by a sample of parents. The skills listed are appropriate across a wide age span. At best, they represent only a sample of the many risks present in home or community settings, with many others not included. Although some are clearly relevant for younger children, most are relevant for adolescents and adults. Referring to the concern that Kirsten's parents expressed in the case study, parents and teachers often assume that students know how to perform most, if not all, of these skills. However, few opportunities (natural or contrived) are arranged to assess them, and few teachers systematically teach them and recommend their inclusion in IEPs. Not surprisingly, many commercially available assessments and curricula include some of these items but not all. Students who cannot perform these skills are potentially at risk for serious injury.

Work Safety

By definition, transition programs are designed to facilitate the transition of students from school to postschool work and living settings, and employment preparation or vocational training receives paramount attention. Such programs are designed to promote the student's employability and later marketability. One skill area that has been virtually ignored, however, is that of work safety. Although safety awareness and safe work behavior are critical job survival needs for employees (Mueller, Wilgosh, & Dennis, 1989), students are not receiving adequate training in work safety skills (Martella & Agran, 1994). Heath (1983) indicated that "not only are workers entering the work force with a minimum of job safety and health knowledge and skills, many of them receive little or no instruction on job risks upon entering the work force" (p. 23). This is problematic for at least two reasons. First, employers might be hesitant to employ individuals with disabilities if they knew they had no safety awareness or had a history of on-the-job injuries (Martella & Marchand-Martella, 1995). Also, lack of these skills (or perceived lack of these skills) may result in a situation in which people with disabilities are denied access to potentially more lucrative and satisfying jobs that may present safety hazards and be placed and maintained in "safer" but less rewarding job tasks. Second, failure to teach students a repertoire of safety skills may put them in a potentially dangerous situation. Although data on the number of injuries sustained by people with disabilities are limited, the available work injury data suggest that injuries for people with disabilities may be comparable to rates reported for people without disabilities. As indicated previously in this chapter, Agran and Madison (1995) reported that close to one third of a sample of supported employees sustained a work injury. Besides the fact that this percentage is unacceptably high, what is troubling is that the number of actual injuries is probably higher because many injuries are not reported, and most of these injuries are preventable.

Work injuries are caused by behavioral or environmental factors (Martella & Agran, 1994). Behavioral factors include an employee's performance of an inappropriate action or a failure to execute an appropriate response (e.g., misusing a tool, not wearing safety goggles). Environmental factors include the

Table 1.   Home and community safety skills

HOME SAFETY

Kitchen
Handling hot stove / oven
Recognizing marked poisons
Safe use of appliances
Safe use of knives
Detecting bad meat / food
Not climbing into refrigerator / freezer
Avoiding sharp corners on cabinets
Reacting to cooking fires

Bathroom
Recognizing marked poisons
Shower / bathtub safety
Adjusting water temperature
Using hot hair appliances
Care on wet floors

OUTDOORS

Yard / Playground
Safe use of tools (lawn mower)
Not climbing trees
Reacting to thunderstorms
Keeping driveway clear
Operating electric garage opener
Safe use of gym equipment
Staying inside boundaries
Not pushing others
Staying away from power sources
Recognizing poisonous plants / berries
Lighting a barbecue grill safely

Bicycle
Reflectors / lights when dark
Not showing off
Using bell / horn
Staying aware of others
Keeping to right of road
Using turn signals
Avoiding drain grates, gravel
Keeping hands / feet out of spokes

Car / Bus
Using seat belts
Not disturbing driver
Keeping head / arms inside vehicle
Knowing emergency exits
Exiting vehicle away from traffic
Not pushing on bus
Staying calm in accident
Proper bus stop behavior
Sitting near bus driver when bus is
    uncrowded
Moving if bothered by strangers
Changing seats in moving bus
Entering / exiting bus
Standing in moving bus

General Home Areas
Picking up toys on stairs
Electric sockets / cords
Dialing emergency telephone numbers
Caution around glass doors / windows
Safe tool / appliance use
Cleaning up broken items
Not using appliances during electric
    storm
Safe use of scissors
Changing light bulb
Locking / unlocking doors
Not playing with matches / lighters

Animals
Reacting to dangerous animals
Being careful around mother with
    young
Being careful around injured animals
Not feeding strange animals
Avoiding animals that are eating
Calling Humane Society about strays
Interacting with familiar animals

Walking Trips
Informing others of one's destination
Asking for directions
Walking on sidewalk
Facing traffic
Carrying address, telephone number,
    money
Following traffic signs
Using crosswalks
Looking both ways before crossing

Water Recreation
Sunburn protection
Swimming in pairs
Communicating with lifeguard
Not pushing others
Using life jacket on boat

Boat safety
Aiding drowner
Leaving water during storm
Avoiding heat exhaustion
Drinking fluids
Wearing hat in hot sun

(continued)

Table 1.   (continued)

Camping / Hiking
  Recognizing poisonous plants
  Staying on trails
  Putting out campfires
  Thunderstorm safety
  Using whistle if lost
  Checking in with others
  Reacting to dangerous animals
  Using insect repellent

Cold Weather
  Dressing warmly
  Avoiding thin ice
  Aiding person who has fallen through
    ice
  Riding sleds
  Recognizing hyperthermia or frostbite
    signs

Night
  Using flashlight
  Staying under street lights

CONCERNS ACROSS CATEGORIES

Fire
  Safe use of fire extinguisher
  Responding to fire / smoke alarms
  Awareness of exit signs
  Feeling doors for heat
  Leaving burning building
  Going to window for help
  Calling fire department
  Keeping gasoline away from heat
  Reacting to person on fire
  Not smoking in bed
  Safe us of matches / lighters

First Aid
  Treating injuries
  Treating burns
  Treating insect bites
  Removing objects from eye
  Removing splinters
  Calling ambulance / 911
  Getting help from others
  Using first-aid kit
  Recognizing signs of illness

Disaster Procedures
  Reacting to floods
  Reacting to earthquakes
  Reacting to hurricanes

Meals
  Chewing before swallowing
  Using utensils properly
  Eating hot foods
  Choking procedures
  Serving hot liquids / foods
  Not eating on floor / ground

Strangers
  Recognizing strangers
  Responding to lures
  Caution in public bathrooms
  Avoiding dangerous areas
  Not talking to strangers
  Avoiding empty elevators
  Attracting attention when attacked

Personal Privacy
  Saying "no" to physical approaches
  Knowing one's private body parts
  Knowledge of safe sex
  Saying "no" to drugs

From Gast, D.L., Wellons, J., & Collins, B. (1994). Home and community safety skills. In M. Agran, N.E. Marchand-Martella, & R.C. Martella (Eds.), *Promoting health and safety: Skills for independent living* (pp. 14–15). Baltimore: Paul H. Brookes Publishing Co.; reprinted by permission.

physical characteristics of a work setting (e.g., objects on floor, exposed wires). Data on work accidents strongly suggest that behavioral factors are most often responsible for injuries. Because most accidents are caused by inappropriate responding, most are thus preventable.

Table 2 lists the most frequently reported causes of accidents reported by a sample of employers in service, manufacturing, wholesale / retail, and food service / distribution occupations (Martella, Marchand-Martella, & Agran, 1992).

Table 2.   Causes of work accidents

Behavioral Causes

Wearing loose or inappropriate clothing around power tools
Throwing objects
Fighting
Inappropriate use of machines or appliances
Play behavior
Lack of knowledge of tool use
Fatigue
Lack of attention span
Tool misuse
Not wearing protective equipment
Lifting heavy objects

Environmental Causes

Exposed wires
Flammables
Poisonous substances
Hot materials
Objects on floor
Slippery floor

Adapted from Martella & Agran (1994).

The behaviors and environmental conditions listed in Table 2 represent generic causes of work accidents of which all employees should be aware and from which they should actively refrain. Other risks associated with specific work tasks may be present, and employees will need to respond safely to them. At the minimum, every student should acquire in his or her transition program a set of generalizable work safety skills and knowledge.

Fire Prevention

The National Fire Protection Association (1991) reported that more than 5,000 Americans are killed each year in fires. Most of these fires occur in single-family homes. Although it is unknown how many people with disabilities die in fires, many fires occur in community residences, including group and foster homes (Juracek, 1994). Most troubling is the fact that many case studies reveal that people without disabilities have great difficulty responding correctly to house fires; thus for people with disabilities, the crisis of dealing with a fire may be even more problematic. Nevertheless, evidence shows that students with disabilities can learn several fire safety skills (see Juracek, 1994).

Table 3 lists critical fire safety skills. Three different classes of responses are involved: exiting from a fire, responding to a contained fire, and preventive fire safety skills. Instructional targets should be based on the individual's instructional needs and capabilities; optimally, skills in each of these classes should be taught.

As Juracek (1994) noted, fire safety skills are most difficult to teach because fires do not occur frequently and when they are taught, they usually are not

Table 3.   Fire safety skills

Responses to Fires

Exiting home/building at sound of alarm
Determining heat of door to decide exiting strategy
Knowing location of alternate exit if first exit is blocked by fire or smoke

Responses to Contained Fires

Extinguishing contained fires
Asking for assistance/help

Preventive Skills

Properly using stove, oven, and microwave
Storing flammables properly
Wearing appropriate clothing while cooking on the stove
Safely using and disposing of smoking materials (e.g., cigarettes, cigars)

Adapted from Juracek (1994).

taught under the actual conditions associated with such a crisis: smoke, fire, and panic. Furthermore, many fires occur at night when people are sleeping. Nevertheless, the self-management skills described later in the chapter may be of value in facilitating the acquisition of fire safety skills.

Crime Prevention

Although exact figures are not available on the number of people with disabilities who have been victimized by crime, available data suggest that they may be particularly vulnerable (Sobsey, 1994). Furthermore, individuals with disabilities may be especially susceptible to sexual or child abuse (Chotiner & Lehr, 1976; Stimpson & Best, 1991). There are several reasons for this situation. First, individuals with disabilities may be viewed as easy prey by criminals who seek to exploit them. Second, because some people with disabilities, like other people in society, may come from unsupportive or dysfunctional families, they may be denied the security and support a more protective family or community can provide. Third, individuals with disabilities who have received little or no instruction in how to respond to a criminal assault may not know how to identify or remove themselves from such a situation. Crime prevention is a critical safety skills domain, but it is one that has regrettably been ignored in transition programs.

Sobsey (1994) suggested that crime prevention involves skills across many different areas: assertiveness, sex education, personal rights, personal safety, social skills, choice making, communication training, self-defense, personal property protection, and money management. Table 4 lists selected skill clusters in these areas.

Acquisition of these skills certainly does not guarantee complete safety, but it is believed that they will minimize the likelihood of being victimized. Without systematic crime prevention instruction, the student may be at great peril. Sobsey's (1994) insistence on teaching students assertiveness skills (see Chapter 10

Table 4.   Crime prevention skills

Knowing one's rights
Asserting one's rights
Appropriate sexual behavior
Knowing how to interact with strangers
Self-defense skills
Friendship building
Pragmatic communication skills
Protecting personal property
Protecting money
Learning the location of the community police station
Knowing who to call for assistance

Adapted from Sobsey (1994).

for strategies to teach assertive behavior) supports the need for more student-managed interventions. In part, students may be made more vulnerable to victimization by our educational insistence on teaching students to be compliant.

> People who are taught to be docile to their caregivers often generalize this docility to those who exploit and abuse them....Not only are students taught to do whatever they are told, they are taught to do it regardless of who gives the order. (Sobsey, 1994, p. 198)

Sobsey (1994) argued that individuals have the right to determine how to protect themselves, to assert their rights, and to determine who and in what manner someone is allowed into their physical and personal space.

HIV/AIDS Prevention

Because of a lack of sex education and HIV prevention training, vulnerability to sexual abuse, and involvement in high-risk sexual behavior, people with disabilities may be particularly vulnerable to becoming infected with HIV (Mason & Jaskulski, 1994). Mason and Jaskulski reported that, among a sample of vocational rehabilitation facilities, approximately one third reported they served consumers who were HIV positive, and 75% of the respondents indicated that they provided no HIV prevention training. Mason and Jaskulski suggested that such instruction be included in students' IEPs. Although professionals may feel uncomfortable discussing such subject matter, information on sexuality, infectious diseases, and hygienic procedures needs to be presented.

Although HIV/AIDS prevention involves many skills, students need to know, at a minimum, that AIDS is a serious disease that can lead to death; that it is transmitted via sexual relationships or intravenous needles; and that it can be prevented by safe sex practices, not sharing needles, or abstinence. Table 5 lists critical HIV/AIDS prevention knowledge and skills.

Mason and Jaskulski noted that

> It is reasonable to expect that as the AIDS epidemic continues to increase, more people with developmental disabilities will be infected. Assuring reduction in the transmission

Table 5.   HIV/AIDS prevention skills

Knowing safe sex practices
Understanding epidemiological information regarding transmission of HIV infection
Knowing about sexually transmitted diseases
Understanding the dangers of sharing needles and syringes
Knowing how to clean needles and syringes
Being aware of local information sources
Being aware of testing services in the community
Possessing skills for coping with the disease

Adapted from Mason & Jaskulski (1994).

of HIV is one of the most pressing priorities facing society today. To date, HIV has not spread to an epidemic level within the population of those with developmental disabilities. However, it is a crisis waiting to happen. (1994, p. 186)

HIV/AIDS prevention education, the authors noted, is "literally a life-saving measure" (p. 186).

Self-Medication and Health Care

Students with significant health care needs are being served increasingly in public schools. Likewise, taking medication is a routine part of the day for many individuals with disabilities. Nevertheless, individuals may have little or no involvement in their own health care. Health care procedures are typically *done to* students, rather than *with* or *by* students (Lehr & Macurdy, 1994). It is unfortunate that individuals are not taught to self-medicate because lack of this skill substantially limits their autonomy and, ultimately, their self-determination. Having another person manipulating and controlling one's physical being and body function is highly intrusive and invasive. If the person with disabilities does not have the skills to administer health care or medication procedures, then having another person perform them is appropriate, as long as such control is extended to the caregiver by the consumer. Increasing evidence shows, however, that people with disabilities can perform many of the procedures that have traditionally been performed by caregivers. Failure to teach self-health care procedures not only promotes the individual's dependence on others (Lehr & Macurdy, 1994) but may also put him or her at greater risk for exposure to sexually transmitted diseases (Jacobs, Samowitz, Levy, Levy, & Cabrera, 1992).

Tables 6 and 7 present self-medication and health care skills that students may be taught to execute, either totally or partially, and that can be included in their IEPs. As noted previously, determination of relevant skills would be contingent on the student's health and instructional needs.

Substance Use Prevention

Substance use among students with disabilities represents a serious yet largely undocumented social problem (Morgan, 1994). Alcohol and other drug use among students with disabilities may be comparable to that in the general population. Students with disabilities appear to be susceptible to the same risk

Table 6. Self-medication skills

Naming medication and stating why it needs to be taken
Locating the correct medication
Knowing when to administer medication
Consuming medication appropriately
Storing the medication appropriately
Being able to problem-solve if necessary (i.e., figuring out what to do if medication is lost, empty, or error is made)

Adapted from Harchik (1994).

factors for substance use as students without disabilities, including peer influence, ready availability, and family history of abuse (Prendergast, Austin, & deMiranda, 1990). In addition, the stressors experienced by students with disabilities (e.g., social isolation, communication impairments) may produce greater risk and predispose them to substance use as a means of coping with their problems. These risk factors are compounded by the fact that many students with disabilities do not receive prevention education in this area.

Table 8 lists a sample of recommended substance use prevention skills (see Morgan, 1994, for detailed information). Although the importance of problem solving and self-management strategies in substance use prevention education should be evident, its importance cannot be emphasized enough. Students with

Table 7. Sample IEP objectives related to special health care procedures

Tube Feeding

Student will explain (orally, in writing, or through other means) reasons for alternative eating method.
Student will describe steps necessary in implementing the procedure.
Student will indicate desire to eat.
Student will measure feeding liquid to be placed in feeding bag or syringe.
Student will pour food in feeding bag or syringe.
Student will direct cleaning of feeding equipment.
Student will clean equipment.
Student will feed self.

Tracheostomy Suctioning

Student will indicate need to be suctioned.
Student will turn on suction machine.
Student will hold suction tube while procedure is being implemented.
Student will describe steps necessary to suction.
Student will explain to others the indicators of need for suctioning.

Catheterization

Student will indicate time to be catheterized.
Student will self-catheterize.
Student will describe steps in implementing the process.
Student will wash materials necessary.
Student will assemble materials necessary.
Student will hold catheter steady during procedure.
Student will describe indicators of problems related to catheterization.

From Lehr, D.H., & Macurdy, S. (1994). Meeting special health care needs of students. In M. Agran, N.E. Marchand-Martella, & R.C. Martella (Eds.), *Promoting health and safety: Skills for independent living* (p. 82). Baltimore: Paul H. Brookes Publishing Co.; reprinted by permission.

Table 8.   Substance use prevention skills

Understanding substance use is harmful
Identifying alcohol and different types of other drugs (legal and illegal) and their effects
Learning various ways to deal with problems (e.g., friendships, stress management)
Knowing the risks of drugs
Knowing how drug use is related to certain diseases and disabilities
Knowing how drugs can affect motor functioning, personal growth, and future opportunities

Adapted from Morgan (1994).

substance use problems have great difficulty because they do not know how to make appropriate choices for themselves and how to manage their behavior adaptively. Instead of knowing how to problem-solve and evaluate the consequences (both immediate and long term) of their use of controlled substances, they opt instead for an outcome that may have deleterious consequences. Prevention programs must present students with sufficient information and experiences so that they can conclude unequivocally that the risks of substance use far outweigh its benefits.

TEACHING SAFETY SKILLS

Self-management strategies function the same way as teacher-directed strategies. The likelihood of a behavior occurring again is promoted by the presence of a consistent cue or stimulus condition, followed by the performance of a target behavior and the delivery of a desired consequence. Generalization is achieved when the response is performed under varying stimulus conditions and consequences. All behaviors are acquired in this manner, including safety skills. When using self-management strategies, the student is responsible for delivering the cues and consequences, rather than the teacher; the instructional process, however, remains the same.

It is not within the scope of this chapter to describe behavioral-instructional strategies to teach health and safety skills (readers are referred to Martella, Marchand-Martella, & Agran, 1994, for detailed information). Suffice it to say that safety skills do not represent good attitudes but rather discrete skills that can be taught using the same procedures you would use to teach any other skill. If the skill can be operationally defined and measured, it can be taught using behavioral technology; and all safety skills for practical purposes can be defined and measured. What is of importance in this chapter is to suggest ways in which safety skills can be taught using various self-management skills. By doing so, the student is provided the opportunity and responsibility for changing his or her own behavior and, ultimately, becoming more self-determined.

PROMOTING INDEPENDENCE
AND RISK-TAKING BEHAVIOR

As mentioned previously, self-determined behavior involves the development and acquisition of a set of component elements, several of which are self-management strategies (e.g., problem solving, self-observation, self-instruction). These strategies, singularly or combined, can be used by students to facilitate their acquisition of safety skills. Although subsequent chapters in the text address these strategies, their applicability to health and safety instruction is described in this section.

Problem Solving

All of the health and safety concerns discussed in this chapter share a common characteristic. Each requires that the individual identify a potential risk or hazard to his or her health or well being and then select and execute a response that will extinguish or at least modify the aversive consequences associated with the identified hazard. In this respect, problem solving is essential to safety skills instruction. Failure to identify a potential hazard and to respond appropriately to it may ultimately result in distress.

As discussed in Chapter 6, problem solving comprises four responses. First, the student is asked to acknowledge that a problem exists and to identify solutions to solve the problem—what he or she needs to do. Following, the student is taught to identify the "best" solution and then to perform the behavior selected. Last, the student is taught to evaluate the consequences of that behavior and to determine whether the behavior solved the problem. This problem-solving sequence can be used for practically any situation. With increased opportunities to problem-solve, students can determine a course of action based on their own experiences—in short, they are behaving in a self-determined manner.

Martella and Agran (1994) taught students a problem-solving strategy to promote their safety at work. After exposing the students to a variety of work hazards (e.g., water spilled on the floor, unlabeled cleaning solvents), the students were taught to ask themselves the following:

1. How would an accident happen?
2. When would an accident be prevented?
3. Who would you talk to?
4. What would you do or say?

This strategy allowed the students to retrieve pertinent information about a potential hazard and make an appropriate response. In another study (Agran et al., 1995), students were taught to respond to the following self-directed questions:

1. What is dangerous?
2. Why is it unsafe?
3. What can I do to make it safe?

The utility of these strategies is that they provide the student with a cognitive structure to process relevant information. They force the student to examine the consequences of his or her actions or failure to act. Whether it is a situation involving work safety (e.g., "What if I use a screwdriver rather than a hammer to remove a nail?"), substance use (e.g., "What should I say if someone offers me a drug?"), HIV/AIDS prevention (e.g., "What would happen if I didn't use a condom?"), or fire safety (e.g., "If I keep the space heater on all night, what could happen?"), problem solving permits students to determine that a problem exists and to come up with a strategy to deal with that problem.

Obviously it is unrealistic to expect a student to repeat the complete problem-solving sequence whenever he or she is confronted with a problem, especially if there is an immediate danger. But it is hoped that with increased opportunities to use such strategies, fluency will be promoted and the student will be more proficient in dealing with many problems with which he or she may be confronted.

Self-Instruction

Self-instruction involves the student's use of his or her own verbal behavior to guide his or her performance (Hughes & Agran, 1994) (see also Chapter 7). In this respect, self-instruction functions like a problem-solving strategy. It provides the student with a self-directed verbal strategy to direct and regulate his or her own behavior, similar to problem solving; to acknowledge that a need or problem exists; and to perform an appropriate behavior to achieve a desired outcome.

For purposes of safety skills instruction, self-instruction can be used by a student to provide self-generated prompts to perform an appropriate response (e.g., dialing 911, assembling catheterization equipment). Rather than relying on the prompts provided by another person, self-instruction allows the student to direct his or her own behavior. It can be used for any safety skill that involves a behavioral sequence. For example, an individual living in a group home may realize that if she does not keep her money or checkbook in a safe place, it may be taken by another person. In such a situation, the individual may be taught to say to herself, "If I don't lock this money away, someone will take it. I need to put this money in a locked bank. I will lock this money away." Like problem solving, self-instruction represents a generative learning strategy. All that is required is to identify the sequence needed to perform a safety skill, develop an appropriate verbal sequence for the student, and reinforce the student for both demonstrating the skill and repeating the self-instructions. It is hoped that over time, as instructional support is faded, the self-instruction will help to promote the durability and generalization of the safety skill.

Self-Monitoring, Self-Evaluation, and Self-Reinforcement

An issue raised earlier in this chapter is the fact that accidents and crises occur infrequently. Unless simulated training is provided, students will have limited opportunities to perform target skills. As long as opportunities are unavailable to assess the student's performance in natural settings, instruction using simulations (e.g., contrived situations, role playing) is recommended. What should be provided in such instruction, however, is to teach the student to monitor and evaluate his or her own behavior (i.e., "Did I follow the prescribed sequence and adequately perform the skill?") (see Chapter 7). Similar to self-instruction, students can be taught to monitor their own behavior for any safety skill involving a behavioral sequence (e.g., exiting a building in case there is a fire, administering and keeping track of medication). The difference, however, is that self-instruction is performed prior to the response whereas self-monitoring occurs afterward. Self-monitoring typically involves the use of a checklist or written schedule, but it may also involve picture cues. Furthermore, the student can be taught to administer reinforcement to him- or herself. That is, after monitoring his or her behavior and meeting an existing standard, a reinforcer (verbal or tangible, based on the student's instructional needs) is delivered by the student. Such self-reinforcement may serve to mediate the desired response, that is, provide immediate reinforcement for a behavior that would typically only receive infrequent, delayed, or indirect reinforcement. These strategies allow the student to monitor, evaluate, and reinforce his or her own safety behavior without external manipulation.

CONCLUSION

Clearly, it is the proposition of this text that maximal opportunities should be presented to students to promote their self-determination. It is crucial for students to realize that the choices they make and the degree to which they can manage and direct their own behavior can provide structure and continuity to their lives and allow them to achieve desired outcomes. The national interest in promoting self-determination has considerable momentum; and many teachers, parents, and professionals are committed to ensuring that students be allowed to exercise free choice. There is, however, a point at which exercise of free choice may be suspended—situations relating to health and safety. Situations that involve potential harm to students may be regarded by service providers as situations in which choice and self-management should rightfully be compromised.

It is our opinion that, just as the rights of individuals should not be suspended because they have a disability, they should likewise not be denied access to situations that contain risk. By doing so, their experiences may be curtailed and the quality of their lives may be greatly compromised. Life, regrettably, is fraught with peril; and, as Perske (1972) indicated, we must use all of our resources to deal with such adversities. Whether we like it or not, we all face this reality and it is a reality that people with disabilities must also face. As Schloss, Alper, and Jayne (1993) recommended, we must make every effort to ensure that people with disabilities have life experiences in which benefits and risks are balanced.

QUESTIONS FOR REVIEW

1. Discuss the reasons students with disabilities have been denied safety skills instruction.
2. Explain why safety skills instruction is particularly difficult to teach. Use as examples one or more safety skills that are discussed in the chapter.
3. Discuss why self-management and problem-solving strategies are particularly effective in teaching safety skills. Cite specific strategies.
4. Select a safety skill and design an intervention using a problem-solving strategy.
5. What are the critical safety skills areas? Select examples from each and discuss their importance for a student with a disability.
6. When used to teach safety skills, how does self-instruction serve a problem-solving function?
7. What is the value of self-reinforcement in teaching safety skills?
8. Why should people with disabilities be given the dignity of risk?

REFERENCES

Agran, M. (Ed.). (1997). *Student-directed learning: Teaching self-determination skills.* Pacific Grove, CA: Brooks/Cole.

Agran, M., & Hughes, C. (1997). Problem solving. In M. Agran (Ed.), *Student-directed learning: Teaching self-determination skills* (pp. 171–198). Pacific Grove, CA: Brooks/Cole.

Agran, M., & Madison, D. (1995). Prevalence of injuries among supported employees. *Journal of Vocational Rehabilitation, 5,* 5–13.

Agran, M., Madison, D., & Bown, C. (1995). Teaching supported employees to prevent work injuries. *Journal of Vocational Rehabilitation, 5,* 33–42.

Agran, M., Marchand-Martella, N.E., & Martella, R.C. (Eds.). (1994). *Promoting health and safety: Skills for independent living.* Baltimore: Paul H. Brookes Publishing Co.

Agran, M., & Moore, S.C. (1994). *How to teach self-instruction of job skills.* Washington, DC: American Association on Mental Retardation.

Brigham, T. (1989). *Self-management for adolescents: A skills training program.* New York: Guilford.

Bryan, E., Warden, M.G., Berg, B., & Hauck, G.R. (1978). Medical consideration for multiple handicapped children in the public schools. *Journal of School Health, 48,* 84–89.

Chotiner, N., & Lehr, W. (1976). *Child abuse and developmental disabilities: A report from the New England regional conference.* Boston: New England Developmental Disabilities Communication Center.

Collins, B.C., Wolery, M., & Gast, D.L. (1991). A survey of safey concerns for students with special needs. *Education and Training in Mental Retardation, 26,* 305–318.

Ferretti, R.P., Cavalier, A.R., Murphy, M.J., & Murphy, R. (1993). The self-management of skills by persons with mental retardation. *Research in Developmental Disabilities, 14,* 189–205.

Foege, W.H. (1988, November). *Newsletter of the Family Health Services Division, Utah Department of Health.* (Available from Stephen McDonald, 288 North 1460 West, Salt Lake City, UT 84116-0650)

Gast, D.L., Wellons, J., & Collins, B. (1994). Home and community safety skills. In M. Agran, N.E. Marchand-Martella, & R.C. Martella (Eds.), *Promoting health and safety: Skills for independent living* (pp. 11–32). Baltimore: Paul H. Brookes Publishing Co.

Haller, J.A. (1970). Problems in children's trauma. *Journal of Trauma, 10,* 269–271.

Harchik, A.E. (1994). Self-medication skills. In M. Agran, N.E. Marchand-Martella, & R.C. Martella (Eds.), *Promoting health and safety: Skills for independent living* (pp. 55–69). Baltimore: Paul H. Brookes Publishing Co.

Heath, E.D. (1983). Youth and safety for the world of work. *Vocational Evaluation, 58,* 23–24.

Hughes, C., & Agran, M. (1994). Teaching persons with severe disabilities to use self-instruction in community settings. *Journal of The Association for Persons with Severe Handicaps, 18,* 261–274.

Hughes, C., & Rusch, F.R. (1989). Teaching supported employees with severe mental retardation to solve problems. *Journal of Applied Behavior Analysis, 22,* 365–372.

Jacobs, R., Samowitz, P., Levy, J.M., Levy, P.H., & Cabrera, G. (1992). Young Adult Institute's comprehensive AIDS staff training program. In A.C. Crocker, H.J. Cohen, & T.A. Kastner (Eds.), *HIV infection and developmental disabilities: A resource for service providers* (pp. 161–169). Baltimore: Paul H. Brookes Publishing Co.

Juracek, D.B. (1994). Fire safety skills. In M. Agran, N.E. Marchand-Martella, & R.C. Martella (Eds.), *Promoting health and safety: Skills for independent living* (pp. 103–119). Baltimore: Paul H. Brookes Publishing Co.

Kazdin, A.E. (1977). Assessing the clinical or applied importance of behavior change through social validation. *Behavior Modification, 1,* 427–451.

Lehr, D.H., & Macurdy, S. (1994). Meeting special health care needs of students. In M. Agran, N.E. Marchand-Martella, & R.C. Martella (Eds.), *Promoting health and safety: Skills for independent living* (pp. 71–84). Baltimore: Paul H. Brookes Publishing Co.

Litrownik, A.J. (1982). Special considerations in the self-management training of the developmentally disabled. In P. Karoly & F.H. Kanfer (Eds.), *Self-management and behavior change* (pp. 315–352). Elmsford, NY: Pergamon.

Martella, R.C., & Agran, M. (1994). Safety skills on the job. In M. Agran, N.E. Marchand-Martella, & R.C. Martella (Eds.), *Promoting health and safety: Skills for independent living* (pp. 121–134). Baltimore: Paul H. Brookes Publishing Co.

Martella, R.C., Agran, M., & Marchand-Martella, N.E. (1992). Problem solving to prevent accidents in supported employment. *Journal of Applied Behavior Analysis, 25,* 637–645.

Martella, R.C., & Marchand-Martella, N.E. (1995). Safety skills in vocational rehabilitation: A qualitative analysis. *Journal of Vocational Rehabilitation, 5,* 25–31.

Martella, R.C., Marchand-Martella, N.E., & Agran, M. (1992). Work-related accident causes: A neglected transitional area. *Canadian Journal of Rehabilitation, 6,* 117–122.

Martella, R.C., Marchand-Martella, N.E., & Agran, M. (1994). Effective behavioral-instructional strategies. In M. Agran, N.E. Marchand-Martella, & R.C. Martella (Eds.), *Promoting health and safety: Skills for independent living* (pp. 1–9). Baltimore: Paul H. Brookes Publishing Co.

Martella, R.C., Marchand-Martella, N.E., Agran, M., & Allen, S. (in press). Using a problem-solving strategy to prevent injuries due to unsafe worker behaviors. *British Columbia Journal of Special Education.*

Mason, C.Y., & Jaskulski, T. (1994). HIV/AIDS prevention and education. In M. Agran, N.E. Marchand-Martella, & R.C. Martella (Eds.), *Promoting health and safety: Skills for independent living* (pp. 161–191). Baltimore: Paul H. Brookes Publishing Co.

Mithaug, D. (1993). *Self-regulation theory: How optimal adjustment maximizes gain.* Westport, CT: Praeger.

Morgan, D. (1994). Preventing substance use. In M. Agran, N.E. Marchand-Martella, & R.C. Martella (Eds.), *Promoting health and safety: Skills for independent living* (pp. 135–159). Baltimore: Paul H. Brookes Publishing Co.

Muccigrosso, L. (1991). Sexual abuse prevention strategies and programs for persons with developmental disabilities. *Journal of Sexuality and Disability, 9*(3), 261–272.

Mueller, H.H., Wilgosh, L., & Dennis, S. (1989). Employment survival skills for entry-level occupations. *Canadian Journal of Rehabilitation, 2,* 203–221.

National Fire Protection Association. (1991). *Life safety code.* Quincy, MA: Author.

National Safety Council. (1988). *Accident facts.* Chicago: Author.

Pelland, M., & Falvey, M.A. (1986). Domestic skills. In M.A. Falvey (Ed.), *Community-based curriculum: Instructional strategies for students with severe handicaps* (pp. 77–99). Baltimore: Paul H. Brookes Publishing Co.

Perske, R. (1972). The dignity of risk. In W. Wolfensberger (Ed.), *Normalization: The principle of normalization in human services* (pp. 194–200). Toronto, Ontario, Canada: National Institute on Mental Retardation.

Peterson, L. (1984). The "safe at home" game: Training comprehensive prevention skills in latchkey children. *Behavior Modification, 8,* 474–494.

Powers, L.E., Wilson, R., Matuszewski, J., Phillips, A., Rein, C., Schumacher, D., & Gensert, J. (1996). Facilitating adolescent self-determination: What does it take? In D.J. Sands & M.L. Wehmeyer (Eds.), *Self-determination across the life span: Independence and choice for people with disabilities* (pp. 257–284). Baltimore: Paul H. Brookes Publishing Co.

Prendergast, M., Austin, G., & deMiranda, J. (1990). *Substance use among youth with disabilities* (Prevention Research Update No. 7). Portland, OR: Northwest Regional Educational Library.

Schloss, P.J., Alper, S., & Jayne, D. (1993). Self-determination for persons with disabilities: Choice, risk, and dignity. *Exceptional Children, 60,* 215–225.

Sobsey, D. (1994). Crime prevention and personal safety. In M. Agran, N.E. Marchand-Martella, & R.C. Martella (Eds.), *Promoting health and safety: Skills for independent living* (pp. 193–213). Baltimore: Paul H. Brookes Publishing Co.

Stimpson, L., & Best, M.C. (1991). *Courage above all: Sexual assault against people with disabilities.* Toronto, Ontario, Canada: DisAbled Women's Network.

West, M.A., Richardson, M., LeConte, J., Crimi, C., & Stuart, S. (1992). Identification of developmental disabilities and health problems among individuals under child protective services. *Mental Retardation, 30,* 221–225.

Westling, D.L., & Fox, L. (1995). *Teaching students with severe disabilities.* Columbus, OH: Charles E. Merrill.

CHAPTER 5

Assessing Preferences
and Teaching Choice Making

After reading this chapter, you will be able to

1. Explain to parents, professionals, and other community members the importance of students with disabilities having the opportunity to express their choices and preferences and have these honored

2. Use six different strategies for assessing the choices and preferences of students with disabilities

3. Use empirically based strategies to teach choice-making skills to students with disabilities

4. Use a variety of strategies to provide a maximum number of opportunities for students to make choices and demonstrate preferences

5. Provide opportunities for students to practice choice making across a variety of situations (e.g., leisure activities, shopping, eating meals, employment)

KEY TERMS

1. Choice
2. Community integration
3. Decision making
4. Empowerment

5. Job sampling
6. Normalization
7. Preferences
8. Quality of life

More than any other component element of self-determined behavior, the right of people with disabilities to make choices has been a focal point in the self-determination movement. Like everyone else, people with disabilities have preferences (Benz & McAllister, 1990; Brown, Belz, Corsi, & Wenig, 1993). Some people prefer to live alone rather than with someone else, some like soft drinks for breakfast, some prefer classical music to rock music, and some prefer to walk across town rather than take the bus. Unlike most citizens, however, people with disabilities too frequently do not have the opportunity to make choices and decisions based on their own preferences. This has certainly been the case for students with disabilities, to such an extent that policy makers believed it necessary to mandate that transition services for students with disabilities include students' interests and preferences (see Chapter 3). The reasons that individuals do not make choices based on individual preferences vary; however, the experience of lacking choice-making opportunities appears to be universal (Wehmeyer & Metzler, 1995).

For individuals with more significant disabilities, multiple barriers to choice making are present. Because many individuals with significant, multiple disabilities have too few opportunities, they do not know how to make choices and need targeted, systematic instruction on this skill. Other individuals with significant disabilities do not express their preferences through conventional means and have limited opportunities to express their choices (Brown et al., 1993; Dattilo & Mirenda, 1987). Instead of asking for ketchup for their french fries, they may act aggressively or stare fixedly at the ketchup bottle. The essence of the problem is not that people with disabilities do not have preferences; rather it is that professionals, family members, and others are not always able to recognize the problematic behavior as an expression of preferences (Dattilo & Mirenda, 1987). What is needed in the field is a technology by which such choices may be made available for interpretation by others, perhaps through inferential means (Goode & Gaddy, 1976; Guess, Benson, & Siegel-Causey, 1985; Shevin & Klein, 1984; Sigafoos & Dempsey, 1992).

Similarly, many individuals who do speak or who have less significant disabilities, such as learning disabilities or mental retardation requiring only intermittent supports, experience lives characterized by equally limited opportunities to make choices or experience the consequences of their decisions (Schloss, Alper, & Jayne, 1993). Choice- and decision-making opportunities are rarely incorporated into instructional curricula for students with mild disabilities (Foxx, Faw, Taylor, Davis, & Fulia, 1993; Kohn, 1993; Wehmeyer, 1992). This situation is due partly to the prevailing belief that these students already possess the skills needed to make good choices or decisions (Brown et al., 1993; Foxx et al., 1993; Northrup, George, Jones, Broussard, & Vollmer, 1996). Postschool outcomes (e.g., unemployment, dependence, segregation) experienced by many students, however, including students with mild disabilities (Blackorby & Wagner, 1996; Harris & Associates, 1994), suggest that many students exiting from secondary education have not learned to exercise choice-

and decision-making skills wisely, and they are unable to navigate the myriad options and situations necessitating decisions during one's daily life in the community (Clark, Field, Patton, Brolin, & Sitlington, 1994; Schloss et al., 1993). If students have not been given the opportunity to learn to make choices based on their own preferences and to experience and learn from the consequences of these choices in the more controlled setting of the school, it is unlikely that they will be able to do so in response to the ever-changing demands of home, community, and work settings. Unwittingly, teachers may believe that they are protecting students by preventing them from experiencing the risks that result from the consequences of poor choices (Bannerman, Sheldon, Sherman, & Harchik, 1990; Brown et al., 1993; Ficker-Terrill & Rowitz, 1991; Perske, 1972). However, they may actually be preventing these students from learning the skills necessary to make independent decisions or to function autonomously, behaviors that are related to success in employment and in the community (Benz & Halpern, 1987; Heal & Rusch, 1995; McGrew, Bruininks, & Thurlow, 1992).

CONCEPTUAL BASIS OF PREFERENCES AND CHOICE MAKING

Preference and choice, although related, are not synonymous. As discussed in the first chapter, the choice-making process consists of two distinct components (Reid, Parsons, & Green 1991). Instruction in choice making focuses attention on these two components: 1) the identification of a preference and 2) the act of choosing. The first component involves "emitting specific behaviors necessary to select one item or event from two or more alternatives" (Reid, Parsons, & Green, 1991, p. 3), and the second directs that action toward the selection of preferred outcomes. Typically, individuals express preferences by verbally identifying the preferred option. For individuals with more significant disabilities and limited communication skills, however, preference must often be inferred from the act of choosing (Skinner, 1971). People, places, or things that are chosen consistently over time typically are considered to be preferred or more highly valued by an individual than other options (Newton, Horner, & Lund, 1991). The following section overviews the importance of expressing preferences and making choices in the lives of people with disabilities. Subsequent sections discuss how to assess preferences for individuals with limited communication skills, how to teach choice-making skills, and how to infuse choice making into day-to-day instruction.

IMPORTANCE OF EXPRESSING PREFERENCES AND MAKING CHOICES

An emerging issue in the area of transition is increasing the opportunity for individuals with disabilities to express preferences and exercise choice (Bannerman et al., 1990; Faw, Davis, & Peck, 1996; Parsons, McCarn, & Reid, 1993;

West & Parent, 1992). Preference and choice as a concept and value are embodied in the principle of normalization (see Chapter 2), the theory of empowerment (Rappaport, 1987), the goal of quality of life (Schalock, 1996), the construct of self-determination (Ward, 1988; Wehmeyer, Kelchner, & Richards, 1996), and the ideal of community integration and participation (Bruininks, Chen, Lakin, & McGrew, 1992). For example, measures that have been used to assess quality of life in empirical investigations include whether a person prefers to spend time alone or with a friend, chooses with whom he or she lives, or chooses how to handle his or her money (Hughes, Hwang, Kim, Eisenman, & Killian, 1995).

Although the freedom to choose should not be approached as a programmatic end in itself (Ferleger, 1994), the opportunity to assert preference and choice are typically viewed as critical to the process of one's personal growth and fulfillment (Deci & Ryan, 1985; Edgerton, 1988; Koestner, Ryan, Bernieri, & Holt, 1984; Lindsay, 1996). Edgerton argued that "[o]ur culture makes the right to choose for oneself a fundamental value. The right—and the necessity—to make crucial choices about one's life must be a central definition of normalization" (p. 332). In addition, legislation (e.g., the Rehabilitation Act Amendments of 1992 [PL 102-569], the Individuals with Disabilities Education Act [IDEA] of 1990 [PL 101-476] and its amendments) mandates incorporating individuals' preferences and choices into the development and implementation of their educational and rehabilitation programs. The current and emerging interest in choice is viewed as an indication of a major shift in federal policy toward incorporating student choice in educational programming and service delivery (Ficker-Terrill & Rowitz, 1991).

Furthermore, the act of making a choice in itself is related to positive outcomes in the educational programming of students with disabilities (Dattilo & Rusch, 1985; Dunlap et al., 1994; Kennedy & Haring, 1993; Mithaug & Mar, 1980; Newton, Ard, & Horner, 1993; Realon, Favell, & Lowerre, 1990). Dunlap and colleagues (1994) found that the opportunity to choose from a menu of academic tasks, rather than simply having access to preferred tasks, resulted in increased task engagement and decreased disruptive behavior for students with emotional and behavioral disorders. In addition, choice making has been related to increased motivation (Foster-Johnson, Ferro, & Dunlap, 1994), academic gains (Cooper et al., 1992), increases in productivity (Mithaug & Mar, 1980), and decreases in aggressive behavior (Dyer, Dunlap, & Winterling, 1990). At the same time, providing access to selected or preferred items, events, or situations has been shown to have positive effects on individuals' performance (Dyer et al., 1990; Fisher et al., 1992; Kennedy & Haring, 1993; Parsons, Reid, Reynolds, & Bumgarner, 1990). Parsons and colleagues (1990) showed that when people with severe disabilities were assigned preferred rather than nonpreferred tasks, their productivity and on-task behavior increased on small assembly jobs (e.g., sanding, staining, and gluing a wooden plaque).

Despite philosophical, legislative, and empirical support for the critical role of preference and choice in improving one's performance, quality of life, and participation in day-to-day experiences, numerous studies indicate that people with disabilities, particularly individuals with more significant disabilities, have limited opportunities to express preferences or make choices in their daily lives, compared with people without disabilities (Crapps, Langone, & Swaim, 1985; Houghton, Bronicki, & Guess, 1987; Kishi, Teelucksingh, Zollers, Park-Lee, & Meyer, 1988; Stancliffe & Wehmeyer, 1995; Wehmeyer & Metzler, 1995). Too often everyday choices, such as what to wear or eat, how to spend free time, or with whom one wants to live, in addition to long-term programmatic goals, such as employment, are made by parents, staff, or teachers (Kishi et al., 1988; Wehmeyer & Metzler, 1995). Stancliffe and Wehmeyer (1995) found that adults with mental retardation had limited opportunities to choose their roommates, where they lived, where they worked, or what they did during their leisure time.

In the following case study, James Watts illustrates how a person whose lack of speech resulted in a daily existence characterized by limited opportunities to express preferences or exercise choice, even regarding what to eat or wear, and the potential benefits of enabling individuals with significant disabilities to learn to express preferences and make choices.

Wednesday seemed like a typical day for James Watts. He was awakened at 6:05 A.M. by his mom. Even though he was already 17 and starting a new school year at West Neck High School, his clothes were already laid out for him on the foot of his bed. After dressing, he had to be told three times by his mom to come to breakfast, where his oatmeal was already prepared and waiting for him. It required an equal amount of badgering from his mom to get him to go up and brush his teeth and hair. On his way out the door, he picked up the lunch his mom had packed and sat on the curb until the bus came. James sensed that his mom was getting tired of doing everything for him; but because she had always cared for him, he assumed she would keep doing so for as long as he needed.

When he entered Mr. Sims's class at West Neck High School, however, James knew something was different. When James walked into class on the first day, Mr. Sims asked James where he would like to sit. It surprised James because he had never been asked where he would like to sit when he was in school; he was always just told where to sit. When James didn't respond, Mr. Sims motioned to several chairs and gestured to James to choose one. The rest of the day was much the same way. Mr. Sims handed James a stack of picture cards and asked James to sort through them and pick the ones that showed activities that he would like to do in class. Then Mr. Sims showed James how to insert the cards in a plastic folder to indicate the order in which James wanted to do the activities. The first thing James picked was playing a game on the classroom computer. James had never had the chance to use a computer before. When it was time to go to lunch, James went to the lunchroom with the rest of the freshman class at West Neck High and was surprised to see that he could choose whatever foods he wanted at the lunch counter.

All he had to do was point to his choice and the cafeteria worker would hand it to him. He decided that maybe the next day he would buy his lunch at school and not bring a lunch. James also could pick with whom he wished to eat lunch, and he decided to sit down next to Jerry.

Throughout the rest of the school year, Mr. Sims took James into the community to try out different jobs and recreational activities. Mr. Sims had explained to James and his parents that, upon entering West Neck High, James had been enrolled in a community-based transition class. Over the next few years, James would have many opportunities to sample different activities in the community to see which he preferred. Mr. Sims would note James's reactions to each of his new experiences to see which he favored and which he might like to spend more time doing.

By the end of James's junior year, it was easy for Mr. Sims to tell that of all his experiences, James really liked being around cars the best. Maybe it was because James's dad worked in an auto body shop. Whatever the reason, James just beamed when he had the chance to vacuum out cars and polish them to make them shine. He also seemed to like to interact with the guys in the shop and kidded and joked with them although he couldn't talk. Mr. Sims thought James might like to get a job at a car wash where he could be part of a crew that cleans and polishes cars as they line up at the car wash. James's mom also had noticed a gradual change in her son's willingness to take responsibility for his behavior. At first she had been concerned that James might not eat a good lunch or might get lost or confused in the community. James soon showed her, however, that he was responsible enough to make reasonable choices, and her concerns soon faded.

When he graduated from West Neck High School, James got a full-time job at the Supreme Car Wash on Eighth Avenue. He chose to walk there from home most days even though he could have taken the bus. James thought it was more fun to watch all the cars as he walked; although, once in awhile when it was raining, he might decide to take the bus. At noon, James and his co-workers at the car wash liked to go to the fast-food restaurant across the street. James liked being able to pick whatever he wanted to eat, although he usually chose a double hamburger and fries by pointing to the pictures on the menu. When work was over, James usually went right home to his apartment that he shared with Jerry, whom he had known since high school. After they fixed dinner, James and Jerry often walked over to the park and shot a few rounds of basketball, or they sometimes decided to take in a movie. Or sometimes James liked to go to visit his parents or one of his friends or maybe go to the mall. There certainly were many different things to choose from in a day!

When one considers that studies indicate that staff or important others' opinions of individuals' preferences frequently do not agree with those individuals' actual preferences (Green et al., 1988; Parsons & Reid, 1990; Stancliffe, 1995), it is especially critical that people with disabilities have the opportunity to express their own preferences and make their own choices. It is particularly important (as well as mandated by law) that students' preferences and interests are incorporated into the transition goals of their individualized education programs (IEPs) and that these preferences are considered in an individual's career planning and experiences. Consideration of an individual's preferences and choices when developing a job match between a worker and a potential job has been associated with enhanced employee satisfaction and performance on the job (Winking, O'Reilly, & Moon, 1993).

Until about the mid-1980s, little research was available to guide teachers, parents, and service providers in assessing people's preferences or providing opportunities for choice making within an individual's educational programming and daily activities (Bannerman et al., 1990; Guess et al., 1985; West & Parent, 1992). For example, Kishi and colleagues (1988) found that group home staff believed that they did not know how to incorporate choices into residents' daily activities and felt constrained by administrative guidelines to limit choice. Fortunately, since the mid-1970s, a growing number of researchers have investigated methods designed to assess the preferences of people with disabilities and teach these individuals choice-making skills. The next two sections overview strategies that have been proven effective at 1) assessing the preferences and choices of students with disabilities and 2) teaching choice-making skills. In addition, recommendations are given regarding future directions and opportunities for incorporating choice into people's everyday lives.

ASSESSING PREFERENCES AND CHOICES

Empirical efforts to assess the preferences and choices of students with disabilities primarily have targeted individuals with significant disabilities and limited language and communication skills. Fewer research efforts have addressed people with milder disabilities, perhaps because these individuals' verbal abilities belie the fact that they, like their counterparts with more significant disabilities, often are not adept at expressing their preferences or do not have their choices honored (Foxx et al., 1993). Therefore, although the research base from which this section draws primarily addresses individuals with severe disabilities, the strategies discussed are intended to apply and can be adapted to individuals with all types of disabilities.

Hughes, Pitkin, and Lorden (1996) conducted a review of the empirical literature on strategies to assess preferences. Because important others' opinions of an individual's preferences may be inaccurate (Stancliffe, 1995), only studies that directly assessed preference through direct observation were included in the review. Therefore, investigations that used only questionnaires or interviews or teacher nomination to identify preferences were not reviewed. In addition, because communication skills relate directly to how an individual expresses choice or preference (Reichle, Sigafoos, & Piche, 1989), only studies that provided sufficient information to determine communication modalities of participants were included. Strategies used in the studies to assess preference or choice are summarized, accompanied by examples to illustrate their implementation by practitioners.

Assessing Students' Responses

Often, students with disabilities, because of limited verbal or communication skills or lack of experience or practice in expressing themselves, cannot tell important others what their preferences are. Sometimes, practitioners must infer preferences from a student's behavior when a student responds to situations in which choices are presented. The type of student response assessed depends on many factors, such as student characteristics, type of choice items or activities presented, and features of the physical environment. Preference and choice were assessed across the 27 studies via six different student responses: activation of a microswitch ($n = 10$ studies); approach toward an object ($n = 9$); verbalizations, signing, gestures, vocalizations, or affect ($n = 9$); physical selection of an item ($n = 6$); task performance ($n = 5$); and time engaged with an item ($n = 1$). (Thirteen studies assessed two types of student responses.)

Activation of a Microswitch   Some students have limited verbal skills as well as very little use of their arms or legs. As such, it is difficult for them to express a preference in a conventional manner (e.g., verbally) or to indicate a choice in the manner in which most people do (e.g., picking up a preferred item, eating a favorite food, engaging in a chosen activity). A strategy that is gaining attention is to teach people with limited use of their bodies to use whatever physical movement they can make to activate a microswitch to indicate a choice among one or two items or activities. Dattilo (1986) taught three students with severe mental retardation, sensory and motor impairments, and no expressive verbal communication skills to activate microswitches that were connected to a computer software program. Activation of a microswitch by a slight movement of a student's body (e.g., raising arm) resulted in the activation of a choice of one of two options (e.g., video scenes, vibrating pad, taped music). Students' choices were tabulated automatically by the computer program. All students indicated preferences for particular choice items, as demonstrated by consistently choosing these items more than others across opportunities to choose.

Approach Toward an Object   Another strategy for assessing the preferences and choices of people with either limited or highly developed verbal skills is to observe whether they approach an object when it is presented as a choice. One or more objects or events can be presented to a student at a time. Pace, Ivancic, Edwards, Iwata, and Page (1985) observed the responses of six individuals with mental retardation and limited communication and adaptive skills when 16 objects (e.g., mirror, hands clapping, juice) were presented one at a time. After each item was presented (e.g., a cup of juice placed in front of the student), the student's approach to the item was assessed. An approach was defined as a student moving toward an object or event with his or her hand or body within 5 seconds of its presentation. Ten opportunities to approach an object were presented for each item; and, following an approach, a student was allowed to interact with the object for an additional 5 seconds. Preferred items were those that were approached on at least 80% of the presentations, and nonpreferred items were those that were approached on 50% or less opportunities. All six students showed definite preferences for some of the 16 items by approaching them at least 80% of the time. Subsequently, the preferred items were demonstrated to serve as reinforcers for the students by increasing their performance on targeted tasks when presented contingently.

Assessing preferences by using the approach strategy may easily be used with any student, with or without a disability. A teacher simply needs to note, across time, which items, activities, materials, or events students tend to approach in a situation in which all choices are equally and readily available (e.g., free time).

Verbalizations, Gestures, and Affect   For students who have expressive communication skills, indications of preferences and choices may include a variety of expressive behavior, including verbalizations, manual signing, physical gestures, vocalizations, or physical affect. For example, Winking and colleagues (1993) observed the expressive behavior of four employees with autism and severe behavior disorders (e.g., aggression, self-injury) as they completed a variety of jobs in a large hotel (e.g., laundry, food service, housekeeping). Observation recorded a range of behaviors for each employee that indicated preference or nonpreference of specific job tasks. For example, for one young woman, preference responses included smiling, singing, and repeating certain words or sounds. Nonpreference responses included wandering, grabbing, or crumbling materials. Employees' preference or nonpreference responses were observed when performing various tasks in the hotel in order to match employees with jobs that they liked to perform. Results showed that individuals had increased work-related skills and decreased inappropriate behavior.

In another study (Newton et al., 1993), residents of group homes were asked which of two activities they preferred to perform from a list of preferred and nonpreferred activities identified by staff (e.g., cook a meal or jog). For those residents who had verbal skills, an affirmative verbal response was considered an indication of preference. Upon making a choice, a resident was given an opportunity to engage in the chosen activity. An advantage of using verbal responses as an indication of a preference is that the preferred item need not always be present in the environment in order to query a student regarding a preference (e.g., asking a student if she would like to go swimming at the lake).

Physical Selection of an Item   The preferences of students with disabilities also can be assessed by observing whether they physically select (e.g., pick up) an item when it is presented. This strategy requires that the item be present in the environment for the student to select, which may limit the variety of choices that can be offered. The range of options can be expanded, however, by presenting items representational of an activity, event, or situation. For example, a ticket to a baseball game could represent the opportunity to see a game, or a book of coupons could represent the opportunity to go grocery shopping. Mithaug and Mar (1980) used physical selection as a preference assessment strategy by presenting employees with a choice of two items representative of different work tasks (e.g., a folded sheet of paper to represent an envelope-stuffing job) and asking the employees to pick up one of the two items to indicate with which item they wished to work. Preferred items (i.e., items chosen more frequently across opportunities) were shown to have reinforcing effects on subsequent work performance of all employees. The physical selection strategy could be used when assessing the preferences of any students with or without disabilities. This strategy is not unlike what occurs if one were to observe a person's choices at a salad bar across many different meals. Foods that are frequently chosen over time are likely those that the person prefers.

Task Performance   Another strategy for measuring preference that requires the physical presence of a choice item is observing a student's performance of a specific task. Wacker, Berg, Wiggins, Muldoon, and Cavanaugh (1985) used task performance as a preference assessment strategy when they observed the performance of five students on instructional tasks (e.g., range-of-motion exercises). When the students performed a targeted behavior, they were given access to a potentially preferred item (e.g., bingo game). Items were varied across performance sessions in order that the effect on performance of different items could be compared. Increases in task performance were associated with access to specific items for all students. Because of the reinforcing effect these items had on task performance, they were considered to be preferred.

The task performance strategy is based on the principle of positive reinforcement, which indicates that people are more likely to perform a behavior if the consequence of the behavior is an activity, event, or item that they prefer. Preference for a particular consequence is inferred from its reinforcing effect on an individual's performance. It would be possible to use the task performance strategy to assess many student preferences. For example, by observing the performance of any student in class, with or without disabilities, a teacher could determine whether getting good grades is a reinforcing (preferred) consequence for the student.

Time Engaged with an Item   Preference for items or activities also has been inferred from the amount of time a student has continued to be engaged with a particular item in comparison to time spent with other items or activities. Kennedy and Haring (1993) used a time engagement strategy when they assessed the preferences of four students with significant, multiple disabilities. Items such as a computer game or jigsaw puzzle were suggested by the students' teachers as likely either to be preferred or not preferred by each student. Subsequently, the items were placed one at a time on each student's wheelchair laptop, and the amount of time the student was engaged with the item during a 1-minute opportunity was noted and compared with time spent with other items. Engagement with an item was defined as a student physically touching the item with his or her hand or arm or facing the item. Findings showed that each student had definite preferences for interacting more with some items than others.

The time engagement strategy for assessing preferences could be used with all students. For example, a teacher or parent could observe the amount of time a student spends on different leisure activities during periods of free time across several weeks. If a student spends considerable time talking with peers on the telephone instead of conversing with family members or watching television during his or her free time, one could assume that talking to peers is a preferred activity for that student.

Observing Students' Responses Over Time

In assessing a student's preferences, it is important to observe the choices a student makes over an extended period of time. The studies reviewed by Hughes and colleagues (1996) indicated that student preferences are not only idiosyncratic to each student, but also that a student's preferences may vary across opportunities to choose (e.g., Kennedy & Haring, 1993). For example, a student may prefer to listen to rock music for several weeks in a row and then change to a preference for country music. Shifts in preference should not be surprising when one considers that, after having recent access to one type of event or activity, a student may become bored or disinterested and wish a change. In addition, whereas some students tend to pick the same options for a lengthy period of time before switching to another, some prefer to vary their choices frequently. Consequently, preferences may not be evident immediately. In order to get a true picture of a student's preferences, it is important to observe the choices a student makes over an extended period of time. A teacher then can estimate the percentage of times a particular option was chosen out of the total number of opportunities from which a student had to choose. Those options chosen a higher percentage of time than others likely are preferred by a student.

Providing Opportunities to Choose

A teacher has a variety of strategies available with which to provide opportunities for students to make choices and demonstrate preferences. Strategies may vary according to the number and type of choices provided as well as the manner of presenting the choices.

Number of Choices   Across the reviewed studies, either one or two items or activities were provided per opportunity to choose. The number of choices presented did not vary according to the level of ability of participants. When preferences were assessed by a participant's physical selection of an item, two options to choose were always presented. In contrast, when preferences were assessed by a participant's task performance, only one choice was offered. Across all other types of preference or choice responses, either one or two choices were presented with equally effective results in identifying preferences. Therefore, if a teacher were assessing a student's preferences by observing his or her approaches to a variety of activities or events, for example, a teacher could present potential preferences either individually or two at a time and note a student's responses.

A teacher also may choose to present an array of options to a student in a less controlled, more naturalistic situation. For example, Koegel, Dyer, and Bell (1987) equipped a large room with many games and toys and allowed three students with autism to choose whichever items they wished to interact with and to change to a new item as frequently as they wished. Results indicated that five preferred and nonpreferred items were identified for each student based on the amount of time each student interacted with the items.

Type of Choices   Theoretically, the types of options a teacher could present to students in order to determine their preferences or choices are limitless. The range of options could vary from choices as simple as what to eat or what to wear to more complex decisions such as what classes to take, whether to get married, or what career to choose. In actuality, empirical studies almost exclusively have assessed preferences that require fairly limited choice- and decision-making skills such as choice of food (e.g., pudding or crackers), music (e.g., rock or soft music), sensory reinforcers (e.g., fan or flashing lights), toys or games (e.g., hand-held toys or computer games), social reinforcers (e.g., hugs or conversation), or video displays (e.g., television shows or video scenes). Reasons for selecting the type of choices assessed in the reviewed studies included 1) availability and ease of presentation, 2) teacher nomination, 3) individualized education program requirements, and 4) replication of previous studies. Although these studies provided guidelines for assessing a variety of potential preferences, they did not systematically address choice in relation to a person's individual lifestyle interests or preferences.

Only a handful of studies have assessed preferences in relation to everyday activities, such as fixing meals or exercising (e.g., Newton et al., 1991), or choice of job tasks, such as housekeeping or food service (e.g., Winking et al., 1993). Even fewer studies have looked at major lifestyle decisions, such as choosing with whom to live, moving to another community, or changing careers (e.g., Foxx et al., 1993). Although few guidelines exist in the empirical literature for assessing lifestyle choices, a few programs have been developed, such as the Foxx and colleagues (1993) strategies for assessing the residential preferences of individuals with mental retardation who are moving from institutions into the community.

Manner of Presenting Choices   In the majority of reviewed studies, choices were assessed by placing a choice item on a table, wheelchair tray, or other surface in front of a participant. Teachers may also demonstrate the use of an item or activity or request a person to perform a task. Or teachers may simply ask people regarding their preference for a particular option, with or without presenting an object representative of the option in question, as needed.

Summary of Findings from the Empirical Literature

The preceding discussion focused on strategies that have been used in the empirical literature for assessing the preferences and choices of students with disabilities. Although most of the strategies have been developed for use with people with more significant disabilities, they may be applied with people with mild disabilities with minimal adaptation, as the previous examples indicate. The next section addresses how teachers may help students with disabilities learn to make choices.

TEACHING CHOICE MAKING

Although a number of strategies, curricula, and programs for teaching individuals to make choices have been developed, few empirical studies have investigated the effectiveness of these strategies. Studies that have investigated the development of choice-making skills stress the importance of systematically providing contingent consequences to emerging choice responses (Dattilo & Mirenda, 1987; Sigafoos & Dempsey, 1992). Sigafoos and Dempsey (1992) argued that behaviors such as approaching or reaching for a preferred item could be shaped as choice-making responses by systematically providing access to the chosen item after the response has been made. For example, to teach students to make choices by manipulating electronic microswitches, Dattilo and Mirenda (1987) used computers to provide immediate access to a chosen item following a student's activation of a microswitch. The principle of providing contingent access to a preferred item or activity following a choice-making response is basic to all programs that teach choice making. A description of some of the developments in choice-making curricula since the 1980s follows.

Making Leisure-Time Choices

A number of studies have used the *choice-training procedure,* developed by Wuerch and Voeltz (1982), to teach students with mental retardation to make choices related to leisure activities (e.g., Nietupski et al., 1986). This procedure comprises providing students with a choice among two or more previously acquired leisure-time activities and reinforcing students when they make a choice or prompting them when they do not. Subsequently, students are given access to the chosen activity, and they are prompted to engage in the activity for increasing periods of time. "Choice charts" were used by Nietupski and colleagues (1986) to provide pictorial and written word examples of leisure activities (e.g., video games, magazines, stationary bicycle) when implementing the choice-training procedure with teenagers with moderate to severe mental retardation. Choice training resulted in increased choice of and sustained engagement in leisure activities with decreased teacher assistance for all participants. In a similar fashion, Bambara and Ager (1992) used cards that contained pictures or words that described leisure activities to help three adults with moderate disabilities choose in which activities they wished to engage. Participants learned to use the cards to choose and schedule weekly leisure activities. Self-scheduling resulted in increased time spent engaged in chosen activities and a wider variety of activities for all participants.

Kennedy and Haring (1993) taught four students with multiple disabilities to use a microswitch communication system to request changes in leisure activities in which they were engaged with a partner. Prompting and reinforcement procedures were used to teach students to press a microswitch that activated a tape-recorded message that requested a change in activities (e.g., "Can we do something else?"). Choice-making training resulted in increases in diversity of activities chosen, time engaged in activities, and interactions with social partners.

Making Shopping Choices

As a component of a consumer education program designed to teach students with mild disabilities to make informed decisions when shopping, Koorland and Cooke (1990) developed a choice-making program for comparative shopping. For example, in teaching students to choose a fast-food restaurant at which to eat, a teacher may begin by leading a class discussion on the characteristics of fast-food restaurants that should be considered in making a choice. Based on this discussion, students develop a rating form to use to rate restaurants on identified characteristics. Subsequently, students dine at selected neighborhood restaurants and rate them. After each student picks his or her favorite restaurant based on the ratings, she visits that restaurant and orders a meal.

Making Mealtime Choices

Several studies have investigated teaching people with significant disabilities to exercise choice at mealtimes. Parsons and colleagues (Parsons & Reid, 1990; Parsons et al., 1993) provided adults with mental retardation opportunities to choose between one of two food or drink items throughout a meal (e.g., applesauce or pudding, coffee with or without cream, bananas or corn chips). Participants were prompted to choose an item if they did not do so independently. Upon choosing a particular item, the item was immediately provided to the participant. Findings of both studies revealed that providing access to a choice immediately following a choice response resulted in increases in choice making by all participants. Gothelf, Crimmins, Mercer, and Finocchiaro (1994) used a similar method to teach mealtime choice making to students who were deaf, blind, and had multiple disabilities. Tactile cues and physical guidance were provided to accommodate for the students' sensory impairments and, upon choosing a sample of an item, students were provided with a full portion of the chosen food.

Making Lifestyle Choices

The Illinois Planning Council on Developmental Disabilities (1992) developed a choice-making model for adults with developmental disabilities to use when making choices regarding lifestyle changes. The model comprises the following steps:

1. Define the problem.
2. Determine options.
3. Evaluate options.
4. Select an option.
5. Develop a plan of action.
6. Experience outcome.
7. Examine the experience.

Individuals are prompted and reinforced for performing each step of the model, and attention is paid to matching choice-making responses to the individual's primary communication mode and skills. Practitioners using these steps taught adults to apply the model to a variety of lifestyle choices such as choosing a job (e.g., "Should I work at a restaurant?"), choosing a hairstyle (e.g., "How should I cut my hair?"), choosing a housemate (e.g., "Should I live with Rick?"), or choosing social relationships (e.g., "Should I date Sarah?").

Faw et al. (1996) replicated the lifestyle choice program developed by Foxx and colleagues (1993) by teaching four adults with mental retardation and mental illness to evaluate available residential options upon leaving an institution. Participants were taught to evaluate options from photographs that depicted residential characteristics. Subsequently, all participants visited the community and successfully made residential choices based on the evaluation criteria they were taught to use.

Making Employment Choices

Several educators have developed curricula for providing students the opportunity to make employment choices by sampling a variety of jobs throughout their high school careers. Hutchins and Renzaglia (1990) developed a longitudinal employment training program in which teachers evaluate students' performance on a variety of jobs over several years. Students have the opportunity to choose jobs that they would like to experience; and, based on a students' job sampling performance, a teacher tries to match a student's job choice to his or her preferences, interests, and performance. Neubert, Danehey, and Taymans (1990) used a similar "job try-outs" program to match the employment choices of students with mild disabilities to job placements. Having the opportunity to sample varied jobs resulted in appropriate job matches for students that honored their vocational choices. Hagner and Salomone (1989) argued that people with disabilities, like all people, base their choices for a career on their work experiences and that the opportunity to sample a variety of jobs must be provided in order for people to gather information needed to make an informed career choice.

Summary of Findings from
Various Choice-Making Programs

Choice-making programs require providing students with disabilities the opportunity to sample many options. For some students, choice-making responses must be shaped. In teaching choice making to students with disabilities, teachers must be careful that choice-making responses consistently are followed by access to the chosen item, activity, or event. Choice-making programs that have been investigated empirically have addressed diverse choices, such as leisure activities, lifestyle choices, and career options.

INFUSING CHOICE MAKING
INTO CLASSROOM INSTRUCTION

Shevin and Klein (1984) emphasized the importance of learning choice-making skills in contexts that promote generalization and provide real-life opportunities to experience choices. They stressed integrating choice-making opportunities throughout the school day and listed five keys to maintaining a balance between student choice and professional responsibility:

1. incorporating student choice as an early step in the instructional process;
2. increasing the number of decisions related to a given activity which the student makes;
3. increasing the number of domains in which decisions are made;
4. raising the significance in terms of risk and long-term consequences of the choices which the student makes; and
5. clear communication with the student concerning areas of possible choice, and the limits within which choices can be made. (Shevin & Klein, 1984, p. 164)

Kohn (1993) suggested that school programs can provide opportunities for meaningful choices in both academic and behavioral areas. In academic areas, students can participate in choosing what, how, and why they learn. The determination of what one learns is fairly straightforward and has become a key element in promoting student involvement in educational planning and decision making (Martin, Marshall, & Maxson, 1993). Allowing a student to choose how they learn certainly entails more dedication and effort on the part of the teacher, but it is reasonable to provide choices in working alone, in small groups, or as a class, or to provide alternatives as to where students sit while they work (Kohn, 1993).

Perhaps the most overlooked aspect of structuring choice in the classroom is getting students involved in a discussion of why they are learning. Deci and Chandler (1986) suggested that providing rationales for activities to learners is one important way of increasing student motivation to learn and participate. Telling students that they have to learn something "because it is for their own good" or other more controlling reasons will limit student self-determination.

Indeed, Deci and Chandler (1986) suggested that being honest and straightforward about rationales for specific learning activities moves an activity from being externally imposed to being self-regulated.

CONCLUSION

Incorporating student preferences and choices into a student's IEP is mandated by current legislation. Historically, students with disabilities have been given limited opportunity to express preferences or exercise choices. A growing empirical research base indicates that students with disabilities, including those with significant disabilities, can communicate their preferences and learn to make choices. The present and future challenge for teachers is to incorporate opportunities for students to express their preferences and make choices throughout their daily activities (Brown et al., 1993). Brown et al. (1993) developed a Model of Choice Diversity for embedding choice-making opportunities throughout the natural course of a student's day. The model delineates seven potential areas of choice within an activity: 1) choice of materials, 2) choice among different activities, 3) choice to refuse to participate in an activity, 4) choice of people to be included or excluded in an activity, 5) choice of location of an activity, 6) choice of time an activity should occur, and 7) choice to end a particular activity. In planning and implementing curricula, teachers should attempt to incorporate opportunities for choice throughout as many of these dimensions as possible. In addition, teachers should be ready to provide instruction in choice making and expressing preferences to those students who have not yet acquired such skills. Furthermore, teachers should evaluate the effects on students of choice making, such as decreases in challenging behavior, increased motivation, and academic improvements (Cooper et al., 1992; Dunlap et al., 1994; Foster-Johnson et al., 1994).

QUESTIONS FOR REVIEW

1. The importance of individuals with disabilities being able to clearly express preferences and make their own choices is highlighted in this chapter. Give an example of how a student's having this ability might benefit each of the following individuals: an employer, the student's parent, and the student.

2. Describe three reasons students with varying levels of abilities may not express their preferences or may not have been provided the opportunity to choose in their daily lives.

3. Briefly describe the difference between the terms *choice* and *preference*.

4. Imagine that you are trying to determine what types of recreational activities James might enjoy (e.g., bowling, fishing, reading, canoeing). Name

two methods that you might use to assess his preferences. Describe how you would use each of these methods.

5. When a student is assessed for his or her preferences, it is important to observe the student's choices over an extended period of time. Briefly explain why.

6. Name and briefly describe the three variables that must be addressed when providing students with opportunities to choose.

7. Describe choice charts or cards (Nietupski et al., 1986) and how they can be of use in teaching students to choose.

8. Explain what is meant by "job sampling." Discuss the importance of preference with respect to job sampling for students with disabilities.

9. As discussed in the chapter, it is important to embed choices for students with disabilities in their everyday activities. Briefly describe four of the seven potential areas of choice within an activity described in Brown et al.'s (1993) Model of Choice Diversity.

10. Refer to the choice-making model of the Illinois Planning Council on Developmental Disabilities (1992). Using the steps described in the model, briefly describe a recent choice or decision you have made in your daily life.

REFERENCES

Bambara, L.M., & Ager, C. (1992). Using self-scheduling to promote self-directed leisure activity in home community settings. *Journal of The Association for Persons with Severe Handicaps, 17,* 67–76.

Bannerman, D.J., Sheldon, J.B., Sherman, J.A., & Harchik, A.E. (1990). Balancing the right to habilitation with the right to personal liberties: The rights of people with developmental disabilities to eat too many doughnuts and take a nap. *Journal of Applied Behavior Analysis, 23,* 79–89.

Benz, M.R., & Halpern, A.S. (1987). Transition services for secondary students with mild disabilities: A statewide perspective. *Exceptional Children, 53,* 507–514.

Benz, M.R., & McAllister, M. (1990). Occupational and leisure preferences of older adults with mental retardation. *Australia and New Zealand Journal of Developmental Disabilities, 16,* 233–244.

Blackorby, J., & Wagner, M. (1996). Longitudinal postschool outcomes of youth with disabilities: Findings from the National Longitudinal Transition Study. *Exceptional Children, 62,* 399–414.

Brown, F., Belz, P., Corsi, L., & Wenig, B. (1993). Choice and diversity for people with severe disabilities. *Education and Training in Mental Retardation, 28,* 318–326.

Bruininks, R.H., Chen, T.H., Lakin, K.C., & McGrew, K.S. (1992). Components of personal competence and community integration for persons with mental retardation in small residential programs. *Research in Developmental Disabilities, 13,* 463–479.

Clark, G.M., Field, S., Patton, J.R., Brolin, D.E., & Sitlington, P.L. (1994). Life skills instruction. A necessary component for all students with disabilities: A position statement of the Division on Career Development and Transition. *Career Development for Exceptional Individuals, 17,* 125–134.

Cooper, L.J., Wacker, D.P., Thursby, D., Plagmann, L.A., Harding, J., Millard, T., & Derby, M. (1992). Analysis of the effects of task preferences, task demands, and adult attention on child behavior in outpatient and classroom settings. *Journal of Applied Behavior Analysis, 25,* 823–840.

Crapps, J.M., Langone, J., & Swaim, S. (1985). Quantity and quality of participation in community environments by mentally retarded adults. *Education and Training of the Mentally Retarded, 20,* 123–129.

Dattilo, J. (1986). Computerized assessment of preference for severely handicapped individuals. *Journal of Applied Behavior Analysis, 19,* 445–448.

Dattilo, J., & Mirenda, P. (1987). An application of a leisure preference assessment protocol for persons with severe handicaps. *Journal of The Association for Persons with Severe Handicaps, 12,* 306–311.

Dattilo, J., & Rusch, F. (1985). Effects of choice on leisure participation for persons with severe handicaps. *Journal of The Association for Persons with Severe Handicaps, 10,* 194–199.

Deci, E.L., & Chandler, C.L. (1986). The importance of motivation for the future of the LD field. *Journal of Learning Disabilities, 19,* 587–594.

Deci, E.L., & Ryan, R.M. (1985). *Intrinsic motivation and self-determination in human behavior.* New York: Plenum.

Dunlap, G., DePerczel, M., Clarke, S., Wilson, D., Wright, S., White, R., & Gomez, A. (1994). Choice making to promote adaptive behavior for students with emotional and behavioral challenges. *Journal of Applied Behavior Analysis, 27,* 505–518.

Dyer, K., Dunlap, G., & Winterling, V. (1990). Effects of choice making on the serious problem behaviors of students with severe handicaps. *Journal of Applied Behavior Analysis, 23,* 515–524.

Edgerton, R.B. (1988). Aging in the community: A matter of choice. *American Journal on Mental Retardation, 92,* 331–335.

Faw, G.D., Davis, P.K., & Peck, C. (1996). Increasing self-determination: Teaching people with mental retardation to evaluate residential options. *Journal of Applied Behavior Analysis, 29,* 173–188.

Ferleger, D. (1994, June). The place of "choice." In C.J. Sundram (Ed.), *Choice and responsibility: Legal and ethical dilemmas in services for persons with mental retardation* (pp. 69–97). Albany: New York State Commission on Quality of Care for the Mentally Disabled.

Ficker-Terrill, C., & Rowitz, L. (1991). Choices. *Mental Retardation, 29,* 63–64.

Fisher, W., Piazza, C., Bowman, L., Hagopian, L., Owens, J., & Slevin, I. (1992). A comparison of two approaches for identifying reinforcers for persons with severe and profound disabilities. *Journal of Applied Behavior Analysis, 25,* 491–498.

Foster-Johnson, L., Ferro, J., & Dunlap, G. (1994). Preferred curricular activities and reduced problem behaviors in students with intellectual disabilities. *Journal of Applied Behavior Analysis, 27,* 493–504.

Foxx, R.M., Faw, G.D., Taylor, S., Davis, P.K., & Fulia, R. (1993). "Would I be able to...?" Teaching clients to assess the availability of their community living style preferences. *American Journal on Mental Retardation, 98,* 235–248.

Goode, D.A., & Gaddy, M.R. (1976). Ascertaining choice with alingual, deaf-blind and retarded clients. *Mental Retardation, 14,* 10–12.

Gothelf, C.R., Crimmins, D.B., Mercer, C.A., & Finocchiaro, P.A. (1994). Teaching choice-making skills to students with dual-sensory impairments. *Teaching Exceptional Children, 26,* 13–15.

Green, C., Reid, D., White, L., Halford, R., Brittain, D., & Gardner, S. (1988). Identifying reinforcers for persons with profound handicaps: Staff opinion versus systematic assessment of preferences. *Journal of Applied Behavior Analysis, 21,* 31–43.

Guess, D., Benson, H.A., & Siegel-Causey, E. (1985). Concepts and issues related to choice-making and autonomy among persons with severe disabilities. *Journal of The Association for Persons with Severe Handicaps, 10,* 79–86.

Hagner, D., & Salomone, P.R. (1989). Issues in career decision making for workers with developmental disabilities. *The Career Development Quarterly, 38,* 148–159.

Harris & Associates. (1994). *N.O.D/Harris survey of Americans with disabilities.* New York: Author.

Heal, L.W., & Rusch, F.R. (1995). Predicting employment for students who leave special education high school programs. *Exceptional Children, 61,* 472–487.

Houghton, J., Bronicki, G.J.B., & Guess, D. (1987). Opportunities to express preferences and make choices among students with severe disabilities in classroom settings. *Journal of The Association for Persons with Severe Handicaps, 12,* 18–27.

Hughes, C., Hwang, B., Kim, J.H., Eisenman, L.T., & Killian, D.J. (1995). Quality of life in applied research: A review and analysis of empirical measures. *American Journal on Mental Retardation, 99,* 623–641.

Hughes, C., Pitkin, S.E., & Lorden, S.W. (1996). *Assessing preferences and choices of persons with severe and profound disabilities.* Unpublished manuscript.

Hutchins, M.P., & Renzaglia, A.M. (1990). Developing a longitudinal vocational training program. In F.R. Rusch (Ed.), *Supported employment: Models, methods, and issues* (pp. 365–380). Sycamore, IL: Sycamore.

Illinois Planning Council on Developmental Disabilities. (1992). *Teaching choices: A curriculum for persons with developmental disabilities.* Naperville, IL: Author.

Individuals with Disabilities Education Act (IDEA) of 1990, PL 101-476, 20 U.S.C. § 3061 *et seq.*

Kennedy, C., & Haring, T. (1993). Teaching choice making during social interactions to students with profound multiple disabilities. *Journal of Applied Behavior Analysis, 26,* 63–76.

Kishi, G., Teelucksingh, B., Zollers, N., Park-Lee, S., & Meyer, L. (1988). Daily decision-making in community residences: A social comparison of adults with and without mental retardation. *American Journal on Mental Retardation, 92,* 430–435.

Koegel, R.L., Dyer, K., & Bell, L.K. (1987). The influence of child-preferred activities on autistic children's social behavior. *Journal of Applied Behavior Analysis, 20,* 243–252.

Koestner, R., Ryan, R.M., Bernieri, F., & Holt, K. (1984). The effects of controlling versus informational limit-setting styles on children's intrinsic motivation and creativity. *Journal of Personality, 52,* 233–248.

Kohn, A. (1993). Choices for children: Why and how to let students decide. *Phi Delta Kappan, 75,* 8–20.

Koorland, M.A., & Cooke, J.C. (1990). Using fast food restaurants for consumer education. *Teaching Exceptional Children, 22,* 28–29.

Lindsay, P. (1996). The right to choose: Informed consent in the lives of adults with mental retardation and developmental disabilities. *Education and Training in Mental Retardation and Developmental Disabilities, 31,* 171–176.

Martin, J.E., Marshall, L.H., & Maxson, L.L. (1993). Transition policy: Infusing self-determination and self-advocacy into transition programs. *Career Development for Exceptional Individuals, 16,* 53–61.

McGrew, K.S., Bruininks, R.H., & Thurlow, M.L. (1992). Relationship between measures of adaptive functioning and community adjustment for adults with mental retardation. *Exceptional Children, 58,* 517–529.

Mithaug, D., & Mar, D. (1980). The relation between choosing and working prevocational tasks in two severely retarded young adults. *Journal of Applied Behavior Analysis, 13,* 177–182.

Neubert, D.A., Danehey, A.J., Taymans, J.M. (1990). Vocational interests, job tryouts and employment outcomes of individuals with mild disabilities in a time-limited transition program. *Vocational Evaluation and Work Adjustment Bulletin, 23,* 17–23.

Newton, J.S., Ard, W., Jr., & Horner, R. (1993). Validating predicted activity preferences of individuals with severe disabilities. *Journal of Applied Behavior Analysis, 26,* 239–245.

Newton, J.S., Horner, R.H., & Lund, L. (1991). Honoring activity preferences in individualized plan development: A descriptive analysis. *Journal of The Association for Persons with Severe Handicaps, 16,* 207–212.

Nietupski, J., Hamre-Nietupski, S., Green, K., Varnum-Teeter, K., Twedt, B., LePera, D., Scebold, K., & Hanrahan, M. (1986). Self-initiated and sustained leisure activity participation by students with moderate / severe handicaps. *Education and Training of the Mentally Retarded, 21,* 259–264.

Northup, J., George, T., Jones, K., Broussard, C., & Vollmer, T.R. (1996). A comparison of reinforcer assessment methods: The utility of verbal and pictorial choice procedures. *Journal of Applied Behavior Analysis, 29,* 201–212.

Pace, G., Ivancic, M., Edwards, G., Iwata, B., & Page, T. (1985). Assessment of stimulus preference and reinforcer value with profoundly retarded individuals. *Journal of Applied Behavior Analysis, 18,* 249–255.

Parsons, M., McCarn, J., & Reid, D. (1993). Evaluating and increasing meal-related choice throughout a service setting for people with severe disabilities. *Journal of The Association for Persons with Severe Handicaps, 18,* 253–260.

Parsons, M., & Reid, D. (1990). Assessing food preferences among persons with profound mental retardation: Providing opportunities to make choices. *Journal of Applied Behavior Analysis, 23,* 183–195.

Parsons, R., Reid, D., Reynolds, J., & Bumgarner, M. (1990). Effects of chosen versus assigned jobs on the work performance of persons with severe handicaps. *Journal of Applied Behavior Analysis, 23,* 253–258.

Perske, R. (1972). The dignity of risk. In W. Wolfensberger (Ed.), *The principle of normalization in human services* (pp. 194–200). Toronto, Ontario, Canada: National Institute on Mental Retardation.

Rappaport, J. (1987). Terms of empowerment / exemplars of prevention: Toward a theory for community psychology. *American Journal of Community Psychology, 15,* 122–143.

Realon, R., Favell, J., & Lowerre, A. (1990). The effects of making choices on engagement levels with persons who are profoundly multiply handicapped. *Education and Training in Mental Retardation, 25,* 299–305.

Rehabilitation Act Amendments of 1992, PL 102-569, 29 U.S.C. § 701 *et seq.*

Reichle, J., Sigafoos, J., & Piche, L. (1989). Teaching an adolescent with blindness and severe disabilities: A correspondence between requesting and selecting preferred objects. *Journal of The Association for Persons with Severe Handicaps, 14,* 75–80.

Reid, D.H., Parsons, M.B., & Green, C.W. (1991). *Providing choices and preferences for persons who have severe handicaps.* Morganton, NC: Habilitative Management Consultants.

Schalock, R.L. (1996). Reconsidering the conceptualization and measurement of quality of life. In R.L. Schalock (Ed.), *Quality of life: Vol. 1. Conceptualization and measurement* (pp. 123–139). Washington, DC: American Association on Mental Retardation.

Schloss, P.J., Alper, S., & Jayne, D. (1993). Self-determination for persons with disabilities: Choice, risk, and dignity. *Exceptional Children, 60,* 215–225.

Shevin, M., & Klein, N.K. (1984). The importance of choice-making skills for students with severe disabilities. *Journal of The Association for Persons with Severe Handicaps, 9,* 159–166.

Sigafoos, J., & Dempsey, R. (1992). Assessing choice making among children with multiple disabilities. *Journal of Applied Behavior Analysis, 25,* 747–755.

Skinner, B.F. (1971). *Beyond freedom and dignity.* New York: Alfred A. Knopf.

Stancliffe, R. (1995). Assessing opportunities for choice making: A comparison of self and staff reports. *American Journal on Mental Retardation, 99,* 418–429.

Stancliffe, R., & Wehmeyer, M.L. (1995). Variability in the availability of choice to adults with mental retardation. *Journal of Vocational Rehabilitation, 5,* 319–328.

Wacker, D., Berg, W., Wiggins, B., Muldoon, M., & Cavanaugh, J. (1985). Evaluation of reinforcer preference for profoundly handicapped students. *Journal of Applied Behavior Analysis, 18,* 173–178.

Ward, M.J. (1988). The many facets of self-determination. *National Information Center for Children and Youth with Disabilities: Transition Summary, 5,* 2–3.

Wehmeyer, M.L. (1992). Self-determination and the education of students with mental retardation. *Education and Training in Mental Retardation, 27,* 302–314.

Wehmeyer, M.L., Kelchner, K., & Richards, S. (1996). Essential characteristics of self-determined behavior of individuals with mental retardation. *American Journal on Mental Retardation, 100,* 632–642.

Wehmeyer, M.L., & Metzler, C.A. (1995). How self-determined are people with mental retardation? The national consumer survey. *Mental Retardation, 33,* 111–119.

West, M.D., & Parent, W.S. (1992). Consumer choice and empowerment in supported employment services: Issues and strategies. *Journal of The Association for Persons with Severe Handicaps, 17,* 47–52.

Winking, D., O'Reilly, B., & Moon, M. (1993). Preference: The missing link in the job match process for individuals without functional communication skills. *Journal of Vocational Rehabilitation, 3,* 27–42.

Wuerch, B.B., & Voeltz, L.M. (1982). *Longitudinal leisure skills for severely handicapped learners: The Ho'onanea curriculum component.* Baltimore: Paul H. Brookes Publishing Co.

CHAPTER 6

Teaching Social Problem-Solving and Decision-Making Skills

After reading this chapter, you will be able to

1. Discuss the similarities and differences between problem solving and decision making

2. Discuss the importance of social problem-solving and decision-making skills to youth with and without disabilities

3. Identify types of problem-solving and decision-making programs and discuss their unique components

4. Identify and give examples of levels of risk taking

5. Identify and distinguish between several problem-solving and decision-making strategies

KEY TERMS

1. Assertiveness training
2. Decision-making skills
3. General cognitive programs
4. General social programs
5. Risk taking
6. Social problem-solving skills
7. Specific cognitive programs
8. Specific social programs
9. Uncertainty

Ineffective decision-making and social problem-solving skills are frequently identified barriers to positive adult outcomes for many individuals with disabilities. The educational literature has emphasized the importance of teaching problem-solving skills to achieve positive vocational, academic, and social outcomes for youth with disabilities (Buser & Reimer, 1988; Izzo, Pritz, & Ott, 1990), as well as stressing the importance of these skills for self-determination. Despite this emphasis, limited research has been conducted into teaching strategies to achieve this outcome. Most people are not taught formal strategies to solve problems and make decisions and instead rely on day-to-day experiences and "on-the-job" training to learn such skills. Unfortunately, many students with disabilities are not provided the opportunities and experiences they need to learn effective problem-solving and decision-making skills and, as illustrated in the following case study, are unprepared for dealing with such circumstances.

Juanita looked at her watch and then looked down the street one more time before giving up and going back in the house. She was supposed to be at work in 15 minutes, but once again she was not going to make it on time. Juanita felt angry and helpless. She had asked her co-worker, George, to pick her up in front of her house a half hour before. It was the third time George had been late. In fact, the last time he hadn't ever arrived. She was afraid she would lose her job, but she didn't know what to do about it. She knew that trusting George was not the best way to solve her problem. He had a history of being late to work as well. Juanita really didn't know what to do and decided that if she lost her job, it wasn't really her fault.

At school the next morning she ran into Maria, who also worked with Juanita. Maria asked where she had been yesterday, and Juanita shared with Maria how George had never shown up to take her to work. Maria listened and when Juanita finished, she asked whether she had considered a way to solve her problem. Juanita admitted she hadn't and Maria volunteered to meet her in the break room at work that evening and help her sort out her problem.

That evening the two friends sat in the break room. Maria pointed out that the first thing Juanita needed to do was to figure out her problem so she could solve it. Juanita was puzzled by this and indicated to Maria that the obvious problem was that George wasn't doing what he was supposed to do, and she didn't know how to solve that problem. When Maria pointed out, however, that the real problem was not that George was unreliable but that Maria needed a reliable way to get to work, she agreed that there were other ways to resolve that problem. Together, Juanita and Maria came up with other ways to get to work. She could have her mom give her a lift, find another co-worker from whom to get a ride, walk, or take the bus. Her mom's work schedule made it tough for her to be there all the time, and Juanita didn't really know anyone else who could help. It wasn't too far to walk, but Juanita didn't want to walk home alone at night. She had thought about the bus, but she wasn't sure how to ride it. Juanita agreed, however, that the bus seemed like a good option if it ran near her home and work.

The next day Juanita got a bus schedule. Sure enough, the bus ran a block from home and she could get off right down the street from work. She checked the time schedule and it looked like she could reliably get to work on time. Juanita felt relieved and good about the fact that, with Maria's help, she had sorted out a big problem. The bus turned out to be the right solution for her. George, however, was fired for being late 3 weeks later.

Problem-solving and decision-making skills are frequently viewed as interchangeable. Although strategies to promote both are discussed in this chapter, differences in the two constructs warrant a quick distinction. As discussed in Chapter 1, a problem is "a task whose solution is not immediately perceived" (Beyth-Marom, Fischhoff, Jacobs Quadrel, & Furby, 1991, p. 20). Problem-solving skills are those skills that enable a person to identify one or more solutions to a problem. Alternatively, decision-making skills refer to a broader set of skills that incorporate problem-solving and choice-making skills in a process to *select* one of several *already identified* solutions. Many instructional programs address both problem-solving and decision-making skills.

Problem-solving and social skills training also frequently overlap. On a daily basis, people encounter situations in which they must decide on a course of action to meet a need or solve a conflict, and these situations frequently involve interactions with other people. Social competence "requires active problem-solving and decision-making behavior, whereby one defines a problematic situation, searches for possible alternative situations, selects the best alternative, and determines its suitability by observing the consequences of its implementation" (Beyth-Marom et al., 1991, pp. 20–21). Social skills training refers to interventions that are designed to increase social behaviors that are absent from an individual's repertoire. Social problem-solving training emphasizes teaching cognitive strategies in such situations, rather than teaching specific behavioral skills.

Beyth-Marom and colleagues (1991) suggested that programs that provide decision-making training can be classified according to 1) their focus, either social or cognitive or 2) their scope, either general or specific. *General social programs* are those that teach interpersonal problem-solving skills, such as coping strategies, assertiveness, and decision-making methods. *Specific social programs* focus on specific problems, such as smoking, peer and family relationships, sexuality, or physical health. Cognitive programs stress thinking skills related to the decision-making process. *General cognitive programs* teach decision making as one of many thinking skills, whereas *specific cognitive programs* teach only decision making. This chapter provides an overview of both social and cognitive decision-making and problem-solving strategies. Chapter 4 discusses problem solving in relationship to safety skills instruction, and Chapter 8 discusses self-instruction strategies, including the use of self-instructional techniques for problem solving, that provide more behavior-based interventions for problem solving in social and other settings (e.g., vocational skills training, community integration skills training).

OVERVIEW OF DECISION-MAKING
AND PROBLEM-SOLVING INSTRUCTION

Because most decision-making procedures incorporate problem-solving strategies, these represent the logical first choice for instructional emphasis. Izzo et
al. (1990) suggested that problem solving is a systematic process involving three
sequential steps: problem identification, problem analysis, and problem resolution. Problem-solving skills, then, include the ability to recognize and define
problems, invent and implement solutions, and track and evaluate results. According to these authors, "problem-solving requires students to think for themselves, make purposeful choices, connect means with ends, identify similarities
and differences, and initiate and follow through with the task at hand" (p. 25).
They suggested a four-step process to approaching a problem:

1. State the problem.
2. List the choices that are available.
3. Identify the consequences of each choice.
4. Select the choice that best meets immediate as well as long-term needs. (p. 25)

Social problem-solving skills, sometimes referred to as interpersonal cognitive problem-solving skills, are particularly important for students to become
self-determined. The following sections overview research in this area and examine the social problem-solving skills of individuals with disabilities. Next,
decision-making skills are discussed.

Research in Social Problem Solving

Until the mid-1970s, problem-solving skills were studied almost entirely from
an impersonal context (Platt & Hermalin, 1989). Most researchers focused on
an individual's ability to complete puzzles and anagrams or solve mathematical
problems. Such problems typically have only one correct solution with answers
remaining the same over time (Wheeler, 1991). In contrast, problems involving
interactions between people are complex, with multiple processing demands and
decision points, and such problems have numerous possible solutions that may
vary according to time or setting. For example, the way an individual would
greet a co-worker if that person has recently been demoted would differ greatly
from a greeting if one knows that the person has been promoted. Likewise, how
one greets a co-worker in front of a supervisor might be very different from
how one might routinely greet that person. Researchers in the area of problem
solving became increasingly concerned that "conceptualizing problem solving as
removed from real-world interactions and applications failed to capture the complexity of social and personal problem solving and was not applicable to practitioners in counseling and education" (Spivack & Shure, 1974, p. 29).

Consequently, research investigating problem-solving skills within a social context emerged, and theorists working in this area began to describe and define social problem solving as a metacognitive process (Elliot, Godshall, Shrout, & Witty, 1990). For the first time, questions were being asked about how a person approached problems. As a result, research in problem solving began to reflect more closely the complexity of social interactions. For example, Heppner and Petersen (1982) suggested that successful social problem solving had three dimensions beyond just a repertoire of behavioral strategies: 1) confidence in one's ability to solve problems, 2) one's approach–avoidance style, and 3) perceptions of personal control.

Platt and Hermalin (1989) were among the earliest researchers to link effective social problem solving with more positive emotional and social outcomes. They proposed that, in order to deal with real-life problems and stay well-adjusted, a person must utilize a set of adaptive social problem-solving skills that include 1) recognition of the problem, 2) optional thinking or the generation of alternatives, 3) causal thinking, 4) means–end thinking or step-by-step planning, 5) consequential thinking, and 6) role taking or metarepresentation.

Social Problem Solving and Individuals with Disabilities

Similar to research efforts with students and individuals without disabilities, investigations of problem solving for individuals with disabilities have moved from impersonal to personal contexts. Much of this research has examined the capacity of individuals with cognitive disabilities, such as mental retardation or learning disabilities, to solve problems. This research has suggested that people with mental retardation exhibit a largely inflexible pattern of problem-solving skills (Ellis, Woodley-Zanthos, Dulaney, & Palmer, 1989; Ferretti & Butterfield, 1989; Ferretti & Cavelier, 1991; Short & Evans, 1990). This pattern, labeled *cognitive rigidity* by Gestalt psychologists, "is characterized by repetition of past strategies to solve current problems without adapting to new stimuli or new task demands" (Short & Evans, 1990, p. 95). Wehmeyer and Kelchner (1995) examined the social problem-solving skills of adults with mental retardation and found that this group generated fewer potential solutions to social problems and that a greater proportion of solutions generated were irrelevant. Likewise, Toro, Weissberg, Guare, and Liebenstein (1990) compared the social problem-solving strategies of students with learning disabilities with those of students without disabilities, and concluded that students with learning disabilities generated fewer alternatives for solving social problem situations.

Although ample research documents the importance of social skills for positive adult outcomes for students with disabilities, little of that research has focused specifically on social problem solving. Healey and Masterpasqua (1992) examined the social problem solving of elementary school students as a function of their adjustment to general education classrooms. These researchers hypothesized that strong social problem-solving skills would be related to more positive peer relations and behavioral adjustment in the classroom. They found that this was indeed the case and that classroom adjustment could be predicted by interpersonal, cognitive problem-solving skills.

Several studies have shown that students with disabilities can acquire effective problem-solving strategies. Castles and Glass (1986) found that training improved social problem-solving skills of youth with mild and moderate mental retardation. Browning and Nave (1993) used an interactive, video-based curriculum to teach social problem-solving skills to youth with mental retardation or learning disabilities. Coleman, Wheeler, and Webber (1993) conducted a review of research in social problem-solving training in school settings with youth with learning or behavior problems. They concluded from this review that "a sequence of social problem-solving steps can be learned by a variety of students with learning or behavior problems" (p. 34). Students in the studies reviewed "consistently demonstrated improvements in knowledge of problem solving on cognitive measures such as role plays or verbal responses to problem situations" (p. 34).

These findings were tempered by mixed results on the effectiveness of such programs when the outcome measure is an observed behavior. Coleman and colleagues (1993) indicated that social problem-solving training does not automatically result in students applying learned strategies to their everyday lives. Park and Gaylord-Ross (1989), however, found that the need to pair skills training with social problem-solving training is reciprocal. That is, not only does social skills instruction need to accompany social problem-solving training in order for students to generalize problem-solving skills, but social skills instruction needs to be coupled with social problem-solving training in order to ensure generalization of social skills. Park and Gaylord-Ross compared social skills training without problem-solving training to a general social skills program that incorporated problem-solving training for youth with developmental disabilities. They found that the social problem-solving training procedure increased generalization and maintenance of the targeted social behaviors.

The classroom environment that needs to be in place to support problem solving is one that is positive in tone, open and allowing of inquiries, supportive, and effective as a role model. Izzo and colleagues (1990) also suggested that two basic criteria must be a part of instruction in problem solving: 1) instruction must be connected to learners' prior knowledge, and 2) instruction should use real-life situations in which social problem solving is important.

Coleman and colleagues (1993) provided several recommendations for teachers interested in using social problem-solving strategies in their classroom but concerned about problems with generalization. First, they suggested, teachers need to individualize instruction by including only students with "demonstrable [social problem-solving] repertoire deficits"(p. 34), instead of assuming that all students lack social problem-solving skills and targeting the entire group.

Second, teachers should be concerned with measuring both the quality as well as the quantity of solutions generated by students with disabilities as a result of problem-solving training. Students may indeed be applying the learned problem-solving process and yet generating solutions that are not appropriate. Finally, these authors suggested that social problem-solving training should be paired with skills instruction, such as that identified in Chapter 8 (i.e., self-instruction).

Decision-Making Skills

Beyth-Marom et al. suggested that the decision-making process includes the following basic steps:

a) listing relevant action alternatives;
b) identifying possible consequences of those actions;
c) assessing the probability of each consequence occurring (if the action were undertaken);
d) establishing the relative importance (value or utility) of each consequence; and
e) integrating these values and probabilities to identify the most attractive course of action. (1991, p. 21)

These steps are similar to those identified in the problem-solving process, except that they start by listing already identified action alternatives; that is, the decision-making process begins with the problem already solved. In addition to these core steps, several others are specific to particular circumstances, including an initial step in which the individual distinguishes among different decision-making models based on circumstances. Simply put, although the core steps remain constant no matter what decisions are made, there are differences in the process based on issues of certainty or uncertainty and the degree of risk.

Beyth-Marom and colleagues (1991) pointed out that uncertainty is a basic element in many decisions. Research indicates that adults and children alike tend to underestimate the uncertainty in most decisions, which often leads to less than optimal outcomes from decisions. Uncertainty in any decision comes from a number of sources. Identifying the consequences of any given alternative is usually a "best guess" situation. This may result either from a lack of information about a particular option or may just be a factor of the type of alternative. It is also often the case that uncertainty exists as to whether a particular alternative is actually available or will be available after a decision is made. The degree of uncertainty in each of these situations should be treated as a factor in reaching a decision, and the fact that such uncertainty typically exists should be a topic of instruction for students with disabilities.

Beyth-Marom and colleagues (1991) suggested that instruction that focuses on teaching students about uncertainty should address questions such as

1. What is uncertainty?
2. What are the different kinds of uncertainty?

3. What is the relationship between uncertainty and amount of available information?

Another factor that has an impact on the decision-making process is the amount of risk involved in making a particular decision. Schloss, Alper, and Jayne (1994) detailed four levels of risk taking associated with making a choice; each of these dimensions is equally relevant when considering alternatives in the decision-making process.

1. *The alternative involves limited potential for immediate risk but little possibility of long-term harm to the individual or others.* Examples include choosing what to eat or wear. This first level of decision making emphasizes that almost no choice is risk free. For example, choosing to wear one's hair in a nontraditional manner may result in others making judgments and holding expectations that are limiting or unfair.
2. *The alternative involves mild risk with minimal possibility of long-lasting harm to the individual or others.* Schloss et al. (1994) provided the example of choosing to spend one's lunch money on a video game and, as a result, having to go without lunch.
3. *The alternative results in a moderate probability for long-lasting harm to the individual or others.* Examples include becoming sexually active without using adequate birth control (moderate risk of becoming pregnant) or choosing to smoke cigarettes (moderate risk of cancer or other illness).
4. *The alternative involves an almost certain outcome that includes personal injury.* Schloss and colleagues (1994) identify daily use of addictive substances as an example of this level. Another example might be unprotected sexual contact with multiple partners over a long period of time (risk of human immunodeficiency virus [HIV] infection).

It is important to note that the great majority of alternatives fall within the first two dimensions and not the latter two. Unfortunately, in many cases these relatively low levels of risk are overemphasized and used to curtail the opportunities students with disabilities have to make choices and decisions. In addition, the risk dimensions must be evaluated with the individual in mind. For example, the consequences of a high-fat diet may be very low risk for some individuals but quite a high risk for others. Because the decision-making process involves balancing risks and benefits to come to an acceptable outcome, it is important that students learn how to judge the relative risk of alternatives and weigh these risks with potential benefits.

PROBLEM-SOLVING AND DECISION-MAKING TRAINING PROGRAMS

Returning to the classification of the types of decision-making training programs and strategies suggested by Beyth-Marom and colleagues (1991), this section describes specific instructional programs and strategies that can be employed to promote student problem-solving and decision-making skills.

General Social Programs

General social programs are those instructional programs and strategies that teach a wide variety of interpersonal problem-solving skills, such as coping strategies, assertiveness, and decision-making methods. The most common of these strategies are assertiveness training programs and social skills training programs. Assertiveness training strategies refer to a number of multicomponent packages built on behavioral rehearsal and including the basic elements of modeling, coaching, feedback, and homework assignments to teach assertive behavior. Social skills training programs incorporate instructional elements that are also involved in the assertiveness training process, such as role playing, modeling, and rehearsal, but they typically share fewer components than those shared by different assertiveness training programs. Social skills training programs are often linked as much by their content (e.g., teaching social skills) as their approach. Assertiveness training strategies are described in detail in Chapter 10 and therefore are not covered in this chapter.

Benjamin (1996a, 1996b) developed two general social programs that address a range of social and problem-solving skills in two different environments—school and work. Benjamin introduced a problem-solving plan designed to get students thinking about problems they encounter. Students are taught the following four steps:

1. Understand: Ask yourself, "What is the problem? What do I need to find out?"
2. Plan and Solve: Ask yourself, "What do I already know? How will I solve this problem?" Then use problem-solving skills to help you and carry out your plan.
3. Check: Look at what happened. Ask yourself, "Have I solved the problem? Does my plan make sense?" If there's still a problem, look over your plan. Change your plan. Try another problem-solving skill to solve the problem.
4. Review: Look at what you did to solve the problem. Ask yourself, "What have I learned? How can I use my plan to solve problems like this in the future?" (Benjamin, 1996a, p. iv)

Lessons in the *Problem Solving in School* materials (Benjamin, 1996a) apply this problem-solving plan to enable students to function more effectively in the school environment. Areas of instruction in which the problem-solving plan is applied are listed in Table 1. As this table shows, the skills that are addressed involve a wide range of social and self-advocacy skills, including goal setting, money management, effective communication, and planning. Likewise, the *Problem Solving on the Job* lessons (Benjamin, 1996b) apply the same problem-solving plan to social skills, vocational skills, and self-advocacy skills training, as seen in Table 2.

Table 1.   Problem-solving areas in the school environment

Unit	Instructional area
Unit 1: Preparing for School	Planning your day
	Getting dressed
	Morning chores
	Getting to school
Unit 2: Managing in School	Being on time
	Following your schedule
	Finishing your schoolwork
	Taking notes
	Doing homework
	Studying
	Class time and personal time
Unit 3: Communication Skills	Talking with a teacher
	Talking with a friend
	Listening
	Asking questions
	Oral reports
Unit 4: Making Judgments and Decisions	Peer pressure
	Problems with students
	Problems in school
	Changes at school
	Setting goals
	School and work
	Planning what schoolwork to do first
Unit 5: Managing Money	Budgeting
	Paying
	Saving

Adapted from Benjamin (1996a).

Specific Social Programs

Unlike general social skills training programs, which are broad in focus, specific social programs focus on specific problems encountered by youth, such as smoking, peer and family relationships, sexuality, or physical health. Problem-solving and decision-making skills instruction occurs only as a component of addressing the specific social problem. There are numerous examples of specific social programs that have been used with individuals with disabilities to address a number of problems, from anger control to community living.

Foxx and Bittle (1989) developed a curriculum for use with students with disabilities called *Thinking it Through*, which teaches a problem-solving strategy for community living. The curriculum focuses on several areas that the authors identify as important to successful community adjustment, including 1) emergencies and injuries, 2) safety, 3) authority figures, 4) peer issues, 5) community resources, and 6) stating one's rights. The program "is designed to teach a

Table 2. Problem-solving areas in the work environment

Unit	Instructional area
Unit 1: Preparing for Work	Getting ready Getting dressed Getting to work
Unit 2: Managing Time	Being on time Your workday Organizing work time Work time and personal life
Unit 3: Managing Job Duties	Completing forms Job duties Planning which job to do first Completing jobs on time Dressing for work Finding information
Unit 4: Communication Skills	Talking with a boss Talking with co-workers Talking with customers Listening Asking questions
Unit 5: Making Judgments and Decisions	Peer pressure Problems on the job Personal issues Change at work
Unit 6: Managing Money	Reading a pay stub Payday Budgeting

Adapted from Benjamin (1996b).

problem-solving strategy by presenting trainees with commonly experienced problems and by guiding them to consider a sequence of problem-solving questions in formulating their solutions" (Foxx & Bittle, 1989, p. 4).

Instead of instructional activities focusing on teaching students a specific cognitive process, *Thinking it Through* teaches students to ask a series of questions in order to formulate solutions to specific problems. The questions are listed below, and one problem situation from each area is presented in Table 3:

1. When will the problem be solved?
2. Where would you or a friend look for help?
3. To whom would you or your friend talk regarding the problem?
4. What would you or your friend say?

Training involves the use of cue cards with one problem situation per card. The facilitator works with three participants, each of whom selects cue cards,

Table 3. Sample problem situations

General category	Sample problem situation
Emergencies and injuries	You feel very dizzy. What should you do?
Safety	You are walking outside and get caught in a thunder and lightning storm. Your friend says, "Let's get under a tree." What should you do?
Authority figures	You just broke your supervisor's favorite mug. He is going to be angry. What should you do?
Peer issues	Whenever you go out with your friend, he burps loudly and then laughs. You are really getting embarrassed. What should you do?
Community resources	A child walks up to you at the fair and says she is lost. What should you do?
Stating one's rights	You have a friend who keeps asking you to go out on a date. You don't want to go. What should you do?

Adapted from Foxx & Bittle (1989).

and, based on the community-living–related problem described, are asked to provide a solution. Through repeated practice and self-monitoring for appropriate solutions, individuals build a repertoire of solutions to community-living–based problems. *Thinking it Through* was designed primarily for use with adults with mental retardation, but the program could be readily adapted for other populations and students.

Tymchuk, Andron, and Rahbar (1988) provided another example of a specific social program used with individuals with disabilities. These authors conducted group training in decision making with women with mental retardation who had children. The training used vignettes describing child-raising situations. The decision-making training involved teaching participants six decision-making components applied to problem situations specific to parenting. The decision-making components that participants learned were 1) decision identification, 2) goal definition, 3) who should make the decision and where help could be obtained, 4) alternatives and weighing risks, and 5) selection of an optimal decision.

Training in the components proceeded by using four vignettes involving common child-rearing decisions (listed in Table 4). Training was conducted in small groups with a professional serving as the trainer. At each session one decision-making component was introduced, with previous components reviewed each time as well. The trainer used a blackboard to help participants visualize each component and its relationship to the other components. Using each training vignette, participants and the trainer discussed the component being introduced, with the trainer verbally reinforcing each appropriate response and providing guided feedback on incorrect or inappropriate responses. Training proceeded through all six component areas. As a means of assessing the efficacy of the training and the participants' ability to generalize the training to other situations, participants were asked to address additional vignettes, examples of

Table 4. Training and sample generalization vignettes involving common child-rearing decisions

Type of vignette	Vignette
Training	Your baby is crying.
	Your son, who has just started the first grade, comes home crying, saying that another boy hit him at school.
	You are feeding your baby, who begins to choke.
	Because you are at home by yourself a lot with your 2-year-old daughter, you are getting more and more upset with her.
Generalization	Your baby seems listless; and when you hold her, she just flops against you.
	Your child never tells you how he is doing at school.
	Someone gives your baby a game with toothpicks in it.
	You are at work and your baby sitter calls to tell you that your 2-year-old is sick.
	Every night around 3 A.M. your baby wakes up crying.
	Your 2-year-old hits you.
	You take away your son's toy, and he says that he hates you.
	Your 4-year-old son likes to sleep in your bed.
	Your child has a trunk full of toys and wants more.

Adapted from Tymchuk, Andron, & Rahbar (1989).

which are listed in Table 4. The investigators found significant improvements in decision-making step identification and use on training and generalization vignettes and improvement in the appropriateness of decisions related to high-risk situations (e.g., when a child is hurt or listless, abusive situations).

The procedure employed by Tymchuk and colleagues (1988) is one that could be easily replicated in classrooms to address a number of specific problem topics, including alcohol use, sexuality and sexually transmitted diseases, safety, hygiene, employment, and independent living. The process did not involve specific curricular materials; instead it employed a lecture/discussion model in which real-world problems were examined by using a consistent decision-making process.

Bullock and Mahon (1992) forwarded a process for teaching students with disabilities a decision-making process specific to decisions in leisure skills. They began instruction with a leisure awareness training program, in which students with disabilities were introduced to five components important to leisure awareness:

1. Concepts of leisure
2. Self-awareness in leisure
3. Knowledge of leisure opportunities
4. Leisure resources
5. Leisure barriers

After students completed the leisure awareness training module, students were taught the Decision Making in Leisure (DML) model. This model's structure was adapted from the Adaptability Instruction model (Mithaug, Martin, & Agran, 1987; described in Chapter 12). The DML model was composed of four steps:

1. Identify a desired leisure experience.
2. Consider alternatives that satisfy the experience desired.
3. Describe the consequences for each alternative, including the amount of enjoyment, whether a partner is required, the cost, where the activity takes place, and the equipment needed.
4. Choose an alternative that satisfies the desired experience.

Instruction using the DML model involves five instructional steps:

1. Introduce the four-step model: Steps are introduced using both oral and pictorial presentation of each step.
2. Teach the child to use the four steps to make a decision: The student is taught to use a schematic representation of the model each time he or she is asked to make a decision.
3. Offer assistance when necessary: The teacher or facilitator allows the student to work through the decision-making process on his or her own but provides verbal cues to support each student as necessary.
4. Provide verbal praise as the student proceeds through making the decision.
5. Remove schematic of the DML model.

Using the DML model, Bullock and Mahon (1992) taught students with mental retardation to make decisions about their leisure time activities in classroom settings independently. They suggested that the teaching approach could also be implemented in a physical education setting or in a student's home.

General Cognitive Programs

Social problem-solving and decision-making programs teach these skills as one aspect of teaching general or specific social skills. In contrast, cognitive problem-solving and decision-making programs focus exclusively on teaching *thinking skills,* either presenting problem solving and decision making as one of many thinking skills or as the sole thinking skill. Considerable overlap occurs between cognitive and social programs, and in many cases the assignment of a particular strategy to one or the other is somewhat arbitrary. The primary difference is one of emphasis—social skills versus thinking skills training. General cognitive programs teach problem solving and decision making as one of many thinking skills, whereas specific cognitive programs teach these skills by themselves. The application of such programs to youth with disabilities has, by and large, not been examined; therefore, this chapter includes only one such program to serve as an example.

The *IDEAL Problem Solver* (Bransford & Stein, 1993) is a general cognitive program that teaches individuals critical thinking, memorization, and problem-solving skills. In this particular program, problem-solving skills take center stage, as it were, over the other thinking skills. Through the program, students learn a five-step problem-solving strategy to approach any problem. The acronym for the strategy is IDEAL, and the steps involve teaching students to

I = Identify problems and opportunities.
D = Define goals.
E = Explore possible strategies.
A = Anticipate outcomes and act.
L = Look back and learn.

What characterizes the *IDEAL Problem Solver* program as a cognitive program is its focus on coupling other thinking skills with the IDEAL problem-solving strategy. In the course of completing the program, participants work on strategies that target several thinking skills, such as memorization skills. Participants learn categorization strategies (i.e., grouping like items together in order to remember them); visualization techniques, such as the method of loci, in which items to be remembered are visualized in a familiar location; or the interactive imagery strategies, in which items to be remembered are paired and visualized in a manner that will be easy to recall (e.g., a dog talking on the telephone to remind one to call the vet). The program then focuses on critical thinking skills, such as using basic comprehension strategies. Bransford and Stein (1993) employed a wide range of instructional strategies to teach these thinking skills, including case-based instruction (i.e., organizing instruction around a situation the student is likely to encounter), project-based instruction (i.e., organizing instruction around a student project), debates, simulations, cooperative learning, and student-directed learning strategies.

Specific Cognitive Programs

Specific cognitive programs are those that teach only problem-solving or decision-making strategies. These programs have evolved from the work of D'Zurilla (D'Zurilla, 1986; D'Zurilla & Goldfried, 1971) and Spivack and Shure (1974). Elias, Branden-Muller, and Sayette (1991) summarized the theoretical approach adopted by D'Zurilla as it applied to educational settings. D'Zurilla's problem-solving model involved five specific stages: 1) problem orientation, 2) problem definition and formulation, 3) generation of alternative solutions, 4) decision making, and 5) solution implementation.

According to Elias and colleagues, the problem orientation stage has four functions:

1. To increase awareness of problems and to introduce the idea of problem solving;
2. To encourage positive expectations for problem-solving and divert attention from negative or preoccupying thoughts;
3. To encourage persistence against emotional stress and difficult situations; and
4. To facilitate a positive emotional state. (1991, p. 168)

Several cognitive variables are targeted within the problem orientation stage. First, instruction focuses on problem perception or the recognition and labeling of problems. Second, instruction focuses on problem attribution skills (e.g., problems attributed to internal or external factors) and problem appraisal skills (i.e., the individual's judgment as to the importance of the problem). D'Zurilla (1986) emphasized issues of self-efficacy and outcome expectancy at this stage, topics that are covered in Chapter 15. Participants also learn how to estimate the time they will need to solve a problem during this stage.

The second stage, problem definition and formulation, is one in which participants learn to gather as much information about the problem as possible, set problem-solving goals, and reexamine the importance of the problem's resolution to their well-being. In stage three, individuals learn to generate alternative solutions to the problem. The generation of alternatives is a step that is often problematic for students with disabilities. As previously mentioned, students with mental retardation or learning disabilities often generate fewer appropriate alternatives than same-age peers without disabilities. Many students with disabilities tend to perseverate on alternatives that are either ineffective or that share a common theme or characteristic. So, for example, students with emotional or behavioral disorders may generate multiple alternatives, all involving aggressive responses. Most people learn about their options based on a combination of learning and experience. Students with disabilities too often do not have the experience base from which to draw when generating alternatives, and "instruction" in this area may be as simple as expanding a student's experiences in relevant areas such as work or leisure.

The emergence of the ability to generate alternatives typically follows a specific sequence (Beyth-Marom et al., 1991). The first stage is the generation of a single alternative. Students who are not able to do so already should be provided instructional opportunities that would enable them to generate at least one alternative for problems relevant to their lives. At the next stage, students learn to generate a small list of alternatives. Again, this may be primarily a rote exercise, learning about and memorizing several alternatives to common problems. In the third stage, students need to learn how to brainstorm new alternatives. The final stages involve the generation of alternatives by classification and criteria standards (i.e., actually inventing alternatives based on characteristics of the problem situation and using past experiences).

The fourth stage of the D'Zurilla (1986) problem-solving model involves decision making. Specifically, participants are taught to consider the value and likelihood of the anticipated consequences, decide whether the alternatives are feasible and acceptable, and examine the cost and benefits of the alternatives. The final stage, solution implementation and verification, incorporates several cognitive/behavioral features (as opposed to strictly cognitive features), including self-monitoring, self-evaluation, and self-reinforcement, all of which are considered in Chapter 7.

Drawing from the previous work of D'Zurilla (D'Zurilla & Goldfried, 1971), Spivack, Shure, and colleagues (Platt, Spivack, Altman, Altman, & Peizer, 1974; Shure & Spivack, 1978; Shure, Spivack, & Jaeger, 1972; Spivack & Shure, 1974) constructed a model of problem-solving thinking with specific emphasis on problem solving and mental health. These researchers focused on a set of cognitively-based problem-solving skills, including

- Problem recognition thinking
- Optional thinking (generation of alternative solutions)
- Causal thinking (identifying consequences)
- Social means–end thinking (step-by-step solutions for goal achievement)
- Emotional means–ends thinking
- Consequential thinking (considering outcomes of interpersonal behaviors)
- Perspective taking

There are several problem-solving programs that have drawn heavily from the work of Spivack and Shure. One such program is *Think Aloud* (Bash & Camp, 1985). In practice, this curriculum is a general social program designed to teach problem-solving and other social skills to students in the elementary and middle school years. The program emphasizes the thinking skills identified by Spivack and Shure, however, and is focused heavily on verbal mediation of problem situations. A second widely available program is *I Can Problem Solve* (ICPS), developed by Shure (1992). This program takes the previous research conducted by the author and translates this to instructional activities to teach pre–problem-solving and problem-solving skills. Shure stated that "the underlying goal of ICPS is to help children learn how to think, not what to think" (p. 1). Again, the program's focus is primarily on elementary-age students.

CONCLUSION

Teaching students to become more effective social problem solvers and decision makers is an important step in the process of teaching self-determination skills. Considerable overlap occurs in this area between teaching assertive behaviors and social skills as well as teaching students to use self-instructional strategies. In fact, it is most likely that teaching students effective social problem-solving skills will be embedded in other instructional areas such as social skills training. It is particularly important that educators attend to the need to provide opportunities for students to generalize learned problem-solving and decision-making behaviors to real-world situations. The educational planning and decision-making process provides one such opportunity, and strategies to involve students in this process are described in Chapter 12. It is equally important that instruction in social problem solving and decision making be coupled with strategies such as self-instruction (Chapter 8), self-evaluation, and self-monitoring (Chapter 7) if such instruction is to be effective.

QUESTIONS FOR REVIEW

1. People with mental retardation exhibit a largely inflexible pattern of problem solving. Discuss some of the factors that have led to this pattern of problem solving.
2. Identify and briefly describe four types of programs or strategies that teach problem-solving and decision-making skills.
3. Define cognitive rigidity and describe how this concept explains the problem-solving strategies of many people with mental retardation.
4. Discuss the steps to effective problem solving.
5. Discuss the role of uncertainty in problem-solving outcomes.
6. Discuss classroom environments that support effective social problem solving.
7. Identify common components of decision-making strategies.
8. Discuss the similarities and differences among choice-making, decision-making, and problem-solving skills.

REFERENCES

Bash, M.A.S., & Camp, B.W. (1985). *Think aloud: Increasing social and cognitive skills—A problem-solving program for children.* Champaign, IL: Research Press.

Benjamin, C. (1996a). *Problem solving in school.* Upper Saddle River, NJ: Globe Fearon Educational.

Benjamin, C. (1996b). *Problem solving on the job.* Upper Saddle River, NJ: Globe Fearon Educational.

Beyth-Marom, R., Fischhoff, B., Jacobs Quadrel, M., & Furby, L. (1991). Teaching decision-making to adolescents: A critical review. In J. Baron & R.V. Brown (Eds.), *Teaching decision making to adolescents* (pp. 19–59). Hillsdale, NJ: Lawrence Erlbaum Associates.

Bransford, J.D., & Stein, B.S. (1993). *The IDEAL problem solver* (2nd ed.). San Francisco: W.H. Freeman.

Browning, P., & Nave, G. (1993). Teaching social problem solving to learners with mild disabilities. *Education and Training in Mental Retardation, 28,* 309–317.

Bullock, C.C., & Mahon, M.J. (1992, Fall). Decision making in leisure: Empowerment for people with mental retardation. *Journal of Physical Education, Recreation, and Dance,* 36–40.

Buser, K.P., & Reimer, D. (1988). Developing cognitive strategies through problem-solving. *Teaching Exceptional Children, 20,* 22–25.

Castles, E.E., & Glass, C.R. (1986). Training in social and interpersonal problem-solving skills for mildly and moderately mentally retarded adults. *American Journal of Mental Deficiency, 91,* 35–42.

Coleman, M., Wheeler, L., & Webber, J. (1993). Research on interpersonal problem-solving training: A review. *Remedial and Special Education, 14,* 25–37.

D'Zurilla, T.J. (1986). *Problem solving therapy.* New York: Springer-Verlag.

D'Zurilla, T.J., & Goldfried, M.R. (1971). Problem solving and behavior modification. *Journal of Abnormal Psychology, 78,* 107–126.

Elias, M.J., Branden-Muller, L.R., & Sayette, M.A. (1991). Teaching the foundations of social decision making and problem solving in the elementary school. In J. Baron & R.V. Brown (Eds.), *Teaching decision making to adolescents* (pp. 161–184). Hillsdale, NJ: Lawrence Erlbaum Associates.

Elliot, T.R., Godshall, F., Shrout, J.R., & Witty, T.E. (1990). Problem-solving appraisal, self-reported study habits, and performance of academically at risk college students. *Journal of Counseling Psychology, 37,* 203–207.

Ellis, N.R., Woodley-Zanthos, P., Dulaney, C.L., & Palmer, R.L. (1989). Automatic effortful processing and cognitive inertia in persons with mental retardation. *American Journal on Mental Retardation, 93,* 412–423.

Ferretti, R.P., & Butterfield, E.C. (1989). Intelligence as a correlate of children's problem-solving. *American Journal on Mental Retardation, 93,* 424–433.

Ferretti, R.P., & Cavalier, A.R. (1991). Constraints on the problem solving of persons with mental retardation. In N.W. Bray (Ed.), *International Review of Research in Mental Retardation* (Vol. 17, pp. 153–192). San Diego: Academic Press.

Foxx, R.M., & Bittle, R.G. (1989). *Thinking it through: Teaching a problem-solving strategy for community living.* Champaign, IL: Research Press.

Healey, K., & Masterpasqua, F. (1992). Interpersonal cognitive problem-solving among children with mild mental retardation. *American Journal on Mental Retardation, 96,* 367–372.

Heppner, P.P., & Petersen, C.H. (1982). The development and implications of a personal problem-solving inventory. *Journal of Counseling Psychology, 29,* 66–75.

Izzo, M.V., Pritz, S.G., & Ott, P. (1990). Teaching problem-solving skills: A ticket to a brighter future. *Journal for Vocational Special Needs Education, 13,* 23–26.

Mithaug, D.E., Martin, J.E., & Agran, M. (1987). Adaptability instruction: The goal of transitional programming. *Exceptional Children, 53,* 500–505.

Park, H.-S., & Gaylord-Ross, R. (1989). A problem-solving approach to social skills training in employment settings with mentally retarded youth. *Journal of Applied Behavior Analysis, 22,* 373–380.

Platt, J.P., & Hermalin, J. (1989). Social skill deficit interventions for substance abusers. *Psychology of Addictive Behaviors, 3,* 114–133.

Platt, J.P., Spivack, G., Altman, N., Altman, D., & Peizer, S.B. (1974). Adolescent problem-solving thinking. *Journal of Consulting and Clinical Psychology, 42,* 787–793.

Schloss, P.J., Alper, S., & Jayne, D. (1994). Self-determination for persons with disabilities: Choice, risk, and dignity. *Exceptional Children, 60,* 215–225.

Short, F.J., & Evans, S.W. (1990). Individual differences in cognitive and social problem-solving skills as a function of intelligence. In N.W. Bray (Ed.), *International review of research in mental retardation* (Vol. 16, pp. 89–123). San Diego: Academic Press.

Shure, M.B. (1992). *I can problem solve.* Champaign, IL: Research Press.

Shure, M.B., & Spivack, G. (1978). *Problem-solving techniques in childrearing.* San Francisco: Jossey-Bass.

Shure, M.B., Spivack, G., & Jaeger, M. (1972). Problem-solving thinking and adjustment among disadvantaged preschool children. *Child Development, 42,* 1791–1803.

Spivack, G., & Shure, M. (1974). *Social adjustment of young children.* San Francisco: Jossey-Bass.

Toro, P.A., Weissberg, R.P., Guare, J., & Liebenstein, N.L. (1990). A comparison of children with and without learning disabilities on social problem-solving skill, school behavior and family background. *Journal of Learning Disabilities, 23,* 115–120.

Tymchuk, A.J., Andron, L., & Rahbar, B. (1989). Effective decision-making/problem-solving training with mothers who have mental retardation. *American Journal on Mental Retardation, 92,* 510–516.

Wehmeyer, M.L., & Kelchner, K. (1995). Interpersonal cognitive problem-solving skills of individuals with mental retardation. *Education and Training in Mental Retardation and Developmental Disabilities, 29,* 265–278.

Wheeler, D. (1991). Metaphors for effective thinking. In J. Baron & R. Brown (Eds.), *Teaching decision making to adolescents* (pp. 309–327). Hillsdale, NJ: Lawrence Erlbaum Associates.

SECTION III

Promoting
Self-Regulated Behavior

CHAPTER 7

Teaching Self-Monitoring, Self-Evaluation, and Self-Reinforcement Strategies

After reading this chapter, you will be able to

1. Discuss the importance of self-regulation and how it affects work performance

2. Identify success behaviors and how they can be taught

3. Identify the components of self-regulation

4. Describe how self-regulation is operative at the biological level and in adaptive responding

5. Discuss the reasons individuals engage in self-regulation

6. Describe how the different self-regulation strategies interact with one another

7. Teach a repertoire of self-regulation strategies to your students

KEY TERMS

1. Actual state
2. Adaptability contract
3. Capacity
4. Goal setting
5. Goal state
6. Just-right matches
7. Opportunity
8. Optimality factors
9. Self-evaluation
10. Self-monitoring
11. Self-regulation
12. Self-reinforcement
13. Success behavior

Transition outcome data for youth with disabilities (see Chapter 3) suggest that these students do not fare well in the adult world, particularly in the world of work. They are employed to a lesser degree and earn lower wages than their peers without disabilities, participate less in postsecondary education, and remain unsure of what their skills or career interests are; in short, they do not know what jobs they want or how to get them (Martin & Marshall, 1997; Mithaug, Martin, Agran, & Rusch, 1988; Wehman, 1996). Furthermore, those variables that are commonly used to measure the quality of an individual's employment status—increases in wage earnings, job satisfaction, and opportunities for advancement—remain irrelevant for a large number of people with disabilities. Many of these individuals have never learned to set goals for themselves, to strive toward meeting self-directed goals, or to take advantage of opportunities to advance their situations. Those qualities that make up the American work ethic—risk taking, striving to get ahead, and exploiting opportunities (Zunker, 1990)—are absent for many people with disabilities. Un- or underemployment is prevalent for the majority of people with disabilities (Wehman, 1996), and many workers with disabilities have resigned themselves to monotonous jobs and ensuing dissatisfaction (Hackman & Oldham, 1981).

In a study conducted by Mithaug et al. (1988) on parental concerns regarding postschool outcomes for their children, the parents surveyed indicated that the most pressing challenges their children faced were lack of independence; problem-solving skills; self-confidence; and an awareness of their needs, interests, and capabilities. Martin and Marshall noted,

> When students with disabilities exit our schools, they leave a pedagogical support system that maximizes learning basic skills. Many of these students participated in academic track, working toward earning the number of academic credits needed for a diploma. But they often are not prepared to respond appropriately to the many problems they encounter when they leave school. Ironically, we adapt educational environments to meet student needs, but we do not teach students to control their lives or adapt to changes in their environments. (1997, p. 229)

The transition outcome data for students with disabilities appears, unfortunately, to support these findings. To reverse these trends, it is useful to examine the characteristics of "successful" people and apply some of those findings to educational programming.

SUCCESS BEHAVIOR

Mithaug et al. (1988) conducted a comprehensive literature review on "success" behaviors, as reported by a sample of notable individuals. More than 40 skills were identified, and four major activities or skill clusters were salient. First, successful individuals *set goals* for themselves and *developed action plans* to achieve these goals. Second, these action plans were *implemented* and *followed*. Third, the individuals *evaluated their actions* and determined how successful they were in achieving their goals. Last, if they did not achieve the desired level of success, they *changed their plans of action.* Mithaug and colleagues suggested that if these skills enabled prominent people to achieve success, why couldn't they also be used by people with disabilities?

Similarly, after interviewing 1,500 people, Garfield (1986) reported that successful people are adept at *making decisions, managing their behavior,* and *adapting to change.* As reported by Mithaug et al. (1988), successful individuals start with a goal, follow an action plan, and then evaluate and change their behavior as needed. Garfield (1986) suggested that such skills serve as the keys to success and can be taught systematically.

As Martin and Marshall (1997) indicated, students with disabilities do not know what to do to achieve success. Instead of behaving independently, making choices that will have a direct impact on their lives, setting goals, and having higher expectations for themselves, they fail to take control. Similarly, Mithaug (1996) noted that often people with disabilities lack both the capacity and the opportunity to seek greater gains. As a result, they have low expectations for themselves and decreased motivation. "The external world, not the individual, is controlling the individual's life" (Mithaug, 1996, p. 152). These low expectations affect people with disabilities in the world of work, in which, as Gajar, Goodman, and McAfee (1993) noted, "certainly employers want workers with initiative, who can assume some measure of autonomy, and who do not require constant supervision" (p. 357). The characteristics of successful people suggest that self-regulated behavior is a critical component of success.

Self-Regulated Behavior

The skills listed previously are referred to as self-regulation strategies, and it is the lack of these skills that has been suggested as one of the greatest problems for students receiving special education services (Agran, Martin, & Mithaug, 1989; Mithaug et al., 1988). Self-regulation skills empower students (Graham, Harris, & Reid, 1992) and enable them to truly take responsibility for their learning (Schuler & Perez, 1987). Self-regulation has been suggested as the central concept in self-management (Karoly & Kanfer, 1977) as well as a key for achieving self-determination (Martin & Marshall, 1997). Without self-regulated performance, the likelihood of an individual achieving success remains small.

Karoly and Kanfer (1977) defined self-regulation as "the aggregate of processes by which psychological variables, both from the person's repertoire and biology and from the immediate environment, are interrelated in order to orient or sustain the organism's goal-directed behavior" (p. 578). In other words, self-regulation allows students to adapt to change (Mithaug, 1993). Most important, it allows students to achieve self-directed goals. As Mithaug (1993) noted, all living organisms self-regulate to varying degrees and with varying degrees of success. As such, living organisms seek a consistent homeostatic level to sustain them and from which they derive sustenance. When environmental conditions change and a discrepancy exists between typical and new conditions (e.g., depletion of sustenance, change in temperature), specific physiological operations occur to accommodate these changes (e.g., organism engages in food gathering, body perspires to regulate temperature).

Similarly, self-regulatory processes function to promote adaptive responding. Karoly and Kanfer (1977) suggested that young children are incapable of self-evaluation. Instead, they imitate the verbal approval of others. As they mature, however, they learn first to reinforce their own behavior; then compare it to a standard (i.e., a desired level of performance); and, finally, monitor their responding. These activities constitute self-regulated performance. Obviously, judgment about oneself is meaningless without a standard, and the comparison of one's performance to such a standard may reveal the nature and size of the discrepancy between an existing and a desired state. With this information, action is needed to reduce such a discrepancy. It is this very process that the student can use to improve his or her work performance and future success.

Theoretical Basis for Self-Regulation

Whitman (1990) suggested that self-regulation involves a response system that enables individuals to examine their environments and their repertoires of responses for coping with those environments to make decisions about how they should act, then to evaluate the adequacy of their actions and to revise their plans as necessary. But what prompts such actions? Why do individuals engage in self-regulation?

Mithaug (1993) suggested that individuals are often in flux between *goal,* or desired, states and existing, or *actual,* states. It is the acknowledgment of this discrepancy—the difference between what one has and what one wants—that provides the incentive for self-regulation and subsequent action. In this respect, self-regulation serves a problem-solving function. The first step in problem solving is to acknowledge that a problem exists. With the realization that a problem or discrepancy exists, the individual then sets out to determine which ends or changes are achievable and which are not. Regrettably, Mithaug noted, people with disabilities often do little to change their situation. Because of a fear of failure or a sense of powerlessness or learned helplessness, these individuals run into difficulty because they either avoid any action or they set expectations that are too low or, in some cases, too high. Negative feelings about oneself produce lower self-expectations and self-confidence. Conversely, higher expectations result in more success and greater capacity in seeking out opportunity for gain.

To promote success, individuals need to enhance or increase their expectations of themselves. The ability to set appropriate expectations is based on the individual's success in matching his or her *capacity* with present *opportunity.* Capacity is the individual's assessment of existing resources (e.g., work skill repertoire, knowledge about task requirements), and opportunity refers to the existing situation that will allow the individual to achieve the desired gain. Mithaug (1996) referred to optimal prospects as "just-right" matches. Such matches involve situations in which individuals are able to correctly match their capacity (i.e., skills, interests) with existing opportunities (e.g., potential jobs). The experience generated during self-regulation "is a function of repeated interaction between capacity and opportunity over time" (Mithaug, 1996, p. 159). Students in transition programs need to be provided such just-right challenges because experience in making these matches will literally define an individual's work success.

The second component of self-regulation is developing and using strategies for optimizing opportunity for gain. These involve self-management strategies that allow individuals to monitor, evaluate, and reinforce their own behavior. For example, a student might express a strong interest in working as a grocery sacker and become involved in instructional activities to achieve this outcome. A personnel representative at the market where instruction has occurred, however, suggests that the student's lack of hygienic practices precludes his employment. When presented with this situation, the student might indicate that he wants the job so badly, he would be willing to pay special attention to his hygiene. In order to accomplish this, he could monitor his own hygienic practice by developing a checklist of recommended activities (e.g., brushing teeth, combing hair), checking off each of these behaviors as they are performed, and then verbally reinforce himself (e.g., "Looking good"). The use of one or more of these self-management strategies will allow students to optimize gain.

The third component of self-regulation is evaluating the effectiveness of the strategy and adjusting one's actions until the goal is achieved. Such adjustment involves either repeating the procedure again, changing the strategy, or changing the criterion level desired. As indicated previously, students with disabilities often do not know how to direct themselves or establish goals for themselves. They also too frequently lack experience in correcting their own behavior; the self-evaluation component in the self-regulation process aims to provide this instruction.

The entire self-regulation process is dynamic, in that the components interact with and influence one another. The ability to identify the option that is more likely to produce the desired gain will create a situation in which the least amount of adjustment would need to be made. As Mithaug (1996) noted, "the more competent we are, the fewer errors we make, and the less time we take, the greater the gain we produce" (p. 156).

Mithaug (1996) suggested that four factors, which he refers to as *optimality factors,* determine the efficacy of self-regulation and, ultimately, the individual's success. These factors are past gain (i.e., previous success experiences), expectations for gain (i.e., just-right matches), choices, and actions (i.e., self-management). With additional experience in self-regulation, students can gain expertise in identifying both short- and long-term goals, the resources and actions needed to achieve these goals, and self-corrective procedures if success eludes them.

In summary, goal-directed behavior occurs during conditions of discrepancy, and self-regulation attempts to reduce such discrepancies (Martin & Marshall, 1997). Also, two important component elements of self-determination are self-efficacy and efficacy expectations (see Chapter 1). Self-efficacy refers to the individual's realization that he or she can execute a specific behavior to produce a desired outcome, and efficacy expectations refer to the belief that execution of this behavior will result in the desired outcome. Self-regulation aids in the development of these perceptions. (See Chapter 15 for more information.)

SELF-REGULATION STRATEGIES

Self-regulation strategies typically include goal setting, self-monitoring, self-evaluation, and self-reinforcement. A description of each follows.

Goal Setting

Chapter 9 provides a comprehensive review of the literature on goal setting, and thus this topic is not covered in detail in this chapter. However, goal setting is critical to self-regulation because it highlights the discrepancy between existing and desired outcomes. With appropriate goals set, the student can then select an activity to achieve desired outcomes. As described in Chapter 3, the Individuals with Disabilities Education Act (IDEA) of 1990 (PL 101-476) and its amendments require that adolescents must be provided transition services and have a major role in instructional goal setting and planning. Clearly, students need to be instructed on how to assume such responsibility effectively. A student's success in setting goals depends directly on the match between the student's assessment of his or her capacity and the available opportunity, but the law underscores the importance of goal setting with respect to self-regulation and, ultimately, self-determination.

Self-Monitoring

Self-monitoring involves teaching a student to observe and record his or her own behavior. It has been used to teach a variety of academic, classroom-related, and social skills (see Smith & Nelson, 1997) and has also been used in transition programs to teach work-task completion (Agran et al., 1989), job-task changes (Sowers, Verdi, Bourbeau, & Sheehan, 1985), and increased productivity (Ackerman & Shapiro, 1984).

Self-monitoring involves two functions. First, the student must learn to discriminate that the desired, or target, behavior did occur. Second, the student must accurately record its occurrence. Interestingly, there are ample demonstrations in the research literature that self-monitoring appears to have a reactive effect (Agran & Martin, 1987; Goetz & Etzel, 1978). That is, the self-monitoring procedure will produce and maintain a desired change without any other intervention. Furthermore, the procedure will produce such an effect even if the student's recordings are not accurate. It has been suggested that self-monitoring has a reactive effect because it functions as a discriminative stimulus to cue desired responding (Baer, 1984) or because it mediates or strengthens weak contingencies (Malott, 1984). For example, as part of his transition program, Louis works several hours each week at a local computer company packing a specified number of computer chips into a plastic tube. He is paid an hourly wage but receives additional compensation if he exceeds a specified number of tubes. Although Louis likes the job and typically exceeds the minimum number of packed tubes, he sometimes is frustrated that he receives his paycheck only once every 2 weeks. Given this potential source of job dissatisfaction, it was suggested that Louis self-monitor the number of tubes he has packed. This enabled him to track how much extra money he earned and potentially to increase his productivity, making the 2-week wait between paychecks less of a strain.

Self-monitoring is also recommended because it promotes generalization and maintenance; self-monitoring serves to cue the desired response, even if a teacher or transition specialist is not present. Also, it provides an easy-to-teach and very practical means to promote independence and self-regulation. Once the student can discriminate the target behavior, teaching the student to record its occurrence is straightforward, and a variety of recording forms can be used (e.g., pencil and paper, wrist counter).

Self-Evaluation

Self-evaluation involves the comparison of the behavior being self-monitored with the performance goal (Smith & Nelson, 1997). It represents a critical component in the self-regulation process because it informs the student whether he or she is meeting the goals established. As Agran and Hughes (1997) noted, having students evaluate their work performance allows them to discern the extent to which they have achieved their goals and to experience a potentially reinforcing event. The procedure can be used as part of a total self-regulation package or independently (Mithaug, 1993; Smith & Nelson, 1997).

As suggested elsewhere in the text, self-evaluation also serves as the final stage in the typical problem-solving model. It provides the student with critical information at two levels. First, it presents data on whether the goal was achieved and at what level. With this information, the student can determine whether either the goal or the planned action needs to be modified. In this sense, self-evaluation functions as a feedback system in which the student can then proceed to provide consequences for appropriate responding or correct the lack thereof.

Instead of waiting on a teacher, self-evaluation allows the student to receive immediate feedback. Figure 1 presents an evaluation form developed by Mithaug

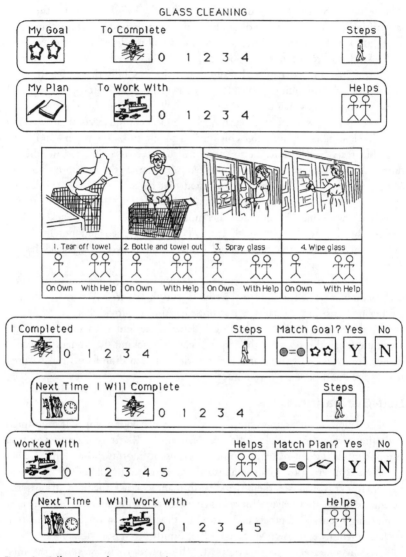

Figure 1.   Self-evaluation form. (From Mithaug, D.E., Martin, J.E., Husch, J.V., Agran, M., & Rusch, F.R. [1988]. *When will persons in supported employment need less support?*, p. 107. Colorado Springs: Ascent Publications; reprinted by permission.)

et al. (1988). Using such a form, students were taught to indicate the level of assistance they thought they needed for a work task (in this case, glass cleaning) and then to evaluate both the number of steps they completed and the level of assistance required. Given this feedback, the student could then set future goals.

Self-Reinforcement

Self-reinforcement represents the major theoretical and procedural component of most conceptualizations of self-management and self-regulation (Brigham, 1989). A number of researchers have suggested that self-reinforcement is as effective, if not more so, than teacher-delivered reinforcement (Deutsch Smith, 1989; Schloss & Smith, 1994). If the purpose of teaching students a repertoire of self-management and self-determination skills is to promote their independence and involvement in their own learning, then self-reinforcement can best serve this purpose. Unlike teacher-delivered reinforcement systems, self-reinforcement involves a system in which students can reinforce their own behavior immediately. The possibility of lost reinforcement opportunities is minimized. Because the student is always present to administer consequences, immediate feedback is essentially guaranteed. Malott (1984) suggested that oftentimes students have difficulty acquiring desired responses because the natural consequences are too delayed or are perceived as being too small or not achievable. In a work experience in which the student is being encouraged to work independently, and therefore external supervision may not be available, self-reinforcement serves as the invaluable link between response and outcome. The more often a student can discriminate a target behavior and consistently reinforce him- or herself for its occurrence, the more likely it will occur in the future.

Functionally, self-reinforcement involves two operations: discrimination and delivery. It is, of course, necessary for the student to discriminate that the target behavior has occurred before the student can reinforce him- or herself. In this respect, self-reinforcement serves a similar function to self-monitoring. Consequently, several researchers have suggested that self-monitoring may be sufficient alone to change the behavior as it appears to involve a reinforcement function (Brigham, 1978; Catania, 1975). Likewise, self-reinforcement may assume stimulus properties and cue appropriate responding. In either case, self-regulation requires that the student has the opportunity to provide consequences for his or her own responding.

To ensure that self-reinforcement is occurring, it is essential that a system be used in which the student has available a pool of reinforcers and is free to deliver them to him- or herself, independent of external manipulation. Reliance on the teacher's administration of the reinforcer will negate the function of the strategy. Effective reinforcers may include self-generated verbal statements (e.g., "Good work, Dante"), tally marks on a recording form to be exchanged later for a delayed reinforcer (e.g., 15 marks equal a trip to the movies), or an immediately awarded tangible reinforcer (e.g., baseball card, school supply, compact disc).

Most investigations of self-reinforcement pertaining to transition-related behavior have addressed the effects of the strategy on work productivity. Helland, Paluck, and Klein (1976) and Wehman, Schutz, Bates, Renzaglia, and Karan (1978) demonstrated that self-reinforcement increased work productivity to levels that were either comparable to or exceeded work levels produced with external reinforcement. The strategy has also been used to teach social skills for or in the workplace (Matson & Andrasik, 1982). As with self-monitoring, as long as the student can discriminate that a target behavior has occurred, self-reinforcement can be used in self-regulation across a wide variety of transition skills.

Examples of Self-Regulation Programs

This section describes how two transition-related programs incorporate self-regulatory procedures. Each is designed to maximize the involvement of the student in goal selection and the implementation and evaluation of goal-directed behavior. Both programs are described in greater detail in Chapter 12, which introduces programs designed to promote student involvement in educational planning and decision making, and are summarized primarily as illustrations of how self-regulation can be incorporated into transition programming.

Adaptability Model   The Adaptability model was developed to promote student self-determination and problem solving (Agran et al., 1989; Mithaug et al., 1988). This model was developed based on observations that students failed to achieve successful transition outcomes because they had been denied autonomy and the opportunity to become active members in educational decision making and in their own learning. The model seeks to empower students and instruct them to become their own advocates and make their own decisions (Martin & Marshall, 1997). The program essentially operationalizes self-management and self-regulation for students in the transition process.

The model consists of four components: 1) decision making, 2) independent performance, 3) self-evaluation, and 4) adjustment. The first component, decision making, involves teaching students how to set work goals, then to develop an action plan to achieve those goals. The student is taught to record the goal on a form called an *adaptability contract*. The form is used for self-monitoring. For example, a student learning to work in a hotel or motel may determine the number of rooms he or she will clean independently. Next, the student is taught to use one or more self-management strategies to guide or direct his or her work behavior. For example, the student may elect to use a checklist to mark off each task completed in a room, picture cues, or self-instructions (i.e., self-directed verbal statements). Following, the student is taught to evaluate whether his or her goal was achieved. This is done by comparing the student's self-recordings with the stated goals. Last, adjustment skills are taught. If the student achieves success, then he or she can choose to keep the same goals or to increase the desired level of independence or productivity.

If the student doesn't achieve the goal, a few options are taught. These include working on the same goals with additional practice, modifying the goals (e.g., selecting easier to achieve goals), or changing the instructional strategy used (e.g., incorporating self-reinforcement into the learning program).

ChoiceMaker Curriculum   The *ChoiceMaker Self-Determination Transition Curriculum* was developed by Martin and Marshall (1995). Like the Adaptability model, it seeks to teach students decision-making, self-management, self-evaluation, and adjustment skills. The ChoiceMaker curriculum provides a valuable addition of a core of skills students can use to take leadership of the individualized education program (IEP) and transition process. The curriculum consists of three major components: choosing goals, expressing goals, and taking action. The "choosing goals" component is designed to acquaint the student with the IEP process and to teach the student to make informed transition decisions based on his or her interests, skills, and skill deficits. "Expressing goals" involves teaching students how to lead their own IEP meetings and to publicly state their interests and goals at these meetings. An 11-step process is taught (see Table 3 in Chapter 11), and lessons include such topics as asking questions and dealing with differences in opinion. The "taking action" component provides students with a planning strategy they can use to achieve their goals. Among the topics addressed are motivational variables, needed supports, and evaluation and adjustment strategies.

Similar to the adaptability model, the ChoiceMaker curriculum aims at teaching students to take control of their lives and design their own futures. It promotes competence. With increased competence, higher goals and expectations can be established and higher levels of achievement will be experienced.

TEACHING RECOMMENDATIONS

The research literature provides ample demonstrations that students with disabilities can learn all of the self-regulatory procedures described in this chapter. Although many people use these skills routinely, they do not come automatically and must be taught, using consistent, systematic, direct instructional methods (Hughes, 1997). The following sections present recommendations on teaching the self-regulation skills of goal setting, self-monitoring, self-evaluation, and self-reinforcement.

Teaching Goal Setting

Goal setting is described in detail in Chapter 9. Suffice it to say in the present context that direct student involvement is critical. As suggested by Mithaug (1996), goals set should exceed the student's present level of performance but be feasible and within reach; in other words, goals should be set for just-right matches that are within the student's capacity and for which an opportunity exists to pursue the goals. Initially, students should set goals that are easily obtainable. With more experience in self-regulation, students can set goals that are more challenging and not as easily or quickly achieved.

Smith and Nelson (1997) recommended a seven-step process for goal setting. First, arrange a conference with the student, his or her parents, and relevant personnel. Second, discuss with the student the purpose of the meeting and the importance of his or her input. Third, discuss and resolve differences regarding the discrepancy between what students want to achieve (i.e., their goal) and their current status. Fourth, propose a solution (i.e., set the goal). Fifth, determine the positive consequences for meeting the goal. (Recommendations on teaching self-reinforcement are presented later in this chapter.) Sixth, develop a self-monitoring plan to assess the student's progress in meeting this goal (see next section). Last, it is recommended that a simple contract or agreement be developed and signed. As described previously in this chapter, an adaptability contract serves this function well.

Teaching Self-Monitoring and Self-Evaluation

The reasons for teaching the student to assume responsibility for self-monitoring his or her progress toward a set goal have been presented throughout this chapter. The value of both formative and summative evaluations and follow-up data on student performance in transition programs is well-documented; and the student is, for all practical purposes, in an ideal situation to collect these data.

In teaching students to monitor and evaluate their transition-related behavior, the following procedure is recommended. After a goal is set, a monitoring or evaluation form needs to be developed. Such forms will vary according to the student's instructional needs and capacity. They may range from pictorial representations of one target behavior to a verbal checklist of multiple target behaviors. Next, the consequences for correct monitoring need to be specified (Smith & Nelson, 1997). This typically involves a three- or four-step sequence. First, the student is reinforced by a teacher for correctly discriminating the target behavior. Both examples of appropriate responses and examples of inappropriate responses should be presented. This can be done through modeling, role plays, or observation of other people displaying the behavior. Corrective feedback is provided as needed. Second, the student is taught how to use the monitoring form and is reinforced for recording occurrence of the behavior. Repeated practice is provided, and expectations for accurate recordings by the student are increased as the student gains fluency in using the form. Third, the student is reinforced for discriminating the target behavior and recording its occurrence. He or she must engage in both actions to receive reinforcement. Last, the student is taught to discriminate the target behavior, record its occurrence, and reinforce him- or herself. The next section describes this last component.

Teaching Self-Reinforcement

On the basis of available data, self-reinforcement is most effective when combined with self-monitoring (Agran, 1997). Although self-reinforcement can be used independently, reported data suggest that it works best when combined with self-monitoring or self-evaluation.

As stated previously in this chapter, students need to be given the responsibility of selecting the reinforcer and the criteria to be met. Failure to do this will negate the very basis for teaching self-regulation. Another issue warrants attention. Many students—with or without disabilities—have had limited or no formal experience in monitoring, evaluating, or reinforcing their own behavior. Indeed, it is the lack of these experiences that contributes to their limited autonomy and self-determination. Consequently, students may feel uncomfortable evaluating their own behavior. Thus, efforts must be made to ensure that students find the use of the self-regulatory strategies reinforcing. It is suggested that a target behavior that is both positive and frequently occurring, such as responding in class or working on task for a short period of time, be identified for initial practice. This allows the student to have repeated practice observing a desirable and consistently occurring behavior.

Similar to the other self-regulatory procedures described previously, the first and second steps to teaching self-reinforcement involve identifying the target behavior and the criterion to be met. The third step is to involve the student in identifying desired reinforcers. Ideally, such reinforcers should be natural consequences (e.g., earnings, positive supervisor evaluations). Next, as stated previously, a self-monitoring procedure needs to be developed. Then, as described in the section on self-monitoring, the student needs to be taught to discriminate the target behavior and to record its occurrence. Following, the student is instructed to use the self-reinforcement procedure. The student is instructed to reinforce him- or herself after performing a desired behavior to a specified level. This is determined by an examination of the self-monitoring form. The student is instructed that accurate recording is critical. Errors in recording, either intentional or accidental, will not provide the student with correct information about his or her performance, will hinder the student's ability to reach his or her goals, and will eventually be discovered. The student is taught to deliver the reinforcer to him- or herself after the target behavior is performed and recorded. Corrective feedback is provided, as needed. The last step involves teaching the student to set new behavioral criteria, as needed, as he or she gains competency.

CONCLUSION

It is clear that the most successful students are those who use self-regulatory strategies consistently. These students not only know what they want, but they also execute actions to achieve these goals. Furthermore, if they do not experience success, they set into motion corrective actions designed to bring them closer to success. These skills, defined in this chapter as self-regulation procedures, comprise strategies that have long been associated with success.

Although most people in the education community would like to be in a situation in which success can be guaranteed for all students, there are many operatives in the greater community that may serve as obstacles and produce inequitable and unfair outcomes. Nevertheless, what educators can do is ensure that students get as fair a chance of achieving success as possible and that they learn to pursue self-directed goals. As Mithaug (1996) noted, "every person deserves an equal chance—a fair prospect—for pursuing a self-determined life" (p. 161).

The self-regulation procedures described in this chapter (and other chapters in this section) are designed to provide students with a dynamic set of skills to define, direct, and modify their lives, their dreams, and their wishes, as they see fit. By using these strategies, students can achieve two very important outcomes. First, they can literally take back their lives. The passive roles they formerly were asked to assume are valid no longer. Second, and most important, as students learn to assume more responsibility for their own learning and living, they will realize that the limits and ceilings placed on them are also no longer valid.

QUESTIONS FOR REVIEW

1. Discuss how lack of self-regulation can have a negative impact on transition outcomes.
2. Explain the similarities between success behavior and self-regulatory procedures.
3. Explain the reasons individuals engage in self-regulation. Provide an example.
4. What is the difference between capacity and opportunity? How do they work together?
5. How can just-right matches be facilitated?
6. What strategies are comprised by self-regulation?
7. For each of the self-regulatory procedures, list the sequence of steps to be taught.

REFERENCES

Ackerman, A., & Shapiro, E. (1984). Self-monitoring and work productivity with mentally retarded adults. *Journal of Applied Behavior Analysis, 17,* 403–407.

Agran, M. (Ed.). (1997). *Student-directed learning: Teaching self-determination skills.* Pacific Grove, CA: Brooks/Cole.

Agran, M., & Hughes, C. (1997). Problem-solving. In M. Agran (Ed.), *Student-directed learning: Teaching self-determination skills* (pp. 171–198). Pacific Grove, CA: Brooks/Cole.

Agran, M., & Martin, J.E. (1987). Applying a technology of self-control in community environments for individuals who are mentally retarded. In M. Hersen, R.M. Eisler, & P.M. Miller (Eds.), *Progress in behavior modification* (Vol. 21, pp. 108–151). Beverly Hills: Sage Publications.

Agran, M., Martin, J.E., & Mithaug, D.E. (1989). Achieving transition through adaptability instruction. *Teaching Exceptional Children, 21,* 4–7.

Baer, D.M. (1984). Does research on self-control need more control? *Analysis and Intervention in Developmental Disabilities, 4,* 211–218.

Brigham, T. (1978). Self-control: Part II. In A.C. Catania & T.A. Brigham (Eds.), *Handbook of applied behavior analysis: Social and instructional processes* (pp. 259–274). New York: Irvington.

Brigham, T. (1989). *Self-management for adolescents: A skills training program.* New York: Guilford Press.

Catania, A.C. (1975). The myth of self-reinforcement. *Behaviorism, 3,* 192–199.

Deutsch Smith, D. (1989). *Teaching students with learning and behavior problems.* Englewood Cliffs, NJ: Prentice Hall.

Gajar, A., Goodman, L., & McAfee, J. (1993). *Secondary schools and beyond: Transition of individuals with mild disabilities.* Columbus, OH: Charles E. Merrill.

Garfield, G. (1986). *Peak performers: The new heroes of American business.* New York: Avon.

Goetz, E.M., & Etzel, B.C. (1978). A brief review of self-control procedures: Problems and solutions. *Behavior Therapists, 1,* 5–8.

Graham, S., Harris, K.R., & Reid, R. (1992). Developing self-regulated learners. *Focus on Exceptional Children, 24*(6), 1–16.

Hackman, J.R., & Oldham, G.R. (1981). Work redesigned: People and their work. In J. O' Toole, J.L. Scheiber, & L.C. Woods (Eds.), *Working changes and choices.* Sacramento: Regents of the University of California.

Helland, C.D., Paluck, R.J., & Klein, M. (1976). A comparison of self- and external reinforcement with the trainable mentally retarded. *Mental Retardation, 14,* 22–23.

Hughes, C. (1997). Self-instruction. In M. Agran (Ed.), *Student-directed learning: Teaching self-determination skills* (pp. 144–170). Pacific Grove, CA: Brooks/Cole.

Individuals with Disabilities Education Act (IDEA) of 1990, PL 101-476, 20 U.S.C. §§ 1400 *et seq.*

Karoly, P., & Kanfer, F.H. (Eds.). (1977). *Self-management and behavior change: From theory to practice.* Elmsford, NY: Pergamon.

Malott, R.W. (1984). Rule-governed behavior, self-management, and the developmentally disabled: A theoretical analysis. *Analysis and Intervention in Developmental Disabilities, 4,* 199–209.

Martin, J.E., & Marshall, L. (1995). ChoiceMaker: A comprehensive self-determination transition program. *Intervention in School and Clinic, 30,* 147–156.

Martin, J.E., & Marshall, L. (1997). Choice making: Description of a model project. In M. Agran (Ed.), *Student-directed learning: Teaching self-determination skills* (pp. 224–248). Pacific Grove, CA: Brooks/Cole.

Matson, J.L., & Andrasik, F. (1982). Training leisure-time social-interaction skills to mentally retarded adults. *American Journal of Mental Deficiency, 86,* 533–542.

Mithaug, D.E. (1993). *Self-regulation theory: How optimal adjustment maximizes gain.* Westport, CT: Praeger.

Mithaug, D.E. (1996). The optimal prospects principle: A theoretical basis for rethinking instructional practices for self-determination. In D.J. Sands & M.L. Wehmeyer (Eds.), *Self-determination across the life span: Independence and choice for people with disabilities* (pp. 147–165). Baltimore: Paul H. Brookes Publishing Co.

Mithaug, D.E., Martin, J.E., Agran, M., & Rusch, F.R. (1988). *Why special education graduates fail: How to teach them to succeed.* Colorado Springs, CO: Ascent Publications.

Mithaug, D.E., Martin, J.E., Husch, J.V., Agran, M., & Rusch, F.R. (1988). *When will persons in supported employment need less support?* Colorado Springs, CO: Ascent Publications.

Schloss, P.J., & Smith, M.A. (1994). *Applied behavior analysis in the classroom.* Needham, MA: Allyn & Bacon.

Schuler, A.L., & Perez, L. (1987). The role of social interaction in the development of thinking skills. *Focus on Exceptional Children, 19*(7), 1–11.

Smith, D.J., & Nelson, J.R. (1997). Goal setting, self-monitoring, and self-evaluation for students with disabilities. In M. Agran (Ed.), *Student-directed learning: Teaching self-determination skills* (pp. 80–110). Pacific Grove, CA: Brooks/Cole.

Sowers, J., Verdi, M., Bourbeau, P., & Sheehan, M. (1985). Teaching job independence and flexibility to mentally retarded students through the use of a self-control package. *Journal of Applied Behavior Analysis, 18,* 81–85.

Wehman, P. (1996). *Life beyond the classroom: Transition strategies for young people with disabilities* (2nd ed.). Baltimore: Paul H. Brookes Publishing Co.

Wehman, P., Schutz, R., Bates, P., Renzaglia, A., & Karan, O. (1978). Self-management programs with mentally retarded workers: Implications for developing independent vocational behavior. *British Journal of Social and Clinical Psychology, 17,* 57–64.

Whitman, T.L. (1990). Self-regulation and mental retardation. *American Journal on Mental Retardation, 94,* 347–362.

Zunker, V.G. (1990). *Career counseling: Applied concepts for life planning* (4th ed.). Pacific Grove, CA: Brooks/Cole.

CHAPTER 8

Teaching
Self-Instruction Skills

After reading this chapter, you should be able to

1. Share the advantages and benefits of using self-instruction with other professionals, parents, and community members

2. Use individualized methods to teach students with disabilities how to self-instruct to achieve desired outcomes in their own lives

3. Use four empirically based methods to teach self-instruction to students with disabilities

4. Employ self-instructional techniques with a variety of behaviors, students, settings, and skills

5. Utilize a variety of instructional techniques to promote generalization of self-instruction

KEY TERMS

1. Antecedent
2. Consequence
3. Direct instructional methods
4. Generalization of behavior
5. Goal setting
6. Self-determination
7. Self-labeling
8. Self-management
9. Self-regulation
10. Self-reinforcement
11. Verbal behavior
12. Verbal correspondence

A major study of the transition of students with disabilities from school to adulthood found that too many such students dropped out of school, ran into trouble with the law, or remained chronically un- or underemployed (Wagner, D'Amico, Marder, Newman, & Blackkorby, 1992). Many students believe that their lives are out of their control, that they are failing, and that they are at risk for these negative outcomes. By and large, however, they do not know what to do or how to change. These students are in desperate need of strategies to help them manage their own lives more effectively.

Self-instruction is a powerful strategy available to teachers to enable them to support students in taking control of and directing their own lives. When students are taught to self-instruct, they learn to use their own verbal behavior to guide their performance (Hughes & Agran, 1993). Self-instruction is a critical self-management strategy that contributes to an individual's self-determination skills.

CONCEPTUAL BASIS OF SELF-INSTRUCTION

How does self-instruction work? How does verbal behavior guide one's performance? For years, the field has speculated on the role of self-instruction in directing performance (e.g., Malott, 1984; Skinner, 1957; Whitman, 1990). Possibly, a self-delivered instruction acts as an environmental cue or stimulus that increases the probability that the targeted behavior will follow (Malott, 1984). Similarly, an individual's self-instructing may be explained by a traditional behavioral paradigm in which an *antecedent,* or environmental cue, prompts an individual's behavior to occur, which is followed by a *consequence* that reinforces the behavior and makes it more likely to occur again (Skinner, 1957). That is, a student may self-instruct by 1) stating a problem situation that serves as an antecedent, 2) stating a possible response, 3) performing that response or behavior, and 4) evaluating the response and verbally reinforcing him- or herself as a consequence.

Self-instruction also may serve as a self-regulation strategy in which language mediates behavior (Hughes & Agran, 1993; Kaplan, 1995; Whitman, 1987). Terms such as *cognitive processing* (Park & Gaylord-Ross, 1989), *verbal mediation* (Kanfer, 1971), and *correspondence training* (Crouch, Rusch, & Karlan, 1984) have been used to describe the process by which language may affect one's behavior. Bandura (1971), Goldfried and Merbaum (1973), and Kanfer (1971) suggested that verbal mediation, language, and thought are critical variables in the self-regulation process. Whitman (1987, 1990) also argued that language is a tool that may be used to label, monitor, analyze, and control one's behavior.

PRACTICAL APPLICATION OF SELF-INSTRUCTION

In a generic sense, self-instruction simply refers to a process in which a person tells him- or herself to do something and then does it. This process would be both foolproof and simple if one's motor performance were always under the control of one's verbal behavior. The process of self-instructing becomes less effective, however, if one's verbal instructions have little influence over one's actual behavior. Because people sometimes fail to use their verbal instructions effectively, the process of self-instructing may require systematic teaching. Direct instructional methods are often used to teach people to self-instruct. These methods typically include modeling, providing opportunities for practice, corrective feedback, and reinforcement presented during brief instructional periods (e.g., one or two 2-hour session, four or five 30-minute sessions). For students with severe or multiple disabilities, extended instructional time may be required before they learn to self-instruct. For example, Hughes (1992) reported that one man with mental retardation in her study required twenty 30-minute training sessions to learn to self-instruct to solve task-related problems related to completing his household chores.

Meichenbaum and Goodman (1971) developed a sequence for teaching self-instruction that has become the prototype for many teaching applications. Their sequence consisted of five steps:

1. Teacher performs task, instructing aloud while student observes.
2. Student performs task while teacher instructs aloud.
3. Student performs task while self-instructing aloud.
4. Student performs task while whispering.
5. Student performs task while self-instructing "covertly."

Contemporary empirical investigations of Meichenbaum and Goodman's teaching sequence typically omit the final two steps because of research requirements for measuring self-instructions verbalized by individuals during observation of performance. Attempts are made by researchers to have individuals "talk aloud," as unobtrusively as possible, in the presence of the researchers alone. When a functional relationship has been demonstrated between self-instructing and correct responding, students are no longer required to self-instruct overtly. The goal for teachers is to provide students with a powerful, self-regulating tool but not to have students draw attention to themselves by using the tool in an obtrusive fashion, such as talking loudly. A comparison between a contemporary model of self-instruction and Meichenbaum and Goodman's training sequence is shown in Table 1 (Hughes, 1991).

MODELS FOR TEACHING SELF-INSTRUCTION

Teachers may choose from several models of self-instruction when teaching students to guide their own behavior. The traditional teaching model is based on Meichenbaum and Goodman's (1971) original sequence and comprises four basic steps: 1) stating a problem, 2) stating a possible response to the problem, 3) evaluating the response, and 4) verbally reinforcing oneself. Some or all of

Table 1.   Comparison between a contemporary model of self-instruction and Meichenbaum and Goodman's (1971) training sequence

Contemporary model	Meichenbaum and Goodman (1971)	Comparison
1. Teacher provides rationale for self-instruction training and tells student to respond as if in response to task demands.	1. Teacher does not provide rationale or tell student to respond as if in response to task demands.	Different
2. Teacher models multiple examples of tasks while self-instructing aloud.	2. Teacher models multiple examples of tasks while self-instructing aloud.	Same
3. Student performs tasks while teacher instructs.	3. Student performs tasks while teacher instructs.	Same
4. Student performs tasks while self-instructing aloud.	4. Student performs tasks while self-instructing aloud.	Same
5. Student does not perform tasks while whispering.	5. Student performs tasks while whispering.	Different
6. Student does not perform tasks while self-instructing covertly.	6. Student performs tasks while self-instructing covertly.	Different
7. Teacher provides corrective feedback and prompting, if needed.	7. Teacher provides corrective feedback and prompting, if needed.	Same
8. Teacher reminds student during training to self-instruct when performing.	8. Teacher does not remind student to self-instruct when performing.	Different

Adapted from Hughes (1991).

these statements are taught to students in variations of self-instructional models. The following case study illustrates how such a model might be used.

It was October 23 and Gwen Jackson was late to her first-period French class again. Actually, her entire freshman year in high school wasn't starting off too well. This was already the eighth time she had been late to school and that meant another day of in-school suspension. Two more days and she wouldn't get any credit in French for the whole semester. But it was just so hard to get up in the morning. Gwen knew she had stayed out too late last night; but, really, what else was there to do? Her older brother George was always out riding around in his car when Gwen got home from school and her mother worked nights. It was just so boring staying home alone and trying to do her homework. It was more fun leaving the house and hanging out with her friends at night. Somehow, she just never could get back home before 1 or 2 A.M., and then the last thing on her mind was doing her homework. And then getting up in the morning—well, that was just too hard. George and her mother were asleep. Why should she get up?

It wasn't that Gwen didn't have goals in her life. She had always wanted to go to beauty college and get her cosmetology license. She was good at working on hair. Everybody said so. She braided and styled all her friends' hair, and her own hair always looked perfect. But, really, it was just getting to be such a drag having to go to school every day—especially considering that she had gotten two Ds, two Fs, and a C– in physical education on her first 6-weeks' report card last week. There really was no way out. She hadn't even started the biology project that was due on Friday. She was afraid to speak in French class because she didn't know any of the vocabulary, and she was sure everyone was laughing at her because she couldn't pronounce the words in French. She had flunked the last two tests in world history and didn't even know where her book was. She had cut Algebra I the last 2 days because she didn't have her homework done, and she had slept through home economics all week and didn't even know what they were doing in there. And the thought of having to go to the office again and sit there for in-school suspension was just too much. For one thing, she didn't know whether she could face seeing Mr. Bailey, the principal, again. Gwen had known him since grade school, and she really didn't want him to see what a mess she was becoming.

Gwen Jackson probably never would have made it through high school if she hadn't been sent to Ms. Summers, the school counselor, for failing grades early in the spring of her freshman year. What Ms. Summers observed in Gwen was a bright student who lacked study skills and self-discipline. Ms. Summers helped Gwen realize that she could gain control of her life by articulating to herself a problem that she was facing and a possible response to the problem. Following her response, Gwen could assess her performance and reinforce herself by saying, "Hey, I did a good job," for having accomplished a task. For example, if the problem was that there was a vocabulary test in English the next day and Gwen didn't know any of the vocabulary, she could say to herself, "Tomorrow's the vocabulary test, and I need to study. I better get the words from Barbara and bring them home tonight and study the definitions. I'll practice writing the definitions down and checking them just like Ms. Summers taught me because I want to pass the test tomorrow. Good for me—I've come up with a good plan and when I learn all the words, I'll go out for a Coke, but only after I've learned them."

Gwen learned that self-instruction could be useful throughout her daily activities. If she got mad at her mother and wanted to yell at her she could say to herself, "I'm mad at Mom but if I yell at her, she'll just punish me and make me stay in my room, and I really don't want to do that. Guess I'll just keep quiet. She's probably had a hard day, too. Hey, you know, that worked a whole lot better. I did great and I bet Mom liked it better, too."

Self-instruction and the support of Ms. Summers started to turn Gwen's life around. Her study skills improved and so did her grades. It looked like she would pass her freshman year in high school after all. Her relationship with her mother improved, and she had a whole new group of friends who, like Gwen, were doing well in school. Because she had more time and energy than when she was out late every night, Gwen decided to try out for the school play in the spring of her freshman year. She was given a small part and found out that she loved being a part of a group that was working together to put on a performance. All in all, Gwen's life was becoming very happy. Whenever she did come up against a problem, Gwen knew she could use her self-instructional strategies to figure out what to do. It felt like she was getting control of her life at last.

One adaptation of the traditional self-instructional model (Meichenbaum & Goodman, 1971) is designed for use with people who have severe disabilities and limited verbal skills. Hughes (1992) taught four adults with mental retardation to verbalize statements, such as those shown in Table 2, while solving problems related to household tasks. In comparison to the statements described previously, these statements were designed to be considerably shorter and simpler in response to the participants' limited verbal skills. However, the four statements are functionally the same as those in the lengthier, more traditional version (i.e., identifying the problem, stating the correct response, evaluating the response, self-reinforcing). Teachers should adapt the length and complexity of self-instructional statements to accommodate a student's needs and skills.

Other models for teaching self-instruction have been investigated by Agran and colleagues. These models include Did-Next-Now, What/Where, and Interactive self-instructional strategies, which may be adapted for students requiring varying degrees of supports. The Did-Next-Now model is especially useful for teaching students to perform a series of tasks in a sequence (e.g., loading a commercial dishwasher). This model involves teaching an individual to state the response just completed ("Did") and the next response to be performed ("Next") and then to direct him- or herself to perform that response ("Now"). A strategy script for designing a Did-Next-Now self-instructional program is provided in Figure 1. The script prompts the teacher to identify a preceding response (e.g., sweeping the floor), a Did-Next-Now verbal sequence (e.g., "I swept the floor," "Next I have to empty the trash," "I need to do it now"), a subsequent target response (e.g., emptying the trash), a reinforcer to follow and maintain the target response (e.g., "Good job. Look at that floor"), and a correction procedure to use in case of error (e.g., "Oops. I was supposed to empty the trash next. Guess I better do that now"). Using this strategy, Agran, Fodor-Davis, and Moore (1986) taught job-sequencing skills to four students with mental retardation enrolled in a hospital work skills program. The students stated the Did-Next-Now verbal sequence when performing a 21-step task sequence for cleaning patient rooms, which included tasks such as dusting and cleaning rest rooms. The sequence was repeated each time the students began a new step of the sequence (e.g., "I just brought the bucket to the room," "Next I need to fill the bucket," "I'm going to fill the bucket now").

The What/Where self-instructional model is used to help guide a student's performance in response to an instruction. Students are taught to select key words from a verbal or written instruction and to determine *what* they are to do and *where* they are to do it. For example, a student worker in a large department store may be told by a supervisor, "These are the juniors' dresses. They go on the sales rack." Using the What/Where strategy, the student would

Table 2.   Self-instructional statements related to household tasks

1.   Identifying the problem (e.g., "not plugged in")
2.   Stating the correct response (e.g., "got to plug in")
3.   Evaluating the response (e.g., "fixed it")
4.   Self-reinforcing (e.g., "good")

Did-Next-Now Strategy Script

Student: _____ Setting: _____

Instructional Target: _____ Task: _____

Preceding Response	Verbalization (What student says)	Target Response (What student should do)	Reinforcer	Correction Procedure
	Did: Next: Now:			
	Did: Next: Now:			
	Did: Next: Now:			

Figure 1. Did-Next-Now strategy script.

163

repeat, "juniors' dresses, sales rack," while beginning to hang the dresses on the correct rack in the juniors' department. For students who have difficulty following instructions, the What/Where strategy provides them with a procedure to identify the relevant information in an instruction that will serve to guide their performance.

The Interactive Self-Instructional Model teaches students to state their self-instructions as questions that are embedded in conversation. This strategy is particularly useful when a student is interacting with customers in public and self-instructing aloud would draw unwanted attention to the student. Agran, Fodor-Davis, Moore, and Martella (1992) taught this strategy to three students with disabilities requiring limited to extensive supports who were learning to work as kitchen assistants. The students were responsible for taking orders from customers for making sandwiches. Agran and colleagues taught the students to repeat the step just completed ("Did"), and then remind themselves that they needed to ask the customer what to do next ("Next"). The students then asked the customer for the next ingredient to be included in the sandwich ("Ask"). For example, one set of interactive self-instructions might be "Did meat" (after placing meat on bread), "Cheese next" (reminding oneself to ask the customer), then "What kind of cheese?" (asking the customer for the next step in the order).

ADVANTAGES OF SELF-INSTRUCTION

Self-instruction has potential as a valuable instructional strategy to promote self-determination. Because most students can learn to use their verbal behavior to guide their own performance even when no one else is around, self-instruction may be an appropriate strategy to teach people to use when they are on their own, outside an instructional setting. Because verbal behavior is often readily available to many people (for recommendations in cases in which verbal behavior is not available or very limited, see Chapter Conclusion with recommendations at the end of this chapter), self-instruction may allow people to act more independently in settings in which instructional support typically is unavailable, such as on the bus, interacting at work, or at the movies with friends. Self-instruction may be especially appropriate for students with disabilities who frequently need support when learning to direct their own behavior independently. For example, Gwen Jackson (see case study presented previously) used self-instruction to help her schedule her studying time at home and to restrict the amount of time she spent visiting with her friends at night. By using self-instruction, Gwen helped direct herself to awaken in time for school each day and, thereby, increased the likelihood that she would improve her grades in school.

TEACHING SELF-INSTRUCTION

This section presents an overview of empirical studies in which self-instructional strategies have been taught to people with disabilities in school, work, and home living environments. Studies are grouped according to skill areas specific to each environment. Variations in methods of teaching self-instruction skills are compared to guide teachers in instructing their students to apply recommended strategies.

Teaching Self-Instruction in School Environments

Self-instruction skills that have been taught in school environments have addressed a variety of student behaviors. Targeted behaviors have included academic skills, community living and working skills, and social and interpersonal skills.

Academic Skills Applications of self-instruction to academic skills typically have targeted performance of traditional academic tasks characteristic of curricula for students with mild disabilities. Most investigations have used the traditional Meichenbaum and Goodman (1971) sequence (i.e., stating a problem, stating a response, evaluating the response, verbally reinforcing oneself) to guide student performance (see Table 2). For example, Whitman and colleagues investigated the effects of self-instruction on mathematics performance in a series of studies. Using the traditional Meichenbaum and Goodman training sequence, Johnston, Whitman, and Johnson (1980) and Whitman and Johnston (1983) taught students with mild mental retardation to add and subtract numbers with regrouping. Self-instructions comprised a series of questions based on a task analysis of the computational process. An example of the self-instructions students used when adding with regrouping and using a number line is shown in Figure 2.

When students were taught to self-instruct, increases were reported in the accuracy of problems completed; however, rate of completion decreased. The authors speculated that, over time, self-instructing might require less effort by students and, subsequently, rate of performance would increase. However, because performance was not assessed after instructional support was withdrawn in these studies, predictions regarding increases in rate could not be verified. Generalization from the instructional to the classroom setting and to similar, untrained problems was reported anecdotally, although not assessed systematically.

Using the same self-instructional format as was presented in Figure 2, Keogh, Whitman, and Maxwell (1988) compared the effects of self-instruction and teacher-delivered instruction on rate and accuracy of adding with regrouping by students with and without mental retardation requiring intermittent supports. Students without mental retardation improved their accuracy following

Q.   What kind of a problem is this?   36
                                        +47

A.   It's an add problem. I can tell by the sign.

Q.   Now what do I do?

A.   I start with the top number in the ones column and I add. Six plus 7 (the child points to the 6 on the number line and counts down 7 spaces) is 13. Thirteen has two digits. That means I have to carry. This is hard, so I go slowly. I put the 3 in the ones column (the child writes the 3 in the ones column in the answer) and the 1 in the tens column (the child writes the 1 above the top number in the tens column in the problem).

Q.   Now what do I do?

A.   I start with the top number in the tens column. One plus 3 (the child points to the 1 on the number line and counts down 3 spaces) is 4. Four plus 4 (the child counts down 4 more spaces) is 8 (the child writes the 8 in the tens column in the answer).

Q.   I want to get it right, so I check it. How do I check it?

A.   I cover up my answer (the child covers the answer with a small piece of paper) and add again, starting with the bottom number in the ones column. Seven plus 6 (the child points to the 7 on the number line and counts down 6 spaces) is 13 (the child slides the piece of paper to the left and uncovers the 3; the child sees the 1 that he or she has written over the top number in the tens column in the problem). Got it right. Four plus 3 (the child points to the 4 on the number line and counts down 3 spaces) is 7. Seven plus 1 (the child counts down 1 more space) is 8 (the child removes the small piece of paper so that the entire answer is visible). I got it right, so I'm doing well. (If, by checking his or her work, the child determines that he or she has made an error, he or she says, "I got it wrong. I can fix it if I go slowly"). The child then repeats the self-instruction sequence, starting from the beginning.

Figure 2.   Self-instructional training sequence for addition with regrouping. (Reprinted from *Applied Research in Mental Retardation, 1,* Johnston, M.B., Whitman, T.L., & Johnson, M., Teaching addition and subtraction to mentally retarded children: A self-instruction program, p. 149, Copyright (1980), with kind permission from Elsevier Science Ltd, The Boulevard, Langford Lane, Kidlington OX5 1GB, UK.)

both instructional conditions and their rate following teacher-delivered instruction only. Only the self-instructional condition resulted in improvements in rate and accuracy for students with mental retardation. The authors argued that these findings suggest that self-instructing may provide individuals with mental retardation the strategies they need in order to attend to and accurately solve problems.

Community Living and Work Skills   Wacker and colleagues (Wacker, Carroll, & Moe, 1980; Wacker & Greenebaum, 1984) adapted the original Meichenbaum and Goodman (1971) self-instructional sequence to teach sorting and assembly skills to students with mental retardation. Their Abbreviated Self-Instructional Method (called "self-labeling") required that students say aloud only the color or shape of cards as they sorted or assembled the cards in sequence.

As in the Meichenbaum and Goodman (1971) training sequence, the teacher demonstrated the correct performance of the required task sequence while stating aloud the color or shape of the cards being sorted or assembled. During subsequent instructional sessions, the students were taught to self-label (i.e., verbalize the names of the colors or shapes without prompting) while completing the assembly steps independently. Students in both studies improved their accuracy on required tasks following training and generalized their skills from the instructional setting to the regular classroom. In addition, using a group comparison design, Wacker and Greenebaum (1984) demonstrated that self-labeling was more effective than direct instruction at producing task acquisition and that only 'self-labeling produced generalization across related responses. Wacker and colleagues concluded that self-labeling may prompt individuals with severe mental retardation to focus on the relevant features of a task, thereby improving task performance.

Hughes, Hugo, and Blatt (1996) combined the Meichenbaum and Goodman (1971) teaching sequence with teaching multiple examples of targeted responses in order to teach a domestic skill (making toast) to five high school students with mental retardation who required extensive supports. The toast-making sequence was divided into 10 tasks. Five problem-solving tasks were used as training examples (i.e., multiple exemplars) and the remaining five served as generalization probes (see Table 3). First, the students were taught to self-

Table 3. Problem-solving sequence and correct response

Problem situation	Activity	Correct response
1. Toaster upside down[a]	Making toast	TURN toaster and insert toast.
2. Toaster unplugged[b]	Making toast	PLUG IN toaster and turn on.
3. Utensil too big[c]	Making toast	FIND correct utensil and butter toast.
4. No towel on table[b]	Cleaning up	FIND towel and dry dishes.
5. No rag on table[d]	Cleaning up	FIND rag and wipe table.
6. Objects on table on top of crumbs[b]	Cleaning up	MOVE objects and clean up crumbs.
7. Vacuum unplugged[d]	Vacuuming rug	PLUG IN vacuum and turn on.
8. Bread crumbs under table[b]	Vacuuming rug	MOVE chair and vacuum crumbs.
9. Game pieces on floor in way of vacuum[d]	Vacuuming rug	MOVE game pieces and vacuum floor.
10. Cord hook in wrong position[d]	Vacuuming rug	TURN hook and wind up cord.

From Hughes, C., Hugo, K., & Blatt, J. (1996). A self-instructional intervention for teaching generalized problem solving within a functional task sequence. *American Journal on Mental Retardation, 100*, p. 569; reprinted by permission of the American Association on Mental Retardation.

[a]Training 1 exemplar for Group 1 students.
[b]Training 2 exemplars for Group 1 students.
[c]Training 1 exemplar for Group 2 students.
[d]Training 2 exemplars for Group 2 students.

instruct in response to one of the five training examples (e.g., toaster upside down when making toast), using statements similar to those in Table 2. When the students were proficient at self-instructing with one example, the remaining four training examples were introduced. All five students learned to self-instruct while performing the training tasks and to generalize their use of the strategy to the untrained tasks, performing all steps of the toast-making task in sequence. In addition, performance across both trained and untrained tasks maintained after instructional support was withdrawn (see Figure 3).

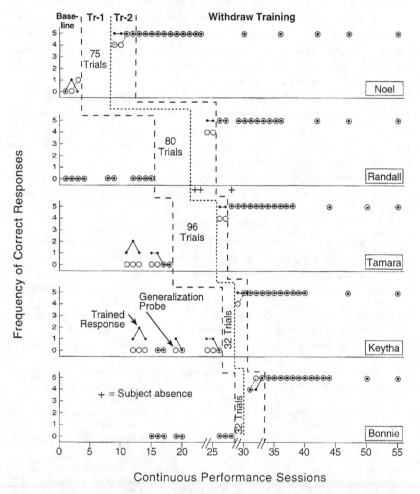

Figure 3.   Frequency of correct responses using self-instruction to trained and untrained problem situations for all participants during performance. (From Hughes, C., Hugo, K., & Blatt, J. [1996]. A self-instructional intervention for teaching generalized problem solving within a functional task sequence. *American Journal on Mental Retardation, 100*, p. 571; reprinted by permission of the American Association on Mental Retardation.)

Social and Interpersonal Skills   Collet-Klingenberg and Chadsey-
Rusch (1991) used an adaptation of traditional self-instruction (i.e., cognitive
processing) to teach appropriate responding to criticism to three high school
students with mental retardation who were receiving vocational training. The
students were taught to verbalize four different types of statements (decoding,
decision making, performing, and self-evaluating) in response to five hand-
drawn pictures depicting social situations in which employees were receiving
work-related criticism from their supervisors. The statements were role-played
by the students and a trainer in response to the scenarios indicated in the
pictures. An example of a scenario and the statements role-played by the students
and their trainer is provided in Figure 4. Findings indicated that two of the
students learned to perform the cognitive process and to generalize appropriate
responding to new role-play scenes involving criticism. No generalization was

---

The trainer says:
"This is a picture of a worker like you. He is working slowly. His boss is telling him to
hurry up and finish mopping because he has other chores to do. You be the worker,
and I'll be the boss. Remember to say the rules out loud and tell me what you would
do. (Student's name), you need to mop faster, you have other chores to do."
The student says:
(Data is collected here)

(Social Decoding Skills)
1.0   "The first rule is understand what is going on.
1.1   So I ask myself, 'What is happening?' Well, the boss is upset with me; I am
       taking too long to mop and have other chores to do.
1.2   Then I think to myself, who is upset with me? The boss is upset with me.
1.3   Next, I think to myself, why is the boss upset with me? He is upset because I am
       taking too long to mop.
1.4   Then I think to myself, how does the boss feel? He's mad."
(Social Decision Skills)
2.0   "The second rule is decide what to do.
2.1   I could ignore the boss or get mad. Those things wouldn't be good, though,
       because the boss would still be mad. Right? So, I am going to tell him that I am
       sorry and that I will try to work faster."
(Social Performance Skills)
3.0   "The third rule is do what I had decided to do.
3.1   So I say, "I'm sorry, I'll work faster."
(Social Evaluation Skills)
4.0   "The fourth rule is what happened when I said I was sorry.
4.1   So, I ask myself, 'How does the boss feel now?' I don't think he's as mad now.
4.2   Then I think, how do I feel now? I feel better because I said I'm sorry.
4.3   Finally, I ask myself, 'Did I do the right thing?' I think saying I'm sorry was a
       good thing to do."

Figure 4.   Training protocol using cognitive processing to teach appropriate responding to criticism. (From
Collet-Klingenberg, L., & Chadsey-Rusch, J. [1991]. Using a cognitive-process approach to teach social
skills. *Education and Training in Mental Retardation, 26,* p. 261; reprinted by permission.)

observed for the student who did not acquire the cognitive process, indicating that this adaptation of the self-instructional process may have been critical to the generalization of social skills.

Hughes, Harmer, Killian, and Niarhos (1995) adapted the Meichenbaum and Goodman (1971) self-instructional training sequence to teach four high school students with mental retardation to initiate and respond to conversations with both familiar and unfamiliar peers with and without disabilities. Peers without disabilities taught the students to self-instruct during conversational skills training, using the statements provided in Table 4. In addition, the peers modeled interactive conversation characteristic of typical high school students and provided corrective feedback and reinforcement to the students as they learned their new conversational skills. Following self-instructional training by peers, all four students learned to initiate and maintain conversation with new conversational partners in a variety of high school settings (see Figure 5). In addition, the students' conversational skills compared favorably to that of a group of typical high school students without disabilities (see range of expected behavior, Figure 5).

Teaching Self-Instruction in Work Environments

Since the 1980s, teaching self-instruction skills has been extended to settings in which people with disabilities are employed. Areas of focus include work skills, productivity, and social and interpersonal skills.

Work Skills   Wacker et al. (1988) adapted the self-labeling strategy used in school settings (e.g., Wacker et al., 1980; see also previous section) for students with mental retardation who were receiving vocational evaluations in a university-based work setting. When entering data into a computer, calculator, or checkbook, the students were taught to "self-label," or say aloud to themselves, each letter, number, or character as it was entered. Following self-labeling training, all students increased their accuracy of data entry across trained and untrained data entry tasks. In addition, when asked if they found self-labeling disruptive, the students' co-workers responded that they were not aware that the students were talking aloud.

Agran, Fodor-Davis, Moore, and Deer (1989) used a What/Where self-instructional strategy script similar to that in Figure 6 to teach instruction-following skills to five students with mental retardation enrolled in a janitorial skills training program. The students were taught to say to themselves what they were supposed to do and where they were supposed to do it after they were

Table 4.   Self-instructional statements for conversational skills training

1. Identifying the problem (e.g., "I want to talk")
2. Stating the correct response (e.g., "I need to look and talk")
3. Evaluating the response (e.g., "I did it; I talked")
4. Self-reinforcing (e.g., "I did a good job")

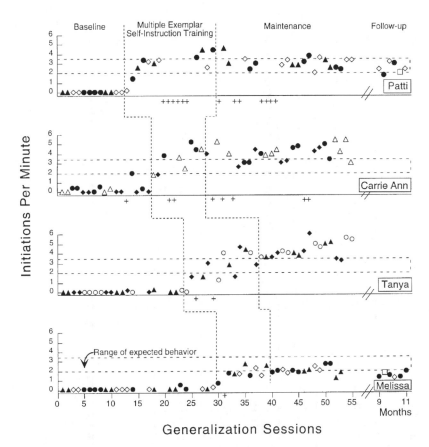

Figure 5.   Conversational initiations per minute by all participants to partners with and without disabilities during generalization sessions. Banded area indicates range of expected performance based upon social comparison data. (□ = gym; ○ = classroom; ◇ = lunchroom; △ = workroom; + = participant absence; open symbols = untrained setting; filled symbols = trained setting.) (From Hughes, C., Harmer, M.L., Killian, D.J., & Niarhos, F. [1995]. The effects of multiple-exemplar self-instructional training on high school students' generalized conversational interactions. *Journal of Applied Behavior Analysis, 28,* p. 210; reprinted by permission.)

given an instruction. For example, the students were taught to say, "Vacuum under table," when they were told to vacuum the carpet under the table, or "Wipe front stove" when given an instruction to wipe the front of a stove. All students were found to improve their instruction-following skills across trained and untrained instructions when they used their self-instruction strategies.

Hughes and Rusch (1989) combined self-instruction with multiple exemplars of targeted responses to teach two workers with severe mental retardation employed in a soap-packaging company to solve work-related problems. First, the work supervisor identified problem situations that were likely to occur during the workday, such as a puddle of soap on a table on which work was to be

What/Where Strategy Script

Student: _____   Setting: _____

Instructional Target: _____   Task: _____

Target Response (What student should do)	Antecedent Stimuli	Verbalization (What student says)	Reinforcer	Correction Procedure
	What: Where:			
	What: Where:			
	What: Where:			

Figure 6.   What / Where self-instructional strategy script.

completed or a paper towel plugging the drain of a sink. Next, the employees were taught to self-instruct in response to five of the identified problem situations, using statements similar to those in Table 2. Acquisition of the problem-solving strategy was demonstrated in addition to generalized use of the strategy in untrained problem situations.

Productivity   An adaptation of self-instruction called verbal correspondence was used by Crouch and colleagues (1984) to improve kitchen workers' start times, productivity, and supervisor ratings when performing kitchen tasks such as sweeping, mopping, and setting up food on a lunch line. Using this procedure, the employees were taught to say the times at which they would start and complete their work (i.e., Step 2 [stating the response] of Meichenbaum and Goodman's [1971] self-instructional sequence). First, they were reinforced for stating the correct times. Next, they were reinforced each time their stated times and actual start and completion times were the same. Stating their start and completion times increased the rate of production of all employees and improved their supervisors' ratings of their performance as well.

Rusch, Martin, Lagomarcino, and White (1987) used an adaptation of self-instructional correspondence called verbal mediation to teach a woman with mental retardation employed in a fast-food restaurant to state her required job sequences (i.e., 23 set-up and clean-up tasks) before performing the tasks. Tasks included clearing tables, taking out trash, wiping tables and counters, and sweeping and mopping the dining area. The verbal mediation strategy required the employee to state in detail each step of the job sequence before performing the required responses. Using verbal mediation, the employee learned to perform tasks in sequence as well as to generalize her skills across scheduled changes in task demands.

Moore, Agran, and Fodor-Davis (1989) examined the effects of a self-management program involving self-instruction, goal setting, and self-reinforcement on the production rates of four employees with severe mental retardation employed in a sheltered workshop. The participants were responsible for a packaging task. They were instructed to set performance goals for themselves (i.e., set timers to specified periods of time), to tell themselves to work faster, and to reinforce themselves with coins when they met their criteria. After training, all participants increased and maintained their production rates at criterion levels for up to 3 months.

Social and Interpersonal Skills   Adaptations of self-instructional procedures have been employed to teach employees with disabilities to seek assistance when needed to complete tasks. Agran, Salzberg, and Stowitschek (1987) taught five employees with moderate to severe disabilities in a vocational training setting to initiate requests when they were out of materials or in need of assistance. The employees were taught to state two steps of the Meichenbaum and Goodman (1971) training sequence (i.e., stating the problem, stating the correct response) when they needed help to complete tasks involved with unpacking cheese, assembling recliner chairs and irrigation wheels, and making candles. For example, employees would say, "I am out of ____" (stating the problem), and "I need to get more ____. I'll ask for ____" (stating the response). Next, the employees would ask a supervisor for assistance. After self-instructional training, participants increased their requests for assistance in both the training and work setting.

Using a teaching format similar to that reported by Agran and colleagues (1987) (i.e., stating the problem, stating the correct response), Rusch, McKee, Chadsey-Rusch, and Renzaglia (1988) taught a young man with severe mental retardation employed in a university-operated film center to make appropriate requests when 1) materials were not available and 2) materials ran out. The employee's job was to receive, fill, and deliver orders for desk supplies to clerical workers. When materials were unavailable or out of stock, the young man was taught to state, "Can't (complete order)." He then would tap a picture of a teacher's aide that was taped to his wheelchair and say, "Tell (the aide)." Next, he was taught to approach the aide; establish eye contact; say, "Excuse me"; and request the missing items by saying, "I need more (name of item)." Following completion of all of the self-instructional steps, the employee was taught to reinforce himself with a nickel. The young man increased his requests for assistance when he performed his self-instructional steps.

The traditional Meichenbaum and Goodman (1971) teaching sequence has been used in employment settings to increase time of on-task behavior among employees with mild to moderate mental retardation. Hughes and Petersen (1989) and Rusch, Morgan, Martin, Riva, and Agran (1985) taught employees with mild to moderate mental retardation to increase their time on task while performing required job-related duties. Employees in these studies were taught to say, "What does (the supervisor) want me to do?" (stating the problem); "I am supposed to wipe the counter and restock the supplies" (stating the response); "Okay, I wiped the counter" (self-evaluating); and "Good, I did that right" (self-reinforcing). To prompt self-instructing, Hughes and Petersen placed on the employees' work tables photographs that showed the employees busy working. Following self-instructional training, increases in time spent working generalized from the training to the work situation for employees in both studies.

Teaching Self-Instruction in Home Living Environments

Two studies investigated the effects of self-instruction in home living environments among people with severe disabilities. These studies addressed community home living skills and recreation and leisure skills.

Community Living Skills   Hughes (1992) combined traditional self-instruction (Meichenbaum & Goodman, 1971) with multiple exemplars to teach four residents of a group home with mental retardation needing extensive supports to solve task-related problems. Four problem situations served as training tasks (i.e., multiple exemplars) and four served as generalization probes. The combined strategy was associated with generalization to untrained problems for all residents as well as maintenance of the problem-solving strategy (i.e., responding to multiple exemplars and self-instructing). Because an analysis of instructional components was not conducted, however, it is not clear which component was responsible for generalization.

Recreation and Leisure Skills   Keogh, Faw, Whitman, and Reid (1984) used self-instruction to teach two adolescent boys with behavior problems who lived in a community residence to play board games. The boys were taught to state Step 2 of the Meichenbaum and Goodman (1971) sequence (stating the correct response) by verbalizing individual moves of the game as they played. Both boys increased performance and verbalization of game moves when instruction was introduced sequentially across games. Prompts and additional instruction were required before generalization occurred in dyad and free-play situations; generalization to three untrained games did not occur. Game skills were maintained, although occasional instructional sessions were required.

Summary of Empirical Studies

As indicated in the previous review, investigations of the effects of self-instruction among people with disabilities have been conducted in school, work, and home living settings. Self-instruction was found to be effective at increasing proficiency in the areas of academics, daily living skills, social skills, recreation and leisure skills, productivity, and employment skills. Applications of self-instruction included replications of the original Meichenbaum and Goodman (1971) teaching sequence as well as variations of the procedure. Self-instruction was effective in producing generalization and maintenance of target behaviors to varying degrees across studies. The following section presents recommendations for teachers who wish to promote the generalized effects of their self-instructional programs.

PROMOTING GENERALIZATION OF SELF-INSTRUCTION SKILLS

A critical aspect of self-determination is independent performance and generalization of socially valued behaviors. Generalization of behavior is demonstrated when students perform targeted skills in situations not associated with prior instruction (i.e., when they encounter unique situations, new people, different tasks or demands) and when their performance continues over time following withdrawal of instruction (i.e., maintenance) (Berg, Wacker, & Flynn, 1990; Pierce & Schreibman, 1994). Although the importance of generalization as an educational goal is widely accepted, strategies to promote generalization rarely are incorporated into instructional programs (Bandura, 1969; Shore, Iwata, Lerman, & Shirley, 1994; Stokes & Baer, 1977). Therefore, it should not be surprising that generalization of targeted skills rarely is demonstrated in instructional settings.

In the following sections, strategies used to promote generalization in the self-instruction studies reviewed in this chapter are identified and discussed. In addition, the reviewed studies are analyzed to identify strategies used to promote generalization as categorized by Stokes and Baer (1977) (i.e., train sufficient exemplars, program common stimuli, mediate generalization, train and hope). Recommendations are provided for teachers to use to increase generalization effects when they teach students to self-instruct.

Instructional Strategies to Promote Generalization

Hughes and Petersen (1989) promoted generalization of on-task behavior among employees by 1) teaching on-task behavior across varied work tasks (i.e., train sufficient exemplars), 2) using a permanent picture cue to prompt self-instructing and telling employees to respond in training as if in response to work demands (i.e., program common stimuli), and 3) reminding employees during self-instructional training to self-instruct when in the work situation (i.e., mediate generalization). Results indicated that on-task behavior for all four employees generalized from the training to the work situation.

Mediating generalization by teaching self-instruction was found to produce generalization over time (i.e., maintenance) (e.g., see Hughes, 1992). In addition, a combination of three factors appeared to account for the effectiveness of self-instructional training in maintaining performance across studies (Hughes, 1991). These factors were 1) length of self-instructional training, 2) number of self-instructional statements taught, and 3) level of ability of participant.

Teaching all four statements of the Meichenbaum and Goodman self-instructional training sequence (i.e., stating the problem, stating the correct response, self-evaluating, and self-reinforcing) appeared to maintain performance without additional assistance across all levels of ability (Hughes & Rusch, 1989; Rusch et al., 1985; Whitman & Johnston, 1983). Saying only Statements 1 and/or 2 (i.e., stating the problem, stating the correct response) required additional instruction or verbal prompting to maintain performance (Rusch et al., 1988). Length of training required appeared to relate to participants' level of ability. Specifically, three to four training sessions, in combination with teaching four self-instructional statements, were sufficient to maintain performance with individuals with mild to moderate disabilities (Whitman & Johnston, 1983), whereas at least 15 training sessions were required to obtain similar effects with individuals with severe disabilities (Hughes & Rusch, 1989).

Recommendations to Promote Generalization

So-called "train and hope" instructional strategies (Stokes & Baer, 1977) were not effective at producing generalization when self-instruction was taught to people with disabilities in the studies reviewed. As suggested by Keogh et al.

(1988), specific programming for generalization must be incorporated into training procedures in order to facilitate generalized effects of self-instruction. Specifically, the combination of training sufficient exemplars, programming common stimuli, and mediating generalization appears to be a particularly powerful strategy for promoting generalization. Recommendations to teachers for promoting generalization when teaching self-instruction skills, therefore, are as follows:

1. Provide many examples of target behaviors that you want students to learn and allow them to practice the behaviors in many different situations (i.e., train sufficient exemplars).
2. Introduce similar environmental cues in all of the settings in which you want students to perform their target behaviors in order to prompt students to self-instruct (i.e., program common stimuli).
3. Remind students to use their self-instructions throughout the day to prompt their independent performance (i.e., mediate generalization).

CONCLUSION

Models of self-instructional training have been utilized across a wide range of behaviors and student populations. Essentially, self-instructing refers to students using their verbal behavior to guide their performance. Because students may not use their verbal behavior effectively to direct their performance, they may need to be taught strategies to do so. This chapter discussed the conceptual basis of self-instruction, practical applications and models of self-instruction, and strategies for teaching and promoting the generalized effects of self-instruction.

Self-instruction holds considerable promise for increasing the independence and self-determination of students with disabilities in school, employment, residential, and community settings. Although the number of self-instruction studies involving students with disabilities remains limited, the studies do support the feasibility of teaching students with disabilities to use self-instructions to acquire, maintain, and generalize skills across a variety of tasks and conditions. The following recommendations are made to guide teachers in increasing the effectiveness of their self-instructional programs.

1. *At present, the most reliable method for teachers to use in determining who will benefit from self-instructional training is to observe a student's preferences and responses* (Browder & Shapiro, 1985). Although some evidence shows that people with higher cognitive abilities may respond better to self-instructional training (Copeland, 1981), it remains uncertain what specific cognitive skills are needed to benefit from such training. In short, the relationship between cognitive level and receptivity to self-instructional training has not been established. Therefore, the wise teacher will carefully observe his or her students' behavior.

For example, does the student talk aloud? Does he or she repeat instructions heard? What words does he or she consistently use? Until we know more about the interaction between student characteristics and the effects of self-instruction, teachers are advised to consider the type and severity of a student's disability as factors in determining methods for teaching self-instruction, *not* whether self-instruction should or should not be taught. Teacher-devised screening assessments, as recommended by Hughes and colleagues (1996), may be used to determine a student's communication skills in relation to self-instructional demands.

2. *Teaching all four statements of Meichenbaum and Goodman's (1971) self-instructional teaching sequence (i.e., stating the problem, stating the response, self-evaluating, and self-reinforcing) and asking learners to verbalize them consistently is recommended in order to produce generalization.* For example, in studies that taught only Step 1 (stating the problem), students required additional assistance to obtain generalization of effects (Rusch et al., 1988). Students should be allowed, however, to adapt statements according to their own functional language abilities. For example, Collet-Klingenberg and Chadsey-Rusch (1991) observed that students in their study had difficulty verbalizing all required cognitive processing statements. Self-labeling is an example of how self-instructional statements may be personalized by students by abbreviating lengthy statements (e.g., Wacker et al., 1988). Hughes and colleagues (e.g., Hughes et al., 1995) demonstrated that simply a noun or verb chosen by a student from a self-instructional statement may relate functionally to behavior change. When teaching students to follow instructions, Meichenbaum and Goodman's (1971) sequence will, no doubt, produce positive outcomes for many students. For students with more marked language impairments, the *what/where* procedure (Agran et al., 1989) may be more appropriate because it requires fewer verbalizations.

3. *Teachers should be aware that the number of training sessions required to achieve proficiency in self-instructing may vary considerably among students.* Individuals have learned to self-instruct effectively in as few as three instructional sessions (Whitman & Johnston, 1983) or as many as 20 instructional sessions (Hughes, 1992). Teachers should establish a criterion for terminating instruction based upon a student's performance in both the training and noninstructional settings. Instruction should be continued until a student has demonstrated clear mastery of self-instructional procedures and behavior change has been observed consistently to ensure that self-instruction will be maintained when instructional support is withdrawn.

4. *Teachers should be flexible in allowing students who are nonverbal or who have limited verbal skills to self-instruct in nontraditional ways.* For example, Hughes and colleagues conducted a series of studies in which students used signing to self-instruct. Peer teachers in these studies modeled self-instructions

both verbally and by signing (Hughes et al., 1995). Signed self-instructions of learners were found to relate to acquisition and generalization of desired responses. An alternative method of self-instructing was demonstrated by Rusch and colleagues (1988) who taught a student to tap and point to a picture in order to seek assistance. The student, a young man whose language was delayed and characterized by echolalic patterns and who had limited mobility, worked in a university-based film center. When he ran out of materials to fill film orders, the student was taught to self-instruct by tapping and pointing to the picture of an aide who could help him get needed materials.

5. *Teachers should use consistent, systematic direct instructional methods such as prompting, modeling, reinforcing, and providing corrective feedback when teaching people to self-instruct,* as illustrated in the studies reviewed in this chapter. Self-instruction is a skill that is taught most efficiently by using sound principles of instruction. If peers are teaching learners to self-instruct, a script may be helpful to ensure that correct protocol is followed by all trainers. Scripts should include instructions for modeling self-instructional statements; the exact training sequence to be used in teaching self-instructing; and rules for prompting, reinforcing, and providing corrective feedback. Peers initially may need to be coached in order to follow the script accurately.

6. *Active participation by a student in a self-instructional program may relate to the effectiveness of instruction* (Meichenbaum, 1975). It may be necessary to modify instructional methods if a first attempt at teaching self-instruction skills is unsuccessful. A teacher should remember, however, that some students will learn more slowly than others and that many sessions may be required before a change in behavior may be readily observed.

7. *The effectiveness of a self-instructional program is ultimately a social validation issue* (Wolf, 1978). A teacher must seek input from a student, her family, and important others in developing instructional goals. If a student's goals are not incorporated into an instructional program, personal preferences and choices may be violated. It is equally important to determine whether self-instructional procedures are acceptable to individuals involved and whether program outcomes are satisfactory to them. In short, teachers must ask whether their instructional and programming efforts have had a positive impact on the actual lives of learners (Johnson & Fawcett, 1994; Schwartz & Baer, 1991). For example, teachers may ask students whether their personal goals have been met by participating in a self-instructional program. Or teachers may observe students self-instructing to determine whether they appear to enjoy using the procedure or whether it is aversive to them. Procedures that are liked and are perceived to have beneficial outcomes are more likely to be adopted by people.

8. *Teachers should not count on "train and hope" methods to produce generalization in their self-instructional programs.* Studies reviewed in this chapter provide considerable evidence that self-instruction alone rarely produces gener-

alized effects. Specific strategies designed to produce generalization, such as teaching with multiple exemplars or programming common stimuli, should be incorporated into self-instructional training.

9.   *Teachers need to evaluate the effects of self-instructional training throughout their intervention efforts* to determine whether students actually are self-instructing and whether self-instruction is correlated with desired behavior change. Repeated measures of target behaviors provide an accurate description of a student's progress and the necessary information to make a decision to initiate, change, or terminate an instructional program.

QUESTIONS FOR REVIEW

1.   Briefly define self-instruction and give an example of its use.
2.   The chapter states that direct instructional methods are most often used to teach individuals to self-instruct. What four strategies do these methods incorporate?
3.   Name and briefly discuss the five steps involved in Meichenbaum and Goodman's (1971) self-instructional training sequence.
4.   Briefly describe the overall goal of self-instruction.
5.   Name and discuss two main differences between Meichenbaum and Goodman's self-instructional training sequence and more contemporary training sequences.
6.   The Did-Next-Now, What/Where, and Interactive self-instructional strategies may be adapted to various levels of abilities. Pick two of the strategies and give an example of how a student could use each of them in doing his or her laundry.
7.   Self-instruction is invaluable in promoting self-determination. Name and discuss two additional benefits of the use of self-instruction by students in community-based work settings.
8.   Self-labeling is an abbreviated self-instructional method developed by Wacker and his colleagues. Briefly describe an example of how self-labeling might be used by a student when completing housekeeping tasks in a hotel.
9.   Give a brief example of how verbal correspondence may be used to improve worker productivity.
10.   Generalization of socially valued target behaviors is critical for the independent functioning of students with disabilities. Explain what generalization is and describe two strategies for promoting generalization of self-instruction skills.

REFERENCES

Agran, M., Fodor-Davis, J., & Moore, S. (1986). The effects of self-instructional training on job-task sequencing: Suggesting a problem-solving strategy. *Education and Training of the Mentally Retarded, 21,* 273–281.

Agran, M., Fodor-Davis, J., Moore, S., & Deer, M. (1989). The application of a self-management program on instruction-following skills. *Journal of The Association for Persons with Severe Handicaps, 14,* 147–154.

Agran, M., Fodor-Davis, J., Moore, S., & Martella, R. (1992). The effects of peer-delivered self-instructional training on a lunch-making work task for students with severe handicaps. *Education and Training in Mental Retardation, 27,* 230–240.

Agran, M., Salzberg, C.L., & Stowitschek, J.J. (1987). An analysis of the effects of a social skills training program using self-instructions on the acquisition and generalization of two social behaviors in a working setting. *Journal of The Association for Persons with Severe Handicaps, 12,* 131–139.

Bandura, A. (1969). *Principles of behavior modification.* New York: Holt, Rinehart & Winston.

Bandura, A. (1971). Vicarious and self-reinforcement processes. In R. Glaser (Ed.), *The nature of reinforcement* (pp. 228–279). New York: Academic Press.

Berg, W.K., Wacker, D.P., & Flynn, T.H. (1990). Teaching generalization and maintenance of work behavior. In F.R. Rusch (Ed.), *Supported employment: Models, methods, and issues* (pp. 145–160). Sycamore, IL: Sycamore.

Browder, D.M., & Shapiro, E.S. (1985). Applications of self-management to individuals with severe handicaps. *Journal of The Association for Persons with Severe Handicaps, 10,* 200–208.

Collet-Klingenberg, L., & Chadsey-Rusch, J. (1991). Using a cognitive-process approach to teach social skills. *Education and Training in Mental Retardation, 26,* 258–270.

Copeland, A.P. (1981). The relevance of the subject variables in cognitive self-instructional programs for impulsive children. *Behavior Therapy, 12,* 520–529.

Crouch, K.P., Rusch, F.R., & Karlan, G.R. (1984). Competitive employment utilizing the correspondence training paradigm to enhance productivity. *Education and Training of the Mentally Retarded, 19,* 268–275.

Goldfried, M.R., & Merbaum, M. (1973). A perspective on self-control. In M.R. Goldfried & M. Merbaum (Eds.), *Behavior change through self-control* (pp. 3–34). New York: Holt, Rinehart & Winston.

Hughes, C. (1991). Independent performance among individuals with mental retardation: Promoting generalization through self-instruction. In M. Hersen, R.M. Eisler, & P.M. Miller (Eds.), *Progress in behavior modification* (Vol. 27, pp. 7–35). Beverly Hills: Sage Publications.

Hughes, C. (1992). Teaching self-instruction utilizing multiple exemplars to produce generalized problem-solving by individuals with severe mental retardation. *American Journal on Mental Retardation, 97,* 302–314.

Hughes, C., & Agran, M. (1993). Teaching persons with severe disabilities to use self-instruction in community settings: An analysis of applications. *Journal of The Association for Persons with Severe Handicaps, 18,* 261–274.

Hughes, C., Harmer, M.L., Killian, D.J., & Niarhos, F. (1995). The effects of multiple-exemplar self-instructional training on high school students' generalized conversational interactions. *Journal of Applied Behavior Analysis, 28,* 201–218.

Hughes, C., Hugo, K., & Blatt, J. (1996). A self-instructional intervention for teaching generalized problem solving within a functional task sequence. *American Journal on Mental Retardation, 100,* 565–579.

Hughes, C., & Petersen, D. (1989). Utilizing a self-instructional training package to increase on-task behavior and work performance. *Education and Training in Mental Retardation, 24,* 114–120.

Hughes, C., & Rusch, F.R. (1989). Teaching supported employees with severe mental retardation to solve problems. *Journal of Applied Behavior Analysis, 22,* 365–372.

Johnson, M.D., & Fawcett, S.B. (1994). Courteous service: Its assessment and modification in a human service organization. *Journal of Applied Behavior Analysis, 27,* 145–152.

Johnston, M.B., Whitman, T.L., & Johnson, M. (1980). Teaching addition and subtraction to mentally retarded children: A self-instruction program. *Applied Research in Mental Retardation, 1,* 141–160.

Kanfer, F.H. (1971). The maintenance of behavior by self-generated stimuli and reinforcement. In A. Jacobs & L.B. Sachs (Eds.), *The psychology of private events: Perspectives on covert response systems* (pp. 39–59). New York: Academic Press.

Kaplan, J.S. (1995). *Beyond behavior modification: A cognitive-behavioral approach to behavior management in the school* (3rd ed.). Austin, TX: PRO-ED.

Keogh, D.A., Faw, G.D., Whitman, T.L., & Reid, D. (1984). Enhancing leisure skills in severely retarded adolescents through a self-instructional treatment package. *Analysis and Intervention in Developmental Disabilities, 4,* 333–351.

Keogh, D.A., Whitman, T.L., & Maxwell, S.E. (1988). Self-instruction versus external instruction: Individual differences and training effectiveness. *Cognitive Therapy and Research, 12,* 591–610.

Malott, R.W. (1984). Rule-governed behavior, self-management, and the developmentally disabled: A theoretical analysis. *Analysis and Intervention in Developmental Disabilities, 4,* 199–209.

Meichenbaum, D. (1975). Self-instructional methods. In F.H. Kanfer & A.P. Goldstein (Eds.), *Helping people change* (pp. 357–391). Elmsford, NY: Pergamon.

Meichenbaum, D., & Goodman, J. (1971). Training impulsive children to talk to themselves: A means of developing self-control. *Journal of Abnormal Psychology, 77,* 115–126.

Moore, S.C., Agran, M., & Fodor-Davis, J. (1989). Using self-management strategies to increase the production rates of workers with severe handicaps. *Education and Training in Mental Retardation, 24,* 324–332.

Park, H., & Gaylord-Ross, R. (1989). A problem-solving approach to social skills training in employment settings with mentally retarded youth. *Journal of Applied Behavior Analysis, 22,* 373–380.

Pierce, K.L., & Schreibman, L. (1994). Teaching daily living skills to children with autism in unsupervised settings through pictorial self-management. *Journal of Applied Behavior Analysis, 27,* 471–481.

Rusch, F.R., Martin, J.E., Lagomarcino, T.R., & White, D.M. (1987). Teaching task sequencing via verbal mediation. *Education and Training in Mental Retardation, 22,* 229–235.

Rusch, F.R., McKee, M., Chadsey-Rusch, J., & Renzaglia, A. (1988). Teaching a student with severe handicaps to self-instruct: A brief report. *Education and Training in Mental Retardation, 23,* 51–58.

Rusch, F.R., Morgan, T.K., Martin, J.E., Riva, M., & Agran, M. (1985). Competitive employment: Teaching mentally retarded employees self-instructional strategies. *Applied Research in Mental Retardation, 6,* 389–407.

Schwartz, I.S., & Baer, D.M. (1991). Social validity assessments: Is current practice state of the art? *Journal of Applied Behavior Analysis, 24,* 189–204.

Shore, B.A., Iwata, B.A., Lerman, D.C., & Shirley, M.J. (1994). Assessing and programming generalized behavioral reduction across multiple stimulus parameters. *Journal of Applied Behavior Analysis, 27,* 371–384.

Skinner, B.F. (1957). *Verbal behavior.* New York: Appleton-Century-Crofts.

Stokes, T., & Baer, D. (1977). An implicit technology of generalization. *Journal of Applied Behavior Analysis, 10,* 349–367.

Wacker, D.P., Berg, W.K., McMahon, C., Templeman, M., McKinney, J., Swarts, V., Visser, M., & Marquardt, P. (1988). An evaluation of labeling-then-doing with moderately handicapped persons: Acquisition and generalization with complex tasks. *Journal of Applied Behavior Analysis, 21,* 369–380.

Wacker, D.P., Carroll, J.L., & Moe, G.L. (1980). Acquisition, generalization, and maintenance of an assembly task by mentally retarded children. *American Journal of Mental Deficiency, 85,* 286–290.

Wacker, D.P., & Greenebaum, F.T. (1984). Efficacy of a verbal training sequence on the sorting performance of moderately and severely mentally retarded adolescents. *American Journal of Mental Deficiency, 88,* 653–660.

Wagner, M., D'Amico, R., Marder, C., Newman, L., & Blackkorby, J. (1992). *What happens next? Trends in postschool outcomes of youth with disabilities.* Menlo Park, CA: SRI International.

Whitman, T., & Johnston, M.B. (1983). Teaching addition and subtraction with regrouping to educable mentally retarded children: A group self-instructional training program. *Behavior Therapy, 14,* 127–143.

Whitman, T.L. (1987). Self-instruction, individual differences, and mental retardation. *American Journal on Mental Retardation, 92,* 347–362.

Whitman, T.L. (1990). Self-regulation and mental retardation. *American Journal on Mental Retardation, 94,* 347–362.

Wolf, M.M. (1978). Social validity: The case for subjective measurement, or how behavior analysis is finding its heart. *Journal of Applied Behavior Analysis, 11,* 203–214.

CHAPTER 9

Teaching Goal Setting and Task Performance

After reading this chapter, you will be able to

1. Explain a conceptual basis for goal setting, including factors related to motivation, self-management, range of personal experiences, and behavioral consequences

2. Describe the reasons that self-selected goals are more effective than teacher-selected goals at enhancing an individual's performance

3. Discuss the effects of goal setting as a component of a treatment package combined with a variety of intervention strategies

4. Use eight empirically based goal-setting treatment packages to teach students with disabilities how to increase their achievement and competence

5. Apply model demonstration programs and conceptual models of goal setting to a variety of behaviors, populations, and settings

KEY TERMS

1. Contingency contracting
2. Effort-attribution training
3. Everyday life experiences
4. Goal actualization
5. Goal attainment
6. Goal setting
7. Immediate and delayed consequences
8. Motivation
9. Recruiting assistance
10. Self-instructional training
11. Self-management
12. Self-recording
13. Strategy training
14. Task performance

Unfortunately, many students with disabilities leave high school without personal goals or direction to guide their future (see the following case study).

> Kevin O'Hara had the distinction of having had the lowest grade point average on record for a first-semester freshman at Midstate Community College. One reason for his poor academic performance was that after the first few weeks of school, he never went to class. College life gave Kevin access to an array of alluring activities much more immediately rewarding than attending class, studying, or going to the library. Classes were boring and studying was too hard. Kevin's philosophy became "if it feels good, do it." Parties and friends provided much more immediate enjoyment than did participation in the long, slow process of obtaining a college degree. The future seemed far away, vague, and unobtainable. All that mattered was the present.
>
> At the end of his first semester at Midstate Community College, Kevin was asked by the college administration to leave. He spent the next few years working in a series of odd jobs, usually staying employed only long enough to pay off the costs of his entertainment and basic personal needs and then move on. Around town he acquired the reputation of being a drifter, wandering aimlessly without any direction or goals. At 35, when most of the friends he had known in high school and college had begun getting married, starting families, purchasing homes, and advancing in their careers, Kevin began to feel like an outsider. In comparison to them, his life seemed stagnant and empty. Without plans or direction, nothing really seemed to matter. Because most of his friends were busy with their own families, careers, and interests, Kevin began to seek companionship more and more in the local pool halls. He felt lonely and discouraged with himself and his lack of accomplishments, interests, and dreams. Kevin spent evenings at home in front of the television, staring blankly at the screen.
>
> Kevin's parents had long been disconcerted by Kevin's apparent lack of ambition. After all, his older brother, Chris, had successfully completed college and had recently been promoted to manager of a small computer business. Kevin's younger sister, Katharine, was enrolled in a pre-med course at Midstate Community College and was planning to become a registered nurse. It was true that Kevin had been diagnosed with a learning disability back in elementary school, but he had taken courses in the resource room and had graduated from high school with a regular academic diploma. Even in high school, however, Kevin seemed to flounder and never seemed to have many interests. After Kevin's graduation, it was his parents' idea that he go to Midstate Community. Not having anything better to do, and because his expenses were to be paid, Kevin had agreed to attend. Once there, however, Kevin realized that he had no interest in attending college or earning a college degree, and he promptly quit going to class.

The lack of personal goals may be one factor related to the high unemployment rate experienced by students receiving special education services after leaving school (Martin & Marshall, 1997). Without a commitment to personal achievement, it may be difficult to pursue a long-term goal for which the immediate benefits seem insignificant and the long-term benefits seem too distant to be worth the effort (Rachlin, 1978). Federal special education legislation (e.g., the Individuals with Disabilities Education Act [IDEA] of 1990 [PL 101-476] and its amendments) mandated that students' goals, interests, and preferences be incorporated into their individualized education programs (IEPs). In addition, whenever a student's transition goals are to be discussed at an IEP meeting, school district personnel are required to invite the student to the meeting to provide his or her input into the development of these goals.

As was discussed in Chapter 3, the potential impact of the legislation supporting student involvement in transition goal setting is far-reaching. A possible pitfall, however, may be that students with disabilities often lack the skills and the variety of experiences needed to set their own goals (West, 1995). They need to learn goal-setting strategies and experience a wide range of situations from which to choose meaningful goals. Few practitioners, however, report that they know how to teach students to set and then act to achieve their own goals (Agran, 1997; Kishi, Telucksingh, Zollers, Park-Lee, & Meyer, 1988; Stancliffe & Wehmeyer, 1995).

This chapter presents a conceptual basis for goal setting and reviews empirical studies designed to teach goal-setting skills. Strategies used in model demonstration programs to promote goal setting are then discussed. Examples that highlight suggested strategies are provided as a guide to teachers who are interested in the application of goal-setting strategies with their students.

CONCEPTUAL BASIS OF GOAL SETTING

A variety of nomenclature has been used to refer to the construct *goal setting* (e.g., self-selection of performance standards, goal attainment, self-determination of contingencies), and varied interpretations of the goal-setting process have been offered (e.g., cognitive, behavioral, psychological). A behavioral explanation of the goal-setting process argues that to set goals, students must be aware of both the consequences of their actions and the contingencies operating in the environment (Miller & Kelly, 1994). For example, in determining a goal for employment (e.g., becoming a maintenance electrician), a student must identify the contingencies required to achieve a goal (e.g., 4 or 5 years of trade school) as well as the possible consequences of achieving the goal (e.g., full-time employment with above-minimum wage and long or irregular hours). In addition, to gain access to the delayed reinforcement of a long-term goal (e.g., graduation from high school in 4 years), a student must relinquish continual access to competing, powerful, immediate consequences (e.g., going skiing for the weekend rather than studying for finals). Over time, acting to obtain immediate reinforcement could result in consequences that would preclude access to long-term goals. In the previous case study, for example, Kevin spent time partying with friends and avoiding studying; consequently, he received poor grades and was asked to leave school, making access to a college degree and postsecondary training at Midstate Community College impossible.

Motivation

The ability to delay immediate reinforcement and act toward the attainment of a long-term consequence may relate to what the layman refers to as *motivation*. Mithaug, Martin, Agran, and Rusch (1988) surveyed the literature on motivation and reported that highly successful, self-determined people are motivated by a definiteness of purpose, which includes

- Deciding on a specific goal in life
- Setting a time limit for reaching that goal
- Choosing specific plans to achieve the goal
- Determining the specific benefits the goal will bring to one's life

According to the literature on motivation, people considered to be highly successful (e.g., individuals who have achieved social prominence) decide on a personal mission that leads to action, envision and communicate that mission, and follow up with an action plan comprising specific goals and benchmarks to evaluate the outcomes of their actions (Agran, 1997). The ability to set goals and act to attain them may relate to a positive mental attitude and the motivation to achieve as well as a sense of self-efficacy (Butler, 1994; Mithaug et al., 1988). As suggested by Bandura (1977), comparing present performance with a desired standard when setting or evaluating goals may enhance motivation to achieve these goals.

Effect of Goal Setting on Self-Management

An individual's ability to set goals may influence the effectiveness of a self-management intervention, such as self-instruction (see Chapter 8). Agran (1997) suggested that without goal setting, self-management programs may be compromised. Unless students have set their own goals or are at least aware of and agree with the goal of a proposed self-management program, they may not implement a self-management strategy with fidelity. For example, teachers may want students to work harder to improve their grades, employers may desire employees to decrease absences, or parents may wish that their children completed their household chores more consistently (Hughes & Lloyd, 1993). If an individual does not want to modify a targeted behavior, however, a self-management program may not be effective in promoting behavior change. Consequently, researchers have suggested that people with disabilities should participate in the selection of their own behavior change goals prior to intervention (e.g., Chadsey-Rusch, 1992; Hughes, Killian, & Fischer, 1996). Involvement in goal setting may increase the active participation of individuals in self-management programs because they may be more likely to change behaviors that they perceive to be important to them (Smith & Nelson, 1997).

Effect of Everyday Experiences on Goal Setting

An individual's ability to set goals also relates to the quality and variety of his or her everyday experiences. Individuals who have lived restricted or sheltered lives with little opportunity to sample a range of employment, social, educational, or community experiences may have a limited repertoire from which to draw when choosing personal goals. For example, during high school Kevin O'Hara may have had little opportunity to sample different kinds of employment. Had he been enrolled in a community-based, school-to-work education program, he may have had the opportunity to sample a variety of careers (e.g., landscaping, data entry, public health). *Job sampling,* which allows students to train on the job at a variety of employment sites, may have helped Kevin identify a career that he would want to pursue by enrolling in vocational training following high school. A prerequisite for appropriate and realistic goal setting, therefore, may be a wide range of everyday life experiences. Without knowledge of a range of possible options, it may be difficult for students to choose personal goals or evaluate their progress toward achieving a goal.

Dilemma of Immediate Versus Delayed Consequences

Individuals face a dilemma when setting and pursuing a goal because they must choose between two or more actions that have different consequences, one immediate and one delayed (Hughes & Lloyd, 1993). For example, a student may have a goal of saving money to purchase a car but may be tempted to use his or her weekly paycheck immediately to buy compact discs (CDs). This situation presents a conflict to the student because the effects of the two alternative responses occur at different times (Rachlin, 1978). In contrast, if opportunities (e.g., a limitless supply of funds) to buy a car or purchase CDs occurred at the same time, there would not be a dilemma; the student would simply choose a purchase based on personal preference. The dilemma occurs, however, because a preferred activity for an individual, such as spending one's money, provides immediate reinforcement, whereas the effect of not saving funds (e.g., not saving enough money to buy a car) is experienced only after a delay (Bandura, 1969). The difference between immediate and delayed consequences makes goal setting and attainment difficult for many individuals. For example, Kevin O'Hara perceived the reinforcing value of friends and parties as more powerful than the action required to obtain postsecondary training and a college degree.

> ***Suggested Solutions***   A potential solution to the dilemma of delayed reinforcers is to make people more aware of the contingencies that are in effect in their environment (Baer, 1984; Rachlin, 1978). This learning may be facilitated by making the consequences of one's actions more salient (Hughes & Lloyd, 1993). For example, to prompt studying, students could be informed that the results of continued poor grades would be academic probation and

eventual dismissal from school. Smokers could be shown X-rays of lungs severely damaged by long-term smoke inhalation to encourage them to stop smoking. Juvenile offenders could be shown jail cells inhabited by convicted criminals to curb petty theft. The long-term outcomes of setting a goal (e.g., returning to school full time to receive training as a carpenter) may seem too improbable, abstract, or inconceivable to compete with more immediately available consequences (e.g., getting a weekly paycheck in an entry-level, minimum-wage job). The benefits of completing a carpentry program could be made more salient to a student by displaying pictures of completed houses or cabinets; informing students of potential salaries, benefits, and opportunities for promotion available upon employment with a major construction company; or having master carpenters visit class to discuss the benefits of the trade with students.

A second solution to the dilemma of the delayed consequences associated with long-term goals is to have a student sign a behavioral contract when the perceived value of a delayed outcome of goal setting is high. For example, Rachlin (1978) suggested that a student might sign a written contract stating a contingency, such as loss of privileges or money for not studying. The contract should be signed when the student's perceived value of studying is high (e.g., when the student's goal of obtaining a scholarship is contingent on maintaining good grades). The contract decreases the student's choice of action due to the impending loss of privileges during those times when the value of studying may wane (e.g., when there are competing reinforcers).

A third suggestion relates to teaching students to use self-management techniques to delay access to reinforcers when pursuing a goal (Hughes & Lloyd, 1993). For example, a dieter could learn that by abstaining daily from fattening desserts, she could reach her goal of fitting into her prom dress next month. Because researchers have analyzed the variables of which behavior is a function, it should be possible to teach individuals to analyze and manipulate variables that influence their own behavior (Skinner, 1953). Through the use of direct instructional principles such as prompting, modeling, practice, and corrective feedback, people have been taught to modify their own behavior by observing instances of their failure to delay reinforcers (e.g., eating three scoops of ice cream when attempting to lose weight) and the environmental events affecting their behavior (e.g., overeating as a result of a stressful day at work). Bandura (1969) emphasized that "the goals that individuals choose for themselves must be specified sufficiently. . . to provide adequate guidance for the actions that must be taken daily to attain desired outcomes" (p. 255). The use of a recording device (e.g., daily log) may help to make environmental events and their consequences more salient to the individual. In addition, a student's actions may be brought under the control of long-term consequences by employing techniques such as the following:

1. Commitment strategies (e.g., arranging to have a wake-up call in order to arrive at an appointment on time) (Rachlin, 1978)
2. Rules and verbal behavior (e.g., raising one's hand before speaking in class to avoid loss of privileges) (Catania, 1984; Malott, 1984)
3. Stimulus control (e.g., eating only when sitting at a table to avoid snacking between meals) (Skinner, 1953)
4. Public announcement of goals (e.g., stating publicly the intention to quit smoking) (Hayes et al., 1985)

Brigham (1978) and Mahoney and Thoresen (1974) proposed that through direct instruction students can be taught to analyze their environments to identify functional variables that influence their behavior. The next step, therefore, is to teach students to modify the variables that control the behavior they wish to change in order to obtain a goal. Brigham (1978) and Skinner (1953) suggested that because any of the variables of which a student's goal-directed behavior is a function may be manipulated, many self-management procedures are available (e.g., self-monitoring, self-instruction, self-recording), and one of these strategies may be chosen that is appropriate for a particular environmental context. For example, at Midstate Community College, Kevin O'Hara might have determined that he would like to obtain a degree in business management in order to get a job managing a small business. The college counselor then could have taught Kevin to set contingencies for studying and completing class assignments (e.g., playing one game of pool only after he has studied for 2 hours and completed all assignments for the day).

EMPIRICAL INVESTIGATIONS OF GOAL SETTING

Researchers have investigated the effects of goal setting as well as the strategies used to teach individuals goal-setting skills. In this section, we review empirical studies to inform teachers about effective methods and materials to use to enhance students' skills at setting realistic and appropriate transition goals. Studies investigating the effects of self-selected versus teacher-selected goals are reviewed first, followed by studies in which goal setting was introduced as a component of a treatment package.

Investigations of Self-Selected Versus Teacher-Selected Goals

Several studies were conducted to compare the effects of having students determine their own performance goals, rather than having these goals selected by teachers. Lovitt and Curtiss (1969) reported that the academic performance of a 12-year-old boy with behavior disorders increased when he chose his own performance contingencies as compared to when contingencies were selected by his teacher. Bolstad and Johnson (1972) observed that self-regulated reinforcement resulted in fewer disruptive episodes for a group of noncompliant, elementary-age children. Farnum, Brigham, and Johnson (1977) found that fifth-graders completed more math problems during a self-selected contingency condition and that they preferred this condition to having their goals determined by teachers. Dickerson and Creedon (1981) observed that students performed better on math and writing tasks when they selected their own performance standards. Schunk (1985) found that sixth-graders with learning disabilities showed more improvement on math skills when they set their own goals as compared to when no goals were set or when teachers set goals for them. In contrast, Felixbrod and O'Leary (1973) and Glynn (1970) reported that students performed equally well on math tasks under self- and experimenter-determined conditions.

Several studies investigated the stringency of performance goals set by students. Felixbrod and O'Leary (1973) reported that students tended to select more lenient performance standards during self-determined contingency conditions (which could account for the fact that they performed equally as well under self- and experimenter-determined conditions). By contrast, stringent standards were maintained in Dickerson and Creedon's (1981) study; however, unlike in the Felixbrod and O'Leary investigation, students remained under the social surveillance of their teachers when setting goals. Similarly, Hayes et al. (1985) observed that public goal setting (i.e., showing written goals to an experimenter) was more effective in increasing study behavior among adults than was private goal setting (i.e., writing down but not showing goals to an experimenter). Dickerson and Creedon and Hayes and colleagues concluded that social consequences associated with making one's goals public may be a critical factor in the effectiveness of goal-setting programs.

Summary   Research suggests that self-selected goals may be as effective or more effective than teacher-selected goals at enhancing individuals' performance (Rosenbaum & Drabman, 1979). Furthermore, establishing more stringent goals is associated with improved performance (Brownell, Colletti, Ersner-Hershfield, Hershfield, & Wilson, 1977). Finally, maintaining stringent performance standards may be enhanced by having individuals announce their goals publicly, a view that is consistent with a behavioral position that suggests that the ultimate controlling factors of anyone's behavior come from the environment and its social context (e.g., Skinner, 1953).

Investigations of Goal-Setting Treatment Packages

A number of investigations were conducted to evaluate the effects of goal setting as a component of a behavioral change treatment program. Flexer, Newbery, and Martin (1979) conducted one of the earliest studies, in which the effects of goal setting on the production rates of adults with mental retardation working in a sheltered workshop were compared across three treatment conditions. Under all conditions, goal setting was combined with a visit to the community so that participants could choose an item that they wished to purchase with their earnings. During the first condition, a photograph of the item was placed at the participants' work stations and used as a reminder of participants' goals. In addition, a money bank was placed at the participants' work stations so that they could monitor the accumulation of their earnings toward their long-term goal of purchasing a particular item. Social praise for meeting an experimenter-determined daily goal was provided under a second condition, and an immediately awarded, tangible reinforcer (i.e., money) was provided under a third condition.

Results indicated that all treatment conditions were superior to a control condition, in which participants did not set goals. Contingent praise for meeting experimenter-determined daily goals in combination with long-term goal setting was found to be superior to either long-term goal setting alone or monetary rewards for meeting daily goals. The authors concluded that the effectiveness of the long-term, goal-setting condition may have been limited because too much time was required to reach the participants' goals and the photograph and money bank may not have served to prompt participants' behavior change. Nevertheless, this study is important because it was one of the earliest demonstrations that individuals with severe mental retardation can work toward long-term goals that they have chosen themselves.

Effort-Attribution Training   Tollefson and colleagues taught junior high school students with learning disabilities to set academic goals by combining goal-setting training and effort-attribution training (Tollefson, Tracy, Johnsen, & Chatman, 1986; Tollefson, Tracy, Johnsen, Farmer, & Buenning, 1984) with self-regulatory training (Tollefson et al., 1986). In both studies, goal setting was taught as a game, in which students could earn tokens to purchase items based on their academic performance. The students set their own performance goals, which were stated in a written contract. In addition, students were taught to evaluate their performance and verbally attribute the reason for the level of their performance to ability, luck, task difficulty, or effort. Tollefson et al. (1986) also taught students to develop a study plan to use to meet their goals and to evaluate their progress by completing a daily progress chart. The authors reported that students in both studies learned to set realistic academic goals (defined as a close correlation between predicted and actual performance), increase their academic performance, and attribute their achievement to the personal effort they expended, rather than to "luck."

Self-Management   Moore, Agran, and Fodor-Davis (1989) taught goal setting in combination with self-management training (i.e., self-instruction and self-reinforcement) and externally managed instruction (i.e., corrective feedback and modeling) to four adults with severe mental retardation who were working in a sheltered workshop. Following self-instruction training, participants were taught to establish production goals for themselves by setting kitchen timers at specified times. Participants were told to instruct themselves to work faster, and praise and corrective feedback were provided, contingent on their performance. Findings indicated that all participants increased their production rates on small assembly tasks. Because a component analysis of the treatment package was not conducted, however, the contribution of the goal-setting component to increases in rate of production could not be identified.

Goal Actualization   Lenz, Ehren, and Smiley (1991) gave instructions in "goal actualization" combined with goal setting to teach secondary-age students with learning disabilities to increase their completion of long-term academic projects (e.g., written reports). The treatment package comprised two phases of instruction: goal setting and goal actualization. During the first phase, students were taught to select and evaluate project-related goals by evaluating task expectation, generating alternatives or options, and clarifying and selecting goals. During the second phase, students were taught to identify steps and strategies to create a plan to facilitate project completion and to monitor step implementation. Goal actualization activities included 1) developing a plan, 2) modifying or expanding the plan, 3) evaluating or analyzing the plan, and 4) monitoring the implementation of the plan through the application of a variety of self-control procedures (e.g., self-reinforcement, self-evaluation, self-monitoring) until the task was completed. Specific strategies for completing each phase were taught through the use of the Student Management Guide (SMG), a form on which students were taught to record their decisions and progress toward goal attainment. A description of the strategies used in each phase of the Goal Attainment System is found in Table 1.

Findings of the study indicated that, following goal attainment training, all students increased the number of academic projects completed successfully and the number of goal-setting and goal-actualization responses made, as described in Table 1. The authors concluded that goal-setting and planning skills can be taught to adolescents with learning disabilities, which may have a positive impact on task completion.

Strategy Training   Planning and writing strategy training was combined with goal setting in a study conducted by Graham, MacArthur, Schwartz, and Page-Voth (1992), which was designed to increase essay-writing skills. Fifth-graders with learning disabilities were taught word processing and composition analysis skills, after which they discussed the goals of training (i.e., learning a strategy for planning and writing better papers) with their instructor and signed a contract indicating they would learn the strategy. The planning and writing strategy comprised three steps:

1. Do PLANS (Pick goals, List ways to meet goals, And, make Notes, Sequence notes).
2. Write and say more.
3. Test goals. (p. 325)

Table 1.   Specific strategies of the SMG goal attainment system

Goal-Setting Component
- **Task Evaluation**
  Identify assignment variables: topic, content, format, length, size, evaluation, resources, location, and time.

  Categorize assignment variables as optional or required.
- **Options Generation**
  Generate options for any of the product-related assignment variables for which an option was given (e.g., topic, content, format, length, size).
- **Goal Specification**
  Create a goal statement that includes the required and optional product-related variables.

Goal Actualization Component
- **Plan Identification**
  List between 6 and 12 major steps to complete the assignment.
- **Plan Expansion**
  Make 6–12 additions to original plan.
- **Demands Consideration**
  Include all of the completion-related assignment variables in the steps (e.g., evaluation, location, resource, time).
- **Self-Monitoring**
  Monitor completion by predicting time for task completion, checking off step completion, evaluating completion of each step, and identifying an appropriate reward for successful task completion.

Adapted from Lenz, Ehren, & Smiley (1991).

The first step, PLANS, involved goal setting, generating possible content for the paper, and sequencing notes. Goal setting focused on three areas: 1) purpose (e.g., writing a paper that will convince my friends), 2) structure (e.g., writing an essay that has all of the necessary parts), and 3) fluency (e.g., writing a paper that is 80 words or longer). Listing ways to meet goals required students to list actual strategies for accomplishing their goals and to attend to the goals when sequencing their notes.

The second step of the strategy (i.e., write and say more) was a self-administered prompt to remind students to continue to plan as they wrote. During the third step (i.e., test goals), students evaluated their papers to determine whether their goals had been accomplished or whether modification in their plans was required. Training of the strategy involved modeling, self-instructing, self-recording, rehearsing, corrective feedback, and verbal praise.

Results indicated that all students improved their writing in three targeted areas: including all basic components in their essays, increasing the length of their papers, and writing convincingly. Improvements also generalized from essay to story writing with the use of short booster training sessions. In addition, social validation measures indicated that students liked the strategy approach and believed that it improved their writing.

Contingency Contracting Miller and Kelly (1994) combined goal setting and contingency contracting to improve the homework performance of elementary school children. Following a parent training session, parents taught the strategies to their own children, using the following method. First, parents recorded whether students brought their homework materials home after school. Next, parents and children divided homework assignments into small, specific goals by using the homework goals worksheet, as shown in Figure 1. Both the parents and children suggested goals, after which a compromise of both their homework goals was recorded (e.g., completing six math problems within the next 10 minutes). Parents and children were instructed to set challenging yet realistic goals and to adjust subsequent goals, as needed. A timer was then set for the amount of time specified in the goal, and the children performed their required tasks. At the end of each goal period, the children determined whether their goal had been met, and their parents confirmed their judgment. The process was repeated until all homework was completed. In addition, each week parents and children negotiated contracts that specified daily and weekly rewards contingent on achievement of homework goals and bringing all homework materials home. An example of a contingency contract is shown in Figure 2.

Findings indicated that overall homework performance improved for all students and that on-task behavior increased for two of the four students. Parent satisfaction data indicated that parents viewed goal setting and contingency contracting as fair and appropriate interventions for improving homework performance and expressed satisfaction with their children's progress. The authors suggested that the strategy may have provided students with a heuristic for completing homework and introduced needed structure into the homework routine. In addition, the students learned to monitor their own behavior, a critical component of self-management programs.

Self-Recording Homework completion was also investigated by Trammel, Schloss, and Alper (1994) in a study that combined self-recording, self-graphing, and goal setting. Secondary education students with learning disabilities were taught to record their assignments on a weekly assignment sheet and were given a piece of gum each day contingent on the accuracy of their recording. Students were then taught to set individual goals for homework completion and to graph their performance. Goals were reviewed every 3 days and adjusted, if necessary. Following training, the number of assignments completed at a prespecified level of accuracy increased for all students. In addition, students and their parents reported satisfaction with the use of the procedure and with the extent of the students' progress. Although the combined strategy was effective, the effects of goal setting could not be separated from the rest of the training package (e.g., self-graphing).

Recruiting Assistance Six youths, ages 17–19 years, with learning disabilities and behavior disorders were taught to set secondary transition goals and to recruit assistance to complete their goals (Balcazar, Keys, & Garate-

Job	Academic subject	Child's goal	Parent's goal	Compromise goal	Time to complete	Achieved goal?
1						
2						
3						
4						

Total number of goals set: _____
Number of goals achieved: _____
Percentage of goals achieved (number achieved/number set): _____

Figure 1. Goal-setting worksheet. (From Miller, D.L., & Kelley, M.L. [1994]. The use of goal setting and contingency contracting for improving children's homework performance. *Journal of Applied Behavior Analysis, 27*, p. 78; reprinted by permission.)

The following materials need to be brought home every day: *homework pad, workbooks, textbooks, pencils*.

If Ann remembers to bring home all of these materials, then she may choose one of the following rewards: *gumballs, 10¢*.

However, if Ann forgets to bring home some of her homework materials, then she: *does not get a snack before bed*.

Ann may choose one of the following rewards if she meets 90%–100% of her goals: *late bedtime (by 20 minutes), 2 stickers* or one of these if she meets 75%–89% of her goals: *soda, 1 sticker*.

If Ann meets *80%* or more of her goals on at least *3* days this week, she may choose one of the following BONUS rewards: *renting a videotape, having a friend from school over to play*.

Child's signature _____   Parent's signature _____

Figure 2.   Sample contingency contract. (From Miller, D.L., & Kelley, M.L. [1994]. The use of goal setting and contingency contracting for improving children's homework performance. *Journal of Applied Behavior Analysis, 27*, p. 79; reprinted by permission.)

Serafini, 1995). The youths were asked to identify several goals of their choice that were functionally related to leaving their residential treatment facility and returning to the community (e.g., finding a job). A sample lesson plan used for teaching goal setting is provided in Figure 3. For each goal, the youths were asked to specify outcomes for three levels of goal attainment: 1) less-than-expected success (e.g., not able to find a job in the community, 2) expected success (e.g., found a job in the community paying minimum wage), and 3) more-than-expected success (e.g., found a job in the community paying above-minimum wage). The youths were then asked to record in a notebook all of the actions they took in order to pursue their goals (e.g., completing a job application). The youths also participated in weekly role-play sessions designed to increase their skills at recruiting assistance in order to complete their goals (e.g., inquiring about job possibilities). In addition, their help-recruiting behaviors were recorded.

Findings indicated that help-recruiting behaviors increased for all youths following training and that, of a total of 17 transition goals generated by the youths (e.g., getting a job), 11 were attained as planned, 4 were still in progress at the end of data collection, and 2 were dropped. The youths also increased the size of their social support networks and reported increased satisfaction with their social skills. Follow-up telephone interviews 1 year later indicated that three of the students were employed and two were receiving training and were working part time. Only one student was not employed or receiving postsecondary education. Although goal setting could not be isolated from the other components of the package (e.g., recruiting assistance), the authors suggested that the

Goal:
Students will understand the concept of a goal and the purpose for setting it.

Method:
Teacher will use the example of a dream to introduce topic; teacher dims lights and explains the process of using your imagination. Students are asked to close their eyes and listen to teacher's voice. Teacher says: "You are asleep, and you wake up 5 years from now. What do you see? Where do you go? Are you alone? How do you get to where you're going?" Teacher gives multiple choices and suggestions to help students see a picture in their minds. Students listen and remember. Students are then asked to share their dreams with a partner in small groups. The sharing of dreams will be audiotaped so that students don't forget their major points. The major points are recorded by teacher, partner, or assistant on large sheets of chart paper with markers. These notes are used to develop specific long-term goals.

Format:
___ Lecture
_X_ Small group
_X_ Large group
___ Role playing
_X_ Discussion/sharing
___ Other

Materials:
___ Overhead projector
___ Video recorder/TV
_X_ Audiotape
___ Slide projector
_X_ Chart paper
___ Markers

Comments:
Next lesson, students will use goals and dreams to develop short-term objectives to set for their specific goals.

Follow-up activity:
_X_ Read/listen pgs.
    (To dream on audiotape)
___ Write:

___ Investigate

___ Practice

Evaluation:
Informal—
_X_ Teacher observation
Formal—Written
_X_ long-term goals

Figure 3. Sample lesson plan for teaching goal setting. (From "Learning to recruit assistance to attain transition goals" by F.E. Balcazar, C.B. Keys, & J. Garate-Serafini, 1995, *Remedial and Special Education, 16,* pp. 245–246. Copyright [1995] by PRO-ED, Inc. Reprinted by permission.)

intervention helped the students focus on their transition goals and understand their own responsibilities and the role others can play in the transition process.

Self-Instructional Training   Hughes et al. (1996) combined goal setting with self-instructional training provided by peers to increase the conversational interactions of four high school students with mental retardation. As suggested by Chadsey-Rusch (1992), interviews were conducted to assess the students' social goals and perceptions of their social skills and social interactions prior to and following intervention. Chadsey-Rusch (1992) argued that participants' goals and self-perceptions rarely are assessed; yet if individuals were more actively involved in setting goals and assessing their needs, social skills instruction may be more effective. Verbal interviews were conducted with the students by asking the open-ended questions shown in Table 2. Interviews were conducted identically pre- and postintervention, with the exception of Question 3, which was asked only after intervention. Preintervention interviews indicated that all four students perceived inadequacies in their social skills and social interactions that they wished to improve. Following peer-delivered, self-instructional training, participants generally indicated that they were satisfied with their performance and had accomplished their goals. For example, participants indicated that it was getting easier to talk to people, that they felt less nervous meeting new people, and that they were beginning to know what to say when meeting someone new. These changes were corroborated by measures of direct observation and behavioral ratings, which indicated that conversational interactions of all participants increased and generalized to new conversational partners following training.

Section Summary

Studies in which goal setting has been introduced as a component of a treatment package have been effective in modifying a variety of behaviors (e.g., rate of production, academic performance, social interaction) across a variety of populations (e.g., adults with mental retardation, elementary school children with learning disabilities, adolescents with behavior disorders) and settings (e.g., school, work, community). Goal setting also was combined with a variety of intervention strategies (e.g., positive reinforcement, self-management training, writing skills training). Although the effects of goal setting were not separated from the other treatment components present in any of the studies, the goal-setting process was shown to be adaptive to many learning situations and participant populations. Further research may help to isolate the effects of goal setting alone on the behavior change process and the extent to which active participation in goal setting influences participant outcomes.

PRACTICAL APPLICATIONS OF GOAL SETTING

In addition to empirical investigations of goal setting, model demonstration programs and conceptual models of goal setting, some of which report explor-

Table 2. Participants' goals and self-perceptions derived from open-ended items on interviews

Question / participant	Preintervention	Postintervention
1. How do you feel when you meet someone new?		
Donna	"Kind of scared."	"Less nervous, now know what to say."
Mandy	"Uncomfortable."	"Fine, I like to talk to new people now."
Daniel	"Meet someone new."	"Feel great when meeting a new student."
Thomas	"I don't know."	"Getting easier to talk to people."
2. What would you like to change about how you act when you meet someone?		
Donna	"Be nicer. Not call them bad words."	"I'm doing good."
Mandy	"Learn to talk."	"I like how I'm doing; I don't need to change."
Daniel	"Meet someone new."	"I'm talking good but want to ask more questions."
Thomas	"Learn to talk to new people."	"I'm doing better."
3. Do you feel you have accomplished your goals being in this project?		
Donna	—	"Yes, I've been doing good, haven't I? I did great on the video."
Mandy	—	"Yes, I'm doing better but want to get better."
Daniel	—	"Yes, I'm doing better at talking and want to talk to new people more."
Thomas	—	"Yes, I can ask more questions and look at them more. I had fun talking to new students."

From Hughes, C., Killian, D.J., & Fischer, G.M. (1996). Validation and assessment of a conversational interaction intervention. *American Journal on Mental Retardation, 100,* p. 498; reprinted by permission of the American Association on Mental Retardation.

201

atory data, have been described in the literature. In this section, we highlight methods and materials that characterize these demonstration programs and conceptual models, which are associated with increases in students' goal-setting skills. Examples are provided to allow teachers to adapt procedures for use with their own students.

Goal-Oriented Approach to Learning (GOAL)

Maher (1982) provided an early demonstration of a goal-setting program, which was designed to facilitate the inclusion of adolescents with learning disabilities into the general education classroom. Eleven high school students with learning disabilities were included in either language arts or mathematics classes. Five students were instructed to apply the Goal-Oriented Approach to Learning (GOAL), and six served as a control group. The GOAL procedure comprises four steps:

1. Goal Setting: Prior to attending the general education class, students and their general education teachers together set an instructional goal for the grading period (e.g., increasing four-digit subtraction skills). The goal is derived from the students' input, past academic performance, and current individualized education program (IEP).
2. Goal Attainment Scaling: Next, the students and teachers develop a scale to evaluate attainment of the goals. The poles of the five-point scale range from "least desired outcome" (e.g., grade point average less than 40%) to "most favored outcome" (e.g., grade point average greater than 69%).
3. Selection of Instructional Strategies: At weekly meetings, the students and teachers discuss the students' academic progress and possible need for changes, and together they develop a written instructional plan for the upcoming week (e.g., implementing a peer tutor program to assist a student).
4. Evaluation of Goal Attainment: At the end of the grading period, students' goal attainment is evaluated, using the goal attainment scale. When a goal has been attained, the students and teachers initiate the GOAL procedure again for the next marking period.

   Preliminary data indicated that the five students who participated in the goal-setting program obtained significantly higher goal attainment scores than did students in the control group. In addition, participating students perceived that the process enhanced their academic achievement as well as their interactions with their teachers.

Goal Setting, Peer Support, and Inclusive Environments

Sherman, Berling, and Oppenheimer (1985) reported findings from a model program in which 14 adolescents diagnosed with physical disabilities (i.e., spina bifida) participated in a summer program to increase their independence and personal growth. At the beginning of the program, the participants identified and prioritized personal goals they wished to achieve during the summer (e.g., developing peer relationships, losing weight, increasing independence in dressing). Next, participants met weekly as a group with program staff to agree on weekly goals and how to reach them. Goal attainment scales ranging from less than expected to greater than expected outcomes were identified, against which the degree of attainment of a goal was evaluated. Attainment of the previous week's goals was acknowledged at the meetings, and successful participants received tokens as awards, which could be cashed in later for small amounts of money. The participants' parents also met weekly with staff to learn how to help their children achieve their personal goals and to build a parent support network. Twenty adolescents served as peer volunteers in the program to assist the participants in achieving their goals (e.g., exercising at a recreation center) and to provide social support. At the end of the summer, participants perceived that they had attained better than expected outcomes on the majority of their goals. Their perceptions were corroborated by direct observation and evaluative feedback from project staff, parents, and volunteers. In addition, the peer volunteers reported that they were developing friendships with the program participants. The authors suggested that the success of the program may have related to the opportunity for participants to establish their own goals, the support provided by the peers, and the inclusive settings in which participants worked on their goals (e.g., community swimming pool).

Goal Setting and Academic Counseling

Kish (1991) combined goal setting with academic counseling to help high school students with learning disabilities achieve academic goals. Kish argued that goal setting is critical to the academic counseling process for students with learning disabilities because

1. Setting goals focuses a student's attention and provides direction in the counseling relationship.
2. The goal-setting process mobilizes the student's energy and effort.
3. Students with clear and realistic goals tend to be more persistent in their efforts to achieve their goals.
4. Setting goals motivates students to search for strategies to accomplish their goals.

Kish (1991) continued that goal statements should be specific and positive (e.g., "I have a right to my feelings and to assert them"). An academic counselor may need to use corrective feedback as students develop their goal statements and, perhaps, ask students to sign a written contract relating to their goals. In addition, the counselor may need to address the following road blocks:

1. Lack of knowledge and information: Some adolescents cannot set goals because they lack information or knowledge. Providing necessary information is an important step in the goal-setting process because it may help students develop a new perspective on their problems.
2. Lack of skills: Lack of skills may prevent students from setting and attaining goals. Counselors may need to help students develop specific skills, such as assertiveness, problem solving, self-management, communication, and decision making.
3. Risk taking: Fear of taking risks may interfere with goal setting. Counselors may need to help adolescents overcome their fear of risk taking through strategies such as role play.
4. Lack of social supports: Adolescents with learning disabilities characteristically have few supportive relationships. Helping them develop support networks may facilitate goal attainment.

Goal Setting and Self-Efficacy

Martino (1993) developed a goal-setting program for middle school students who were at risk for school failure or dropout. Martino argued that the goals adolescents set become their standards for evaluating performance and that their sense of self-efficacy influences the goals they set. If adolescents are fearful or unsure, their future goals are likely to be nonexistent or unrealistic. Teacher assistance is needed to help students who are at risk set realistic short-term goals that are attainable and provide a sense of accomplishment.

Consequently, Martino (1993) developed a structured system of goal setting, goal attainment, and evaluation, which was used successfully in dropout prevention programs at the middle school level. Martino recommended that goals be related to classroom performance, such as punctuality and assignment completion, and that they be set for an entire scholastic grading period (e.g., semester). Goals should be changed during that time only if they are attained or if they are too difficult to achieve. Teachers should try to prevent students from setting goals that are unattainable and that would result in a student's sense of failure. Goals should be scored weekly (e.g., every Friday). Martino recommended that goals be set privately with students, but that scoring should be done publicly within a group of students (unless doing so may embarrass or frighten a student). When scoring publicly, students may share goal achievements or nonachievements and specifics about what was done or what was not done to attain a goal. Teachers should check students' goal attainments in other classes; and at the end of the grading period, the student and teacher should record the total weekly goals achieved throughout the period. Percentage of goals attained should be recorded as a permanent record, and attainment and nonattainment of goals should be discussed by the student and teacher. In addition, new performance goals should be set for the next grading period. Martino reported that middle school students who followed the goal setting and attainment process achieved higher levels of performance than those who did not. Based on classroom observations, Martino argued that for middle schools students who are at risk, use of the goal-setting strategy may be a critical factor in producing consistently higher student achievement.

Goal Setting and Feelings of Self-Competence

Goal setting has also been used to help college students with learning disabilities achieve academic goals. Butler (1994) developed a model program in which participants were taught to recognize important features in a learning task, set appropriate learning goals, select and implement task strategies, monitor goal progress, and adapt goals or strategies, as needed. In addition, the program addressed students' knowledge and beliefs in relation to the task (e.g., perceptions of competence, knowledge of task performance, strategy awareness). Students were taught to define their goals (e.g., "What am I trying to do?"), select a goal strategy (e.g., "How can I achieve my objectives?"), and evaluate goal progress (e.g., "How well do the approaches I use work?"). Butler argued that as students develop and implement effective strategies and monitor the positive impact of their performance, their feelings of competence and self-control should increase. Such an increase was demonstrated through multiple measures in a case study of six college students with learning disabilities who participated in the model program (Butler, 1994).

Section Summary

Model demonstration programs and implementations of conceptual models have provided the practical application of goal setting in addressing a variety of problems related to a successful transition into adulthood for students with disabilities. Goal setting has been shown to be an effective procedure related to increases in students' achievement and perceptions of competence. In its practical application, goal setting typically is an element of an instructional program that allows students to be actively involved in their educational process. Teachers may find that by incorporating goal setting into their current teaching procedures, students may increase their performance achievements.

CONCLUSION

Federal special education legislation (e.g., the Individuals with Disabilities Education Act of 1990) requires educators to consider students' goals and preferences when designing their educational programs. Many students, however, may not have had the opportunity or may lack the skills to set their own goals. In this chapter, we have provided a conceptual basis for goal setting, including factors related to motivation, self-management, range of personal experiences, and behavioral consequences. Empirical and practical applications of goal-setting programs were reviewed, with illustrations to guide teachers in implementing the procedures with their own students. In general, across applications, teaching students to set their own goals was found to increase the effectiveness of instructional programs.

Teachers who are interested in incorporating goal setting into their students' IEPs may be pleasantly surprised to learn that goal setting is relatively easy to implement. The applications reviewed indicate that excessive time or materials are not needed to teach students goal-setting skills. For limited investment on the part of the teacher, the effects of a goal-setting program may be pervasive for a student (e.g., successfully passing a class, learning a new job skill, developing friendships). Furthermore, there is some indication that students' sense of self-esteem, competence, and confidence may improve as a result of attaining their goals (e.g., Butler, 1994).

Based on our review of goal-setting applications, we have several recommendations:

1.   Much of the published work in the area of goal setting has focused on students with mild disabilities, such as students with learning disabilities. We suggest that an increased emphasis be placed on increasing the goal-setting skills of students with more severe disabilities, such as those with mental retardation who require limited to extensive supports or those with serious emotional disturbance. The few investigations that have been conducted with students with more severe disabilities (e.g., Balcazar et al., 1995; Flexer et al., 1979) have demonstrated that teaching goal setting relates to a variety of favorable outcomes (e.g., increasing productivity, delaying immediate gratification in favor of long-term goals, maintaining employment).

2.   Few investigators have asked students to compare their goals before and after participation in an educational program (e.g., Chadsey-Rusch, 1992; Hughes et al., 1996). If students are to be active participants in their educational programming, it is critical that they not only have the opportunity to set their own goals, but that they also continually evaluate whether they are achieving their goals.

3.   Future research should attempt to isolate the effects of goal setting from other components of an intervention package. Goal setting in combination with other procedures (e.g., self-management, contingency contracting, planning strategy training) has been found to be effective in achieving instructional objectives. The role of goal setting in the behavioral change paradigm, however, has not yet been identified. Furthermore, the effects of having individuals state their goals publicly should be investigated further (e.g., Hayes et al., 1985).

With a focus on goal setting and task attainment, it is possible that outcomes for students receiving special education services, such as Kevin O'Hara, will more closely resemble the positive situation described in the following case study, rather than the negative outcomes described for him previously (see previous case study).

When Kevin O'Hara turned 14 and entered the ninth grade, he was asked by his resource room teacher, Ms. Martin, to attend his annual individualized education program (IEP) meeting. Although Kevin had been diagnosed with a learning disability when he was in elementary school, this was the first time he had been asked to attend his own IEP meeting. When he asked his mother about it, she said something about the new IDEA legislation requiring that students be invited to attend IEP meetings when transition goals were being discussed. Kevin, however, had no idea what she meant by transition goals.

The next week, when he arrived at the meeting with his mother, Ms. Martin asked Kevin what sort of job he would like to get or what school he would like to attend when he graduated from high school. Kevin was surprised because no teacher had asked him that before. He suddenly realized that he had no idea what he wanted to do after high school. Ms. Martin also asked him what personal goals he wished to achieve during high school. Kevin had really never thought about what he wanted to achieve before and didn't know what to say. Kevin's IEP team then decided that it would be helpful if Kevin visited with Mr. Brinker, the ninth-grade counselor, before his long-term goals were developed for his IEP. The team wanted Kevin to provide input into his educational goals, and Mr. Brinker had recently developed a program that helped students with learning disabilities, like Kevin, to set, attain, and evaluate their own goals. The IEP team agreed that they would reconvene the meeting after Kevin was clearer about what he hoped to accomplish during his high school years.

During their first meeting, Mr. Brinker helped Kevin explore his immediate goals for the semester. Kevin began to realize that he really wanted to enroll in a general education math class, instead of the resource class. Together, Kevin and Mr. Brinker outlined the outcomes Kevin hoped to achieve in the class and a strategy that would help him achieve these outcomes. They decided that a peer tutor from the math class would be the most helpful. Kevin and Mr. Brinker agreed to meet weekly to determine the extent to which Kevin was achieving his goals and to adjust his goals, if necessary. They decided that, for now, Kevin would try to maintain a 75% average in the class and would have all assignments done on time. Kevin realized that being in the general education classroom was something he had wanted for a long time but never had admitted to himself.

During subsequent visits, Kevin continued to monitor his progress in his math class with Mr. Brinker. They were both pleased that he was actually exceeding his expected goal by maintaining an 80% average. Another goal was added for Kevin to begin to make friends with some of the students in his class. Also, Mr. Brinker and Kevin began to discuss some of Kevin's long-term goals after graduation. They decided that one goal would be for Kevin to attend a career education class next semester in order for Kevin to begin to find out a career in which he was interested. The career education class was geared toward giving students an opportunity to visit different community businesses, trade schools, and local colleges.

During the next few years, Kevin was able to gain enough experience in the community to realize that what he really wanted to do was become an electrician. He set a long-term goal to attend the local technical school when he graduated from high school and to become trained in his chosen field. Now that he knew where he was going in life, Kevin felt much happier. Because he had learned to evaluate his own progress, he felt motivated to set and work toward one goal after another. He was pleased, too, that he had made lasting friendships in his general education classrooms and that he no longer felt lost and confused about his future. He couldn't wait to graduate from high school and get started on his way to becoming an electrician!

QUESTIONS FOR REVIEW

1. Briefly describe the behavioral explanation of the goal-setting process.
2. Mithaug et al. (1988) surveyed the literature on motivation. Give four specific strategies used by highly successful, self-determined people in order to set goals and act to attain them.
3. Agran (1997) suggested that without goal setting, self-management programs may be compromised. Briefly discuss the effect of goal setting on self-management.
4. The chapter states that an individual's ability to set goals relates to the quality and variety of his or her everyday life experiences. Explain the effect of everyday life experiences on goal setting by using a brief example of an individual who has lived a restricted or sheltered life.
5. Explain the reasons individuals face a dilemma when setting and pursuing a goal, and give three methods with which to solve the dilemma.
6. Several studies were conducted to compare the effectiveness of self-selected versus teacher-selected goals. Briefly summarize the research results, and give their rationale for these findings.
7. A number of investigations evaluated the effects of goal setting as a component of a treatment package combined with a variety of intervention strategies (e.g., effort-attribution training, self-management training, goal-attainment training, planning and writing strategy training, contingency contracting, self-recording training, self-instructional training). Choose two treatment packages and briefly describe the overall procedure and findings of each treatment package.
8. Lenz et al. (1991) developed a goal-attainment training program to teach secondary students with learning disabilities to increase their completion of long-term academic projects. Briefly describe two phases of instruction: goal setting and goal actualization.
9. The chapter describes several model demonstration programs and conceptual models that are associated with increases in student's goal-setting skills. Apply one specific model program for a student who has a lack of goal-setting skills and describe the overall procedure.
10. List recommendations for future studies in the area of goal setting.

REFERENCES

Agran, M. (Ed.). (1997). *Student directed learning: Teaching self-determination skills.* Pacific Grove, CA: Brooks/Cole.

Baer, D.M. (1984). Does research on self-control need more control? *Analysis and Intervention in Developmental disabilities, 4,* 211–218.

Balcazar, F.E., Keys, C.B., & Garate-Serafini, J. (1995). Learning to recruit assistance to attain transition goals. *Remedial and Special Education, 16,* 237–246.

Bandura, A. (1969). *Principles of behavior modification.* New York: Holt, Rinehart & Winston.

Bandura, A. (1977). *Social learning theory.* Englewood Cliffs, NJ: Prentice Hall.

Bolstad, O.D., & Johnson, S.M. (1972). Self-regulation in the modification of disruptive classroom behavior. *Journal of Applied Behavior Analysis, 5,* 443–454.

Brigham, T.A. (1978). Self-control: Part II. In A.C. Catania & T.A. Brigham (Eds.), *Handbook of applied behavior analysis: Social and instructional processes* (pp. 259–274). New York: Irvington.

Brownell, K.D., Colletti, G., Ersner-Hershfield, R., Hershfield, S.M., & Wilson, G.T. (1977). Self-control in school children: Stringency and leniency in self-determined and externally imposed performance standards. *Behavior Therapy, 8,* 442–455.

Butler, D.L. (1994). From learning strategies to strategic learning: Promoting self-regulated learning by postsecondary students with learning disabilities. *Canadian Journal of Special Education, 9,* 69–101.

Catania, A.C. (1984). *Learning* (2nd ed.). Englewood Cliffs, NJ: Prentice Hall.

Chadsey-Rusch, J. (1992). Toward defining and measuring social skills in employment settings. *American Journal on Mental Retardation, 96,* 405–418.

Dickerson, E.A., & Creedon, C.F. (1981). Self-selection of standards by children: The relative effectiveness of pupil-selected and teacher-selected standards of performance. *Journal of Applied Behavior Analysis, 14,* 425–433.

Farnum, M., Brigham, T.A., & Johnson, G. (1977). *A comparison of the effects of teacher determined and student determined contingencies on arithmetic performance.* Unpublished manuscript, Washington State University, Department of Psychology, Pullman.

Felixbrod, J.J., & O'Leary, K.D. (1973). Effects of reinforcement on children's academic behavior as a function of self-determined and externally imposed contingencies. *Journal of Applied Behavior Analysis, 6,* 241–250.

Flexer, R.W., Newbery, J.F., & Martin, A.S. (1979). Use of goal setting procedures in increasing task assembly rate of severely retarded workers. *Education and Training of the Mentally Retarded, 14,* 177–184.

Glynn, E.L. (1970). Classroom applications of self-determined reinforcement. *Journal of Applied Behavior Analysis, 3,* 123–132.

Graham, S., MacArthur, C., Schwartz, S., & Page-Voth, V. (1992). Improving the compositions of students with learning disabilities using a strategy involving product and process goal setting. *Exceptional Children, 58,* 322–334.

Hayes, S.C., Rosenfarb, I., Wulfert, E., Munt, E.D., Korn, Z., & Zettle, R. (1985). Self-reinforcement effects: An artifact of social standard setting? *Journal of Applied Behavior Analysis, 18,* 201–214.

Hughes, C., Killian, D.J., & Fischer, G.M. (1996). Validation and assessment of a conversational interaction intervention. *American Journal on Mental Retardation, 100,* 493–509.

Hughes, C., & Lloyd, J.W. (1993). An analysis of self-management. *Journal of Behavioral Education, 4,* 405–425.

Individuals with Disabilities Education Act (IDEA) of 1990, PL 101-476, 20 U.S.C. §§ 1400 *et seq.*

Kish, M. (1991). Counseling adolescents with LD. *Intervention in School and Clinic, 27,* 20–24.

Kishi, G., Teluicksingh, B., Zollers, N., Park-Lee, S., & Meyer, L. (1988). Daily decision-making in community residences: A social comparison of adults with and without mental retardation. *American Journal on Mental Retardation, 92,* 430–435.

Lenz, B.K., Ehren, B.J., & Smiley, L.R. (1991). A goal attainment approach to improve completion of project-type assignments by adolescents with learning disabilities. *Learning Disabilities & Practice, 6,* 166–176.

Lovitt, T.C., & Curtiss, K.A. (1969). Academic response rate as a function of teacher- and self-imposed contingencies. *Journal of Applied Behavior Analysis, 2,* 49–53.

Maher, C.A. (1982). Learning disabled adolescents in the regular classroom: Evaluation of a mainstreaming procedure. *Learning Disability Quarterly, 5,* 82–84.

Mahoney, M.J., & Thoresen, C.E. (1974). Behavioral self-control. In M.J. Mahoney & C.E. Thoresen (Eds.), *Self-control: Power to the person* (pp. 20–26). Monterey, CA: Brooks/Cole.

Malott, R.W. (1984). Rule-governed behavior, self-management, and the developmentally disabled: A theoretical analysis. *Analysis and Intervention in Developmental Disabilities, 4,* 199–209.

Martin, J.E., & Marshall, L.H. (1997). Choice making: Description of a model project. In M. Agran (Ed.), *Student directed learning: Teaching self-determination skills* (pp. 224–248). Pacific Grove, CA: Brooks/Cole.

Martino, L.R. (1993). A goal-setting model for young adolescent at risk students. *Middle School Journal, 24,* 19–22.

Miller, D.L., & Kelly, M.L. (1994). The use of goal setting and contingency contracting for improving children's homework performance. *Journal of Applied Behavior Analysis, 27,* 73–84.

Mithaug, D.E., Martin, J.E., Agran, M., & Rusch, F.R. (1988). *Why special education graduates fail: How to teach them to succeed.* Colorado Springs, CO: Ascent Publications.

Moore, S.C., Agran, M., & Fodor-Davis, J. (1989). Using self-management strategies to increase the production rates of workers with severe handicaps. *Education and Training in Mental Retardation, 24,* 324–332.

Rachlin, H. (1978). Self-control: Part I. In A.C. Catania & T.A. Brigham (Eds.), *Handbook of applied behavior analysis: Social and instructional processes* (pp. 246–258). New York: Irvington.

Rosenbaum, M.S., & Drabman, R.S. (1979). Self-control training in the classroom: A review and critique. *Journal of Applied Behavior Analysis, 12,* 467–485.

Schunk, D.H. (1985). Participation in goal setting: Effects on self-efficacy and skills of learning disabled children. *Journal of Special Education, 19,* 307–317.

Sherman, R.G., Berling, B.S., & Oppenheimer, S. (1985). Increasing community independence for adolescents with spina bifida. *Adolescence, 20,* 1–13.

Skinner, B.F. (1953). *Science and human behavior.* New York: Macmillan.

Smith, D.J., & Nelson, J.R. (1997). In M. Agran (Ed.), *Student directed learning: Teaching self-determination skills* (pp. 80–110). Pacific Grove, CA: Brooks/Cole.

Stancliffe, R., & Wehmeyer, M.L. (1995). Variability in the availability of choice to adults with mental retardation. *Journal of Vocational Rehabilitation, 5,* 319–328.

Tollefson, N., Tracy, D.B., Johnsen, E.P., & Chatman, J. (1986). Teaching learning disabled students goal-implementation skills. *Psychology in the Schools, 23,* 194–204.

Tollefson, N., Tracy, D.B., Johnsen, E.P., Farmer, A.W., & Buenning, M. (1984). Goal setting and personal responsibility training for LD adolescents. *Psychology in the Schools, 21,* 224–233.

Trammell, D.L., Schloss, P.J., & Alper, S. (1994). Using self-recording, evaluation, and graphing to increase completion of homework assignments. *Journal of Learning Disabilities, 27,* 75–81.

West, M.D. (1995). Choice, self-determination and VR services: Systemic barriers for consumers with severe disabilities. *Journal of Vocational Rehabilitation, 5,* 281–290.

Promoting
Self-Advocacy
and Leadership Skills

CHAPTER 10

Teaching Assertiveness and Effective Communication Skills

After reading this chapter, you will be able to

1. Define assertive behavior and discuss its role in expressing one's rights

2. List skills that are critical for the development of assertive behavior

3. Discuss four methods of assessing assertive behavior skills and their utility in intervention

4. Discuss the differences among assertive, nonassertive, and aggressive behavior

5. Identify other key communication skills that are important to self-determination

KEY TERMS

1. Aggressive behavior
2. Assertive behavior
3. Assertiveness training
4. Behavior change requests
5. Behavior rehearsal
6. Coaching
7. Covert assertive behavior skills
8. Generalization
9. Listening skills
10. Modeling
11. Nonassertive behavior
12. Nonverbal behavior
13. Overt assertive behavior skills
14. Paralinguistic elements of assertive behavior
15. Social skills training programs

Self-advocacy skills are critically important if students with disabilities are to become independent, self-determined young people. Two of the most frequently identified self-advocacy skills are assertive behavior and effective communication skills. These two essential self-advocacy skills are, in practice, so closely linked that they are often discussed as one entity...assertive communication (Wilson, 1994).

George and Rosa (see the following case studies) approach problem situations with different strategies. George is passive and nonassertive, whereas Rosa responds aggressively. Although their responses are very different, they both find that their strategies share a common characteristic...they are largely unsuccessful. Both students could benefit from instruction in assertive behavior and effective communication skills to learn to resolve their problems successfully. These skills become particularly important during the transition years. From negotiating for a raise at one's job to interacting with other people in the community, successful adults use effective and assertive communication skills almost daily. This chapter describes instructional strategies to teach assertive behaviors and to promote more effective communication skills.

George is a junior this year. One of his favorite classes is gym class. He likes almost everything about gym class...except picking up the wet towels in the locker room every day. The physical education teacher, Coach Lofton, gave the responsibility for handing out locker room duties to Brian, who is also a junior. One of the duties is to pick up the towels left around the locker room. All of the class members are supposed to pick up their own towels and put them in the laundry cart. No matter how many times class members are told, however, there are always towels draped over benches or hanging from empty lockers, and someone has to pick them up. George doesn't mind taking his turn picking up the towels, but he is beginning to suspect that he and one other student are handling towel duty more than any other class members. In fact, he is pretty certain that some of his classmates, who just happen to be buddies with Brian, are not doing their share of the work around the locker room.

George likes Brian all right, except for his suspicion that Brian is taking advantage of him. However, George is concerned about talking about the problem and figures it is easier just to do what he is told...pick up towels. George is afraid that Brian won't like him or will get angry with him if he talks to him about the situation. George hates when people get angry with him, but he sure doesn't like doing everyone else's job. He wishes he could figure out a better way to deal with the situation.

Now that she has calmed down, Rosa is beginning to feel bad about blowing up at Drew. Drew and Rosa share a homeroom class and third-period math. After third period, they usually leave campus and go down to the taco place at the end of the block for lunch. Rosa just can't stomach the school cafeteria food!

Anyway, Drew has a bad habit of borrowing money for lunch and then not paying it back. The person she often borrows that money from is Rosa, and Rosa was getting tired of loaning her money and then never seeing it again. The last time that Drew had hit her up for some cash, Rosa had exploded. She had called Drew a lot of names, told her that she wanted all of the money she owed her right then, and then stomped off in a rage.

Rosa felt that she was right to be angry about Drew's borrowing habit. Rosa worked part time at the downtown grocery store to earn some spending money. Drew didn't work and seemed to think that money was easy to come by. However, Drew and Rosa had become pretty good friends, and she hated to risk losing a friend. When Rosa had stormed off, she had looked back at Drew, who was standing in the taco place looking uncomfortable and red-faced.

Now Rosa was thinking that maybe yelling and becoming angry wasn't the best way to handle the situation. It wasn't like this was the first time that Rosa had flown off the handle. It seemed like things got her angry, but she let them sit and broil until she finally blew her top. There must be a better way to handle her anger; she wished she could figure something out.

CONCEPTUALIZING ASSERTIVE BEHAVIOR

Like self-determination, assertiveness has been conceptualized in a number of ways, including 1) as a basic human right, 2) as the expression of honest or appropriate emotions, 3) as a specific response class, and 4) as based on functional properties of the response class (Rakos, 1991). The earliest definitions developed for intervention purposes focused on assertiveness as the expression of emotions. Wolpe (1969) defined assertiveness as "any overt expression of spontaneous and appropriate feelings other than anxiety" (p. 19). Rimm and Masters (1979) defined assertive behavior as "interpersonal behavior involving the honest and straightforward expression of thoughts and feelings" (p. 63). Rimm and Masters described the intent of their definition as "to convey a sense of what most writers and practitioners mean when they use the term assertive behavior" (p. 63). These definitions were limited, however, because they were not intended to provide direction for practitioners and, consequently, had limited pragmatic utility.

Definitions that identified assertive behavior based on a specific response class provided more practical direction. Rakos (1991) provided one of the first such attempts, defining assertive behavior as "the ability to say 'no,' the ability to ask for favors or to make requests, the ability to express positive and negative feelings, the ability to initiate, continue and terminate general conversations" (p. 697). The primary drawback of these definitions lies in the fact that any attempt to define assertiveness by listing behaviors will not only be cumbersome but also will almost certainly omit some behaviors. Later definitions tried to overcome this limitation by expanding the list of assertive responses from specific behaviors to categories of assertive behavior, such as defining assertive behavior as refusal, request, or commendatory responses (Rakos, 1991).

For the same reasons that we have defined self-determination based on the functional properties (i.e., essential characteristics) of individual responses or behaviors, it seems most useful to define assertive behavior based on the functional properties of a specific response class of behaviors, instead of by the behaviors themselves. Rakos suggested that a functional definition offered by Rich and Schroeder (1976) has particular utility for practice. Rich and Schroeder defined assertive behavior as

> the skills to seek, maintain, or enhance reinforcement in an interpersonal situation through the expression of feelings or wants when such expression risks loss of reinforcement or even punishment. The degree of assertiveness may be measured by the effectiveness of an individual's response in producing, maintaining or enhancing reinforcement. (1976, p. 1084)

Rakos (1991) identified several performance implications in this functional definition. First, the definition identifies assertiveness as a learned skill and as a function of the situation and the interaction of the person and that situation. Second, according to Rakos, the definition makes clear that "assertion is an expressive skill, composed of verbal and nonverbal response components and performed in an interpersonal context in which there is some risk of negative reaction by the recipient" (p. 10). Finally, Rakos noted that assertiveness is both defined and measured by outcomes of the behavior.

Research has indicated that there are both overt (i.e., observable) behavioral components and covert (i.e., nonobservable) behavioral components of assertive behavior. This chapter focuses primarily on the overt behavioral components; however, many of the covert components important to assertive behavior are described elsewhere in the text, including perceptions of control (Chapter 14) and positive attributions of efficacy (Chapter 15), problem-solving skills (Chapter 6), self-monitoring skills (Chapter 7), and self-instructional skills (Chapter 8).

Overt Response Components

Rakos proposed three categories for overt response components of assertive behavior:

1. Content: the verbal behavior of the asserter, or what the individual says to the other person(s).
2. Paralinguistic elements: the vocal characteristics of the verbal behavior, or how the asserter sounds.
3. Nonverbal behaviors: the body movements and facial expressions that accompany the verbal behavior, or how the asserter appears. (1991, p. 25)

The content of assertive behaviors reflects two response categories: the expression of rights and the expression of elaborations. Elaborations are the "extra" aspects of the content that are part of successful assertive communications. Examples of these extras include explanations as to why one is expressing a specific right; an acknowledgment of the feelings or rights of the other person; compromises and alternatives; and, in some circumstances, apologies.

The expression of rights is, according to Rakos (1991), the core of any assertion. The content of any assertion will contain a verbalization of desire, affect, or opinion. Rakos proposed that the expression of rights can take several forms, including the following:

- Refusals (e.g., "No, thank you, I am not interested in contributing at this time")
- Behavior change requests (e.g., "I would like you to ____")
- Expression of an unpopular or different opinion (e.g., "I disagree with ____")

Students with disabilities vary in the degree to which they need instruction in expressing rights or in employing elaborations. Students with behavior disorders may be perfectly capable of expressing their opinions, wants, or needs, yet have very limited skills using appropriate elaborations so that they can actually achieve their desired outcome. Students with mental retardation, however, may have had limited opportunities to express their needs, and they may need instruction in that particular area.

Paralinguistic elements refer to the verbal characteristics of assertive behaviors. Instruction focuses on topics like voice characteristics (e.g., how loudly or softly the assertion is made, voice intonation and inflection, voice firmness) and characteristics of the response, including duration and fluency. Nonverbal behavioral components include eye contact, facial expressions, gestures, and body language. Students with disabilities typically can benefit from instruction in both paralinguistic and nonverbal components of assertive behavior. (More details about nonverbal behaviors are provided later in this chapter.)

Rakos (1991) also identified a series of process skills that affect the success of assertive behaviors. Such skills include response timing, or the degree to which a person responds to the situational cues during the interaction. Unskilled or inexperienced individuals fail to time their vocalizations and gestures, allowing long periods of silence or responding too quickly (Rakos, 1991). The degree to which someone both initiates an assertive behavior and persists in actions to achieve a desired outcome is also important in the relative success of the interaction.

Covert Response Components

We have indicated that there are critical cognitive skills that must be gained for students to become self-determined. This is true for assertive behaviors as well. Rakos (1991) listed the following covert skills as being necessary to asserting oneself:

- Interpersonal problem-solving skills
- Knowledge
- Philosophical beliefs

- Self-efficacy and outcome expectations
- Self-instruction skills
- Self-monitoring skills
- Social perception skills

One can easily see where other self-management skills, such as self-reinforcement or self-evaluation skills, are also needed to become assertive. Although most of these covert response components are not addressed in this chapter because they are topics of other chapters (see Chapters 7, 8, 9, and 14), they should be considered when providing instruction in assertive behavior.

TEACHING ASSERTIVE BEHAVIOR

There are several strategies that can be used to teach assertive behavior. The most commonly cited strategy is assertiveness training (AT). This strategy and others are discussed in this section.

Assertiveness Training

Assertiveness training originated with the work of Salter (1949) and Wolpe (Wolpe, 1969; Wolpe & Lazarus, 1966) and quickly became one of the most widely used interventions to promote assertive behaviors (Rakos, 1991). Social skills training programs, which are frequently used to teach social skills such as assertive behavior to students with disabilities, essentially were formed based on the assertiveness training model (Bates, 1980; Bornstein, Bellack, & Hersen, 1977). The term *assertiveness training* has been applied to several intervention programs that share similar, though not identical, procedures (Rimm & Masters, 1979). At the core of AT is a multicomponent package built on behavioral rehearsal and including the basic elements of modeling, coaching, feedback, and homework assignments (Rakos, 1991).

Joyce and Weil (1980) noted that AT, as a teaching model, is based on behavioral models of learning and instruction. Teaching models in this family—which in addition to AT include contingency management, self-control through operant methods, stress reduction, and systematic desensitization—were developed based on research in behavior theory, including both operant and counter-conditioning (Joyce & Weil, 1980).

Roffman (1993) summarized the basic elements of AT as including 1) modeling, 2) behavior rehearsal, 3) reinforcement, 4) feedback and coaching, 5) positive self-statement training, 6) relaxation training, and 7) homework assignments. Table 1 provides a summary of these elements and some activities involved in their performance, particularly as they pertain to transition. A practical example of how to use AT to teach assertiveness skills to George (see previous case study) is provided in Figure 1.

Assertiveness training has been widely used and its efficacy documented in the general population and within targeted populations, including people with

Table 1.   Assertiveness training model for transition

Basic element	Activities
Modeling	Instructor or other exemplar models inappropriate and appropriate behavioral responses. Models can be presented live, on video, or audio. Most effective model is someone close to the trainees in age, gender, and social characteristics but with a slightly higher social status. Modeling is most effective when models focus on coping skills and start at the level of the trainee (e.g., express same fears).
Behavior rehearsal	Generally involves role playing or acting out situation with feedback and suggestions for improvement from trainer or (if used in group setting) other group members.
Reinforcement	Acknowledging or praising assertive behaviors in clear, nonjudgmental manner and specific to the behavior performed.
Feedback and coaching	Corrective feedback involving specific suggestions for improving assertive responses. Often better received if positive aspects of performance are articulated first.
Positive self-statement training	Teaching participants to engage in self-directed verbalizations that are positive and reinforce use of assertive behaviors.
Relaxation training	Teaching participants strategies to decrease physiological (and physical) arousal and stress inherent in assertive communications.
Homework assignments	Provide opportunities for skills generalization and repeated practice sessions.

Adapted from Roffman (1993).

substance abuse problems, depression, anxiety disorders and other psychiatric disorders, as well as with populations defined by demographic characteristics (e.g., women, children, older adults) (Rakos, 1991). Individuals with disabilities have also been shown to benefit from AT, although the literature base is limited compared with studies of AT with other groups of people.

Bates (1980) conducted weekly group training sessions with adults with mental retardation. The purpose of the sessions was to increase several social skills, including one skill important to assertiveness—differing with others. The training strategies included modeling, behavior rehearsal, coaching, structured feedback, contingent incentives, and homework assignments. Participants acquired each of the social skills successfully. Kirkland and Caughlin-Carver (1982) recruited 28 adults with mental retardation to examine the efficacy of AT with this population. Participants were randomly assigned to an experimental and a control group. The experimental group received AT and was judged (based on ratings of videotaped role-play responses to specific problem situations) to be more assertive than the control group. Participants in the control group then took assertiveness training and showed significant improvement in

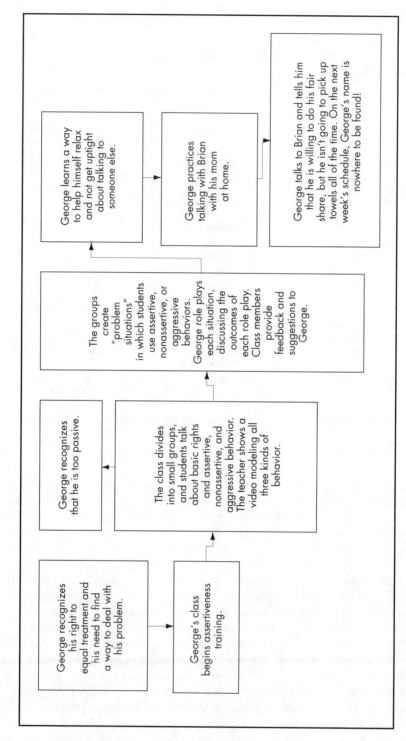

Figure 1. Assertiveness training strategy with George.

their assertiveness skills. Bregman (1984) used assertiveness training with 128 adults with mental retardation, with participants showing enhanced assertiveness skills and a more internalized locus of control. Glueckauf and Quittner (1992) used assertiveness training to improve the assertiveness skills of adults who used wheelchairs, and they determined that the intervention had the additional benefits of improving acceptance of disability by the participants and of enhanced efficacy expectations. Morgan and Leung (1980) also used AT with students with physical disabilities to increase acceptance of disability.

Other Instructional Strategies

Although the most common strategy identified in the literature to teach assertive behaviors is AT, it may be more appropriate in some circumstances to focus on individual skill areas and to teach these skills using another teaching strategy instead of implementing an entire AT program. Some students may already be competent in most skill areas related to assertive behavior and require instruction in one area only. For example, a student may need to learn how to use body language more effectively, yet not need instruction in expressing feelings or providing elaborations. Many AT strategies, however, require that students employ skills that some students with special learning needs may lack. Thus, a student with mental retardation may need instruction to understand basic rights, as described subsequently, before learning to assert those rights.

Social Skills Training   Social skills training programs emerged as a response to consistent findings that students with disabilities lacked essential social skills, one of which is assertive behavior, and that such deficits resulted in diminished social competence. Social skills training programs have their historical roots in AT (Bates, 1980), and most social skills training programs incorporate instructional elements that are also involved in the AT process, such as role playing, modeling, and rehearsal. Unlike assertiveness training, social skills training typically refers more to the content of the instructional effort (e.g., specific social skills) than to a specific process or procedure. Thus, social skills training programs share fewer components than those shared by different AT programs and often employ only one strategy as opposed to a series of basic elements, as is the case with AT.

The starting point for social skills training is to identify the skill(s) a student needs and then match the identified skill(s) with effective instructional activities. Table 2 provides a list of some assertive behavior skills. The identification of target assertive behavior skills for intervention purposes involves a combination of assessment strategies, including

Observation of naturally occurring behavior: Perhaps the simplest assessment procedure, and the logical first step, is to observe a student's behavior in situations in which opportunities to display assertive behavior are available. It is advisable to code these observations in some manner, either through longhand

222 Promoting Self-Advocacy and Leadership Skills

Table 2. Skills needed for assertiveness

Skill area	Discrete skills
Expression of rights	Identifies and articulates rights
	Identifies and articulates associated responsibilities
	Discriminates conflicts between rights of individual(s) and groups
	Identifies and articulates personal beliefs and values
	Identifies and articulates differences among assertive, non-assertive, and aggressive behaviors
	Discriminates among statements of wants, needs, opinion, and fact
	Understands inherent risk factor in assertion
Verbal assertion skills	Expresses rights statement in brief, concise, and direct manner
	Communicates rights statement in first person
	Discriminates between and employs refusals and behavior change requests
	Communicates opinions and beliefs appropriately
	Employs appropriate tone of voice
	Uses intonation and timing effectively
	Responds appropriately to aggression and persists in assertion
Nonverbal assertion skills	Uses and understands body language
	Uses gestures and facial expressions appropriately
	Makes eye contact appropriately
	Uses appropriate posture and body positioning
Expression of elaborations	Communicates understanding of others' feelings, opinions, or experiences
	Employs negotiation, compromise, and persuasion skills
	Modulates voice characteristics to match elaboration
Conversation skills	Practices active listening skills

records, event recording, or behavioral counts. Such observations can form the basis for developing behavioral checklists, which could be used both to code future natural observations and to create teacher, parent, and student self-report checklists.

Completing behavioral checklists: Another means of gathering information about assertiveness is to complete behavioral checklists. Such lists of assertive behaviors can be generated from observations or compiled from behaviors reported in the literature. Items should be worded in an active voice (e.g., Sara makes eye contact with other person). In addition to using checklists as coding sheets for student observations, such lists can be completed by the teacher, student, and/or his or her family members.

Role-play assessments: One drawback to observations in natural settings (e.g., school settings) is that the opportunities to observe students interacting in an assertive manner are relatively limited. In addition, simply the presence of an observer in specific settings can alter the behavior. One alternative is to develop role-play scenarios in which students respond to a scripted problem situation. Teachers can identify areas of strengths and limitations across a number of settings in which assertive behavior would be useful.

Self-monitoring: Student self-monitoring of behavior can be both an effective assessment tool and intervention strategy. Teachers can work with students to identify assertive behaviors and ask students to monitor and in some manner record when they use such behaviors. It is prudent not to use self-monitoring as the sole assessment strategy because having students attend to specific behaviors will probably increase the likelihood that they will perform those behaviors, making the assessment less useful.

There are other assessment strategies, including sociometric ratings (e.g., asking classmates and peers to identify fellow students who are assertive), standardized self-report measures, and analogue assessments (i.e., situations in which a student will need to be assertive are contrived within the typical environment). It is likely that educators will need to employ more than one of these methods in order to determine which behaviors warrant instructional intervention.

Korinek and Polloway (1993) synthesized the instructional strategies employed across a variety of social skills training programs to teach social skills as part of a general instructional sequence, which is presented in Table 3. The similarity in this training sequence and assertiveness training is readily apparent.

Numerous examples appear in the literature where these social skills training strategies, in various combinations and with additions or alterations, have been used effectively to promote assertive behavior for individuals with disabil-

Table 3. Social skills training instructional steps

Instructional step	Activities
Introduce skill and rationale.	Tell student what the skill involves, how it relates to other skills they know, and why they should learn the skill.
Discuss situations and examples.	Provide guided discussion, using frequent examples of situations in which the skill is useful, and discuss consequences of not employing skills. Students should be guided to identify alternative options for action and the consequences of each option.
Identify skill steps.	Provide in-depth analysis of each step of the skill, including verbal and nonverbal behaviors. Skill steps can be listed and then checked off to encourage self-evaluation and self-monitoring.
Model the skill.	Appropriate and inappropriate responses can be modeled, either live or through video, audio, or print materials.
Rehearse with feedback and reinforcement.	Student practices skill until mastery is achieved. Instructor may include role-play and massed-trial procedures.
Generalize to other settings and situations.	Student has opportunities to perform behavior in additional settings, preferably within the student's typical environment.

Adapted from Korinek & Polloway (1993).

ities, including children and adolescents with hearing impairments (Lemanek, Williamson, Gresham, & Jensen, 1986), adults and students with mental retardation (Bornstein, Bach, McFall, Friman, & Lyons, 1980; Korinek & Polloway, 1993; Senatore, Matson, & Kazdin, 1982), and adults and students with emotional and behavior disorders (Bornstein, Bellack, & Hersen, 1980; Liberman, DeRisi, & Mueser, 1989).

A common problem associated with both assertiveness and social skills training for some students with disabilities is the lack of generalization to natural environments (Bates, 1980). Specific skills training and discrimination activities do not automatically generalize to natural environments. It is important to include a systematic plan for the generalization of assertive behavior skills to people, settings, and circumstances different from artificial settings such as role-play situations.

Role Playing   Role playing is a frequently applied social skills training strategy, both within instructional programs and as a sole instructional activity. The primary instructional purpose of role playing is to provide students with the opportunity to learn to deal with problems through actions. In a role-play situation, a problem is presented, a potential solution is acted out, and the outcomes of that solution are discussed. As depicted in Table 4, Joyce and Weil

Table 4.   Implementing role playing

Phase	Activities
I. Warm up the group.	• Identify or introduce problem. • Discuss and elaborate problem issues. • Explain role-playing process.
II. Select participants.	• Analyze roles. • Select role players.
III. Set the stage.	• Describe action of role play. • Restate roles.
IV. Prepare the observers.	• Describe what to look for. • Assign observation tasks.
V. Enact.	• Begin role play. • Complete role play.
VI. Discuss and evaluate.	• Review action of role play. • Discuss major focus. • Discuss solutions/outcomes. • Develop alternative enactment.
VII. Reenact.	• Play revised roles, incorporating previous suggestions. • Change roles to provide alternative perspectives.
VIII. Discuss and evaluate.	• Repeat steps in Phase VI.
IX. Share experiences and generalize.	• Relate problem situation to real experience and current problems. • Explore general principles of behavior.

Adapted from Joyce & Weil (1980).

(1980) provided suggestions for using role playing as an instructional tool. It is important to note that role playing is intended to be beneficial both for students acting out the problem scenario and for students observing the scenario.

Implementing role playing requires some specific skills on the part of the teacher. Role-play situations are generally less structured than other instructional activities, so the teacher must maintain a balance between too much and too little control. This primarily means starting the phases and guiding students through the discussion and evaluation activities. Questions and comments need to encourage a free and honest expression of ideas and feelings, particularly in the discussion phases. In most circumstances, the teacher will identify the problem issues, script the role-play scenario, and generate the questions and options for alternative responses. Students can become involved in many of these activities as well.

Joyce and Weil provided the following guidelines to teachers regarding their reactions to students during the role play:

1. Accept student responses and suggestions in a nonevaluative manner;
2. Respond in such a way as to help students explore multiple sides and perspectives in a situation;
3. Summarize student responses and incorporate those into the discussion in order to make students more aware of their own views and feelings;
4. Emphasize that there are different ways to play the same role and different consequences that may arise from these various ways;
5. Emphasize that there are often alternative ways to solve problems and no one way may be absolutely correct. (1980, p. 253)

Assertive, Nonassertive, and Aggressive Behaviors Most strategies to promote assertive behaviors teach students to discriminate among assertive, nonassertive, and aggressive behaviors and to express their wants, needs, or feelings in an assertive, rather than aggressive, manner. Aggressive behavior is behavior that is hostile and intended to hurt another person. It is inappropriate, however, to characterize aggressive or nonassertive behaviors as always bad and assertive behaviors as always good. Students should recognize that, although occasions arise in which nonassertive or aggressive behaviors are more appropriate, these actions are typically less helpful options to achieve their desired outcomes.

One way to communicate the differences among assertive, nonassertive, and aggressive behaviors is to discuss the outcomes of each type of behavior, as illustrated in Table 5. Using strategies such as role playing, it is easy to illustrate the differences among these three response classes and to highlight the outcomes associated with each. It is important, however, to emphasize that acting assertively does have a risk factor involved. For example, whenever a person is expressing his or her opinion or belief or requesting that someone change his or her behavior, one runs the risk that others will disagree, become upset, or act aggressively in response. A nonassertive response in a situation might minimize

Table 5.   Outcomes of assertive, nonassertive, and aggressive responses

Type of response	Outcome of response
Assertive	• Communicates knowledge of individual right • Acknowledges rights of others and value of those rights • Enhances mutual respect • Minimizes potential conflict • Leads to enhanced self-confidence and internal control
Nonassertive	• Fails to communicate knowledge of one's rights • Invites others to take advantage of individual • Limits potential for achieving desired outcome • Completely avoids conflict
Aggressive	• May hurt others and damage potential for collaboration and compromise • Elicits defensive reactions and positioning • Provides opportunity for temporary release of anger • Limits potential for achieving desired outcome

the potential for disagreement or conflict at the risk of not achieving the desired outcome. If, however, a person is fairly certain that his or her assertive behavior will result in problems created by aggressive responses, he or she may chose a nonassertive course of action. Behaving assertively involves a constant evaluation of the risks and benefits of acting in an assertive manner.

Rights and Responsibilities

Expressing one's rights is the core element of any assertive expression; it stands to reason, therefore, that students with disabilities should learn about rights and identify the responsibilities that accompany them. Strategies to teach assertive behavior, such as assertiveness training or social skills programs, focus on teaching students *how* to be assertive. Instruction in rights and responsibilities turns the focus toward the issue of *what* to advocate or assert.

Many times instruction on rights focuses solely on citizenship training—for example, voting skills, understanding the constitution, and knowledge of laws and the legislative process. Although issues important in citizenship training certainly overlap with assertiveness and effective communication (and are discussed in detail in Chapter 11), it is probably more important to promote assertiveness by focusing instruction on basic human rights and building the confidence to assert one's rights. The identification of such rights has the reciprocal benefit of encouraging assertive behavior. Kelley pointed out that

1.   Talking about human rights often helps individuals feel more comfortable about their right to be assertive; and
2.   The concept of rights helps individuals feel that they can justify their assertive acts. (1979, p. 14)

The identification of basic human rights is, in many ways, an individual process. Certainly governmental bodies have enunciated legally protected rights and pseudogovernmental bodies, such as the United Nations, have declarations of basic human rights. However, in our society many more "rights" exist that, although generally accepted, are not yet civilly protected. In many cases the need to be assertive relates to these unprotected rights. Kelley provided a series of questions that a student could ask to identify his or her basic human rights:

1. What are some of the basic things I believe people are entitled to be, have, or do because they are human beings?
2. Is this something that can be given to all people; do I accord this right to others?
3. What rights are necessary for all involved to be treated fairly, with dignity, and as people of worth?
4. What rights do people need in order to make their own decisions and to live their own lives without violating the rights of others? (1979, p. 16)

Teaching students to identify the basic human rights that are important to them begins with an understanding of those civilly protected rights and then expands to those rights that are important to the student based on his or her beliefs and values and the beliefs and values of the student's cultural experiences. Table 6 provides a list of basic human rights identified in one such process (Kelley, 1979). As a quick scan of this sample list indicates, this process is not designed to list all potential human rights. For example, there is nothing on the list about the rights to free association or free speech. An understanding of such rights, however, is the basic primer to developing rights lists that are specific to the student. If a student understands that she has the right to free speech, she can apply that to an understanding that she has the right to state her own feelings and opinions. Likewise, if a student understands the right to free association, he may extend that to his own circumstances and declare his right to live or work with other people in the community.

Students need to further understand that rights are coupled with responsibilities and that others have rights that may, in some ways, conflict with their own rights. Students should understand that just because they have a certain

Table 6.   Examples of basic human rights

I have the right to state my opinions and my feelings.
I have the right to refuse requests.
I have the right to make my own decisions.
I have the right to decide what to do with my property and time.
I have the right to ask for information.
I have the right to make choices based on my beliefs, values, and interests.
I have the right to be treated with dignity and respect.
I have the right to stand up for my own needs.
I have the right to be listened to and taken seriously.
I have the right to be alone when I wish.
I have the right to a free, appropriate public education.

Adapted from Kelley (1979).

right, or indeed just because they view something as a right, does not give them a free ticket to do as they please or mean that others will automatically recognize that right. It is for this reason that skills such as negotiation and compromise, effective elaboration skills (e.g., acknowledging others' rights), and effective verbal and nonverbal skills are important.

TEACHING EFFECTIVE COMMUNICATION SKILLS

Throughout the previous section we stressed the importance of effective communication skills to assertive behaviors. Effective communication skills are, in and of themselves, important skills for self-advocacy. For example, in a job interview a potential employee needs to advocate on his or her own behalf that he or she is the most appropriate candidate for the job. In this setting, the interviewee will have to employ a number of communication skills, including assertiveness, to convince the employer that he or she is the right choice. These skills include conversation skills, listening skills, and body language skills. This section describes the types of communication skills that warrant attention in self-advocacy instruction.

Conversation Skills

We have already discussed the importance of voice tone, volume, intonation, and inflection in assertive communication exchanges. These skills are equally important within the context of learning effective conversation skills. Understanding the dynamics of conversations can be important for students to effectively achieve the outcomes targeted by self-advocacy efforts. In addition to the nonverbal components of conversations and the paralinguistic aspects discussed previously, effective conversation skills include responding to a conversation partner's question or statement with a relevant statement or answer, initiating conversations at appropriate times, appropriate turn taking, and showing continued interest in a conversation by employing brief speech acknowledgers (e.g., "yes, I see," "right"). Ineffective conversation skills include frequent silences following a conversation partner's questions or statements; short, abrupt responses; frequent interruptions; off-topic responses; inappropriate tone (e.g., making a joke in response to a partner's expressed concern or problem); and mumbling or otherwise unintelligible responses.

Many studies have shown that conversation skills can be promoted using social skills training and role-playing strategies. Kelly, Furman, Phillips, Hathorn, and Wilson (1979) and Kelly, Wildman, Urey, and Thurman (1979) successfully used videotape modeling, coaching, and behavior rehearsal strategies to increase conversation skills of students with mental retardation (e.g., asking/answering conversational questions, reinforcing/complementing conversational partners) and found evidence that the training generalized to naturally occurring conversations. Bradlyn et al. (1983) employed group conversation skills training, focusing on discrete social behaviors (e.g., asking questions, talking about oneself, making speech acknowledgers) with adolescents with mental retardation and, using a multiple-baseline design, showed the efficacy of these strategies to increase conversation skills. Plienis et al. (1987) used a similar group process to teach students with emotional disorders conversation skills. Gajar, Schloss, Schloss, and Thompson (1984) used feedback (i.e., a signal indicating the occurrence of a positive or negative social interaction) and self-monitoring to teach appropriate conversation skills to youths with severe head trauma. Hunt, Alwell, and Goetz (1988) taught three students with severe disabilities to initiate a conversation independently and employ appropriate turn-taking skills by using communication books that served as an alternative conversation medium.

Nonverbal Communication Skills

Nonverbal behaviors, such as eye contact, facial expressions, gestures, and body language, are important components of communicative interactions. There are a number of ways that humans communicate by using nonverbal messages that are discussed in the following sections.

Eye Contact   Eye contact can indicate mood, emotions, and feelings and transmit warning, challenging, or reassuring messages (Banbury & Hebert, 1992). Students can be taught to discriminate among messages sent by types of eye contact. Engaging in frequent eye contact and having one's eyes open wide with raised eyebrows are indicators of acceptance, approval, or assertiveness. Alternatively, squinting or glaring and frequently averting eye contact can indicate disapproval; avoiding eye contact, looking down, or staring blankly indicates indifference (Banbury & Hebert, 1992).

Facial Expressions   Facial expressions work in conjunction with eye contact to communicate emotions. A smile transmits feelings of approval and happiness; a frown communicates unhappiness or dissatisfaction; and anger is communicated by pursed or tightly closed lips, clenched teeth, and scowls (Banbury & Hebert, 1992). Students with disabilities often have difficulty interpreting emotion from facial expressions (Hobson, Ouston, & Lee, 1989; Nabuzoka & Smith, 1995; Wigg & Harris, 1974), and practice may be necessary, via role playing or social skills training, to strengthen these skills.

Gestures and Body Movements   Banbury and Hebert (1992) pointed out that gestures and body movements do not, in and of themselves, have specific meaning. Instead, such movements must be considered within the context of the accompanying verbal message and the situation. Arm and hand motions can be used to augment verbal messages. Approval or acceptance can be expressed by head nodding, an open stance (e.g., arms/legs uncrossed, arms at side), orienting one's body toward the other person, and other body movements or gestures. Shaking one's head from side to side, folded arms, and physical distance all express disapproval. Pointing or shaking a finger at a person, getting too close, or thrusting one's chin out can indicate aggression; and leaning away from a person, folding one's hands behind one's back, and tapping one's feet indicates indifference or boredom.

Listening Skills

Students should learn that listening skills may be as important to self-advocacy as are assertiveness or conversation skills. Although students spend a great deal of time in education settings listening, they often do not do so effectively. The same is true in conversations and other circumstances in which communication is important, such as while negotiating, persuading, and asserting. According to Wallace, Cohen, and Polloway (1987), there are several purposes for listening, including

- Discrimination: discriminating among and identifying words and sounds
- Comprehension: identifying information in messages
- Therapy: helping a person work through a problem
- Analysis: deciding whether a statement is fact or opinion, determining reasons for action, predicting outcomes, and generalizing
- Appreciation: listening for pleasure

Mandlebaum and Wilson (1989) identified three steps in the listening process:

1. Receiving aural stimuli (e.g., hearing)
2. Attending to the message
3. Assigning meaning to what is heard and understanding the message

Students with disabilities may need instructional emphasis in either or both of the last two steps. However, teachers should ensure that problems with listening are not, in fact, related to a student's difficulty in actually hearing the message. Students with hearing impairments need to have accommodations made for them (e.g., seating arrangements, interpreter, hearing device). In Step 2, students need to be able to select the relevant stimuli, sometimes tuning out other stimuli, and to sustain their attention to this stimuli over time. Skills needed to succeed in Step 3 include cognitive strategies to recognize and remember what is said, categorize information, compare it with what is already known, and sequence and interpret the information (Mandlebaum & Wilson, 1989).

Mandlebaum and Wilson (1989) have summarized practices that teachers can incorporate to improve listening skills. These include providing direct instruction in listening skills; planning lessons so that students immediately use the information they extract from a communication; teaching students to self-monitor their listening behavior; teaching students to pay attention to cues that signal the presentation of important information; and, after a listening activity, asking students questions that require more than just recalling facts. McShane and Jones (1990) also provided suggestions for activities to improve listening skills. To increase students' attention to auditory stimuli, teachers can

> Teach the sequential nature of a conversation by using words like first, last, finally, etc.
> Direct students' attention to details by having the student perform an action (tap the desk, clap, mark a checklist) each time a piece of information is given
> Pair auditory and visual stimuli together, then fade out the visual aid (McShane & Jones, 1990, p. 444).

Active Listening Strategies   Active listening is a strategy that has been employed to enhance listening skills in circumstances in which self-advocacy skills might be employed. Instruction in active listening techniques instruct students to do the following:

1. *Look at the person who is speaking.* Stress that when someone looks at a person while that person is speaking, it tells the speaker that he or she is listening to what the speaker has to say.
2. *Ask questions.* Emphasize that when a person is actively listening, the speaker is likely to say something about which the listener can ask a question. Questions can clarify something the speaker has said or confirm a speaker's statement. In both cases, the listener can gather more information and, at the same time, let the speaker know that he or she is listening.
3. *Don't interrupt.* Although it is a good idea to ask some questions to show that one is listening, it is a bad idea to continually interrupt the speaker. A good listener lets another person speak without interrupting unless it is really necessary. Repeated interruptions send a message to the speaker that the listener does not really want to hear what he or she has to say.
4. *Take notes.* In some circumstances it is appropriate to take notes. Note taking can assist the listener to remember what he or she learned in the conversation and, once more, lets the speaker know that he or she is listening.

Structuring the Educational Environment to Improve Listening Skills   Because many students with disabilities have problems with discrimination, comprehension, and analysis skills, it is important to structure classrooms so that students can benefit from the information being presented to them and improve their listening skills. McShane and Jones provided a number of suggestions for teachers to better promote listening skills:

1. Make sure you have the student's full attention before initiating a communication.
2. Establish eye contact with the student before talking to the student.

3. Speak in a quiet voice so that the student will have to attend more closely.
4. Keep sentences short, separate phrases, slow down speech within and between words, and speak with distinct emphasis and clear intonation patterns.
5. Provide information in small communicative packets, not large chunks.
6. Be aware of room conditions such as lighting, temperature, and seating comfort. [Lighting that is too low, room temperatures that are too low or too high, or hard, uncomfortable seats make for poor listening conditions.]
7. Make recall as easy as possible by presenting material at a rate learners can handle, grouping items that are to be repeated, and emphasizing key words. (1990, p. 440)

CONCLUSION

Assertive behaviors and effective communication skills are critical components of self-advocacy. Students with disabilities frequently need instruction in these areas to improve interactions and to achieve self-selected goals. Strategies such as assertiveness training, social skills training, and role playing have been validated as effective for increasing the assertiveness behavior and conversation skills of youths with disabilities. These skills represent, in many ways, the entry-level skills to becoming self-advocating and provide a solid foundation for the development of other self-advocacy skills.

QUESTIONS FOR REVIEW

1. Define assertiveness and the various ways in which it has been conceptualized.
2. Discuss the "performance implications" of a functional definition of assertiveness:
   - Assertiveness is a learned skill.
   - Assertiveness is a function of the interaction between the person and his or her situation.
   - Assertiveness is an expressive skill composed of verbal and nonverbal responses components.
   - Assertiveness is performed in an interpersonal context in which there is some risk of negative reaction by the recipient.
   - Assertiveness is defined and measured by the outcomes of the behavior.
3. The expression of rights is the core of any assertion. Discuss why this is central to assertiveness.
4. Describe assertiveness training and the components of most assertiveness training programs.
5. Describe the two focal points for the instruction of rights and responsibilities (e.g., how to advocate and for what to advocate). Discuss the role of education in each.
6. List and discuss effective communication skills.

7. Discuss how assertiveness training and social skills training are similar and how they differ.

REFERENCES

Banbury, M.M., & Hebert, C.R. (1992). Do you see what I mean? Body language in classroom interactions. *Teaching Exceptional Children, 25,* 34–38.

Bates, P. (1980). The effectiveness of interpersonal skills training on the social skill acquisition of moderately and mildly retarded adults. *Journal of Applied Behavior Analysis, 13,* 237–248.

Bornstein, P.H., Bach, P.J., McFall, M.E., Friman, P.C., & Lyons, P.D. (1980). Application of a social skills training program in the modification of interpersonal deficits among retarded adults: A clinical replication. *Journal of Applied Behavior Analysis, 13,* 171–176.

Bornstein, M., Bellack, A.S., & Hersen, M. (1977). Social skills training for unassertive children: A multiple baseline analysis. *Journal of Applied Behavior Analysis, 10,* 183–195.

Bornstein, M., Bellack, A.S., & Hersen, M. (1980). Social skills training for highly aggressive children: Treatment in an inpatient psychiatric setting. *Behavior Modification, 4,* 173–186.

Bradlyn, A.S., Himadi, W.G., Crimmins, D.B., Christoff, K.A., Graves, K.G., & Kelly, J.A. (1983). Conversational skills training for retarded adolescents. *Behavior Therapy, 14,* 314–325.

Bregman, S. (1984). Assertiveness training for mentally retarded adults. *Mental Retardation, 22,* 12–16.

Gajar, A., Schloss, P.J., Schloss, C.N., & Thompson, C.K. (1984). Effects of feedback and self-monitoring on head trauma youths' conversation skills. *Journal of Applied Behavior Analysis, 17,* 353–358.

Glueckauf, R.L., & Quittner, A.L. (1992). Assertiveness training for disabled adults in wheelchairs: Self-report, role-play, and activity pattern outcomes. *Journal of Consulting and Clinical Psychology, 60,* 419–425.

Hobson, R.P., Ouston, J., & Lee, A. (1989). Recognition of emotion by mentally retarded adolescents and young adults. *American Journal on Mental Retardation, 93,* 434–443.

Hunt, P., Alwell, M., & Goetz, L. (1988). Acquisition of conversation skills and the reduction of inappropriate social interaction behaviors. *Journal of The Association for Persons with Severe Disabilities, 13,* 20–27.

Joyce, B., & Weil, M. (1980). *Models of teaching* (2nd ed.). Englewood Cliffs, NJ: Prentice Hall.

Kelley, C. (1979). *Assertion training: A facilitator's guide.* LaJolla, CA: University Associates, Inc.

Kelly, J.A., Furman, W., Phillips, J., Hathorn, S., & Wilson, T. (1979). Teaching conversational skills to retarded adolescents. *Child Behavior Therapy, 1,* 85–97.

Kelly, J.A., Wildman, B.G., Urey, J.R., & Thurman, C. (1979). Group skills training to improve the conversational repertoire of retarded adolescents. *Child Behavior Therapy, 1,* 323–336.

Kirkland, K., & Caughlin-Carver, J. (1982). Maintenance and generalization of assertive skills. *Education and Training in Mental Retardation, 17,* 313–318.

Korinek, L., & Polloway, E.A. (1993). Social skills: Review and implications for instruction for students with mild mental retardation. In R.A. Gable & S.F. Warren (Eds.),

Strategies for teaching students with mild to severe mental retardation (pp. 71–97). Baltimore: Paul H. Brookes Publishing Co.

Lemanek, K.L., Williamson, D.A., Gresham, F.M., & Jensen, B.J. (1986). Social skills training with hearing-impaired children and adolescents. *Behavior Modification, 10,* 55–71.

Liberman, R.P., DeRisi, W.J., & Mueser, K.T. (1989). *Social skills training for psychiatric patients.* Needham, MA: Allyn & Bacon.

Mandlebaum, L.H., & Wilson, R. (1989). Teaching listening skills in the special education classroom. *Academic Therapy, 24,* 449–459.

McShane, E.A., & Jones, E.L. (1990). Modifying the environment for children with poor listening skills. *Academic Therapy, 25,* 439–446.

Morgan, B., & Leung, P. (1980). Effects of assertion training on acceptance of disability by physically handicapped university students. *Journal of Counseling and Clinical Psychology, 27,* 209–212.

Nabuzoka, D., & Smith, P.K. (1995). Identification of expressions of emotions by children with and without learning disabilities. *Learning Disabilities Research and Practice, 10,* 91–101.

Plienis, A.J., Hansen, D.J., Ford, F., Smith, S., Stark, L.J., & Kelly, J.A. (1987). Behavioral small group training to improve the social skills of emotionally-disordered adolescents. *Behavior Therapy, 18,* 17–32.

Rakos, R.F. (1991). *Assertive behavior: Theory, research and training.* London: Routledge.

Rich, A.R., & Schroeder, H.E. (1976). Research issues in assertiveness training. *Psychological Bulletin, 83,* 1084–1096.

Rimm, D.C., & Masters, J.C. (1979). *Behavior therapy: Techniques and empirical findings.* New York: Academic Press.

Roffman, A. (1993). Social skills training. In C.A. Michaels (Ed.), *Transition strategies for persons with learning disabilities* (pp. 185–211). San Diego: Singular.

Salter, A. (1949). *Conditioned reflex therapy.* New York: Farrar, Strauss & Giroux.

Senatore, V., Matson, J.L., & Kazdin, A.E. (1982). A comparison of behavioral methods to train social skills to mentally retarded adults. *Behavior Therapy, 13,* 313–324.

Wallace G., Cohen, S.B., & Polloway, E.A. (1987). *Language arts: Teaching exceptional students.* Austin, TX: PRO-ED.

Wigg, E.H., & Harris, S.P. (1974). Perception and interpretation of nonverbally expressed emotions by adolescents with learning disabilities. *Perceptual and Motor Skills, 38,* 239–245.

Wilson, G.L. (1994). Self-advocacy skills. In C.A. Michaels (Ed.), *Transition strategies for persons with learning disabilities* (pp. 153–184). San Diego: Singular.

Wolpe, J. (1969). *The practice of behavior therapy.* Oxford, England: Pergamon Press.

Wolpe, J., & Lazarus, A.A. (1966). *Behavior therapy techniques: A guide to the treatment of neuroses.* Oxford, England: Pergamon Press.

CHAPTER 11

Teaching Leadership, Teamwork, and General Self-Advocacy Skills

After reading this chapter, you will be able to

1. Identify the rights or protections guaranteed under the Individuals with Disabilities Education Act (IDEA) of 1990 and its amendments for students with disabilities

2. Discuss strategies to teach students about civil rights

3. Identify and discuss some barriers to leadership for people with disabilities

4. Identify reasons for holding meetings, particularly educational planning meetings

5. Identify skill areas in which students could receive instruction in order to assume a leadership role in their planning meeting

6. Discuss three strategies or programs that promote general self-advocacy skills

KEY TERMS

1. Briefing meetings
2. Citizenship skills
3. Consultative meetings
4. Cooperative learning strategy
5. Decision-making meetings
6. Group dynamics skills
7. Informed consent
8. Instructional meetings
9. Leadership skills
10. Legal rights
11. Participation skills
12. Ritualistic meetings
13. Self-advocacy skills
14. Teamwork skills

Although assertive behavior and effective communication skills are important if students are to become self-advocating, a number of other critical skills are needed if students are to achieve this end. McTaggert and Gould (1988) suggested that secondary-age instruction in self-advocacy should include instruction and practice in some or all of the following areas:

- Assertive behavior
- Communication
- Decision-making skills
- Goal setting and attainment
- Leadership skills
- Legal and citizenship rights and responsibilities
- Problem-resolution skills
- Public speaking skills
- Transition planning
- Use of community resources

Several of these elements (i.e., decision making, problem solving, and goal setting) are discussed in separate chapters (see Chapters 6, 8, and 9). This chapter overviews content areas and strategies for teaching those self-advocacy skills not addressed elsewhere, including teaching leadership and teamwork skills, and legal and citizenship rights and responsibilities. Also overviewed here are several strategies that have been used to promote global self-advocacy.

PROMOTING SPECIFIC SELF-ADVOCACY SKILLS

Leadership, teamwork, and general self-advocacy skills (including understanding one's legal rights and practicing citizenship skills) are important aspects of self-advocacy. This section addresses strategies to promote each of these important areas.

Legal Rights and Citizenship Skills

Gould (1986) suggested that the primary emphasis in teaching self-advocacy should be "sensitizing transition-age students to their own needs and rights and ways of pursuing them" (p. 39). Gould described the issue of rights as central to self-advocacy, and the author listed two types of rights: 1) legal or statutory rights that apply to citizens by virtue of laws or regulations enacted by political representatives, and 2) personal or human rights that apply to everyone by common agreement. We have discussed the importance of the latter in assertive behavior as well (see Chapter 10). Key areas of training in citizenship rights include

- Defining legal and citizenship rights for all citizens
- Important legal or civil rights for individuals with disabilities
- Responsibilities associated with citizenship
- How laws are made and how citizens can be involved
- What safeguards apply in cases of limitations of rights
- How rights are protected and by whom
- What someone should do when their legal rights are violated (Gould, 1986)

A number of successful strategies are available for teaching civil and legal rights to students with disabilities. Sears, Bishop, and Stevens (1989) implemented strategies to teach students with mental retardation their Miranda rights so that they might better advocate for themselves if they encountered the criminal justice system. They suggested starting with efforts to increase literal comprehension of rights (e.g., using written materials such as textbooks or other training materials) and then developing vignettes and role-playing potential situations in which the knowledge of civil and legal rights might be used. Brolin (1993) suggested a career education approach to learning and exhibiting responsible citizenship, focusing instructional efforts on 1) identifying basic civil rights when questioned by law enforcement officials, 2) identifying actions to take when a crime has been witnessed, 3) listing local laws and consequences of violating these laws, and 4) learning about the court system and its procedures. Cronin and Patton (1993) stressed a life skills approach to instruction in citizenship.

Teaching students about the Constitution of the United States and the Bill of Rights is one means of increasing student knowledge of civil and legal rights. This is typically an activity undertaken in secondary social studies, government, or political science classes. In many cases students with disabilities have few, if any, opportunities to learn about these issues, either because they are not included in classes in which the topics are covered or because it is not considered important to the student's educational program. Successful strategies have been developed, however, to teach these topics to youths with disabilities. For example, Howard (1988, 1991) developed two sets of material that enable secondary teachers to teach students with special needs, particularly students with mental retardation, about the Constitution and Bill of Rights. The first set, *We the People,* is a teaching unit on the Constitution for high school students with disabilities. Materials in this set include a student-directed workbook, audio and videotapes, and student booklets on the Constitution and voting rights. The second set of materials, the *Bill of Rights Series,* incorporates multimedia elements to further students' understanding of the Bill of Rights, including cartoon-style booklets on the First Amendment, Arrest and Trial, and Voting Amendments as well as a card and board game. These materials stress a cooperative learning strategy, in which students work together in groups of two to five members. Howard (1991) made the following suggestions for augmenting instruction on civil rights:

- Visit the city council or county board of supervisors (or commissioners).
- Visit a voter registration office and practice filling out forms in class.
- Take a tour of the state capitol building or legislative offices. Ask a legislator to speak to students if possible.
- Watch C-SPAN when programming takes place in the Congress.
- Write to the League of Women Voters for information about local elections.
- Analyze newspaper articles and editorials for opposing views.
- Hold a mock trial.

A third area of focus is to teach students about their rights and responsibilities under specific laws or regulations that particularly affect their lives, such as Individuals with Disabilities Education Act (IDEA) of 1990 (PL 101-476) and its amendments, which are laws that are pertinent to all students receiving special education services. Students can learn what the Act of 1990 and its amendments were written to achieve, what the Act and its amendments require in the way of educational meetings and program delivery, what the laws say about transition services and require in terms of student involvement, and what procedural guidelines are in place to ensure compliance. Similar instructional efforts could target Section 504 of the Rehabilitation Act of 1973 (PL 93-112) or the Americans with Disabilities Act (ADA) of 1990 (PL 101-336). Valenti (1989) suggested teaching students with learning disabilities that IDEA and its amendments:

- Guarantee the availability of special education instruction to all youths with disabilities
- Ensure fairness and appropriateness in decision making with regard to providing these services
- Establish clear management requirements and procedures at all levels of government
- Establish federal aid for the efforts of state and local governments providing special services

In addition, Valenti (1989) identified three rights or protections guaranteed under IDEA and its amendments:

1. A free, appropriate public education for all children with disabilities
2. The maintenance of a written individualized education program (IEP) that must include a statement of transition planning

3. Educational services that must be delivered to students in the least restrictive environment

Leadership and Teamwork Skills

Abery, Smith, Sharpe, and Chelberg suggested that most people, with or without a disability, do not view themselves as leaders, in part because of the images of "leader" in our society. Leaders, contend Abery and colleagues, are

> viewed as charismatic individuals who inspire others to action through fiery speeches. Leaders are thought of as unusually attractive, intelligent, powerful, talented and/or prosperous. Still others think of leaders as martyrs who sacrifice all for a cause. (1995, p. 1)

At least in part because of this grandiose view, people with disabilities are rarely perceived as leaders (Abery, et al., 1995; Wehmeyer & Berkobien, 1996). Disability and leadership are, in fact, often viewed as being mutually exclusive. Consequently, there have been few efforts to promote leadership for students with disabilities. Given that the role of leader is one that is valued by most adults in our society, this omission serves to further marginalize adults with disabilities. However, most people probably have the capacity to become a leader, if one examines more closely what it means to lead. Leaders are people who guide or direct others on a course of action, influence the opinion and behavior of other people, and show the way by going in advance. Leadership can take many forms, and many leaders do not fit the stereotypes described previously. The types of skills that leaders need to possess are varied and, in some cases, redundant to skills discussed in the chapter on assertive behavior. Table 1 presents skills typically associated with leaders.

Leadership, by definition, is contextual (Bolden, 1995). That is, a leader guides or directs others in defined settings or circumstances. The most common opportunities to experience leadership roles are in group settings, such as at

Table 1. Basic leadership skills

- Locate and use resources that will be of benefit to the individual or group.
- Communicate effectively with the group and the public.
- Help the group describe and communicate a common goal, objective, or vision.
- Understand group and individual needs.
- Be goal oriented and organized, and have strategic planning skills.
- Set an example for others.
- Teach and mentor others.
- Facilitate teamwork and cooperation.
- Provide feedback and evaluation.
- Resolve conflicts and solve problems.
- Direct group activities and distribute resources and responsibilities equitably.

meetings and in clubs, volunteer organizations, religious or charitable organizations, and other groups or entities. Within an organization or group, the types of leadership roles can vary considerably. For example, taking the lead to ensure that a mailing gets out to the members of a volunteer organization requires different skills and actions than chairing a governmental committee or volunteer board of directors.

Although skills development is an important part of learning to be a leader, it is also important that students have opportunities to learn to lead by leading. The educational planning process is an ideal venue in which to teach leadership skills and to provide opportunities for students to assume some leadership responsibilities, as discussed next. Chapter 12 provides an overview of student involvement in educational planning and decision making as a means of teaching self-advocacy skills, specifically identifying programmatic efforts to increase student involvement. In addition, there are a number of school and community-based extracurricular activities, such as clubs or sports, in which students can assume leadership roles.

Barriers to Leadership   Many barriers have been erected that limit the degree to which people with disabilities have become leaders. Wehmeyer and Berkobien (1996) identified several:

- A self-fulfilling prophecy exists that, because of the existence of the disabling condition, people with disabilities are not capable of leading and thus are not provided opportunities to lead.
- Accommodations are rarely in place to support people with disabilities in leadership roles.
- A double standard is frequently applied to people with disabilities in leadership positions, and they are excluded for shortcomings that may represent inadequacies in the system as much as personal incompetence.
- People with disabilities are not provided the lifelong experiences in making choices and decisions that lead to more effective problem solving.

The lack of supports or accommodations represents a significant barrier to people with disabilities assuming leadership roles. It is important that students are provided *both* adequate accommodations that will enable them to learn leadership skills and opportunities to learn what accommodations they need so that they can communicate these to others. Wehmeyer and Berkobien (1996) identified a number of such support mechanisms and accommodations to overcome specific barriers:

1. Pair the individual with someone in the organization who can serve as a mentor and a contact person.

2. Allow the person with a disability to select a support person to assist him or her and to identify the level of support he or she requires to succeed. This person should be someone the individual believes will best represent his or her viewpoints and attitudes.

3. Prior to meetings or other organizational activities, provide tutorials on issues and procedures that will be addressed in the meeting.

4. Provide cognitively accessible materials for individuals with mental retardation and other cognitive impairments. This includes minimizing the use of written materials, presenting such materials orally in the meeting or beforehand, tape recording discussions, and using pictures or color-coding handouts and agenda items.

5. Set up co-leadership situations in which an additional person (with or without disabilities) helps the individual by assuming some responsibilities normally contained in a single position or activity.

6. Help the student identify his or her individual strengths, and match committee, board, or agency responsibilities according to these skills.

Educational Planning Meetings as a Learning Opportunity

If a student receives special education services, he or she must also have an annual IEP meeting at which an educational program is designed. These meetings emphasize collaboration and teamwork and provide excellent opportunities to learn and practice leadership and teamwork skills. To become effective leaders, students need to learn the purposes of meetings, types of meetings, and the various roles associated with meetings.

Purposes of Meetings   To be effective leaders (and participants, for that matter), students need to learn why meetings are useful. Wehmeyer and Kelchner (1995) identified several reasons to hold meetings, particularly educational planning meetings:

1. Meetings are a good way to share information about something of interest to a lot of people. In the case of IEP meetings, that information involves the student's educational progress, needs, and program.

2. Meetings are an effective way to build unity and establish teamwork. Educational planning meetings provide an opportunity to identify areas of mutual interest and build a team to achieve some common objectives.

3. Meetings provide an opportunity to bring several people together to examine a problem and to problem-solve. No matter how effective any given person is at problem solving, it is often useful to have more than one person looking at a problem to make sure that all options are identified.

4. Meetings provide a good context in which to come to decisions that have support among stakeholders and that meet the various needs of participants.

Types of Meetings   Students will participate in different kinds or types of meetings both in school and as adults. These different meeting types also have differing expectations and intentions and require different skills, or more precisely, differential use of various leadership skills. Bormann and Bormann (1972) identified types of meetings and their purposes (see Table 2).

The responsibilities of leaders in each type of meeting vary greatly, as do the responsibilities of meeting participants. IEP meetings are, theoretically, decision-making meetings, although in reality many such meetings resemble more closely ritualistic or briefing meetings! When conducted as decision-making meetings, however, in which participants have the opportunity to contribute and to share in decision-making and planning activities, educational planning meetings provide chances for students to put into practice the leadership and teamwork skills they have acquired.

Running a Meeting   The basic skills required to run an efficient decision-making meeting involve the skills to get a meeting started, keep participants on track, move the meeting along, and enable the participants to reach a decision. The first problem that the leader of a meeting faces is getting the group focused on the business at hand. One strategy is to ask questions, particularly open-ended questions that cannot be answered with a simple yes or no. A leader may want to start a meeting with a brief set of comments upon which to base such questions. To keep participants focused on business, Bormann and Bormann (1972) suggested that leaders keep the agenda to a manageable length, typically no more than 2 hours, and determine the appropriateness of the discussion to the topic. Finally, the leader should summarize the discussion, identify the options arising from such discussions, and assist the group in actually

Table 2.   Types of meetings

Meeting type	Primary purpose
Ritualistic meeting	Usually designed to promote cohesiveness within an organization. The purpose of the meeting is to assure participants that adequate leadership is in place and, often, to rubber-stamp decisions that have already been made.
Briefing meeting	Designed to provide participants with information to carry out plans that are already in place.
Instructional meeting	Designed to teach people in order to make them more proficient at their assigned tasks.
Consultative meeting	Designed to enable a person responsible for the meeting to elicit advice and direction from meeting participants. Participants are often experts or consultants. The meeting organizer remains responsible for the final decision.
Decision-making meeting	Designed to make decisions and formulate a course of action. Participants should be involved in problem solving; decision making; and, eventually, plans to put decisions into action.

Adapted from Bormann & Bormann (1972).

making a decision. The group dynamics skills discussed in the next section provide more examples of the skills needed to run a meeting.

Martin, Marshall, Maxson, and Jerman (1993) provided an example of how a student might take a leadership role in his or her IEP team meeting. Table 3 identifies eleven steps in which a student could receive instruction to assume a leadership role effectively. More information about this process is provided in Chapter 12.

Leadership and Teamwork Skills Acquisition   Specific skills instruction to promote leadership focuses on individual skills components such as teaching students how to set goals, resolve conflicts, be assertive, foster teamwork and participation, communicate effectively, and run a meeting. These skills can be taught using a social skills training model or employing procedures such as modeling, role playing, and behavioral rehearsal.

Teamwork and Participation Skills   If it is true that too many chefs spoil the broth, then certainly too many leaders ruin the meeting! Although virtually anyone can lead in one way or another, it is hardly useful to have everyone trying to lead at once! One important role of a leader is to promote teamwork and effective participation skills. Students need to learn both to be effective team members and participants and, in the role of leader, to facilitate teamwork and participation. The goal of teamwork building is to get all participants working together to achieve a common objective or goal. The goal of participation skills building is to get each individual involved and contributing.

Effective team members

- Have a positive attitude about the team process, can trust and rely on other team members, and approach issues in a problem-solving mode
- Follow through on what they promise

Table 3.   Steps to student leadership of planning meeting

Step	Activity
1	Begin meeting by stating purpose.
2	Introduce everyone.
3	Review past goals and performance.
4	Ask for others' feedback.
5	State your school and transition goals.
6	Ask questions if you don't understand.
7	Deal with differences in opinion.
8	State what support you'll need.
9	Summarize your goals.
10	Close meeting by thanking everyone.
11	Work on IEP goals all year!

Adapted from Martin, Marshall, Maxson, & Jerman (1993).

- Make sure that they get the information they need to contribute by talking to other team members and doing their homework

Students should learn that they can be good team members at meetings by

- Getting to the meeting on time
- Dressing neatly and appropriately
- Bringing any information that has been sent to them
- Working positively with other team members
- Staying throughout the meeting
- Listening without interrupting
- Talking only about the topic under discussion
- Following through on their commitments

Good participant skills and effective teamwork skills overlap considerably. Participation skills usually focus on the individual's ability to contribute to the discussion and the decision-making/problem-solving process as a whole. Thus, teaching students to be more effective decision makers or problem solvers will increase their participation skills. Likewise, effective small-group communication skills, as discussed in the next chapter, contribute to more effective participation skills. A frequently mentioned participation skill is the ability to critique ideas, proposals, and outcomes in a constructive manner. Effective critiquing skills develop as individuals have more opportunities to participate. Instructional activities also can promote the emergence of these skills. For example, Balcazar, Seekins, Fawcett, and Hopkins (1990) taught members of a self-help organization how to identify and report on disability-related issues to the group. Training included 1) teaching members to identify disability-related issues from various sources; 2) how to report, evaluate, and critique the particular issue or practice; and 3) how to present this information to the group. This instruction included some role-playing and self-directed learning activities. Issues identified and reported included a need for curb cuts for wheelchairs, the lack of an emergency alarm safety system to protect people with severe disabilities in their home, and concerns over the fire safety of people with disabilities in a local nursing home.

Participants generated actions that could be taken to resolve the issues and monitored outcomes. As a result, team members showed increased ability to identify and report issues of interest to the group, and, for each of the issues identified, positive outcomes were achieved (e.g., curb cuts installed, alarm systems purchased, fire drills planned).

Group Dynamics Skills   Group dynamics skills are the skills that one has to use to work successfully with groups and to enable individuals within a group to work together successfully. Although skills such as goal setting, decision making, problem solving, and assertiveness receive the largest share of attention as leadership skills, a number of skills that fall under the category of group dynamic skills may be just as important. Gardner, DePalma, and Zastowny (1982) conducted a survey to identify the most important behaviors that leaders exhibited. Among those that were in the top 15 skills were 1) appropriate use of silence, 2) providing reassurance and approval, 3) subtle guidance, 4) the ability to clarify questions and issues, and 5) motivating the group. Morris (1993) also identified several group dynamic skills as critical to leadership among student leaders, including compassion, integrity, and effective listening.

Because leadership activities, by definition, involve interactions with groups of people, group dynamic skills become especially important. Again, meetings are frequently the settings in which effective group dynamics skills must be used. Table 4 provides a list of strategies to address problems created by a specific individual in a group. These authors also made suggestions for circumstances in which it is the group as a whole that is the problem. If a group responds apathetically and appears to lack interest, the leader should use humor and small talk to cajole members into participation. The leader should model enthusiasm by his or her actions and not give up after initial attempts to motivate the group

Table 4.   Involving a participant and keeping a meeting moving

Problem	Solutions
A team member won't participate.	• Involve member in the conversation by asking open-ended questions. • Make sure participant has adequate information about the topic and is receiving adequate accommodations. • Use other times to find out personal interests / issues and include those issues in the discussion. • When member does contribute, listen carefully and make special note of the contribution.
A member is constantly joking and disrupting the discussion.	• Support efforts if meeting is tense and members need a release. • At times when interruptions are inappropriate, ignore the intrusion and redirect the discussion to the topic.
One member monopolizes the discussion.	• Interrupt politely and direct the conversation to another member by asking that member a specific question. • Take advantage of natural pauses in the person's speech to elaborate on what the person has said and redirect the conversation to another person.
A member is argumentative.	• Don't lose your temper! Stay in control. • Acknowledge the person's position, find merit if possible, and solicit other opinions or move the discussion on to other members. • If necessary, talk with the member privately before the next meeting.

Adapted from Bormann & Bormann (1972).

fail. It may also be necessary to explain the purpose of the meeting, the expected outcomes, and to provide more information about the topic of discussion.

If a group is openly hostile, it is the leader's responsibility to determine the cause for the hostility (e.g., members do not like one another, members do not like topic); identify appropriate roles for each member; focus the group on a commonly agreed-upon objective; and, if necessary, bring the hostility into the open for discussion and resolution. If a group seems continually off-track or confused, or if members feel that their time is being wasted, the leader needs to step in and suggest an alternative means of achieving the common objective, examine the work allocation and redistribute work if necessary, and provide a specific agenda for further action.

Conflict Resolution Skills   One of the more difficult challenges to teamwork that a leader must address is conflict in a group. Conflicts arise for a variety of reasons from personality clashes to power grabs. One common feature of conflicts, however, regardless of origin, is that they are disruptive to effective teamwork and must be addressed. The first response to conflict on the part of the leader is to make sure that it is not a result of ineffective leadership. Leaders should examine the degree to which they have fostered good participation skills, communicated a common purpose or objective, and fostered teamwork. Given that the conflict has not been manufactured by ineffective leadership, Guerra, Moore, and Slaby (1995) provided a series of steps students could learn (in a self-directed manner) that would enable them to resolve conflicts:

1. *Why is there a conflict? Checking facts and beliefs.* In this step, students learn the importance of obtaining the factual information necessary to resolve the conflict and to explore their own beliefs about a situation. Guerra and colleagues stressed the importance of teaching students to look out for their own and other people's biases.
2. *Why is there a conflict? Taking another's perspective.* Students need to learn to think about a conflict situation from the perspective of all parties in order to craft a response that will resolve the conflict to the satisfaction of everyone involved.
3. *Generating possible solutions.* Based on the information gathered in the previous two steps, students need to learn to generate possible solutions to the problem. Guerra et al. stressed that leaders should be assertive and involve all parties in the generation of solutions.
4. *Deciding on a solution.* Students should apply decision-making skills to identify the most satisfactory solution to the conflict. At this point in the process students need to employ effective negotiation, compromise, and persuasion skills as well.
5. *Evaluate results.* Once a conflict has been resolved, students need to learn to monitor ongoing interactions and keep a similar situation from boiling up again.

PROMOTING GENERAL SELF-ADVOCACY

A number of instructional strategies and programs have been developed to promote general self-advocacy, as opposed to targeted self-advocacy skills. These strategies often cluster a group of self-advocacy behaviors, and instruction targets all of these behaviors. This section reviews these instructional strategies and programs and suggests ways to provide opportunities for students to practice self-advocacy skills.

Direct Instruction

Durlak, Rose, and Bursuck (1994) used direct instruction to teach students with learning disabilities a set of seven self-advocacy skills. Eight students with learning disabilities were involved in the instruction. The authors used a multiple-baseline design, recording student performance of self-determined behaviors across all phases of baseline and intervention. Training procedures were adapted from the direct instruction literature, and instructional procedures for the study included seven steps:

1. The trainer described the target behavior while the student followed on his or her instruction sheet.
2. The trainer demonstrated the behavior.
3. The trainer gave students the opportunity to ask questions and clarify procedures.
4. Students rehearsed the target behavior.
5. Peers and staff gave students immediate feedback.
6. Students repeated the task until mastery was demonstrated.
7. Following mastery, additional practice was conducted in the natural environment.

Self-Advocacy Plan

Phillips (1990) taught students with learning disabilities self-advocacy skills, using a process called the *Self-Advocacy Plan,* which was designed to "stimulate the transition from parent advocacy to self-advocacy by providing students with practice in assuming responsibility for planning and decision-making" (p. 466). The teacher's role in this process is described as being a mediator of learning, as opposed to a remedial educator. Phillips defined a mediator of learning as someone who is interposed between the learner and the environment who intentionally influences the interaction. Students involved in the *Self-Advocacy Plan* process participate in a learning disabilities seminar. Meeting once a week for 10 weeks, students discuss a series of topics, including

-   The concept of a learning disability
-   Information about specific learning disabilities
-   School and social relations issues that relate to learning disabilities

- Specific learning strengths and weaknesses
- People who have a learning disability who have also succeeded in careers
- Laws pertaining to learning disabilities (IDEA, Section 504)
- Availability of post-secondary education supports
- Community resources (Phillips, 1990, p. 467)

During the seminar, students hear from successful adults with learning disabilities and visit colleges to examine what support services are available. After the seminar is over, students form small groups to discuss their learning styles and strategies. Students keep *learning logs* (i.e., personal observations of what works for them in terms of self-advocating) and, in subsequent stages of the plan, participate in a career awareness seminar, identify modifications that will assist them to succeed in the classroom, and self-evaluate progress on their educational goals and objectives. Phillips (1990) used the *Self-Advocacy Plan* with 15 students with learning disabilities and determined that the process improved students' knowledge of services for which they might qualify; increased students' awareness of their strengths, limitations, and potential accommodations; and improved awareness of career and educational opportunities.

Self-Advocacy Seminars

Brinckerhoff (1993, 1994) developed a 6-week training session, composed of seven topical workshops, to promote self-advocacy for youth with learning disabilities who are college bound. The general intent of the workshops was to "give participants a greater understanding of their learning disabilities, their rights under the law, how to effectively advocate and negotiate with college-faculty members, and how to use accommodations that compensate for their learning disabilities" (1993, p. 231). The curriculum was designed to be team taught by a learning disabilities specialist and two adults with learning disabilities who attend college. Table 5 summarizes the workshops and their content.

The self-advocacy seminar process incorporates instruction in disability-related laws, self-directed activities to increase student self-awareness and identify accommodations, group sessions, and role-playing activities. It also incorporates one feature of a student-directed transition planning program called the *Self-Advocacy Strategy* (see Chapter 12). Students in this process use a strategy called I–PLAN (see Chapter 12, Table 4) to teach them how to participate in their transition planning program.

Providing Opportunities for Practicing Self-Advocacy Skills

Skills acquisition is only the first step in the learning process. Students with disabilities must be provided opportunities to practice these skills in order to maintain and generalize their use. Role playing provides opportunities for practicing self-advocacy skills in a variety of scenarios. West et al. (1992) suggested that teachers could have students role-play transition-related situations that would utilize self-advocacy skills, such as the following:

- Setting up a class schedule
- Moving out of the home
- Asking for accommodations needed for a course
- Meeting with a rehabilitation counselor or social services coordinator
- Meeting with a medical provider
- Working with a personal care attendant
- Interviewing for a job
- Making choices at an IEP meeting

Once students feel comfortable with specific self-advocacy skills and strategies, they should be encouraged to move beyond role playing. The educational

Table 5.   Self-advocacy seminars

Session title	Activities
Session 1: LD 101: What is your learning disability in plain language?	• Definition of learning disability • Glossary of common terminology • Types of tests to determine learning disabilities • Famous people with learning disabilities • Research on successful adults with learning disabilities
Session 2: Legal rights under IDEA, Section 504, and the ADA	• Overview of key provisions of IDEA • Overview of key provisions of Section 504 • Overview of the ADA • Comparisons, benefits, and limitations of legislation
Session 3: Self-advocacy basics	• Importance of self-advocacy in college • Determining what, where, when, and why • Using support services to your benefit
Session 4: Determining reasonable accommodations in the classroom	• What factors are affecting your performance in college? • What kinds of accommodations can help you compensate? • Guidelines for contacting college instructors • Pyramid process—a guide to independent decision making
Session 5: Independence versus dependence issues	• The parent's perspective • The service provider's perspective • The college faculty's perspective
Session 6: Strategy instruction and self-advocacy role playing	• The fine art of negotiating • I–PLAN training • I–PLAN initiation • Modeling by presenters with students
Session 7: Self-advocacy role play and direct application	• Student role play with support staff and faculty • Self-advocacy and students' self-evaluation

Adapted from Brinckerhoff (1994).

and transition planning process provides an ideal learning environment in which to put such skills into action. In the process of developing and implementing a transition plan, students have the opportunity to actually call their local vocational rehabilitation agency and set up a meeting with a rehabilitation counselor; go to the local community college and identify potential accommodations; or, if appropriate, set up job interviews. All of these can provide functional, real-world ways to apply self-advocacy skills.

Another important way for students to apply self-advocacy skills is to become involved in organizations and clubs, both internal and external to the school system. There are almost an endless number of such outlets, from self-advocacy and self-help groups for people with disabilities, to cause-related organizations such as the Sierra Club, to a fund-raising campaign to build a local library. Students can identify their interests and abilities and become involved in activities that apply their leadership and self-advocacy skills in settings with others who share a common goal and who may provide support and encouragement.

Self-advocacy and self-help organizations may be particularly important for many individuals with disabilities. As described in Chapter 2, self-advocacy and self-help groups are consumer-organized and run organizations that typically provide support for members; support individual and group advocacy activities; and, in some cases, provide a vehicle for socialization and interaction.

CONCLUSION

The image of people with disabilities as leaders, as well as effective team members, may be incongruous to some people. This, however, is because of the pervasive effects of stereotypes—stereotypes about people with disabilities and stereotypes about leaders in our society. When one moves beyond these stereotypes, it becomes evident that people with disabilities can assume leadership roles and can become effective team members and decision makers. The next chapter describes ways in which this can occur for students with disabilities in one important setting, the educational and transition planning and decision-making process. Skills that students learn in that setting and through other instructional efforts will be useful across the life span. Such leadership skills become particularly important as consumers of services gain more of a voice in the types of services and supports available to them.

QUESTIONS FOR REVIEW

1. Identify supports or accommodations that could overcome barriers to leadership for students with disabilities.
2. Describe the general benefits of holding meetings.
3. What are some of the specific benefits of educational planning meetings?

4. Describe different types of meetings.
5. Discuss reasons people with disabilities have not traditionally been able to assume leadership roles.
6. Discuss the types of meetings and the role of leaders and participants in each.
7. What are some basic leadership skills?

REFERENCES

Abery, B., Smith, J., Sharpe, M.N., & Chelberg, G. (1995). From the editors. *IMPACT: Feature Issue on Leadership by Persons with Disabilities, 8*(3), 1.

Americans with Disabilities Act (ADA) of 1990, PL 101-336, 42 U.S.C §§ 12101 *et seq.*

Balcazar, F.E., Seekins, T., Fawcett, S.B., & Hopkins, B.L. (1990). Empowering people with physical disabilities through advocacy skills training. *American Journal of Community Psychology, 18,* 281–296.

Bolden, J.A. (1995). The impact of gender and race on leadership by persons with disabilities. *IMPACT: Feature Issue on Leadership by Persons with Disabilities, 8*(3), 6–7.

Bormann, E.G., & Bormann, N.C. (1972). *Effective small group communication.* Edina, MN: Burgess.

Brinckerhoff, L.C. (1993). Self-advocacy: A critical skill for college students with learning disabilities. *Community Health, 16,* 23–33.

Brinckerhoff, L.C. (1994). Developing effective self-advocacy skills in college-bound students with learning disabilities. *Intervention in School and Clinic, 29,* 229–237.

Brolin, D. (1993). *Life-centered career education: A competency-based approach.* Reston, VA: Council for Exceptional Children.

Cronin, M.E., & Patton, J.R. (1993). *Life skills instruction for all students with special needs: A practical guide for integrating real-life content into the curriculum.* Austin, TX: PRO-ED.

Durlak, C.M., Rose, E., & Bursuck, W.D. (1994). Preparing high school students with learning disabilities for the transition to postsecondary education: Teaching the skills of self-determination. *Journal of Learning Disabilities, 27,* 51–59.

Gardner, K.G., DePalma, D.M., & Zastowny, T.R. (1982). Toward a comprehensive assessment of leadership behavior in groups. *Psychological Reports, 51,* 991–998.

Gould, M. (1986). Self-advocacy: Consumer leadership for the transition years. *Journal of Rehabilitation, 27,*39–42.

Guerra, N.G., Moore, A., & Slaby, R.G. (1995). *Viewpoints: A guide to conflict resolution and decision making for adolescents.* Champaign, IL: Research Press.

Howard, E. (1988). *Bill of Rights series: Teacher's guide.* Arlington, TX: The Arc National Headquarters.

Howard, E. (1991). *Handbook for high school teachers: Staff development on the topic of constitutional government.* Arlington, TX: The Arc National Headquarters.

Individuals with Disabilities Education Act (IDEA) of 1990, PL 101-476, 20 U.S.C. §§ 1400 *et seq.*

Martin, J.E., Marshall, L.H., Maxson, L., & Jerman, P. (1993). *Self-directed IEP: Teacher's manual.* Colorado Springs, CO: University of Colorado at Colorado Springs, Center for Educational Research.

McTaggert, K., & Gould, M. (1988). *Self-advocacy curriculum.* Unpublished manuscript.

Morris, G.B. (1993). Adolescent and adult female leaders: Comparisons on measures of valued leadership traits and irrational thinking. *Psychological Reports, 72,* 565–566.

Phillips, P. (1990). A self-advocacy plan for high school students with learning disabilities: A comparative case study analysis of students', teachers' and parents' perceptions of program effects. *Journal of Learning Disabilities, 23,* 466–471.

Rehabilitation Act of 1973, PL 93-112, 29 U.S.C. §§ 701 *et seq.*

Sears, J., Bishop, A., Stevens, E. (1989). Teaching Miranda rights to students who have mental retardation. *Teaching Exceptional Children, 21,* 38–42.

Valenti, R.A. (1989). *Developing self-advocacy.* Columbia, MO: Hawthorne Educational Services.

Wehmeyer, M.L., & Berkobien, R. (1996). The legacy of self-advocacy: People with cognitive disabilities as leaders in their community. In G. Dybwad & H. Bersani (Eds.), *New voices: Self-advocacy by people with disabilities* (pp. 246–257). Cambridge, MA: Brookline Books.

Wehmeyer, M.L., & Kelchner, K. (1995). *Whose future is it anyway? A student-directed transition planning program.* Arlington, TX: The Arc National Headquarters.

West, L.L., Corbey, S., Boyer-Stephens, A., Jones, B., Miller, R.J., & Sarkees-Wircenski, M. (1992). *Integrating transition planning into the IEP process.* Reston, VA: Council for Exceptional Children.

CHAPTER 12

Self-Advocacy
Through Student Involvement

After reading this chapter, you will be able to

1. Discuss the educational benefits of student involvement in the planning and decision-making process

2. Briefly discuss the reasons students may be left out of the transition planning process

3. Discuss the Adaptability Instruction model, student activities in the model, its "essential components," and its influence on later models for promoting student involvement

4. Discuss several programs to promote student involvement in educational planning and decision making, the skills each addresses, and unique aspects of each program

KEY TERMS

1. Adaptability Instruction model

2. ChoiceMaker Self-Determination Transition Curriculum and program

3. Deficits model

4. Education for All Handicapped Children Act of 1975 (PL 94-142)

5. Partial participation

6. Self-efficacy

7. Self-evaluation

8. Self-instruction

9. Self-modeling

10. Self-reinforcement

11. Student involvement

12. Student-directed learning

As discussed in Chapter 3, the student involvement requirements in the Individuals with Disabilities Education Act (IDEA) of 1990 (PL 101-476) and its amendments have provided impetus to efforts to promote self-determination as an educational outcome. In addition to justifying the need for instruction in self-determination, however, student involvement in educational planning meetings and the educational planning process provides an ideal environment in which students with disabilities can learn and practice self-advocacy skills. This chapter describes ways in which the educational planning process can be used to teach self-advocacy and highlights several curricular strategies that can be used to promote self-advocacy through student involvement.

WHAT IS STUDENT INVOLVEMENT?

Promoting student involvement has too frequently been misinterpreted as giving students absolute control over the educational process. Involvement in educational planning and decision making can take many forms, from students generating their own individualized education program (IEP) goals and objectives to introducing members of the IEP team. The degree to which students, when provided adequate support, can or will want to participate in educational planning and decision making varies significantly from one student to another. Regardless of the role the student assumes, the key to student involvement is that the student is an active, rather than passive, participant in his or her educational program.

Agran (1997) defined *student-directed learning* as instructional activities in which students have control over their learning, experience opportunities to set goals, define actions based on those goals, implement the chosen actions, evaluate their outcomes, and adjust their performances. Student involvement in transition planning and decision making is the intuitive antecedent to student-directed learning; the student is actively involved in his or her educational planning and decision-making process. As such, the definitional criteria for student involvement is not that students have absolute control over their planning, decision-making, and learning process; but that they are active participants, indeed equal partners, in this process.

In addition to promoting the development of self-advocacy skills, there are a number of educational benefits to student involvement. Strickland and Turnbull (1990) listed several benefits, including

1. Students can contribute firsthand information regarding areas that present the greatest and least amount of difficulty for them and identify strategies that enable them to overcome these difficulties.
2. The student's presence at the IEP meeting can personalize the meeting for team members, particularly if they do not know the student. This also enables other team members to ask the student directly about interests, skills, accommodations, and so forth.

3. By including students in the decision-making process, team members communicate to them that they are expected to behave maturely and responsibly. Students may be more motivated to pursue goals that they have had a hand in selecting.

HOW INVOLVED ARE STUDENTS WITH DISABILITIES?

The emphasis on student involvement in planning and decision making contrasts with the historical role of students in educational planning and decision making, a role that has been associated with passivity and inactivity. Prior to the passage of the Education for All Handicapped Children Act of 1975 (PL 94-142), decisions about the educational program a student with a disability received (in those cases in which an educational program was even available) were made by educational and psychological professionals, typically the school psychologist or diagnostician (Yoshida, Fenton, Maxwell, & Kaufman, 1978). PL 94-142 opened the door for parental and family involvement in educational planning and decision making, and although the actual implementation of this component remains inconsistent (Wehmeyer & Davis, 1995), parental involvement became a more visible factor in educational placement and program decisions.

PL 94-142 suggested that students' involvement in IEP decisions take place "whenever appropriate"; however, as Gillespie and Turnbull (1983) have pointed out, this was too frequently interpreted to mean that student involvement was not appropriate or necessary. As a result, student involvement in educational planning and decision making became haphazard at best, and students were essentially outsiders to the educational decision-making process (Van Reusen & Bos, 1990, 1994; Wehmeyer & Lawrence, 1995). Van Reusen and Bos (1990) concluded that "student involvement [in educational planning], even at the secondary level, is for the most part either nonexistent or passive" (p. 30). This is the case in spite of evidence that shows that student involvement can have positive effects on student achievement, outcomes, and motivation, as detailed subsequently, and that, for the most part, educators agree that students can benefit from greater involvement in transition planning. Walker and Shaw (1995) found that special educators perceived student involvement in transition planning to be low but felt such involvement to be desirable.

Field, Hoffman, and Sawilowsky (1994) conducted a pilot study of student involvement in transition planning. They interviewed 41 students, classified as having a disability and being eligible for special education services, regarding their involvement in their last educational planning meeting. Seventy-one percent of these students indicated that they attended their last IEP meeting. However, 56% indicated they had not been told the purpose of the meeting, 63% indicated that they had not been told things to think about before the meeting, 76% said they had not prepared for the meeting, and only 41% indicated that they had helped to identify goals that were included in their IEP.

BARRIERS TO STUDENT
INVOLVEMENT IN TRANSITION PLANNING

Students with disabilities are left out of the transition planning process for a number of reasons. One common factor that has led to the assumption that student involvement, particularly in educational planning and decision making, was not appropriate was the presence of a severe disabling condition. Until the 1980s, issues of student choice and preference for students with severe, multiple disabilities have been largely ignored by most educators (Guess, Benson, & Siegel-Causey, 1985). In a study of students with severe disabilities, for example, Houghton, Bronicki, and Guess (1987) determined that classroom staff responded with very low rates to student-initiated expressions of preference or choice during the school day. The assumption that students with severe disabilities cannot be involved in educational planning and decision making is not consistent with findings from the self-management literature that shows that students with severe disabilities can direct their own learning (Agran, 1997). Many of these studies showed that students and adults with severe disabilities can self-regulate all or a portion of the learning process.

Furthermore, exclusion from educational planning and decision making is not restricted solely to students with severe disabilities. Students with learning disabilities, emotional disorders, mental retardation requiring only intermittent supports, and other higher incidence populations have not gained adequate access to the planning process. For example, when Gilliam and Coleman (1981) conducted a survey of participants in IEP meetings for students with learning disabilities and emotional disorders to determine who most influenced IEP committee decisions, students were not even included in the list of "influential committee members" from whom survey respondents could select!

A number of additional issues stand as barriers to student involvement. One such issue is a societal distrust of the competence of most minors to make decisions in an informed and effective manner (Adelman, MacDonald, Nelson, Smith, & Taylor, 1990). Many educators also point to the lack of student motivation to participate in the educational process, particularly the IEP meeting, as a barrier to student involvement. Finally, there is a pervasive belief that the educational planning and decision-making process is, inherently, too complex for students and, thus, should be handled by someone with specific expertise in control. Sufficient evidence is available, however, to discount these objections and to actively involve students in the transition process. As discussed in Chapter 1, research has shown that students with disabilities can make competent decisions (e.g., Salend, 1983; Taylor, Adelman, & Kaser-Boyd, 1983, 1985; Van Reusen & Bos, 1994) and can adequately take into account the degree of risk involved with various options (Grisso & Vierling, 1978)

The suggestion that the transition process is too complex for students with disabilities has some face validity given the complexity of most school procedures. Perhaps the strongest evidence to the contrary is that a number of re-searchers have shown that students can be involved effectively in the transition planning and decision-making process despite complex procedures (Martin & Marshall, 1995; Van Reusen & Bos, 1994; Wehmeyer & Lawrence, 1995). Turnbull, Anderson, Turnbull, Seaton, and Dinas (1996) showed that students with severe cognitive and multiple disabilities could be involved in transition planning and decision making. These programs succeed because they enable students to "maximally participate" in their transition program. In many cases, such maximal participation is achieved by use of the principle of partial partic-ipation, forwarded by Baumgart and colleagues (1982). This principle was orig-inally forwarded in relationship to the participation of students with severe disabilities in educational programs and, simply put, suggests that most students can be at least partially involved in virtually any activity. In the case of transition planning, a student with mental retardation may not be able to complete the complicated IEP form mandated for use by the school district, but the student could introduce his or her team members, be responsible for listing the previous year's goals, and identify new goals or objectives.

In summary, there seems to be clear evidence that student involvement in transition planning and decision making can have multiple benefits, including opportunities to teach self-advocacy skills; yet, despite this evidence, student involvement is minimal. Traditional barriers to student involvement are based primarily on beliefs about minors and students with disabilities that are, at best, incorrect and serve to limit the degree to which educators and family members seek to involve students in transition programming.

STRATEGIES TO PROMOTE STUDENT INVOLVEMENT

The utility of the educational planning meeting to promote leadership, team-work, and participation skills was discussed in Chapter 11. This section reviews programmatic efforts to achieve student involvement, including a number of model programs that have been developed to involve students in the educational planning and decision-making process.

Adaptability Instruction Model

One of the first models for promoting student involvement and self-determination was the Adaptability Instruction model forwarded by Mithaug, Martin, and Agran (1987). These authors proposed that students should learn to become "more independent in understanding what they need and want, how to set personal goals...and to select action plans that will lead to desired out-comes" (Mithaug, Horiuchi, & McNulty, 1987, p. 59). The Adaptability In-struction model incorporated findings from problem-solving, self-management, and self-regulation literature (Agran & Martin, 1987; Bandura, 1986; Kanfer & Goldstein, 1986; Martin, Burger, Elias-Burger, & Mithaug, 1988; Mithaug,

1993) and provided a framework through which student involvement could be achieved. The core tenets of the Adaptability Instruction model were that students should be involved in activities promoting decision making, independent performance, self-evaluation, and adjustment. This model operationalizes, and thus exemplifies, the key elements of student involvement in transition programming. Students involved in activities based on the Adaptability Instruction model identify their own needs, interests, and abilities; consider options and alternatives for transition-related outcomes; and select goals and objectives related to the selected outcomes. Students then work with teachers to design and implement student-directed learning activities that enable them to achieve these goals and objectives, including self-instruction and other antecedent procedures, such as picture cues, written prompts, and verbal labeling (Wehmeyer, Martin, & Sands, 1997).

While working on these tasks, students self-evaluate by monitoring and recording performance outcomes, and then comparing their results with goals and performance objectives set during the decision-making process. Students adjust their performance by using their self-evaluations to decide what to do next time. These adjustments "are the essential component of the Adaptability Instruction model. They connect future actions with past performance. Before beginning another task or project, students review feedback from previous adjustment decisions and select goals, plans, and performance objectives accordingly" (Wehmeyer et al., 1997, p. 555).

Perhaps the essential component of student involvement across virtually all programs is that the preferences, interests, abilities, wants, and needs of the student are the starting point for all activities. Although some students with more severe disabilities may have considerable difficulty with the decision-making, goal-setting, or problem-solving aspects of student involvement, all students express some preferences and can become involved from that aspect. The degree to which student preferences and interests are used to enable students to make meaningful choices for educational programs is, essentially, dependent on the creativity and motivation of educators and family members.

It is not taken for granted, however, that students will be able to identify their own interests, abilities, limitations, and strengths. This may be especially true for students receiving special education services, for which a deficits model has too frequently emphasized student weaknesses (Wehmeyer, 1992). To combat this deficits model, most programs to promote student involvement focus on enabling students to identify interests based on their preferences, understand their unique abilities and limitations, and learn to apply these strengths and interests to identify future plans and goals. Additional themes common to student involvement programs, illustrated by the Adaptability Instruction model, include having students learn to identify problems, identify and evaluate options or solutions to the problems, and identify and contact resources that enable them to implement selected options. Student involvement programs frequently teach students how to generate, evaluate, and track educational goals and objectives; express leadership and self-advocacy skills; communicate effectively by using negotiation, compromise, and persuasion, and self-regulate their behavior. The latter includes the employment of student-directed learning strategies, such as self-instruction, self-modeling, self-evaluation, and self-reinforcement (see Chapters 7 and 8).

Student-Directed IEP Programs

Several programs apply the key elements introduced in the Adaptability Instruction model to programmatic efforts to involve students in transition planning. These programs employ two basic strategies, student-directed transition planning programs and self-advocacy programs, although most programs incorporate aspects of both. Student-directed transition planning programs emphasize student direction of the educational planning process, and they are often written expressly for students to implement and use the IEP or transition planning meeting as the fulcrum for activities. Self-advocacy programs tend to emphasize the development of skills related to leadership, assertive communication, individual rights and responsibilities, and advocacy efforts; they are less likely to use the IEP meeting itself as a central focus and are generally implemented by someone other than the student (e.g., the classroom teacher). Most of the latter are discussed in Chapter 11. However, one self-advocacy program, The Self-Advocacy Strategy for Education and Transition Planning (Van Reusen, Bos, Schumaker, & Deshler, 1994), uses the IEP meeting as the focal point for the development of self-advocacy skills and is presented later in this chapter.

ChoiceMaker Self-Determination Transition Curriculum
The ChoiceMaker program (overviewed in Martin & Marshall, 1996) emerged from a federally funded self-determination grant and teaches self-determination through student self-management of the IEP process. The *ChoiceMaker Self-Determination Transition Curriculum* (Martin & Marshall, 1995) consists of three sections: 1) Choosing Goals, 2) Expressing Goals, and 3) Taking Action. Each section contains from two to four teaching goals and numerous teaching objectives addressing six transition areas. Included are 1) an assessment tool, 2) Choosing Goals lessons, 3) the Self-Directed IEP, and 4) Taking Action lessons.

The ChoiceMaker materials are built around a socially validated transition curriculum. The first step in the validation process involved a comprehensive literature review and interview process. This resulted in a list of 37 self-determination concepts, which the authors grouped into seven areas:

- Self-awareness
- Self-advocacy
- Self-efficacy
- Decision making

- Independent performance
- Self-evaluation
- Adjustment

Table 1 lists the 37 self-determination concepts in the seven areas. After this initial identification phase, the concepts were defined, expanded, and placed into a curriculum matrix. At this time, teachers, adults with disabilities, parents, and university-based transition experts from around the United States validated the concepts and the matrix. Finally, a comprehensive field test of the materials was conducted. Figure 1 provides a graphic example of the flow between the transition domains of the ChoiceMaker IEP process. The *ChoiceMaker Self-Determination Transition Curriculum* sections, goals, and lessons are provided in Table 2.

The Choosing Goals lessons enable students to learn the necessary skills and personal information needed to articulate their interests, skills, limits, and goals in one or more self-selected transition areas. The Self-Directed IEP lessons enable students to learn the leadership skills necessary to manage their IEP meeting and publicly disclose their interests, skills, limits, and goals identified through the Choosing Goals lessons. Rather than be passive participants at their IEP meetings, students learn to lead their meeting to the greatest extent of their ability. These lessons teach students 11 steps for leading their own meeting (see Table 3 in Chapter 11).

The Taking Action materials enable students to learn how to break down their long-range goals into specific goals that can be accomplished in a week. Students learn how they will attain their goals by deciding 1) a standard for goal performance, 2) a means to get performance feedback, 3) what motivates them to accomplish a goal, 4) the strategies they will use, 5) needed supports, and 6) schedules. Instead of teachers, parents, or support staff telling students what to do, when to do it, and how they did, students assume these responsibilities. This requires a learning process that fades teacher instruction as students learn the crucial skills. Martin and Marshall (1995) reported that the ChoiceMaker materials were field-tested and revised with students with behavioral and learning disabilities across several school districts.

Whose Future Is it Anyway?   The Arc, with funding from the U.S. Department of Education, has developed and field-tested a student-directed transition planning program for adolescents with mental retardation and other cognitive and developmental disabilities entitled *Whose Future Is it Anyway?* (Wehmeyer & Kelchner, 1995). This curriculum consists of 36 sessions introducing students to the concept of transition and transition planning and enabling students to self-direct instruction related to 1) self-awareness and disability awareness; 2) making decisions about transition-related outcomes; 3) identifying and securing community resources to support transition services; 4) writing and evaluating transition goals and objectives; 5) communicating

Table 1.   ChoiceMaker self-determination constructs

Core area	Self-determination construct
Self-awareness	• Identify needs. • Identify interests. • Identify and understand strengths. • Identify and understand limitations. • Identify own values.
Self-advocacy	• Assertively state wants. • Assertively state rights. • Determine support needs. • Pursue needed support. • Obtain and evaluate needed support. • Conduct own affairs.
Self-efficacy	• Expect to obtain goals.
Decision making	• Assess situational demands. • Set goals. • Set standards. • Identify information needed to make decisions. • Consider past solutions for new situations. • Generate new, creative solutions. • Consider options. • Choose best option. • Develop plan.
Independent performance	• Initiate tasks on time. • Complete tasks on time. • Use self-management strategies. • Perform tasks to standard. • Follow through on own plan.
Self-evaluation	• Monitor task performance. • Compare performance to standard. • Evaluate effectiveness of self-management strategies. • Determine whether plan is completed and goal met.
Adjustment	• Change goals. • Change standards. • Change plan. • Change strategies. • Change support. • Persistently adjust. • Use environmental feedback to aid adjustment.

effectively in small groups; and 6) developing skills to become an effective team member, leader, or self-advocate.

The materials are student directed in that they are written for students as end-users. The level of support needed by students to complete activities varies a great deal. Some students with difficulty reading or writing need one-to-one support to progress through the materials; others can complete the process independently. The materials make every effort to ensure that students retain some control while at the same time receiving the support they need to succeed. For example, although there is a *Coach's Guide* (Wehmeyer & Lawrence, 1995a) to assist teachers in providing adequate support, the identification of the person to serve as coach is left to the student. Students are instructed to identify a teacher or other person to serve as a coach and to take the *Coach's Guide* to that person.

Section 1 of *Whose Future Is it Anyway?* (titled "Getting to Know You") introduces the concept of transition and educational planning; provides information about transition requirements in IDEA; and enables students to identify who has attended past planning meetings, who is required to be present at such meetings, and who they want involved in their planning process. Later in the section, they are introduced to four primary transition outcome areas (employment, community living, postsecondary education, and recreation and leisure). Activities throughout the process focus on these transition outcome areas.

The remainder of the sessions in the first section discuss the topic of disability and disability-awareness. Students are encouraged to identify their own unique characteristics, including their abilities and interests. Participants then identify specific learning needs related to their disability. This process begins with a discussion of stereotypes associated with disability and the possible negative impact of such stereotypes.

The second section ("Making Decisions") introduces a decision-making process called "DO IT!" (see Table 3) that students then apply toward making

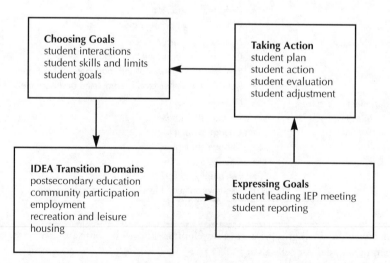

Figure 1.   The flow between transition domains and the ChoiceMaker IEP process. (Adapted from Martin & Marshall [1996].)

Table 2.   *ChoiceMaker Self-Determination Transition Curriculum* sections, goals, and lessons

Section	Goals	Lessons
1. Choosing Goals	A. Student Interests B. Student Skills and Limits C. Student Goals	• Choosing Employment Goals • Choosing Personal Goals • Choosing Post–High School Goals • Choosing Secondary School Goals • Choosing Housing and Daily Living Goals • Choosing Community Participation Goals
2. Expressing Goals	D. Student Leading Meeting E. Student Reporting	• Self-Directed IEP
3. Taking Action	F. Student Plan G. Student Action H. Student Evaluation I. Student Adjustment	• Take Action

Adapted from Martin & Marshall (1996).

decisions about the four transition outcome areas. Students learn a simple problem-solving process by working through each step in the process to make a decision about a potential living arrangement, and they then apply the process to make decisions about the three other transition outcome areas. In the final session in this section, students learn to use the DO IT! process to give informed consent and apply this specifically to the transition planning meeting.

The third section ("How to Get What You Need, Sec. 101") enables students to locate community resources identified in previous planning meetings that are intended to provide supports in each of the transition outcome areas. Students identify such supports, if available, then gather information about each community resource. Section 4 ("Goals, Objectives and the Future") enables learners to apply a set of rules to identify transition-related goals and objectives that are currently on their IEP or transition planning form, evaluate these goals based on their own transition interests and abilities, and develop additional goals to take to their next planning meeting. Students learn what goals and objectives

Table 3.   DO IT! Problem-solving strategy from *Whose Future Is it Anyway?*

D	**D**efine the problem.
O	**O**utline your options.
I	**I**dentify the outcome of each option.
T	**T**ake action.
!	Get excited**!**

are, how they should be written, and ways to track progress on goals and objectives.

The fifth section ("Communication") introduces effective communication strategies for small-group situations, such as the transition planning meetings. Students work through sessions that introduce different types of communication (e.g., verbal, body language) and how to interpret these communicative behaviors, understand the differences between aggressive and assertive communication, learn how to effectively negotiate and compromise, when to use persuasion, and other skills that will enable them to be more effective communicators during transition planning meetings.

The final section ("Thank You, Honorable Chairperson") enables students to learn types and purposes of meetings, steps to holding effective meetings, and roles of the meeting chairperson and team members. Students are encouraged to work with school-district personnel to take a meaningful role in planning for and participating in the meeting, including eventually chairing a transition planning meeting themselves.

Students are encouraged to work on one session per week during the weeks between their previous transition planning meeting and the next scheduled meeting. The final two sessions review the previous sessions and provide a refresher for students as they head into their planning meeting. After all development activities were completed, the *Whose Future Is it Anyway?* process was field-tested with almost 60 students with cognitive disabilities attending high school (Wehmeyer & Lawrence, 1995b). Analyses of pre- and postintervention student assessments indicated significant changes in students' scores on self-efficacy and outcome expectancy for educational planning, indicating that students believed they possessed more skills necessary to participate in their planning meeting and felt that if they exhibited these actions, preferred outcomes related to their involvement in the meeting would occur. In addition, students provided consistent positive feedback about the process and its importance to their lives, a finding replicated with these students' teachers.

Next S.T.E.P.: Student Transition and Educational Planning   Halpern et al. (1997) developed a student-directed transition planning program called the *Next S.T.E.P.* curriculum. The two main purposes of this curriculum are to "teach students the skills they need to do transition planning" and "engage students successfully in this process" (Halpern et al., 1997, p. 1). The curriculum uses video and print materials developed for specific audiences (e.g., students, teachers, family members) to help students become motivated to engage in transition planning, self-evaluate transition needs, identify and select transition goals and activities, assume responsibility for conducting their own transition planning meeting, and monitor the implementation of their transition plans.

The curriculum consists of 16 lessons, clustered into four instructional units, with each lesson designed to be delivered in a 50-minute class period. These lessons include teacher and student materials, videos, guidelines for involving parents and family members, and a process for tracking student progress. Unit 1 ("Getting Started"), which introduces and overviews transition planning, is intended to enable students to understand the transition planning process and to motivate them to participate. Unit 2 ("Self-Exploration and Self-Evaluation") includes six lessons that focus on student self-evaluation. Students work through activities that identify unique interests, strengths, and weaknesses in various adult-outcome oriented areas. At the end of this unit, students complete the student form of the Transition Skills Inventory, a 72-item rating instrument assessing how well the student is doing in four transition areas: 1) personal life, 2) jobs, 3) education and training, and 4) living on one's own. The student's self-evaluation of these areas are combined with similar evaluations by his or her teacher and a family member to form a basis for future transition planning activities. Students are encouraged to discuss differences of opinion between the teacher or family member evaluations and their own self-evaluation and to resolve these discrepancies either before or during the transition planning meeting.

Unit 3 ("Developing Goals and Activities") includes five lessons regarding transition goal identification in the four areas considered in the Transition Skills Inventory. Students identify their hopes and dreams, then select from a broad range of potential goals in each area, narrowing the total set of transition goals to four or five goals that they prefer. In addition, students choose activities that will help them pursue the goals they have selected. Unit 4 ("Putting a Plan into Place") includes three lessons preparing students for their transition planning meeting. The lessons emphasize the implementation of their plan and help students to ensure that they monitor their progress and, if necessary, make adjustments. Halpern and colleagues (1997) have successfully field-tested and validated the use of the curriculum with more than 1,000 students with disabilities.

Self-Advocacy Strategy for Education and Transition Planning

Van Reusen et al. (1994) developed a procedure that incorporates both student-directed transition planning and self-advocacy instruction. The program stresses the importance of self-advocacy to enhance student motivation and is "designed to enable students to systematically gain a sense of control and influence over their own learning and development" (p. 1). Students progress through a series of lesson plans focusing on seven instructional stages. Stage 1, titled "Orient and Make Commitments," broadly introduces education and transition planning meetings, the program itself, and how participation can increase student power and control in this process. Stage 2, titled "Describe," defines and provides detailed information about transition and education planning meetings and the advantages students experience if they participate. In this stage the "I–PLAN" steps of student participation are introduced. These steps provide a simple algorithm that students can use to chart their participation in planning meetings. Table 4 illustrates the I–PLAN steps.

In Stage 3, "Model and Prepare," the teacher models the I–PLAN steps so that students can see the process in action. Students complete an Inventory, step 1 in the I–PLAN process, resulting in information that they can use at

Table 4.   I–PLAN steps for a successful transition planning meeting

I	**I**nventory your strengths, areas in which to improve or learn, and goals and choices for learning or accommodations.
P	**P**rovide your inventory information.
L	**L**isten and respond.
A	**A**sk questions.
N	**N**ame your goals.

their conference. Stage 4 is "Verbal Practice," during which students are asked questions to make sure they know what to do during each step of the I–PLAN strategy, and then students verbally rehearse each of the steps. In Stage 5, "Group Practice and Feedback," once students have demonstrated mastery of the steps in I–PLAN, they participate in a simulated group conference. The student receives feedback from the teacher and other students, and the group generates suggestions on where the student might improve. The simulated conference is audio- or videotaped for future reference.

Stage 6, "Individual Practice and Feedback," allows the student to meet independently with the teacher for practice; feedback; and, eventually, mastery. The audio- or videotape from the previous stage is reviewed and students provide a self-evaluation of their performance. The student and instructor work together to improve areas of self-identified need and engage in another simulated conference that is also audio- or videotaped and used to document improvement and reevaluate performance. Stage 7, "Generalization," is intended to generalize the I–PLAN strategy to actual conferences. This stage has three phases: 1) preparing for and conducting the planning conference, 2) preparing for other uses of the strategy, and 3) preparing for subsequent conferences. Van Reusen and colleagues (1990, 1994) have shown that the I–PLAN strategy can be successfully implemented with students with disabilities and results in increased motivation and participation.

TAKE CHARGE for the Future   *TAKE CHARGE for the Future* (Powers, 1996) is a student-directed, collaborative model to promote student involvement in educational and transition planning. The model is an adaptation of a validated approach, referred to as *TAKE CHARGE,* to promote the self-determination of youth with and without disabilities (Powers, Sowers, Turner, Nesbitt, Knowles, & Ellison, 1996). TAKE CHARGE uses four primary components or strategies to promote adolescent development of self-determination: skill facilitation, mentoring, peer support, and parent support. TAKE CHARGE introduces youth to three major skills areas needed to take charge in one's life: achievement skills, partnership skills, and coping skills. Table 5 shows the skills addressed in each of these areas.

Youth involved in the TAKE CHARGE process are matched with successful adults of the same gender who experience similar challenges and share common interests; the youth are also involved in peer support activities through-

Table 5. Strategies and skills in the TAKE CHARGE model

Skills areas	Specific skills
Achievement	Dream.
	Set goals.
	Problem-solve.
	Prepare.
	Do it!
Partnership	Schmooze.
	Be assertive.
	Negotiate.
	Manage help.
Coping	Think positive.
	Focus on accomplishments.
	Manage frustration.
	Track and reward progress.

out the program (Powers et al., 1996). Parent support is provided via information and technical assistance and written materials.

TAKE CHARGE for the Future uses the same set of core strategies to enable learners with disabilities to participate in their transition planning meeting. Students are provided self-help materials and coaching to identify their transition goals; to organize and conduct transition planning meetings; and to achieve their goals through the application of problem-solving, self-regulation, and partnership management strategies. Concurrently, youth participate in self-selected mentorship and peer support activities to increase their transition-focused knowledge and skills. Their parents are also provided with information and support to promote their capacities to encourage their son's or daughter's active involvement in transition planning.

Goal Action Planning   Turnbull and colleagues (1996) developed the *Goal Action Planning* (Anderson, Seaton, Dinas, & Satterfield, 1995) procedure to enable youth with mental retardation and developmental disabilities who require extensive supports to become involved in their educational planning. Goal Action Planning incorporates strategies from future planning models to achieve this end. Students, family members, professionals, and others complete a process, which begins with identifying the student's dreams and hopes, to identify goals, resources, and obstacles to achieving the student's desired outcomes. Using this information, the student with a disability, supported by the group, formulates action plans across eight areas of daily life: domestic, transportation, employment, financial, recreational, social relationships, behavioral patterns, and community participation. The program was developed through a model demonstration program and was field-tested and validated with learners with significant learning needs.

CONCLUSION

The programs described in this chapter offer specific programs that could be implemented and, more important, serve as guides for teacher-initiated efforts to improve student involvement. These programs share common activities, including efforts to increase student self-awareness; awareness of the educational and transition planning process; goal-setting, decision-making, and planning skills; self-advocacy; and leadership skills. They take as their basic vision the importance of getting students actively involved to the greatest extent possible.

QUESTIONS FOR REVIEW

1. What is the key to student involvement?
2. Discuss what IDEA has to say about student involvement. Should this language be stronger?
3. Identify the essential component of student involvement across virtually all programs.
4. Briefly cite characteristics of student-directed planning programs and self-advocacy programs that emphasize their differences.
5. Discuss the advantages of teaching self-determination by emphasizing student self-management of the IEP process.
6. Discuss the disadvantages of coupling the IEP process and self-determination.
7. Identify the steps to running an IEP meeting as discussed in the ChoiceMaker program.
8. What is the DO IT! process? Discuss the importance of using metacognitive strategies to promote decision making.
9. Discuss the similarities and differences among various student involvement programs.

REFERENCES

Adelman, H.S., MacDonald, V.M., Nelson, P., Smith, D.C., & Taylor, L. (1990). Motivational readiness of children with learning and behavior problems in psychoeducational decision making. *Journal of Learning Disabilities, 23,* 171–176.

Agran, M. (Ed.). (1997). *Student-directed learning: Teaching self-determination skills.* Thousand Oaks, CA: Brooks/Cole.

Agran, M., & Martin, J.E. (1987). Applying a technology of self-control in community environments for individuals who are mentally retarded. In M. Hersen, R.M. Eisler, & P.M. Miller (Eds.), *Progress in behavior modification* (pp. 108–151). Beverly Hills: Sage Publications.

Anderson, E.L., Seaton, K., Dinas, P., & Satterfield, A. (1995). *Group Action Planning: An innovative manual for building a self-determined future.* Lawrence, KS: Full Citizenship., Inc.

Bandura, A. (1986). *Social foundations of thought and action: A social cognitive theory.* Englewood Cliffs, NJ: Prentice Hall.

Baumgart, D., Brown, L., Pumpian, I., Nisbet, J., Ford, A., Sweet, M., Messina, R., & Schroeder, J. (1982). Principle of partial participation and individualized adaptations in educational programs for severely handicapped students. *Journal of The Association for Persons with Severe Handicaps, 7,* 17–27.

Education for All Handicapped Children Act of 1975, PL 94-142, 20 U.S.C. §§ 1400 *et seq.*

Field, S., Hoffman, A., & Sawilowsky, S. (1994). *Student involvement in transition planning: A proposal submitted to the U.S. Department of Education.* Detroit, MI: Wayne State University.

Gillespie, E.B., & Turnbull, A.P. (1983). It's my IEP! Involving students in the planning process. *Teaching Exceptional Children, 29,* 27–29.

Gilliam, J.E., & Coleman, M.C. (1981). Who influences IEP committee decisions? *Exceptional Children, 47,* 642–644.

Grisso, T., & Vierling, L. (1978). Minor's consent to treatment: A developmental perspective. *Professional Psychology, 9,* 412–427.

Guess, D., Benson, H.A., & Siegel-Causey, E. (1985). Concepts and issues related to choice-making and autonomy among persons with severe disabilities. *Journal of The Association for Persons with Severe Handicaps, 10,* 79–86.

Halpern, A.S., Herr, C.M., Wolf, N.K., Lawson, J.D., Doren, B., & Johnson, M.D. (1997). *NEXT S.T.E.P.: Student transition and educational planning.* Austin, TX: PRO-ED.

Houghton, J., Bronicki, G.J.B., & Guess, D. (1987). Opportunities to express preferences and make choices among students with severe disabilities in classroom settings. *Journal of The Association for Persons with Severe Handicaps, 10,* 87–95.

Individuals with Disabilities Education Act (IDEA) of 1990, PL 101-476, 20 U.S.C. §§ 1400 *et seq.*

Kanfer, F.H., & Goldstein, A.P. (1986). *Helping people change: A textbook of methods* (3rd ed.). Elmsford, NY: Pergamon Press.

Martin, J.E., Burger, D.L., Elias-Burger, S., & Mithaug, D. (1988). Application of self-control strategies to facilitate independence in vocational and instructional settings. In N.W. Bray (Ed.), *International review of research in mental retardation* (Vol. 15, pp. 155–193). San Diego, CA: Academic Press.

Martin, J.E., & Marshall, L.H. (1995). ChoiceMaker: A comprehensive self-determination transition program. *Intervention in School and Clinic, 30,* 147–156.

Martin, J.E., & Marshall, L.H. (1996). ChoiceMaker: Infusing self-determination instruction into the IEP and transition process. In D.J. Sands & M.L. Wehmeyer (Eds.), *Self-determination across the life span: Independence and choice for people with disabilities,* (pp. 215–236). Baltimore: Paul H. Brookes Publishing Co.

Mithaug, D.E. (1993). *Self-regulation theory: How optimal adjustment maximizes gain.* New York: Praeger.

Mithaug, D.E., Horiuchi, C.N., & McNulty, B.A. (1987). *Parent reports on the transitions of students graduating from Colorado special education programs in 1978 and 1979.* Denver: Colorado Department of Education.

Mithaug, D.E., Martin, J.E., & Agran, M. (1987). Adaptability instruction: The goal of transitional programs. *Exceptional Children, 57,* 6–14.

Powers, L.E. (1996). *TAKE CHARGE transition planning project.* (Grant No. H H158U50001 from the U.S. Department of Education and Oregon Health Sciences). Portland: Oregon Health Sciences University.

Powers, L.E., Sowers, J., Turner, A., Nesbitt, M., Knowles, E., & Ellison, R. (1996). TAKE CHARGE: A model for promoting self-determination among adolescents with challenges. In L.E. Powers, G.H.S. Singer, & J. Sowers (Eds.), *On the road to auton-*

omy: Promoting self-competence for children and youth with disabilities (pp. 291–322). Baltimore: Paul H. Brookes Publishing Co.

Salend, S.J. (1983). Self-assessment: A model for involving students in the formulation of their IEPs. *Journal of School Psychology, 21,* 65–70.

Strickland, B.B., & Turnbull, A.P. (1990). *Developing and implementing individualized education programs.* Columbus, OH: Charles E. Merrill.

Taylor, L., Adelman, H.S., & Kaser-Boyd, N. (1983). Perspectives of children regarding their participation in psychoeducational decisions. *Professional Psychology: Research and Practice, 14,* 882–894.

Taylor, L., Adelman, H.S., & Kaser-Boyd, N. (1985). Minor's attitudes and competence toward participation in psychoeducational decisions. *Professional Psychology: Research and Practice, 16,* 226–235.

Turnbull, A.P., Blue-Banning, M.J., Anderson, E.L., Turnbull, H.R., Seaton, K.A., & Dinas, P.A. (1996). Enhancing self-determination through Group Action Planning: A holistic emphasis. In D.J. Sands & M.L. Wehmeyer (Eds.), *Self-determination across the life span: Independence and choice for people with disabilities* (pp. 237–256). Baltimore: Paul H. Brookes Publishing Co.

Van Reusen, A.K., & Bos, C.S. (1990). I Plan: Helping students communicate in planning conferences. *Teaching Exceptional Children, 22*(4), 30–32.

Van Reusen, A.K., & Bos, C.S. (1994). Facilitating student participation in individualized education programs through motivation strategy instruction. *Exceptional Children, 60,* 466–475.

Van Reusen, A.K., Bos, C.S., Schumaker, J.B., & Deshler, D.D. (1994). *The self-advocacy strategy for education and transition planning.* Lawrence, KS: Edge Enterprises.

Walker, J.H., & Shaw, S.F. (1995, October). *Perceptions of team members regarding the involvement of students with learning disabilities in transition planning.* Paper presented at the International Conference of the Division on Career Development and Transition, Raleigh, NC.

Wehmeyer, M.L. (1992). Self-determination and the education of students with mental retardation. *Education and Training in Mental Retardation, 27,* 302–314.

Wehmeyer, M.L., & Davis, S. (1995). Family involvement. In D. Brolin (Ed.), *Career education: A functional life skills approach* (pp. 91–116). Columbus, OH: Charles E. Merrill/Prentice Hall.

Wehmeyer, M.L., & Kelchner, K. (1995). *Whose future is it anyway? A student-directed transition planning program.* Arlington, TX: The Arc National Headquarters.

Wehmeyer, M.L., & Lawrence, M. (1995a). *Coach's guide: Whose future is it anyway? A student-directed transition planning program.* Reston, VA: Council for Exceptional Children.

Wehmeyer, M.L., & Lawrence, M. (1995b). Whose future is it anyway? Promoting student involvement in transition planning. *Career Development for Exceptional Individuals, 18,* 69–83.

Wehmeyer, M.L., Martin, J.E., & Sands, D.J. (1997). Self-determination for children and youth with developmental disabilities. In A. Hilton & R. Ringlaben (Eds.), *Best practices in educating students with developmental disabilities* (pp. 549–569). Austin, TX: PRO-ED.

Yoshida, R.K., Fenton, K.S., Maxwell, J.P., & Kaufman, M.J. (1978). Group decision-making in the planning team process: Myth or reality. *Journal of School Psychology, 16,* 237–244.

Promoting
Self-Realization and
Psychological Empowerment

CHAPTER 13

Strategies to Promote Student Self-Awareness and Self-Knowledge

After reading this chapter, you will be able to

1. Describe the development of self-awareness and its importance to youth with disabilities

2. Discuss how individuals with more significant disabilities can achieve self-determination

3. Discuss the reasons efforts to promote self-awareness should focus on self-acceptance

4. Describe the role of assessment in self-awareness

5. Teach self-awareness and disability awareness skills by using several strategies

KEY TERMS

1. Anosognosia
2. Anticipatory awareness
3. Career education
4. Disability awareness
5. Dispositional states
6. Emergent awareness
7. Empowerment evaluation
8. Intellectual awareness
9. Metacognitive self-knowledge
10. Self-awareness
11. Self-knowledge
12. Self-realization
13. Self-understanding

If students with disabilities are to become self-determined, they need both to possess the skills to act in a self-determined manner and to hold perceptions and beliefs about themselves and their environment that are conducive to using those skills. Although most of the chapters in this text focus on component elements of self-determination related to the former (i.e., skills development), the chapters in this section address how to promote the latter (positive perceptions and beliefs about oneself and one's environment).

As discussed in Chapter 1, psychological empowerment is a term referring to the multiple dimensions of perceived control, including its cognitive (personal efficacy), personality (locus of control), and motivational domains (Zimmerman, 1990). Essentially, people acting in a psychologically empowered manner do so on the basis of a belief that they 1) have control over circumstances that are important to them (internal locus of control); 2) possess the skills necessary to achieve desired outcomes (self-efficacy); and 3) if they choose to apply those skills, the identified outcomes will result (outcome expectations).

Self-realization refers to the fact that people who are self-determined use a comprehensive and reasonably accurate, knowledge of themselves and their strengths and limitations to act in such a manner as to capitalize on this knowledge. This self-knowledge and self-understanding forms through experience with and interpretation of one's environment and is influenced by evaluations of significant others, reinforcement, and attributions of one's own behavior.

This chapter overviews strategies that support the emergence of positive self-awareness and self-knowledge, including how to promote positive disability awareness. Subsequent chapters in this section explore how to promote positive perceptions of control, efficacy, and expectations of success. In each of these chapters the developmental aspect of self-determination is explored in greater detail than in previous chapters. This is because the emergence of a positive self-awareness; comprehensive self-knowledge and self-understanding; and positive perceptions of control, efficacy, and achievement attribution relies on lifelong learning experiences and opportunities to experience control, make choices and decisions, and experience successes. Too often students with disabilities have not had such experiences and opportunities because others have made decisions for them; and, as a result, these students do not typically see themselves as actors in their own lives. It is important that teachers, including teachers working with transition-age students, understand the development of these important perceptions and beliefs in order to adequately promote their emergence through instruction and environmental modifications.

DEVELOPMENT OF SELF-KNOWLEDGE AND SELF-UNDERSTANDING

Doll and colleagues (Doll, Sands, Wehmeyer, & Palmer, 1996; Sands & Doll, 1996) have described the development of self-determination, including the development of self-awareness. These authors suggested that if students are to act in a self-determined manner they must possess a basic understanding of their individual strengths, abilities, limitations, and unique learning needs, and they must know how to use these unique attributes to enhance their quality of life. The development of both self-awareness and self-knowledge requires the acquisition of a categorical sense of self, that is, an understanding of one's uniqueness and separateness from others. As is described briefly in the following paragraphs, this typically occurs early in child development. In subsequent years, self-awareness and self-knowledge require an accurate sense of the cognitive self or an understanding of one's own thinking and reasoning acts, as well as the capacity to deliberately manipulate these to suit one's purposes.

Until the mid-1980s, most researchers agreed that infants fail to recognize themselves as distinct beings from their caregivers until they are between 8 and 12 months of age (Lewis & Brooks-Gunn, 1979). Newer studies of infant behavior, using technologically advanced measures and sophisticated experimental designs, suggest instead that infants experience a sense of an emergent self beginning at birth, with no confusion between self and others at any point during infancy (DeCasper & Spence, 1986; Stern, 1985). In either case, as early as 3 months of age infants begin to display an interest in and act intentionally toward caregivers and other social objects. This intentional behavior is the catalyst for the growing recognition that they are distinct beings from their caregivers (at 8–12 months of age) and that they can control or cause specific outcomes through their own actions. Most children have a fully developed categorical sense of self by the age of 15–18 months (Lewis & Brooks-Gunn, 1979), providing a foundation on which future self-awareness and self-knowledge can be built.

The emergence of self-awareness and self-knowledge that are both positive and realistic requires an understanding of emotions, feelings, and other within-person states that are common to all individuals. Children have a rudimentary understanding of their own internal states by no later than 3 years of age and can begin to understand that others experience these as well at roughly the same age (Bretherton & Beeghly, 1982; Eder, 1989). For example, 3-year-olds are able to decide when a pictured person is happy, and 4-year-olds can identify both happy and sad (Moore, 1979; Shantz, 1975). By 6 or 7 years of age, children can accurately label four emotional states: happy, sad, afraid, and angry (Shantz, 1975). With age and experience, children's understanding of affective states becomes more differentiated, and they are more accurate in predicting the affect of other people (Selman, 1980).

Dispositional states are frequent, enduring tendencies that are used to characterize people. Unlike internal states, dispositional states are not shared by all people but may represent important differences among them. For example, whereas some children may be thoughtful and reflective when facing a problem, others tend to be agitated and impulsive. Understanding these dispositional states occurs somewhat later in children, emerging in its most simple form around 3 years of age (Eder, 1990). At that age, most children understand that people familiar to them have characteristic ways of being that are stable over time. By ages 7 or 8, children have developed a more complex understanding of these dispositional characteristics, with a sense of how such characteristics might or might not be expressed across different situations or events (Rholes & Ruble, 1984). It is not until ages 9–10, however, that children begin to use these dispositional characteristics to predict the behavior of others (Rholes & Ruble, 1984).

Metacognitive self-knowledge refers to children's ability to reflect on their own mental processes and is evidenced when children take increasing control over the cognitive processes that they use. Ample evidence illustrates that the accuracy of children's metacognitive knowledge increases with age, as does children's propensity to use that understanding to actively direct and control their cognitive processes (Belmont, 1989; Chi, 1981; Fabricius & Hagen, 1984; Garner, 1987). Preschoolers and kindergartners do not attend to their own thinking, do not always notice when they are being either ineffective or effective, and so tend not to revise or fine-tune their cognitive approaches to tasks, even when these are unsuccessful (Forrest & Walker, 1980; Ghatala, 1986; Paris & Lindauer, 1982). Early elementary students do a better job of matching their strategies to the problem than kindergartners and are more likely to plan ways to approach a task that takes advantage of their own competencies (Forrest & Walker, 1980; Paris & Lindauer, 1982). By sixth grade, students actively seek information so that they can judge their task success and adjust their task approach as necessary (Ruble & Flett, 1988). The impact of metacognitive self-knowledge on task performance can be seen in a set of studies showing that the performance of young children can equal that of adolescents if they are directed to pay attention to metacognitive information. The young children in these studies were provided with training in the use of appropriate strategies, feedback regarding the usefulness of the strategy in enhancing task performance, and frequent and very directive reminders to use the strategies in subsequent problem-solving tasks (Cornaldi, 1987; Cornaldi, Gobbo, & Mazzoni, 1991; Ghatala, 1986).

It is a mistake to assume that because many of the developmental processes underpinning self-awareness and self-knowledge are in place prior to transition age, this information is unimportant to instruction with transition-age students. First, adolescence is the time during which individuals form a coherent personal identity. The onset of puberty and the physical and emotional changes (and turmoil) surrounding that process mark the onset of the process through which adolescents will form a self-identity and, essentially, move from childhood to adulthood. During this period, adolescents turn to peers and other sources outside the family for communication and support, yet adolescents remain largely reliant on the support and guidance of their parents (Damon, 1983). It is in adolescence that individuals finally begin to see themselves as volitional with the ability to effectively control their destinies. In short, it is during adolescence that students piece together the disparate aspects of themselves that developed prior to adolescence into a coherent, systematic organized self-conception (Damon, 1983).

Second, transition is a lifelong process that begins early in life and, most likely, continues throughout adulthood. Clark, Carlson, Fisher, Cook, and D'Alonzo (1991) emphasized this in the position statement of the Council for Exceptional Children's Division on Career Development and Transition for students with disabilities in elementary school. This position statement highlighted several basic principles for transition:

1. Education for career development and transition is for individuals with disabilities of all ages.
2. Career development is a process begun at birth and continues throughout life.
3. Early career development is essential for making satisfactory choices later.
4. Significant gaps or periods of neglect in any area of basic human development affects career development and the transition from one stage of life to another. (Clark et al., 1991, p. 118)

As the last basic principle suggests, the development of self-awareness has more than just academic relevance to teachers working with adolescents with disabilities because gaps in development can, and do, have an impact on students' capacities later in life. Many students with disabilities, particularly students with cognitive disabilities, have neither the learning opportunities nor day-to-day experiences that enable them to develop the rudimentary essentials for a positive, realistic self-awareness. As such, students may be ineffective at predicting the emotional states of other people and thus function poorly in job-related situations that require frequent social interactions, be unable to use metacognitive strategies to solve problems or make decisions, resulting in poor job performance, or may establish unrealistic expectations for future transition-related outcomes.

The latter (unrealistic expectations for transition outcomes) is a common experience for many teachers working with adolescents with disabilities. Students frequently seem unaware of the link between specific abilities and job requirements. Whereas such unrealistic expectations are not uncommon for young adolescents, they may be more pronounced for students with disabilities because these students have not learned, through experience and instruction, about their unique abilities and limitations; nor may they have received instruction in such areas as self-management or social problem solving and decision making that enable them to apply metacognitive strategies to their actions. Just as research has borne out that younger students can perform more like adolescents on tasks if they are provided instruction in and support for the use of metacognitive strategies (Cornaldi, 1987; Cornaldi et al., 1991; Ghatala, 1986), so too do we suspect that students with disabilities might perform more like their peers without disabilities if afforded similar opportunities and supports.

Significant Cognitive Disability and Self-Determination

This chapter, and subsequent chapters in this section, describes the developmental course of component elements of self-determination, specifically those that lead students to act in psychologically empowered or self-realizing ways. Historically, a reliance on a developmental model has resulted too frequently in cases in which adolescents, particularly individuals with more significant cognitive disabilities, spend their days involved in childlike activities associated with their mental, rather than their chronological, age. We are not advocating for the use of chronological age–inappropriate activities to define the curriculum and content of instruction for students with disabilities by detailing specific developmental milestones. Instead, we adopt the position that there are universal principles of development that can inform our work with adolescents with disabilities (see, e.g., Giaia, 1993; Hodapp, Burack, & Zigler, 1990; Weisz & Zigler, 1979).

Unfortunately, there remains an a priori assumption by many people, including professionals in the field of disability services, that people with significant disabilities cannot become self-determined (Wehmeyer, 1996b). It may be particularly important to debunk these assumptions before discussing how to promote positive self-awareness and self-knowledge because too many people view people with significant disabilities, particularly significant cognitive disabilities, as unable to be self-aware and, thus, self-determined.

Cognitive impairments that impede an individual's rate of learning; ability to generalize; and development in learning, memory, and language have an undeniable impact on his or her relative self-determination. As can be seen in each chapter in this book, however, such impairments do not unequivocally preclude the development and acquisition of the component elements of self-determined behavior. People with significant disabilities may experience limits in the number and complexity of skills they acquire that are important to becoming fully self-determined. However, for the most part, given adequate supports and accommodations, opportunities to express preferences and make choices, learn problem-solving and decision-making strategies, learn and practice self-management strategies, and experience control, the vast majority of people with even the most significant disability can become more self-determined.

This is not to suggest that all individuals with severe cognitive and intellectual disabilities will be able to take *full* control of decisions that affect their lives. It seems evident that many people with significant intellectual impairments will need considerable support in financial and medical decision making, social interactions, and many other domains. As pointed out in Chapter 1, however, causal agency is not synonymous with absolute control over decisions. Human beings are not completely autonomous or independent; they are interdependent on many others.

People who have significant physical disabilities may rely on a personal care attendant to perform specific actions that they cannot accomplish themselves because of the limits placed on them by their disabling condition. As long as the person with the disability is the causal agent in this process, however, in that the personal care attendant is acting based on the preferences and instructions of the person with the disability, there is no reason to suggest that they are not self-determined simply because they do not actually perform the action. Likewise, there is no reason that the same is not true for people with significant cognitive disabilities. As illustrated in the following case study, such accommodations may be quite extensive for some individuals with significant disabilities and may go beyond a "curb cut" mentality for accommodations; however, people with significant disabilities can be the causal agent in their lives. No evidence from the literature supports the assumption that individuals with significant disabilities cannot use, to some extent, metacognitive strategies and understand many aspects of dispositional characteristics to direct their lives the way that they wish them to be.

In 1992, The Arc awarded its national Bill Sackter Award to William Crane, who lives in Minneapolis, Minnesota. The Sackter award recognizes someone with mental retardation who has become an achieving, integrated member of society after having left an institutional setting. Bill Crane lived at the Faribault State Hospital in Minnesota for 20 years. Bill experienced significant challenges in his efforts to improve his life. He was born with cerebral palsy, was labeled as having severe mental retardation, and was deaf. He lacked a systematic means of communication. He exhibited behaviors that were deemed too disruptive for the community. Bill was even denied services in a sheltered workshop because of the severity of his disability and his behaviors. His psychological report described him as "functioning in the severe to moderate range, having no survival skills and needing constant supervision." In a very real sense, Bill was powerless to control his life because the system that was designed to serve his needs controlled his life instead.

The accommodation to overcome these barriers came in the form of legislation and advocacy. Christine Boswell, who at the time was Executive Director of the local chapter of The Arc, became Bill's advocate. Together, Bill and Christine forged a working relationship, then a friendship. Christine took the time to listen to Bill; to decipher what he was trying to communicate; and, finally, to begin to advocate on his behalf. He was afforded the opportunity to move into the community. He learned some basic sign language. He worked with his advocate to gain access to employment, first sheltered, then supported. Bill's contribution to this process was simple but essential. He simply never gave up. He never gave up hope. He never gave up expressing his preferences. He never gave up telling anyone who would listen what he wanted.

When awarded the Sackter Award, the nominating form chronicled the achievements of a man who lives a self-determined life. Bill works 30 hours per week as a clerk in a Minneapolis nonprofit agency with the support he needs. He has received commendations from his employer as a valued employee. He lives independently in a supported living home in a suburban neighborhood. He has two roommates whom he selected. He interviewed the support service personnel who were chosen to come into their home on a daily basis. He enjoys mountain camping, whitewater river rafting, hockey, and visiting friends and relatives. He was reunited with his mother after 15 years and travels to visit her when he can make room in his schedule. Bill cooks with a microwave, shops, and is responsible for his own self-care needs.

The final sentence in the application sums up Bill's current existence quite neatly. It states that "IQ labels have been disregarded as irrelevant to Bill's potential and capabilities." Bill's accommodations went beyond simply a personal care attendant or a technological device. Without systems changes, in the form of legislation and changing perspectives on how to provide services, and strong advocacy, it is probable that Bill would have been unable to overcome the barriers in his way. But, as all of those who spoke during the award ceremony that recognized his achievement, there was never any doubt as to who the causal agent in this process was...it was Bill.

PROMOTING SELF-AWARENESS AND DISABILITY AWARENESS

Too frequently, the only time the issue of student self-awareness comes to the forefront in education is when people other than the student question the degree to which he or she has "accepted" his or her disability or, in less positive terms, accepts what he or she *cannot do* because of the disability. When self-awareness is seen only in terms of students accepting what they cannot do, the course of treatment is too often "forcing" students to "accept" their disability. Although disability awareness is an important part of self-awareness, understanding one's disability and its effects on how one interacts with the environment and other people should not be the goal of educational efforts to promote self-awareness. Instead, such efforts should be focused on promoting student self-acceptance through self-understanding and self-knowledge and on enabling students to use their unique skills and abilities to their greatest advantage. Wolman (1973) defined self-acceptance as "a healthy attitude toward one's worth and limitations consisting of an objective recognition of each quality and an acceptance of each as being part of the self" (p. 342). Thus, although this section includes a discussion about promoting disability awareness, the emphasis of any intervention should be on assisting students to identify in what ways they are unique and how they can best take advantage of their uniqueness.

In her poem titled, "A Conversation with Cerebral Palsy," Jill Allen (1996) illustrates both the enabling power of self- and disability awareness and the potential negative consequences of focusing attention exclusively on a student's disability:

Well, cerebral palsy—
Do you mind if I call you CP for short?—
You've been with me for fourteen years:
My constant companion.

I accept that you are with me,
Yet I resist you,
I ignore you most of the time CP,
I hope you don't mind.

But if I devoted every waking hour to you,
I'd be miserable and get nowhere in life. (p. 93)

Later in the poem, Allen writes,

I must thank you, though, CP.
If it wasn't for you,
I wouldn't be me.

Because of you,
I am more determined than ever
To make something of myself:
To succeed. (p. 94)

Allen (1996) explained that her poem underscored two crucial points for teens with disabilities, points that educators would be wise to note. First, she says, in order for teens to become independent, they must not let their disabilities take too much control of their actions. Otherwise, Allen stated, "teens may start to view themselves as 'disabled teens,' rather than as 'teens with disabilities'" (p. 95). Second, Allen emphasized that a teen's disability

> shouldn't be treated as an obstacle that has to be overcome. Instead, it should be viewed merely as something to be dealt with. If seen as something insurmountable, then the disability is always cast in a negative light. This hurts the outlook of the person with the condition. (p. 95)

The term self-awareness refers to one's conceptualization of oneself as a unique individual and is often used in conjunction (if not synonymously) with the terms self-understanding and self-knowledge. This includes the process referred to as disability awareness, which involves the capacity of an individual to appraise his or her own abilities as a function of a specific disabling condition. Although Allen (1996) showed in her poem that she has a realistic awareness of her disabling condition, this is not always the case.

In the medical rehabilitation literature the issue of disability awareness, or more appropriately, impaired awareness, is a topic of particular concern regarding the rehabilitation of individuals who have experienced traumatic brain injury. DeLuca, Tiersky, and Diamond (1996) identified two forms of impaired awareness from this literature: 1) neurologically based unawareness of a disability and 2) psychological denial. The first category, known as *anosognosia*, refers to a lack of knowledge about an impairment due to the nature of the impairment. Willer (1996) described a case of a man who was cortically blind, yet when asked whether he could see, replied, "of course!" When asked to describe the person standing in front of him, the man went on to describe the person as "black, with black hair, and a black background." This man was not denying his blindness, rather he was genuinely unaware of his condition. There are several levels of severity in anosognosia:

1. Intellectual awareness: This is the most basic level in which the person does not understand that a given deficit exists.
2. Emergent awareness: The person acknowledges a specific problem but may be unable to recognize it when it is occurring.
3. Anticipatory awareness: Individuals cannot anticipate a potential problem that may result from a specific impairment.

Treatment or intervention for anosognosia is most likely out of the domain of education and best left to specialists in medical rehabilitation. It is useful, however, to note that much of what teachers and others complain about regarding students' lack of disability awareness can often be conceptualized as problems with anticipatory awareness. That is, students do not anticipate a problem related to their specific disability. So, for example, an adolescent with a learning disability may not take into account his or her unique learning needs and supports when entering a test situation and, consequently, performs poorly.

It is equally insufficient to describe the issues that face many students with disabilities related to disability awareness as a result of psychological denial. Although many students may, indeed, deny the existence of their disability label because they are reacting to negative stigmas and stereotypes associated with that label, they are frequently quite capable of describing their specific learning problems. Within the educational context, it is more appropriate to consider disability awareness as a process of students understanding their unique strengths and limitations related to how they learn or interact with the environment, as opposed to either a neurologically based phenomenon or a function of denial. Intervention in this circumstance will include learning about individual strengths, limitations, and supports.

Teaching Self- and Disability Awareness

Several attempts have been made to establish curricula pertaining to self-awareness, many of which are embedded in broader efforts to teach self-determination, self-advocacy, or independent living. For example, several of the strategies to involve students in their educational planning and decision-making process, which are listed in Chapter 12, incorporate exercises in self-awareness. Wehmeyer and Kelchner (1995) introduced the concept that each individual is unique by having students think about how their transition preferences differed from other students' preferences. Students answer a series of questions asking them to identify their favorite food, the last movie they saw, who taught them to swim, and numerous other similar questions, then compare their profile from the answers with that of other students. Next, students identify their abilities and interests and discuss how these will have an effect on what they want to do. Only after several sessions on these topics do students begin to talk about disabilities, and even then within the framework that a disability is just one more thing that makes individuals unique. The emphasis is not on being different, per se, but on being unique and capable. Students identify their unique learning needs, based on a better understanding of their abilities and limitations, then apply this knowledge to identify supports they might need to succeed (referred to as "My Unique Learning and Educational Supports," or MULES). One of the reasons the process enables students to focus on positive aspects of disability awareness is because it is self-directed instead of other directed. It is all too human to react to someone else telling you what you need to do to overcome a disability with defensiveness and, potentially, denial. In fact, it seems likely that much of the "denial" that contributes to student unawareness of disability is a function of defensiveness engendered by other-directed attempts at disability awareness!

Yuan (1994) reported on the use of a college-level course developed to help students with learning disabilities build self-understanding, disability awareness, and acceptance as well as self-advocacy skills. The course goals were to

- Provide students with answers to basic questions about learning disabilities
- Process information regarding each student's own learning style, strengths and weaknesses, and strategies for capitalizing on strengths and compensating for weaknesses
- Teach self-advocacy skills and help students use them in their immediate and future lives (Yuan, 1994)

The course was held twice weekly for 13 weeks and involved 50 minutes per session. The course was introduced as a "quest," and students were encouraged to be active participants and to utilize their own experiences as sources of information. Course topics included

- Feelings about learning disabilities
- What are learning disabilities?
- What causes learning disabilities?
- How are learning disabilities diagnosed?
- Learning disabilities and testing
- What are common characteristics of people with learning disabilities?
- What are different types of learning disabilities?
- Cognitive styles
- Identifying strengths
- Compensating for learning disabilities

- Developing an individualized learning profile
- Learning disabilities and self-advocacy

In addition to group discussion and individual worksheets related to the various topics, participants complete an individualized learning profile (ILP). The ILP outlines the student's learning strengths and limitations and identifies specific strategies for capitalizing on strengths and compensating for limitations. Although Yuan (1994) conducted her work with students in college, the format could be easily replicated with high school students with a variety of disabilities. Teachers working with transition-age students could modify the topic discussion and activities to be more focused on transition issues. For example, instead of focusing just on identifying "learning strengths," participants could identify specific strengths related to important transition areas, such as employment, residential living, or transportation.

Steps to Self-Determination   The self-determination curriculum developed by Field and Hoffman (1996), titled *Steps to Self-Determination,* brings considerable focus to the issue of self-awareness. Field and Hoffman based the curriculum on a definition of self-determination as the ability to define and achieve goals based on a foundation of knowing and valuing oneself (Field & Hoffman, 1994). Students involved in the *Steps to Self-Determination* curriculum work to promote self-awareness and self-acceptance through a series of individual, parent–student, and group activities. First, students complete a worksheet titled, "How I See Myself," while at the same time, parents or others complete a worksheet called, "How I See You." On the "How I See Myself" worksheet, students identify two strengths and one limitation in each of five areas: 1) physical, 2) mental, 3) emotional, 4) social, and 5) beliefs. The "How I See You" worksheet asks parents or friends paired with the student to identify two of the students' strengths in each area (no limitations are listed). When these are completed, students and parents or friends discuss the worksheet responses and identify where they were in agreement and disagreement. Students are encouraged to discuss the reasons they see themselves in the way they reported. Likewise, parents and friends discuss the reasons they see the students' strengths as reported.

The participants subsequently work through a series of activities related to self-acceptance. Students complete a self-acceptance worksheet discussing what they perceived as their limitations on the "How I See Myself" worksheet. Students identify previously unconsidered strengths they have to deal with these limitations.

Career Education Approach   Promoting self-determination and self-awareness within a career education framework seems particularly promising for youth with disabilities. Career education refers to a purposeful sequence of planned educational activities that assist individuals in their career development. Career education is a lifelong process that includes many settings (e.g., home, school, employment, community) and roles (e.g., student, worker, consumer, citizen, family member). Career education refers to the totality of a student's life experiences, vocational and avocational, and incorporates strategies generally agreed upon as important for youth with disabilities, such as goal-oriented programming, functional curricula, and community-referenced instruction (Brolin, 1993).

Wehmeyer (1995) identified one widely used career education curriculum, the *Life Centered Career Education* (LCCE) curriculum (Brolin, 1993), as having potential utility to promote self-determination. The LCCE is organized into 22 competencies in three primary instructional categories: daily living skills, personal-social skills, and occupational guidance and preparation. Each of the 22 competencies is further divided into subcompetencies, for a total of 97 subcompetency areas. Comprehensive goals, objectives, and lesson plans are provided for each subcompetency. Wehmeyer (1995) identified a total of four competency areas and 17 subcompetency areas that seemed pertinent to self-determination. Two of these competency areas, constituting roughly half of the instructional activities, involved teaching self-awareness and self-confidence. Table 1 lists the LCCE competency and subcompetency areas for these lessons.

Using the LCCE, instruction in self-determination begins with instruction on issues of self-awareness. When students acquire a broader sense of themselves, they learn to apply that knowledge to building a positive self-image and gaining self-confidence. Only then do they begin to learn skills related to choice and decision making, goal setting, and self-organization. Instruction in self-awareness begins with the identification of basic physical and psychological needs, interests, and abilities. Given the emphasis of the Individuals with Disabilities Education Act (IDEA) of 1990 (PL 101-476) on basing transition services on individual student interests and preferences (see Chapter 3), these lessons are particularly important. Students learn to distinguish between their physical and psychological needs and then learn ways to meet these needs. They use role-playing and brainstorming procedures to explore interests and abilities, including those com-

Table 1. LCCE competency and subcompetency areas for promoting self-awareness

Competency	Subcompetency
Achieving self-awareness	Identify physical and psychological needs.
	Identify interests and abilities.
	Identify emotions.
	Demonstrate knowledge of physical self.
	Develop awareness of how behavior affects others.
Acquiring self-confidence	Express feelings of self-worth.
	Describe others' perceptions of self.
	Accept and give praise.
	Accept and give criticism.
	Develop confidence in oneself.

mon to most people as well as those unique to themselves. Students then discuss common emotions, such as fear, love, hate, and sadness; how these affect their behavior and the behavior of others; and how to cope with such emotions.

Moving from the emotional domain to basic physical awareness, students learn to demonstrate a knowledge of their physical self and how their physical health has an impact on the ways they act. Students need to learn that there are physical causes for the way they feel and that how they feel affects the way they behave. This is an opportune time to import additional materials involving health and body systems. The final subcompetency teaching self-awareness involves demonstrating how one's behavior affects others. The students explore appropriate ways to act in a variety of situations and how to use cues to regulate their behavior.

The next set of lessons apply self-awareness to acquiring self-confidence and self-acceptance. Students first learn to express feelings of self-worth. They identify their own positive physical and psychological attributes, how these make them feel, and how other people's actions affect their feelings of self-worth. Students move on to explore others' perceptions of them, listing potential reactions of others, constructing a view of how others see them, and describing how their behaviors affect others' reactions. As one component of this process, students discuss differences among people, including interests and abilities. Students then learn to give and accept praise and criticism. They learn appropriate and inappropriate ways to respond to each of these, list the effects and purposes of praise and criticism, and practice strategies to give and receive both. Finally, students identify their own positive characteristics, ways to express confidence in themselves, how to react to others' expressions of confidence, and how to appropriately make positive statements about themselves.

These approaches illustrate some of the ways that teachers could promote the self-awareness, self-understanding, and self-knowledge of students with disabilities. Common threads run through each of these approaches, including the types of activities that are implemented. Perhaps the most common thread, however, is that in all such efforts, the student must be the catalyst for change. Students need to be actively involved in identifying their interests, abilities, strengths, and unique learning needs, as well as applying this knowledge to identify strategies and supports that can enable them to overcome limitations.

Empowerment Evaluation and Self-Awareness

One of the universal experiences of students with disabilities is that, at some point during their school career, they have undergone standardized testing to determine their educational needs and eligibility for special education. Unfortunately, in far too many circumstances, assessment experiences are negative for students; they result in lists of things students with disabilities do not do well or lead to diagnostic labels that set them apart from other students. This is the paradox of educational testing. On one hand, knowledge about one's educational strengths and limitations can be empowering, enabling the learner and those working with him or her to individualize instruction and identify supports. On the other hand, the over-reliance of many educators on standardized testing that is conducted by highly trained professionals and emphasizes conformity and rigid testing standards has resulted in experiences that limit student empowerment.

It is neither the intent nor the purpose of this section to provide a comprehensive treatment of assessment and its uses and abuses. Nonetheless, assessment and instruction are necessarily linked in virtually all successful educational efforts, and this may be particularly so in promoting self-awareness. This is only the case, however, if assessment is approached with the intent of providing students with the knowledge they need to act to better their own lives. One assessment strategy that has emerged that emphasizes this outcome is called *empowerment evaluation.* Fetterman (1996) defined empowerment evaluation as "the use of evaluation concepts, techniques and findings to foster improvement and self-determination" (p. 4). Whereas many traditional assessment orientations mandate that the evaluator maintain impartiality and distance, "empowerment evaluation has an unambiguous value orientation—it is designed to help people help themselves and improve their programs using a form of self-evaluation and reflection" (p. 5).

Within an empowerment evaluation framework, assessment becomes a collaborative effort, combining the input of the student and other significant parties and incorporating an evaluation of the environment. In other words, in empowerment evaluation, the focal point is student self-evaluation and self-directed interpretation of assessment findings. Students work collaboratively with significant others to identify strengths and limitations and to chart a course for intervention.

By necessity, empowerment evaluation typically incorporates some form of student self-report. Although there are self-report measures of virtually every psychological and educational construct conceptualized, from locus of control to self-esteem and autonomy, very few of these instruments have been used with students with disabilities, particularly students with cognitive impairments. One of the reasons for this is the pervasive skepticism regarding the validity of perceptions of students with cognitive and other disabilities. It is widely recognized, for example, that students with mental retardation tend to be outerdirected, heavily influenced by adults, and overly acquiescent. The prevailing sentiment, based on an assumption of deficits, has been that people with cognitive disabilities are not reliable or valid reporters of their own perceptions.

Although issues related to the validity and reliability of self-report measures with individuals with disabilities, particularly mental retardation, are of serious concern, it is frequently the case that when professionals question the validity of the perceptions of students with cognitive disabilities, what they often mean is that these students hold unrealistic perceptions. Although this may be true, it does not negate the validity of the student's perception. A perception is invalid when it does not match the student's true beliefs or feelings, rather than when it is unrealistic. Thus, student perceptions are a particularly important aspect to understand when trying to promote self-determination and self-awareness.

Assor and Connell (1992) provided a number of suggestions for improving the validity of students' self-reports:

1. Remember and communicate that what you want is for students to report what they truly believe about themselves. Accurate reports do not necessarily reflect real or actual performance.
2. Question students in a way that helps them understand what you are after in the assessment process. There is nothing hidden or secret about the process. We are not seeking some psychologically defined variable but simply what the student feels or believes.
3. Emphasize that, no matter what students answer, as long as it is truly what they believe or feel, it is the right answer. Ensure confidentiality and put students at ease.
4. Communicate to students what the information will be used for and why they are being asked these questions. Get students involved in the interpretation process as well as the assessment process.

The key to ensuring valid self-reports is to convince students that what they believe is very important. In order to convince students, one must genuinely believe this him- or herself. This means acting on students' perceptions in a manner that is respectful, nonjudgmental, and promotes student involvement.

The Arc's Self-Determination Scale   One example of the use of self-report measures to promote empowerment evaluation is *The Arc's Self-Determination Scale* (Wehmeyer & Kelchner, 1995). This scale is a student self-report measure of self-determination designed for use by adolescents with disabilities, particularly students with mental retardation and learning disabilities who require intermittent supports. The Scale was constructed based on a definitional framework of self-determination as an educational outcome proposed by Wehmeyer and colleagues (Wehmeyer, 1992, 1996a; Wehmeyer, Kelchner, & Richards, 1996), described in Chapter 1 of this text.

This instrument is a 72-item self-report scale that provides data on each of the four essential characteristics of self-determination as well as a more general overview. Students indicate the degree to which they perform certain behaviors. Section 1 measures student autonomy, including the student's independence and the degree to which he or she acts on the basis of personal beliefs, values, interests, and abilities, using a Likert-type format. Items relating to independence include actions in routine personal care and family-oriented functions and interaction with the environment. Items measuring acting on the basis of personal beliefs, values, interests, and abilities focus on recreational and leisure time activities, community involvement and interactions, personal expression, and postschool directions. Higher scores in this section reflect greater autonomy.

The second section measures student self-regulation. This section is composed of two subdomains: interpersonal, cognitive problem solving and goal-setting and task performance. In the first subdomain, students are presented a series of stories in which a problem is described and then an outcome is provided. Students are asked to identify the action that best resolved the problem, resulting in the outcome indicated. Answers are scored based on the degree to which students' solutions achieved the outcome. High scores reflect more effective social problem-solving abilities. In the second subdomain, students are asked to identify goals they have in three areas that will be important after they graduate (e.g., where they live, where they work, what transportation they use). If students identify a goal, they are asked to list one to four steps they need to take to achieve this goal. Higher scores reflect goal-oriented behaviors.

The third section of the scale is an indicator of psychological empowerment. Students choose from items measuring psychological empowerment by using a forced-choice method. High scores reflect positive perceptions of control and efficacy. The final section of *The Arc's Self-Determination Scale* measures student self-realization. Students respond to a series of statements reflecting low or high self-realization by indicating that they agree or disagree with items such as "I know how to make up for my limitations" and "I know what I do best." High scores reflect high levels of self-realization.

There are a total of 148 points available on the scale, and higher scores reflect higher self-determination. *The Arc's Self-Determination Scale* was normed with 500 students with and without cognitive disabilities in rural, urban, and suburban school districts in five states. One of the primary purposes for the scale is to serve as a vehicle to enable students to identify areas of strengths and educational needs in self-determination and to work collaboratively with teachers to identify educational goals and objectives to address these needs. In this process, the student becomes the focal point for all phases of assessment activities. The role of the teacher is to provide the support the student needs to participate in the assessment process successfully. The level of support needed will vary according to the student's individual characteristics, and some students may need considerable support, from having the items read to marking responses and scoring. With adequate support, students can become the causal agent for assessment by directing assessment activities; participating in scoring; and, perhaps most important, working collaboratively with teachers to identify interventions and potential goals. This model could be adopted for a number of self-report measures as well as measures that may typically have been completed by the teacher or a parent.

CONCLUSION

The emergence of a positive self-awareness and self-knowledge and the application of this knowledge to act in a self-determined manner is a process that begins very early and continues throughout adulthood. Education's role in this process is to work collaboratively with families and the community to provide students with the experiences that enable them to learn more about themselves, their strengths, and the accommodations they may need to be successful.

QUESTIONS FOR REVIEW

1. Discuss the reasons it is important to hold positive beliefs about oneself in order to become self-determined.
2. Define psychological empowerment and self-realization.
3. Why is it important to understand the development of self-awareness? Give examples of how disruptions in development can have an impact on later functioning.
4. Describe how people with significant disabilities show self-determination.
5. What should the outcome of instruction in self-awareness be for youth with disabilities?
6. What is Allen trying to say in her poem about cerebral palsy?
7. Describe some features common to most attempts to promote self-awareness.
8. Discuss the reasons students need to be the focal point for instruction in self-awareness.
9. Define career education.
10. Define empowerment evaluation and describe how it might be used to promote self-determination.

REFERENCES

Allen, J. (1996). A conversation with cerebral palsy. In L.E. Powers, G.H.S. Singer, & J. Sowers (Eds.), *On the road to autonomy: Promoting self-competence in children and youth with disabilities* (pp. 93–95). Baltimore: Paul H. Brookes Publishing Co.

Assor, A., & Connell, J.P. (1992). The validity of students' self-reports as measures of performance affecting self-appraisals. In D.H. Schunk & J.L. Meece (Eds.), *Student perceptions in the classroom* (pp. 25–47). Hillsdale, NJ: Lawrence Erlbaum Associates.

Belmont, J.M. (1989). Cognitive strategies and strategic learning: The socio-instructional approach. *American Psychologist, 44,* 142–148.

Bretherton, I., & Beeghly, M. (1982). Talking about internal states: The acquisition of an explicit theory of mind. *Developmental Psychology, 18,* 906–921.

Brolin, D. (1993). *Life centered career education: A competency-based approach.* Reston, VA: Council for Exceptional Children.

Chi, M. (1981). Knowledge development and memory performance. In M. Friedman, J. Das, & N. O'Connor (Eds.), *Intelligence and learning* (pp. 34–62). New York: Plenum.

Clark, G.M., Carlson, B.C., Fisher, S., Cook, I.D., & D'Alonzo, B.J. (1991). Career development for students with disabilities in elementary schools: A position statement of the division on career development. *Career Development for Exceptional Individuals, 14,* 109–120.

Cornaldi, C. (1987). Origins of intentional strategic memory in the child. In B. Inhelder, D. De Caprona, & A. Cornu-Wells (Eds.), *Piaget today* (pp. 183–201). Hillsdale, NJ: Lawrence Erlbaum Associates.

Cornaldi, C., Gobbo, C., & Mazzoni, G. (1991). On metamemory–memory relationship: Strategy availability and training. *International Journal of Behavior Development, 14,* 101–121.

Damon, W. (1983). *Social and personality development.* New York: Norton.

DeCasper, A.J., & Spence, M.J. (1986). Prenatal maternal speech influences newborns' perception of speech sounds. *Infant Behavior and Development, 9,* 133–150.

DeLuca, J., Tiersky, L., & Diamond, B.J. (1996). Impaired awareness following brain injury: Suggested remediation techniques. *i. e. Magazine, 4*(2), 14–19.

Doll, B., Sands, D.J., Wehmeyer, M.L., & Palmer, S. (1996). Promoting the development and acquisition of self-determined behavior. In D.J. Sands & M.L. Wehmeyer (Eds.), *Self-determination across the life span: Independence and choice for people with disabilities* (pp. 65–90). Baltimore: Paul H. Brookes Publishing Co.

Eder, R. (1989). The emergent personologist: The structure and content of 3-, 5-, and 7-year-olds' concepts of themselves and other persons. *Child Development, 60,* 1218–1228.

Eder, R. (1990). Uncovering young children's psychological selves: Individual and developmental differences. *Child Development, 61,* 849–863.

Fabricius, W., & Hagen, J. (1984). Use of causal attributions about recall performance to assess metamemory and predict strategic memory behavior in young children. *Developmental Psychology, 20,* 975–987.

Fetterman, D.M. (1996). Empowerment evaluation: An introduction to theory and practice. In D.M. Fetterman, S.J. Kaftarian, & A. Wandersman (Eds.), *Empowerment evaluation: Knowledge and tools for self-assessment and accountability* (pp. 3–46). Beverly Hills, CA: Sage Publications.

Field, S., & Hoffman, A. (1994). Development of a model for self-determination. *Career Development for Exceptional Individuals, 17,* 159–169.

Field, S., & Hoffman, A. (1996). *Steps to self-determination: A curriculum to help adolescents learn to achieve their goals.* Austin, TX: PRO-ED.

Forrest, D.L., & Walker, T.G. (1980, April). *What do children know about their reading and study skills?* Paper presented at the annual meeting of the American Educational Research Association, Boston.

Garner, R. (1987). *Metacognition and reading comprehension.* Norwood, NJ: Ablex.

Ghatala, E.S. (1986). Strategy-monitoring training enables young learners to select effective strategies. *Educational Psychologist, 21,* 43–54.

Giaia, G.A. (1993). Development and mental retardation. In R. Smith (Ed.), *Children with mental retardation: A parents' guide* (pp. 51–87). Rockville, MD: Woodbine House.

Hodapp, R.M., Burack, J.A., & Zigler, E. (1990). The developmental perspective in the field of mental retardation. In R.M. Hodapp, J.A Burack, & E. Zigler (Eds.), *Issues in the developmental approach to mental retardation* (pp. 3–26). New York: Cambridge University Press.

Individuals with Disabilities Education Act (IDEA) of 1990, PL 101-476, 20 U.S.C. §§ 1400 *et seq.*

Lewis, M., & Brooks-Gunn, J. (1979). *Social cognition and the acquisition of the self.* New York: Plenum.

Moore, S.G. (1979). Social cognition: Knowing about others. *Young Children, 34,* 54–61.

Paris, S.G., & Lindauer, B.K. (1982). The development of cognitive skills during childhood. In B. Wolman (Ed.), *Handbook of developmental psychology* (pp. 333–349). Englewood Cliffs, NJ: Prentice Hall.

Rholes, W.S., & Ruble, D.N. (1984). Children's understanding of dispositional characteristics of others. *Child Development, 55,* 550–560.

Ruble, D.N., & Flett, G.L. (1988). Conflicting goals in self-evaluative information seeking: Developmental and ability level analyses. *Child Development, 59,* 97–106.

Sands, D.J., & Doll, B. (1996). Fostering self-determination is a developmental task. *Journal of Special Education, 30,* 58–76.

Selman, R.L. (1980). *The growth of interpersonal understanding.* New York: Academic Press.

Shantz, C.U. (1975). The development of social cognition. In E.M. Hetherington (Ed.), *Review of child development research* (Vol. 5, pp. 257–323). Chicago: University of Chicago Press.

Stern, D. (1985). *The interpersonal world of the infant.* New York: Basic Books.

Wehmeyer, M.L. (1992). Self-determination and the education of students with mental retardation. *Education and Training in Mental Retardation, 27,* 302–314.

Wehmeyer, M.L. (1995). A career education approach: Self-determination for youth with mild cognitive disabilities. *Intervention in School and Clinic, 30,* 157–163.

Wehmeyer, M.L. (1996a). Self-determination as an educational outcome: Why is it important to children, youth and adults with disabilities? In D.J. Sands & M.L. Wehmeyer (Eds.), *Self-determination across the life span: Independence and choice for people with disabilities* (pp. 17–36). Baltimore: Paul H. Brookes Publishing Co.

Wehmeyer, M.L. (1996b). Self-determination for youth with significant cognitive disabilities: From theory to practice. In L.E. Powers, G.H.S. Singer, & J. Sowers (Eds.), *On the road to autonomy: Promoting self-competence in children and youth with disabilities* (pp. 115–134). Baltimore: Paul H. Brookes Publishing Co.

Wehmeyer, M.L., & Kelchner, K. (1995). *The Arc's self-determination scale.* Arlington, TX: The Arc National Headquarters.

Wehmeyer, M.L., & Kelchner, K. (1995). *Whose future is it anyway? A student-directed transition planning program.* Arlington, TX: The Arc National Headquarters.

Wehmeyer, M.L., Kelchner, K., & Richards. S. (1996). Essential characteristics of self-determined behaviors of adults with mental retardation and developmental disabilities. *American Journal on Mental Retardation, 100,* 632–642.

Weisz, J., & Zigler, E. (1979). Cognitive development in retarded and non-retarded persons: Piagetian tests of the similar sequence hypothesis. *Psychological Bulletin, 80,* 831–853.

Willer, B. (1996). Editorial. *i. e. Magazine, 4*(2), 5.

Wolman, B.B. (Ed.). (1973). *The dictionary of behavioral science.* New York: VanNostrand Reinhold.

Yuan, F. (1994). Moving toward self-acceptance: A course for students with learning disabilities. *Intervention in School and Clinic, 29,* 301–309.

Zimmerman, M.A. (1990). Toward a theory of learned hopefulness: A structural model analysis of participation and empowerment. *Journal of Research in Personality, 24,* 71–86.

CHAPTER 14

Strategies to Promote Positive Perceptions of Control in the Classroom

After reading this chapter, you will be able to

1. Define locus of control and discuss its importance to positive educational outcomes

2. Discuss the impact of the learning environment and teacher-control orientation on student perceptions

3. Identify ways to involve parents and family members in promoting student self-determination

4. Identify strategies to promote positive perceptions of control for students with disabilities

KEY TERMS

1. Attributional approach
2. Causal unrealist
3. Coercive power
4. Communicator style
5. Cooperative learning
6. Expert power
7. Intentionality bias
8. Legitimate power
9. Locus of control
10. Peer mediation
11. Privacy
12. Referent power
13. Reward power
14. Teacher-control orientation

Since the mid-1980s, the mainstream educational literature has placed increasing emphasis on the importance of adaptive student perceptions for positive educational outcomes (Schunk & Meece, 1992). Schunk (1992) identified this emphasis as emerging from theories of learning and motivation that "assume that students are active information processors who affect classroom events as much as they are affected by them" (p. 3). These theories, according to Schunk,

> portray students as individuals who formulate achievement goals, selectively attend to events, engage in activities, and employ strategies they believe will help them attain goals, process information in meaningful ways and create and maintain a positive psychological climate in accomplishing goals. (1992, p. 3)

This research highlights the importance of promoting students' positive beliefs about themselves and their environment to facilitate learning. Among the most important of such beliefs are beliefs about control in the classroom. This chapter describes the issues related to promoting positive perceptions of control, identifies barriers to this outcome, and discusses curricular and non-curricular strategies.

DEVELOPING POSITIVE PERCEPTIONS OF CONTROL

Locus of control refers to the degree to which a person perceives contingency relationships between his or her actions and outcomes. The locus of control construct provides a way to conceptualize the degree to which individuals believe that they have control over and can influence outcomes in their lives, or whether such outcomes are controlled by others, fate, or circumstances. The construct is represented by two dichotomous orientations: internal versus external locus of control. Mercer and Snell characterized these orientations as follows:

> When a person is characterized as having an internal locus of control, he views reinforcement as primarily the consequence of one's own actions; whereas, if a person is characterized as having an external locus of control, reinforcement is viewed as the result of outside forces such as luck, fate, chance and/or powerful others. (1977, p. 183)

Research with children and adolescents has linked locus-of-control orientation with a variety of academic, motivational, and personality-related variables and outcomes. One of the most closely scrutinized of these has been the relationship between locus of control orientation and academic achievement. Researchers in the field hypothesize that an internal locus-of-control orientation is one factor that contributes to positive academic achievement. Findley and Cooper (1983) reviewed the literature testing this hypothesis, and the authors concluded that internal perceptions of control were positively associated with greater academic achievement (as measured on standardized achievement tests), with the strength of this relationship being weak to moderate. In an earlier review, Bar-Tal and Bar-Zohar (1977) also concluded that "the perception of locus of control is related to academic achievement" and "that the more internal the orientation, the higher the individual's achievement" (p. 182).

In addition to academic achievement, locus-of-control orientation has been associated with other educationally relevant outcomes. Scores related to internal locus of control have been linked to greater attention to information pertaining to valued goals, extended time of deliberation when making difficult decisions or choices, and increased attentiveness to environment-based cues (Lefcourt, 1976). Boggiano, Main, and Katz (1988) determined that children's self-reported perceptions of academic competence and personal control were positively related to their interest in schoolwork and preferences for challenging school activities. External control orientations have been found to be correlated with distractibility, impulsive decision making, and sociometric rating of rejection from peers (Ollendick, Green, Francis, & Baum, 1991; Ollendick & Schmidt, 1987).

There appear to be predictable relationships between age and locus of control, with orientations becoming increasingly internal as children enter adolescence and young adulthood. The developmental framework undergirding the emergence of perceptions of control and causality in typical child development involves a process of differentiation in children's understanding of the meaning of causal concepts; contingency relationships; and the role of effort, ability, and luck in securing outcomes (Skinner, 1990). In children's earliest conceptualizations of causality, ability and luck are not distinguished from beliefs about effort. Children basically believe that effort and hard work account for success and the lack thereof is the explanation for failure (Skinner, 1990). Eventually, children begin to distinguish between effort and chance. Weisz (1980) found that 8- and 9-year-old children believed that practice could improve their chances of winning a chance task while older children (10- to 11-year-olds) differentiated between effort and luck and regarded the latter as noncontingent and uncontrollable. Effort and ability remained undifferentiated, however, until 11 or 12 years of age. Until then, children inferred ability from effort and viewed other children as smart based more on the amount of effort exerted than actual performance or outcomes.

Nicholls (1978) proposed four hierarchically organized, sequentially invariant levels between ages 5 and 13 in the differentiation of effort, ability, and luck. At the first level, very young children emphasized the superiority of effort in explaining performance outcomes. Consistently at this level, and inconsistently at the second level, children inferred high ability equally from either high effort or high performance. The next step came as children began to comprehend that effort and ability contribute independently to performance outcomes. In level three children's understanding of the differentiation is partially established, and at level four this differentiation is complete. Skinner described the developmental course of perceived control and causality as "an early, global and diffuse view of causes as contingent and controllable to successively more differentiated causal categories: contingent causes are distinguished from noncontingent ones and then ability from effort" (Skinner, 1990, p. 1883).

STUDENTS WITH DISABILITIES AND PERCEPTIONS OF CONTROL

Lawrence and Winschel (1975) argued that "internality in locus of control must become a conscious goal in the education of ...children [with disabilities]" (p. 484). This contention was based on the assumption that students with disabilities are more externally oriented and thus hold maladaptive perceptions of control. Subsequent research has supported this contention. Dudley-Marling, Snider, and Tarver (1982) determined that six of seven studies of students with learning disabilities found that these students were more externally oriented when compared with children without disabilities. Additional studies since this review have replicated this finding (see, e.g., Grolnick & Ryan, 1990; Lewis & Lawrence-Patterson, 1989; Rogers & Saklofske, 1985).

Similarly, students with mental retardation appear to be more externally oriented. Mercer and Snell (1977) determined that four of five studies attributed more externally based scores to students with mental retardation than to peers without disabilities (Fox, 1972; Gruen, Ottinger, & Ollendick, 1974; Riedel & Milgram, 1970; Shipe, 1970). In the 1990s, we have conducted a series of studies examining the locus-of-control orientation of youth with mental retardation (Wehmeyer & Kelchner, 1994, 1996). These studies show that students with mental retardation hold more external orientations than both peers with learning disabilities and peers without disabilities. Based on this research, we have suggested that students with disabilities may be *causal unrealists,* in that they hold unrealistic or incorrect understandings of causality. This "causal unreality" is characterized by an overreliance on luck and chance, less mature beliefs about the role of ability and effort on outcomes, and an inability to judge competence and ability in themselves and others (Wehmeyer & Kelchner, 1994).

TEACHER VARIABLES AND STUDENT PERCEPTIONS OF CONTROL

Students' perceptions of their learning environment and others in that environment are factors that have also been identified as important for positive achievement outcomes and internal control orientations. Research on students' perceptions of their classroom environment show that they are related to student locus-of-control orientation and self-concept (Madonna, Bailey, & Wesley, 1990). Students' perceptions of their classroom environment are linked to the teaching style and orientation of the classroom teacher. Research has linked excessive teacher-control orientations with maladaptive student motivation and self-esteem (Deci, Spiegel, Ryan, Koestner, & Kauffman, 1982), lower academic achievement (Boggiano & Katz, 1991), and decrements in performance (Flink, Boggiano, & Barrett, 1990).

Research on social influences in educational classrooms and on the impact of instructional communication styles has focused on the issue of teacher control, specifically teachers' use of power in the classroom. Richmond and Roach noted that

> the role of a teacher, almost by definition, involves social influence. The tasks of a teacher are manyfold. An instructor is responsible for presenting subject content, explaining difficult concepts, modeling and stimulating problem-solving skills, promoting both cognitive and affective learning in students, motivating students toward academic achievement, and providing an environment conducive to learning. Simply stated, a teacher's job is to influence students. One can quickly see the importance and operation of power in the instructional setting. (1992, p. 58)

They concluded that the use of power is an inherent part of the teaching process, with that power focused on influencing students toward educational ends. Different types or bases of power come into play in the classroom. Barraclough and Stewert identified five types of power:

1. *Reward power,* based on the target's perception that the agent has the ability to mediate reward for her or him;
2. *Coercive power,* based on the target's perceptions that the agent has the ability to mediate punishments for her or him;
3. *Legitimate power,* based on the target's perception that the agent has a legitimate right to prescribe and/or proscribe behavior for her or him;
4. *Referent power,* based on the target's identification with the agent; and
5. *Expert power,* based on the target's perception that the agent has some special knowledge or expertise (1992, pp. 4–5)

Richmond and Roach (1992) pointed out that using these various types of powers to create an effective learning climate is a difficult tightrope for teachers to have to walk. This may be particularly so for teachers who work with students with disabilities, who frequently need more structure, guidance, and direction than other students. Given the potential detrimental impact of overly controlling teaching styles, however, this is an area that warrants consideration.

Few efforts have been made to examine the perceptions of students with cognitive disabilities about their classroom environment. Wehmeyer and Kelchner (1996) measured the perceptions of students without disabilities, students with mental retardation, and students with learning disabilities about their classroom, specifically the degree to which they perceived their teacher as being controlling and the relative organization of the classroom itself. The authors

then examined these beliefs as a function of student locus of control and academic achievement attributions; they found that students with mental retardation and learning disabilities hold perceptions of themselves and their classroom
environment that are maladaptive and could contribute to limited self-
determination and student involvement. As previous research had suggested,
there were significant differences in locus-of-control scores among students without disabilities and students with mental retardation and learning disabilities.
Students with mental retardation scored almost 33% more external scores than
peers without disabilities, and students with learning disabilities were not far
behind.

On the measures of teacher control and classroom management, students
with learning disabilities perceived their classroom environment as the most
controlling, followed by students with mental retardation and students without
disabilities. For all students, teacher-control scoring was one of only two variables that contributed to overall locus-of-control orientation; the other being
scores from the measure of academic achievement attribution (discussed in
Chapter 15). Students who perceived their classroom as noncontrolling had
significantly lower, thus more adaptive, locus-of-control scores than peers who
perceived their classroom as controlling. The same was not true for the measure
of classroom organization, which did not contribute to less positive control
orientations.

It is important to distinguish between excessive teacher control and effective classroom management, organization, and structure. The tendency is to
confuse issues of structure with control, and there is a belief on the part of
many educators that promoting self-determination is synonymous with giving
up all structure in the classroom. This is simply not true, and in fact could not
be further from the truth. As Deci and Chandler (1986) noted, promoting self-
determination is not the same as allowing chaos. In classrooms with little structure and no expectations for appropriate behavior, students cannot learn.
However, special education environments are often too tightly structured and
controlling (Ianacone & Stodden, 1987; Wehmeyer, 1992) and limit any meaningful opportunities to achieve self-determination or to promote positive perceptions of control.

TEACHING STRATEGIES
TO PROMOTE PERCEIVED CONTROL

Instructional strategies to promote positive perceptions of control focus on examining teacher-control orientation, promoting student autonomy in the classroom, and creating a classroom environment that provides opportunities for
students to develop an internal orientation. Nunn and Nunn (1993) provided
several suggestions for teachers who want to achieve this outcome. These are
summarized in Table 1 and discussed in the following paragraphs.

Table 1.   Strategies to promote positive perceptions of control

Ensure that conditions for successful learning experiences are in place.
Emphasize to students the relationship between their behavior and their performance.
Have clearly stated, high expectations for behavior and performance.
Systematically bring students into "participatory ownership" of their learning experience.
Enlist the assistance of parents to promote reinforcement of internal characteristics.
Make sure that learning tasks and goals have credible value and relevance.
Provide students with a real choice in how, when, and why they learn within a structured
    framework of student-centered teaching.

Adapted from Nunn & Nunn (1993).

Ensure that conditions for successful learning experiences are in place. The importance of success and, conversely, of learning from failure experiences, to promote student self-efficacy are discussed in Chapter 15. Previous learning experiences affect a student's expectations for subsequent learning experiences; thus, if students succeed, they begin to expect to do so in the future. In addition, experiences of success in learning provide the conditions for the development of an internal locus of control.

Emphasize to students the relationship between their behavior and their performance. As defined previously, locus of control refers to the degree to which an individual perceives contingency relationships between his or her actions and outcomes. We have suggested that students with cognitive disabilities are often causal unrealists because they either do not understand the contingency relationships between their behavior and outcomes or because they have an immature understanding of such causal relationships. Teachers need to reinforce the link between the student's behavior and specific outcomes. Based on findings from the developmental literature, Doll, Sands, Wehmeyer, and Palmer (1996) suggested a sequential strategy, described in Table 2, to strengthen the link between student performance and outcomes.

Table 2.   Steps to linking student performance and outcomes

Step 1	• Begin by providing opportunities for students to learn to self-evaluate task performance by comparing their work to a model. Point out what they've done that is like the model (e.g., the word you wrote looks just like the word on the chalkboard).
	• Ask directive questions so that the student compares his or her performance to a model.
Step 2	• Provide opportunities for students to systematically evaluate their own work by comparing them to a model. Guide students through this process, though avoid actually comparing the work for the student.
Step 3	• Provide opportunities for students to evaluate task performance in affectively "safe" ways: identifying their own strengths and weaknesses in performance, reflecting on ways to improve performance, trying out some ways and reevaluating performance to check for improvement.

Adapted from Doll et al. (1996).

Have clearly stated, high expectations for behavior and performance. As Feldman, Saletsky, Sullivan, and Theiss (1983) pointed out, "one of the best supported findings in recent years demonstrates that the expectations that teachers hold about student performance are related to subsequent student outcomes" (p. 27). Those outcomes include student perceptions about themselves and their control over their lives. By setting and communicating high expectations, teachers communicate to students that they think they are capable and competent. Such expectations should be established based on the individual student's abilities and should emphasize the importance of effort to meet expectations.

Systematically bring students into "participatory ownership" of their learning experience. Nunn and Nunn (1993) stressed the importance of getting students to become self-directed learners instead of passive recipients of information. This involves implementing many of the strategies described throughout this text, from increased problem-solving, self-management, and decision-making skills to involvement in goal-setting and self-advocacy activities. As student learning becomes increasingly self-directed, so too will students increasingly believe they have control over outcomes in their lives.

Enlist the assistance of parents to promote reinforcement of internal characteristics. The family and the home environment have a significant impact on student perceptions of themselves and others. An effective parent–school partnership is critical if students are to develop positive perceptions of control. Cook, Brotherson, Weigel-Garrey, and Mize (1996) detailed the critical role that a student's home plays in the development of self-determination. Just as is the case in the classroom, features of the physical environment of the home, as well as the attitude of parents, can influence the development of positive perceptions of control. Cook and colleagues identified several ways in which the home environment has an impact on self-determination and locus of control:

- Sense of territory: When a person claims control over a specific area, be it a room, the garage, or a fort in the yard, he or she is exhibiting territorial behavior. Having control over such a space or area is an important part of developing positive perceptions of control. Families should be encouraged to set aside areas over which their son or daughter has control. Such control means a greater voice in when (and if) the area gets cleaned, control over entry and exit, and control over how the space is decorated.
- Privacy: An important aspect of the use of a personal space is the experience of privacy. Experiencing privacy and learning how to make private times enjoyable and fulfilling are important components of the development of autonomy. Children need some defined space of their own that they can regulate to ensure privacy.
- Nurturance: Children develop positive perceptions of control by becoming actors in their day-to-day lives. This involves risk taking and, occasionally, experiencing failure. Homes provide a safe environment in which to take risks and learn from failure, as well as a place to receive praise for successes.

Davis and Wehmeyer (1991) suggested 10 steps that parents can implement to promote self-determination in the home. These steps are listed in Table 3; teachers could share these or similar suggestions with families to enable them to better assist their son or daughter to develop positive perceptions of control and increased self-determination.

Make sure that learning tasks and goals have credible value and relevance. One way to make sure that students see the link between their behavior and outcomes is to make sure that the tasks in which they participate are tied to outcomes that are relevant to the student. Deci and Chandler noted that teachers

Table 3.   Ten steps to self-determination in the home

Step   1:   Walk the tightrope between protection and independence. Allow your son or daughter to explore his or her world. This may mean biting your lip and watching from the kitchen window when your child first meets the neighbor's kids, instead of running out to supervise. Although there are obviously limits to this, all parents have to "let go," and it is never easy.

Step   2:   Children need to learn that what they say or do is important and can have influence on others. This involves allowing risk taking and exploration. Encourage your child to ask questions and express opinions. Involvement in family discussions and decision-making sessions is one way of providing this opportunity to learn.

Step   3:   Self-worth and self-confidence are critical factors in the development of self-determination. Model your own sense of positive self-esteem to your child. Tell your child that he or she is important by spending time with your child and involve your child in family decisions.

Step   4:   Don't run away from questions about differences related to your child's disability. That doesn't mean, however, that you should focus on the negative side of the condition. Stress that everyone is unique, encourage your child's abilities, and help him or her to accept unavoidable limitations.

Step   5:   Recognize the process of reaching goals; don't just emphasize outcomes. Children need to learn to work toward goals. For older children, encourage skills like organization and goal setting by modeling these behaviors. Make lists or hang a marker board in the laundry room that shows the daily schedule.

Step   6:   Schedule opportunities for interactions with children of different ages and backgrounds. This could be in child care centers, schools, churches, and when playing in the neighborhood. Start early in finding chances for your son or daughter to participate in activities that help all children realize that everyone is unique.

Step   7:   Set realistic but ambitious expectations. The adage that our goals should extend just beyond our reach is true here. Take an active role in your child's educational experience. Be familiar with his or her reading ability and identify books that provide enough challenge to move to the next reading level. Be sure you don't just force activities that lead to frustration, but don't assume that all of the progress should occur at school.

Step   8:   Allow your child to take responsibility for his or her own actions...successes and failures. Provide valid reasons for doing things, instead of simply saying "because I said so!" Providing explanations provides the opportunity for the child to make an activity his or her own.

Step   9:   Don't leave choice-making opportunities to chance. Take every opportunity to allow your child to make choices: what she wears, what is served for dinner, or where the family goes for vacation. When offering choices, make sure that the child's selection is honored.

Step 10:   Provide honest, positive feedback. Focus on the behavior or task that needs to be changed. Don't make your child feel like a failure.

Adapted from Davis & Wehmeyer (1991).

should explain to students the reasons they are being asked to perform activities. These authors suggested that

> it is important [when asking students to take on tasks] to be clear and honest about why they are being asked to do them....they need a rationale for the activity. "It's for your own good" is not a rationale; it's a control. (1986, p. 591)

Provide students with a real choice in how, when, and why they learn within a structured framework of student-centered teaching. Most of the strategies in this text provide ways that educators can establish a structured framework of student-centered teaching. Brown, Belz, Corsi, and Wenig (1993) suggested seven ways to infuse choices into instructional activities:

1. Choosing within an activity
2. Choosing between two or more activities
3. Deciding when to do an activity
4. Selecting the person with whom to participate in an activity
5. Deciding where to do an activity
6. Refusing to participate in a planned activity
7. Choosing to end an activity at a self-selected time

Differentiating Among Ability, Effort, and Chance

If students with disabilities are causal unrealists, that is, if they do not fully differentiate between the influences of a person's ability or effort and the role of chance or circumstance in a given outcome, instructional efforts should be focused on teaching students to make these causal attributions. An emerging approach to address a specific educational problem, aggression, exemplifies both the importance of considering student perceptions in the classroom and the need to provide instruction enabling students to become more effective at attributing causes to situations. As anyone who has read a newspaper in the last decade will recognize, the problem of violence in the school has emerged as a topic of intense interest, both on the part of educators and the general population. Dodge and Crick (1990) have examined the causes of aggressive behavior in school children. One factor that contributes to aggressive behavior is the child's attribution of the cause of a negative event. That is, children who act in a more aggressive manner are more likely to infer a hostile intent to a negative event than children who do not act aggressively. Graham and Hudley (1992) gave as an example the finding that when asked to imagine if another child spilled milk on them in the lunchroom, aggressive children are more likely to report that the peer spilled the milk on purpose. Such an intentionality bias, explained Graham and Hudley, leads to an increased probability of retaliation and aggression.

Graham and Hudley (1992) developed a school-based cognitive intervention program to address problems in the attribution of causality with adolescent students who exhibited aggressive behaviors. They employed several instructional strategies, including group discussions, introspection exercises, and role playing. Students role-played situations in which an aggressive action occurred or discussed personal experiences. Through these role plays and subsequent discussions and exercises, students were taught to search for, interpret, and properly categorize verbal and behavioral cues present in most social situations that are critical for causal attribution. Students also produced videotaped scenarios depicting situations in which the intent of the negative event was altered (e.g., prosocial, accidental, hostile, or ambiguous peer intent). Students participating in the program showed marked progress in ascribing causal intent across a variety of situations.

Peer-Mediated and Cooperative Learning

As is the case for virtually every aspect of school, peers play a significant role in the development of a student's perceived control. Many school policies established to ensure discipline and classroom management have the unfortunate side effect of suppressing peer relations in the classroom and, in some cases, result in social isolation. Some teachers do not let students sit near their friends or make students who talk with peers change seats. While these steps may be necessary to deal with specific situations, they may inadvertently lead to less positive perceptions of the school experience and limit opportunities for students to acquire more positive perceptions of control. One means of countering this is to utilize peer-mediated and cooperative learning strategies, in which students work in collaboration with peers. Research suggests that systematic use of cooperative learning can improve attitudes toward school, improve academic achievement, and increase socialization (Berndt & Keefe, 1992).

Cooperative learning involves situations in which students work together to reach common goals (Putnam, 1993) (e.g., students working collaboratively on a science project, students working together to generate word problems in math). If implemented effectively, cooperative learning offers many benefits. It teaches students cooperation skills, provides excellent conditions for students to learn goal-oriented behavior, and creates opportunities for social interactions and the establishment of friendships. In addition, cooperative learning groups can provide an ideal support system for a student with special learning needs.

Teacher Communicator Style

The construct called *communicator style* refers to "the way one verbally and paraverbally interacts to signal how literal meaning should be taken, interpreted, filtered or understood" (Nussbaum, 1992, p. 146). A teacher's communicator style is the way he or she presents content to the class. Research in this area has linked teacher communicator style to teacher efficacy, including students' perceptions about their control in the classroom and other outcomes related to learning. The suggestions from this research are fairly straightforward and simple. Teachers who teach with enthusiasm and energy, who use a variety of strategies (e.g., humor, the use of surprise) to grab students' attention, and who are confident in trying new techniques in their classroom are the most effective.

Creating a Positive Classroom Environment

In summarizing research in community psychology that focused on the area of environment assessment, Trickett, Leone, Fink, and Braaten (1993) concluded that "(a) environments can be meaningfully conceptualized and measured and (b) environments affect behavior in systematic ways" (p. 411). As described previously, this is particularly true for the learning environment. The strategy described next can enable teachers to create a learning environment that supports the emergence of positive perceptions of control.

Book and Putnam (1992) identified three stages in the development of a positive classroom learning community. The first stage in the process, "Beginnings," focuses on five primary tasks. Teachers should

1. Inform students about life in a classroom learning community, with the emphasis on class members as a community;
2. Help students learn each others' names, become acquainted and begin to build trust among community members;
3. Foster appreciation of other students' multiple abilities;
4. Promote students developing a voice in the learning community;
5. Assess what students know and can do and use as a database for reflection (Book & Putnam, 1992, p. 23)

As Book and Putnam (1992) described it, "life in a classroom learning community" emphasizes the value of differences among students, participation, open communication, the importance of learning from mistakes, and the need to learn from and respect others in the community. To foster an appreciation of other students' abilities, they recommend designing group projects in which each student contributes something unique to the completion of the project. In such circumstances, students learn that their own goals and objectives can be reached by working with others who have different talents and abilities. Teachers need to reinforce the importance of open communication and the value of students' opinions and input to the learning community. Students are encouraged to ask questions, both of the teacher and their peers, and are encouraged to show ongoing respect for themselves and others in the course of these interactions. Finally, this first stage of building a learning community focuses on determining what students *know* and do *well,* and works from that vantage point, as opposed to identifying deficiencies and starting there.

The second stage in the process of building a learning community is to establish expectations. Book and Putnam described this stage as one

in which the teacher and students build shared understanding through making norms, roles, rules and procedures explicit by providing students with
(a)   descriptions,

(b)   reasons for their existence,
(c)   illustrations of what they look like in the learning community,
(d)   practice opportunities,
(e)   feedback to individuals and groups, and
(f)   consequences to the individual and community when they are not used (1992, p. 26)

At this stage, teachers work with students to establish appropriate behavioral norms for interactions within the community. Such norms include demonstrating respect for one another by listening, responding, questioning, and working cooperatively to solve problems and achieve mutually identified goals. The roles of each student within the community are defined and assigned. There are individual roles (e.g., small-group facilitator, timer, recorder) and group roles. Group roles involve those roles that all students are expected to undertake, including contributing to discussions, giving information, or asking questions. Based on these established norms and roles, community rules and classroom procedures can be established.

The next stage in the process of building a community learning environment is to identify and resolve the inevitable conflicts that emerge in any group. A key feature of a learning community is that power is distributed among members of the class as well as among teachers. It is still the teacher's role, however, to use power to facilitate learning. One such use of power will be to resolve behavior problems. Conflict resolution strategies, discussed in Chapter 10, become important ways to solve problems and support a learning environment. The fourth stage of building a learning community is to expand the community. This involves the use of a wider variety of instructional strategies across different environments outside of the classroom. Students may engage in project-related activities in alternative learning environments, such as a museum. Students could learn about a science topic, such as the reasons dinosaurs died, using the museum as the learning environment, rather than just as a field trip. Other topics could be covered in community-based settings, such as learning about personal finance in a bank.

CONCLUSION

It is not easy or straightforward to "teach" students positive perceptions of control. Strategies to support this end require teachers to examine their communication style, the ways in which they are using power to control classroom interactions, the impact of these interactions on students' perceptions, and the learning environment they create. Unless teachers undertake such efforts, many of their instructional efforts will go for naught. Students who do not believe that they have control over outcomes in their lives are much less likely to utilize skills that they have learned and less likely to achieve outcomes that are valued by students, families, and teachers alike.

QUESTIONS FOR REVIEW

1. What is an internal locus-of-control orientation?
2. Discuss the use and potential misuse of power in the classroom.
3. When asking students to perform tasks, it is important to provide a rationale. Why is this true and how should such a rationale be provided?
4. Identify ways to infuse choice into instructional activities.
5. Discuss the development of the understanding of causality. What is meant by the term *causal unrealist*?
6. How are students' perceptions of control related to the classroom environment?
7. How do current practices for students receiving special education services affect students' perceptions?
8. What can teachers do to promote positive student perceptions of control?

REFERENCES

Bar-Tal, D., & Bar-Zohar, Y. (1977). The relationship between perception of locus of control and academic achievement: Review and some educational recommendations. *Contemporary Educational Psychology, 2,* 181–199.

Barraclough, R.A., & Stewert, R.A. (1992). Power and control: Social science perspectives. In V.P. Richmond & J.C. McCroskey (Eds.), *Power in the classroom: Communication, control, and concern* (pp. 1–18). Hillsdale, NJ: Lawrence Erlbaum Associates.

Berndt, T.J., & Keefe, K. (1992). Friends' influence on adolescents' perceptions of themselves at school. In D.H. Schunk & J.L. Meece (Eds.), *Student perceptions in the classroom* (pp. 51–74). Hillsdale, NJ: Lawrence Erlbaum Associates.

Boggiano, A. K., & Katz, P. (1991). Maladaptive achievement patterns in students: The role of teachers' controlling strategies. *Journal of Social Issues, 47*(4), 35–51.

Boggiano, A.K., Main, D.S., & Katz, P.A. (1988). Children's preference for challenge: The role of perceived competence and control. *Journal of Personality and Social Psychology, 54,* 134–141.

Book, C.L., & Putnam, J.G. (1992). Organization and management of a classroom as a learning community culture. In V.P. Richmond & J.C. McCroskey (Eds.), *Power in the classroom: Communication, control, and concern* (pp. 19–34). Hillsdale, NJ: Lawrence Erlbaum Associates.

Brown, F., Belz, P., Corsi, L., & Wenig, B. (1993). Choice diversity for people with severe disabilities. *Education and Training in Mental Retardation, 28,* 318–326.

Cook, C.C., Brotherson, M.J., Weigel-Garrey, C., & Mize, I. (1996). Homes to support the self-determination of children. In D.J. Sands & M.L. Wehmeyer (Eds.), *Self-determination across the life span: Independence and choice for people with disabilities* (pp. 91–110). Baltimore: Paul H. Brookes Publishing Co.

Davis, S., & Wehmeyer, M.L. (1991). *Ten steps to independence: Promoting self-determination in the home.* Arlington, TX: The Arc National Headquarters.

Deci, E.L., & Chandler, C.L. (1986). The importance of motivation for the future of the LD field. *Journal of Learning Disabilities, 19,* 587–594.

Deci, E. L., Spiegel, N. H., Ryan, R. M., Koestner, R., & Kauffman, M. (1982). Effects of performance standards on teaching styles: Behavior of controlling teachers. *Journal of Educational Psychology, 74,* 852–859.

Dodge, K., & Crick, N. (1990). Social information-processing bases of aggressive behavior in children. *Personality and Social Psychology Bulletin, 16,* 8–22.

Doll, B., Sands, D.J., Wehmeyer, M.L., & Palmer, S. (1996). Promoting the development and acquisition of self-determined behavior. In D.J. Sands & M.L. Wehmeyer (Eds.), *Self-determination across the life span: Independence and choice for people with disabilities* (pp. 65–90). Baltimore: Paul H. Brookes Publishing Co.

Dudley-Marling, C.C., Snider, V., & Tarver, S.G. (1982). Locus of control and learning disabilities: A review and discussion. *Perceptual Motor Skills, 54,* 503–514.

Feldman, R.S., Saletsky, R.D., Sullivan, J., & Theiss, A. (1983). Student locus of control and response to expectations about self and teacher. *Journal of Educational Psychology, 75,* 27–32.

Findley, M.J., & Cooper, H.M. (1983). Locus of control and academic achievement: A literature review. *Journal of Personality and Social Psychology, 44,* 419–427.

Flink, C., Boggiano, A.K., & Barrett, M. (1990). Controlling teaching strategies: Undermining children's self-determination and performance. *Journal of Personality and Social Psychology, 59,* 916–924.

Fox, P.B. (1972). Locus of control and self-concept in mildly retarded adolescents (Doctoral dissertation, University of Minnesota, 1972). *Dissertation Abstracts, 33,* 2807B.

Graham, S., & Hudley, C. (1992). An attributional approach to aggression in African-American children. In D.H. Schunk & J.L. Meece (Eds.), *Student perceptions in the classroom* (pp. 75–94). Hillsdale, NJ: Lawrence Erlbaum Associates.

Grolnick, W.S., & Ryan, R.M. (1990). Self-perceptions, motivation and adjustment in children with learning disabilities: A multiple group comparison study. *Journal of Learning Disabilities, 23,* 177–184.

Gruen, G.E., Ottinger, D.R., & Olliendick, T.H. (1974). Probability learning in retarded children with differing histories of success and failure in school. *American Journal of Mental Deficiency, 79,* 417–423.

Ianacone, R.N., & Stodden, R.A. (1987). Transition issues and directions for individuals who are mentally retarded. In R.N. Ianacone & R.A. Stodden (Eds.), *Transition issues and directions* (pp. 1–7). Reston, VA: Council for Exceptional Children.

Lawrence, E.A., & Winschel, J.F. (1975). Locus of control: Implications for special education. *Exceptional Children, 41,* 483–490.

Lefcourt, H.M. (1976). *Locus of control: Current trends in theory and research.* Hillsdale, NJ: Lawrence Erlbaum Associates.

Lewis, S.K., & Lawrence-Patterson, E. (1989). Locus of control of children with learning disabilities and perceived locus of control by significant others. *Journal of Learning Disabilities, 22,* 255–257.

Madonna, S., Bailey, G.K., & Wesley, A.L. (1990). Classroom environment and locus of control identifying high and low self-concept in fourth and fifth graders. *Psychological Reports, 66,* 1152–1154.

Mercer, C.D., & Snell, M.E. (1977). *Learning theory research in mental retardation: Implications for teaching.* Columbus, OH: Charles E. Merrill.

Nicholls, J.G. (1978). The development of the concepts of effort and ability, perception of academic attainment, and the understanding that difficult tasks require more ability. *Child Development, 49,* 800–814.

Nunn, G.D., & Nunn, S.J. (1993). Locus of control and school performance: Some implications for teachers. *Education, 113,* 636–640.

Nussbaum, J.F. (1992). Communicator style and teacher influence. In V.P. Richmond & J.C. McCroskey (Eds.), *Power in the classroom: Communication, control, and concern* (pp. 145–158). Hillsdale, NJ: Lawrence Erlbaum Associates.

Ollendick, T.H., Greene, R.W., Francis, G., & Baum, C.G. (1991). Sociometric status: Its stability and validity among neglected, rejected and popular children. *Journal of Child Psychology and Psychiatry, 32,* 525–534.

Ollendick, T.H., & Schmidt, C.R. (1987). Social learning constructs in the prediction of peer interaction. *Journal of Clinical Child Psychology, 16,* 80–87.

Putnam, J.W. (Ed.). (1993). *Cooperative learning and strategies for inclusion: Celebrating diversity in the classroom.* Baltimore: Paul H. Brookes Publishing Co.

Richmond, V.P., & Roach, K.D. (1992). Power in the classroom: Seminal studies. In V.P. Richmond & J.C. McCroskey (Eds.), *Power in the classroom: Communication, control, and concern* (pp. 47–66). Hillsdale, NJ: Lawrence Erlbaum Associates.

Riedel, W.W., & Milgram, N.A. (1970). Level of aspiration, locus of control and n-achievement in retardates and normal children. *Psychological Reports, 27,* 551–557.

Rogers, H., & Saklofske, D.H. (1985). Self-concepts, locus of control and performance expectations of learning disabled children. *Journal of Learning Disabilities, 18,* 273–278.

Schunk, D.H. (1992). Theory and research in student perceptions in the classroom. In D.H. Schunk & J.L. Meece (Eds.), *Student perceptions in the classroom* (pp. 3–23). Hillsdale, NJ: Lawrence Erlbaum Associates.

Schunk, D.H., & Meece, J.L. (Eds.). (1992). *Student perceptions in the classroom.* Hillsdale, NJ: Lawrence Erlbaum Associates.

Shipe, D. (1970). Impulsivity and locus of control as predictors of achievement and adjustment in mildly retarded and borderline youth. *American Journal of Mental Deficiency, 76,* 12–22.

Skinner, E.A. (1990). Age differences in the dimensions of perceived control during middle childhood: Implications for developmental conceptualizations and research. *Child Development, 61,* 1882–1890.

Trickett, E.J., Leone, P.E., Fink, C.E., & Braaten, S.L. (1993). The perceived environment of special education classrooms for adolescents: A revision of the Classroom Environment Scale. *Exceptional Children, 59,* 411–420.

Wehmeyer, M.L. (1992). Self-determination and the education of students with mental retardation. *Education and Training in Mental Retardation, 27,* 303–314.

Wehmeyer, M.L., & Kelchner, K. (1994). Perceptions of self-determination and psychological empowerment of adolescents with mental retardation. *Education and Training in Mental Retardation and Developmental Disabilities, 29,* 9–21.

Wehmeyer, M.L., & Kelchner, K. (1996). Perceptions of classroom environment, locus of control and academic attributions of adolescents with and without cognitive disabilities. *Career Development for Exceptional Individuals, 19,* 15–30.

Weisz, J.R. (1980). Developmental change in perceived control: Recognizing noncontingency in the laboratory and perceiving it in the world. *Developmental Psychology, 16,* 385–390.

CHAPTER 15

Strategies
to Promote Self-Efficacy
and Outcome Expectations

After reading this chapter, you will be able to

1. Discuss the relationship among people's actions, self-efficacy, and outcome expectations

2. Identify the primary sources for the emergence of efficacy expectations

3. Discuss the effects of age on students' perceptions of ability and/or competence

4. Identify ways to increase the effectiveness of modeling

5. Recognize the impact of teacher expectations on student perceptions and identify strategies to counter these effects

KEY TERMS

1.	Causality	6.	Positive self-efficacy
2.	Emotional arousal	7.	Relaxation training
3.	Modeling	8.	Self-efficacy
4.	Negative self-efficacy	9.	Verbal persuasion
5.	Outcome expectations	10.	Vicarious experiences

In Chapter 1, psychological empowerment was defined as a construct reflecting the multiple dimensions of perceived control. This chapter discusses the cognitive component of perceived control: self-efficacy and outcome expectations. An overview of the research on self-efficacy and outcome expectations is presented, their relevance and importance to youth with disabilities is examined, and strategies are presented to promote these outcomes.

SELF-EFFICACY AND OUTCOME EXPECTATIONS

Bandura (1977a) proposed two related constructs that lead to perceptions of efficacy: self-efficacy and outcome expectancies. Bandura defined self-efficacy as "the conviction that one can successfully execute the behavior required to produce a given outcome" (Bandura, 1977a, p. 193). Simply put, self-efficacy refers to "one's beliefs about one's capabilities to perform a given behavior" (Hackett & Betz, 1992, p. 230). Outcome expectancies refer to an individual's belief that if he or she does perform a given behavior, it will lead to the expected outcome. Outcome expectations are an individual's probability assessments of the likelihood that a predicted outcome will occur.

People who act in a self-determined manner do so based on positive self-efficacy and outcome expectancies. That is, they believe that they can perform the behaviors needed to produce a given outcome (if such behaviors are in their repertoire); and they also believe that if they do perform the behavior, the predicted or desired outcome will occur. It is important that both sets of beliefs are in place, as illustrated in the following case study. Ramona may believe that she can perform a given behavior, in this case typing or math skills (positive self-efficacy); yet because she believes that doing well will not affect her chances of getting a good grade (negative outcome expectations), she has chosen not to exhibit the behavior.

> Stephanie was puzzled by the behavior of her friend, Ramona. Both classmates were juniors at Nathan Hale High School and had been lifelong neighbors. Stephanie felt like she knew Ramona almost as well as she knew herself. Both of them had played soccer in elementary school, joined the drama club in junior high, and run on the track team in high school. Several years ago Ramona had started having some problems reading and had to go through some testing. Since then, Ramona had received some special assistance in several of her subjects because she had what the psychologist called a learning disability. She and Ramona had talked a lot about it at first, but after a while it became less important. Ramona even joked about it, calling the school psychologist a "psy-school-agist" and claiming that she called him this because of her learning disability!
>
> Ramona's junior year seemed to be more difficult than her first year in high school. She and Stephanie saw each other a lot less because it was a bigger school and they had fewer classes together. Stephanie went out of her way to eat lunch with Ramona every chance she got; and, of course, they still saw each other at home a lot. That was what was puzzling Stephanie. At home, Ramona did a lot of things well that she seemed to avoid doing at

school. For example, they spent a lot of time surfing the Internet at home, and Stephanie knew that Ramona was a very good typist. However, in the introductory business class that they had together during fifth period, Ramona was failing the typing unit. Also, Ramona had always been good at math, but at lunch the other day she mentioned that she was not doing well in her business math class either. When Stephanie asked Ramona one day about her typing performances, Ramona just shrugged her shoulders. When she pressed the subject, Ramona had said that it did not make any difference whether she tried or not, she was not going to get higher than a "C" in her course. Stephanie asked why she thought this was the case, and Ramona said that it had something to do with her learning disability and students in special education not being able to get higher than a certain grade. Stephanie hardly thought that was fair and decided she could not really blame Ramona for not trying. She just hoped that she would soon go back to being the good-time Ramona she used to know.

Bandura (1982) proposed that self-efficacy and outcome expectancies are important determinants of how (and why) people behave, rather than "simply inert estimates of future action" (p. 122). Self-efficacy judgments influence an individual's choice of activities, where and with whom such activities will occur, how much effort the individual will expend and how long he or she will persist at a task, and how much preparation time will be invested in an activity. Quite simply, if a person doubts that he or she can perform a specific behavior or task or doubts that if he or she does perform that task the desired outcome will occur, that person is less likely to take on the task, work hard to achieve the task, and persist at the task when difficulties are encountered (Schunk, 1992). Success in transition obviously relies on persistence, preparation, and positive expectations. For example, if a student thinks he or she wants a job in the area of computers but goes to the interview unprepared, expecting not to get the job, and then gives up after one unsuccessful interview, it is unlikely that he or she will ever get a job in that area. Conversely, if the student believes that he or she has the skills to succeed in a computer job, prepares for the interview, and persists despite setbacks, odds are good that he or she will, eventually, succeed.

Bandura (1977a) identified four primary sources for the emergence of efficacy expectations (i.e., self-efficacy and outcome expectancies): 1) performance accomplishments, 2) vicarious experiences, 3) verbal persuasion, and 4) emotional arousal. Performance accomplishments refer to personal mastery experiences—"successes raise mastery expectations; repeated failures lower them" (Bandura, 1977a, p. 195). Vicarious experiences involve learning by watching others. Verbal persuasion refers to the role of verbal reinforcement and encouragement in promoting perceptions of efficacy, and emotional arousal refers to the effects of stressful or otherwise emotional circumstances on behavior. Specific ways in which these sources for efficacy expectations work, and what this means for instructional emphasis, are discussed in a subsequent section.

Like the locus of control construct, efficacy and outcome expectations have been hypothesized to interact with social and instructional factors to have an impact on academic and social outcomes for students with and without disabilities. Higher efficacy expectations are predictive of college achievement, persistence at academic activities, effective decision making, and academic achievement in secondary education (Schunk, 1992). Self-efficacy beliefs may be particularly important for students in the transition process. Lent and Hackett applied the self-efficacy construct to vocational behavior, proposing that "career self-efficacy refers to judgments of personal efficacy in relation to the wide range of behavior involved in career choice and adjustment" (1987, p. 349). Subsequent research has found that self-efficacy beliefs are predictive of more effective career decision making and persistence in achieving career outcomes (Niles & Sowa, 1992).

Development of Self-Efficacy and Outcome Expectations

Doll, Sands, Wehmeyer, and Palmer (1996) described the development of self-evaluation and attributions of efficacy. One antecedent to positive self-efficacy and outcome expectations is for students to self-evaluate (i.e., recognize their own actions and the outcomes of those actions clearly and without bias). Through self-evaluation, individuals can recognize personal strengths or confront limitations that conflict with their image of themselves as capable people. Resolving this tension so that one's self-evaluation is both accurate and empowering is one of the key challenges to the development of self-determination. Moreover, candid self-evaluation of personal strengths, weaknesses, and needs is an emotionally charged task that becomes difficult for individuals who are insecure about their capacity or their acceptance by significant others. Because children tend to become less self-confident and less secure in their relationships with age, self-evaluation becomes affectively more difficult for older children. Consequently, unlike other developmental tasks, resolving the conflict between accurate self-evaluation and empowering self-efficacy is a task one faces relatively late in the developmental sequence underlying self-determination (Doll et al., 1996).

Rudimentary self-evaluation skills have been observed in preschool children as they predict whether they might succeed at a task (Butler, 1990). These early self-descriptions are strikingly inaccurate and are often highly inconsistent from one task or situation to another (Frey & Ruble, 1987). Nevertheless, they represent an emerging understanding by the preschooler that specified kinds or levels of performance are valued by others and merit the effort required to achieve them (Higgins, 1989). It is not until the early elementary years that children's estimates of their own ability become stable and global across tasks (Dweck & Elliott, 1983; Rholes & Ruble, 1984), although children are unlikely to use normative comparisons (see next paragraph) spontaneously until the age of 10 years (Nicholls, 1978; Ruble, Boggiano, Feldman, & Loebl, 1980). By the middle elementary school grades, students' spontaneous self-evaluations are stable across time and settings, are relatively accurate, and could become appropriate foundations for self-determination.

Judging one's performance against a normative standard is a more complex cognitive task than making comparisons with mastery standards. In one study, preschoolers struggled to describe their own competence when asked to use normative standards (i.e., standards established based on some indication of typical or average performance across a population) that ranked their performance against those of their peers (Butler, 1990), but they were as accurate as fifth graders when judging their task performance against fixed mastery standards exemplified in models or templates (Stowitschek, Ghezzi, & Safely, 1987). Similarly, preschool children were adept at judging the degree to which their copy of a drawing matched the original but overestimated their performance when asked whether their drawing was the best copy in their group (Butler, 1990). It is not until the early elementary grades that students begin to understand their own ability as a point on a peer continuum of task performance. By third grade, students become more adept at comparing their performance to that of a normative group and are less likely to inflate their achievements (Butler, 1990). Only after fifth grade are students likely to use these self-evaluations as the basis for appropriate decisions to request instructional assistance or utilize cognitive strategies (Ghatala, 1986; Nelson-Le Gall, Kratzer, Jones, & DeCooke, 1990).

With increasing age and experience, children's self-evaluations become less optimistic and more congruent with their actual task performance. The overoptimism that characterizes preschool self-evaluations has led some theorists to suggest these self-evaluations represent wishful thinking, rather than actual expectations of success (Butler, 1990; Eccles, Midgeley, & Adler, 1984; Frey & Ruble, 1987). They attribute age-linked declines in children's estimates of their own competence to an increasing ability to overcome an emotional press to "congratulate oneself." Alternatively, Butler (1990) points to parallels between the erroneous self-assessments of preschoolers and the similar overestimates of adults who are provided with insufficient information about their performance or information that is difficult to organize and understand. She suggested instead that the cognitive complexity of self-evaluation biases children toward overestimating their likelihood of success.

Concurrent with their increasingly accurate self-evaluations, children develop an understanding of causality, including the development of the understanding of contingency relationships and the different roles that effort, ability, and luck play in outcomes (described in Chapter 14). These two developments contribute to children's ability to make realistic attributions and self-evaluations and, consequently, to develop a positive self-efficacy.

Self-Efficacy, Outcome Expectations, and Students with Disabilities

Research examining self-efficacy and outcome expectancies for youth with disabilities has been very limited. Schunk (1989) reviewed the literature pertaining to self-efficacy, cognitive achievement, and students with learning disabilities, most of which focused on changes in efficacy expectations contingent on environmental or methodological modifications. This literature suggested that students with disabilities held generally lower self-efficacy and outcome expectations than peers without disabilities. This supposition was confirmed by Wehmeyer (1994), who found that self-efficacy scores for youth with mental retardation and youth with learning disabilities were significantly less adaptive than same-age peers without disabilities. In addition, Wehmeyer found that the developmental progression of self-efficacy and outcome expectations for youth with cognitive disabilities differed from that seen in typical development. For most youth, self-efficacy expectations are higher in early adolescence and actually become lower over time as the previously unrealistic estimations of ability are replaced with more realistic estimations. Outcome expectations, however, start lower and become higher over time, based largely on increased opportunities to experience success. For youth with cognitive disabilities, self-efficacy expectations were lower initially and remained basically stable (e.g., lower) over time, and outcome expectations started at levels roughly comparable to students without disabilities and actually declined over time. In essence, youth with cognitive disabilities became less sure of their capacity to act in a situation and less convinced that if they do act, the predicted outcome will occur. This developmental course is obviously detrimental to self-determination and its emergence and, consequently, detrimental to positive transition outcomes.

PROMOTING POSITIVE SELF-EFFICACY AND OUTCOME EXPECTATIONS

Bandura's theory of self-efficacy (1977a) posits four primary sources of efficacy expectations (i.e., performance accomplishments, vicarious experience, verbal persuasion, emotional arousal), which were previously discussed. Each of these sources has multiple modes of induction, or more simply, ways in which different interventions operate to create expectations of mastery.

Performance Accomplishments and Vicarious Experiences

To paraphrase an old adage...nothing succeeds to promote positive self-efficacy and outcome expectancies like success! Ensuring that students with disabilities succeed is an important way to promote perceptions of efficacy and constitutes the first and most important way of establishing efficacy expectations: performance accomplishments. A fine line exists, however, between ensuring that students succeed and allowing students to learn from failure. Although it is generally true that successes raise mastery expectations and repeated failures lower them, the accent in that statement needs to be on *repeated*. Research has noted, and Bandura (1977a, 1977b) suggested, that occasional failures that are mitigated and later overcome can promote self-efficacy and increase persistence on tasks. Another factor to consider when allowing students to take risks, and thus increasing the chances that students will fail, is the strength of the student's efficacy beliefs. If students already strongly believe in their capacity to perform and achieve, then occasional failures (that the student then uses to learn to overcome the failure) will not have an impact on his or her efficacy expectations. If, however, a student's efficacy expectations are fairly fragile, even infrequent failures may be detrimental to that emerging sense of self-efficacy.

Bandura (1977a) suggested four modes of induction, or strategies, leading to personal mastery. The first mode, modeling, is a focal point of Bandura's social learning theory (Bandura, 1977b), and it is also the central strategy for the second way to establish efficacy expectations: vicarious experience. Although other chapters have touched on the use of modeling as an instructional strategy because it is central to the promotion of self-efficacy, it is discussed in detail in this section.

Vicarious Experiences: Modeling as an Instructional Strategy
According to social learning theory, there are several component processes that govern the degree to which an individual learns through modeling. Teachers employing modeling as a strategy need to keep aspects of each of these components in mind to ensure success. First, there are several *attentional* processes, pertaining to both the model and the observer, that govern observational learning. Table 1 lists these processes, and we selectively discuss those particularly relevant to promoting self-determination.

As shown in Table 1, several characteristics of the model stimuli (i.e., the behavior that is being modeled) influence learning. Perhaps most important, the stimuli should be distinct, and observers must be able to clearly differentiate the

Table 1. Component processes of learning from modeling

Attentional processes	Retention processes	Motor production processes	Motivational processes
Modeling stimuli distinctiveness	Symbolic coding	Physical capabilities	External reinforcement
Affective valence	Cognitive organization	Component responses	Vicarious reinforcement
Complexity	Symbolic rehearsal	Self-observation	Self-reinforcement
Prevalence	Motor rehearsal	Accuracy feedback	
Functional value			
Observer characteristics			
Sensory capacities			
Arousal level			
Perceptual set			
Past reinforcement			

modeled behavior. The purpose of using modeling as a teaching strategy is to transmit information about how to perform a specific behavior or action to observers. It seems self-evident that the success of that information transmission will be related to how clearly the behavior is modeled.

The success of modeling is also influenced by the affective valence of the model, that is, the complexity of the modeled behavior and the frequency with which the student sees the behavior modeled. The affective valence, or the emotional strength, of the model can be influenced by the choice of the model or the circumstance under which the behavior is modeled. As Bandura (1977b) noted, within any social group some individuals command greater attention than others, and behaviors modeled by such individuals may be more salient than if modeled by others. Likewise, behaviors modeled in circumstances that are motivating, interesting, and reinforcing to students may have more impact than behaviors modeled in less reinforcing situations. Like other areas of learning, the key is to make sure that learning is functional and that situations in which learning occurs promote generalization.

Observer characteristics also play into the success of modeling at the attentional phase, as would be expected. First, teachers need to take into account the capacity of the student to perceive the modeled behavior. Particularly important for students with visual, hearing, or physical impairments, students may need accommodations to benefit from modeled behavior. Such accommodation may be as simple as making sure that a student with a visual or hearing impairment is seated close to the model, or as sophisticated as providing a videotape of the modeled behavior with appropriate supports (e.g., closed captioning, large screen). Similarly, accommodations may be necessary for students with cognitive impairments, which may not have an impact on the sensation or perception of the event (e.g., whether the student sees or hears the event) but instead on the actual cognitive processing of the modeled behavior. Such accommodations include making the modeled behavior simple and highly differentiated from other behavior; providing repeated exposures to the modeled behavior; or, in some instances, providing specific training on observation or imitation skills.

Behavior complexity and repetition are important variables to the success of modeling for all students. The more complex the behavior, the more important it is that students have multiple opportunities to observe the modeled behavior. Thus, modeling goal-setting, problem-solving, or decision-making behavior is most likely to be effective only if students see repeated examples of these behaviors. An additional consideration when using modeling as a strategy would be to model a behavior in multiple environments to promote generalization. Past reinforcment history also affects the efficacy of modeling.

The second process influencing the impact of modeling involves student *retention* of the modeled behavior. Simply put, if students do not remember what they see, they will be unlikely to learn that behavior! As indicated in this text, a number of self-management strategies can be used to enhance retention (e.g., self-instructions, picture prompts on self-monitoring forms). What is probably the best way to ensure that students remember the modeled behavior or action, however, is by having students rehearse that behavior. This could include motor practice (e.g., physically repeating the behavior as modeled immediately after the model performs the behavior) or verbal practice (e.g., repeating a metacognitive strategy to solve problems).

The third process, *reproduction* processes, does not deal with practicing the behavior but with the actual reproduction of the behavior in other settings removed from the actual modeling situation. In order to replicate the preferred behavior pattern, students need to have adequate social and behavioral skills in their repertoire. Again, students with disabilities may require some accommodations to achieve adequate reproduction of the desired behavior. Bandura (1977b) also emphasized the importance of self-regulated learning in this phase and the next, *motivational* processes. In both phases, students need to learn self-observation and self-reinforcement skills.

One criticism of the use of modeling is that students are expected to simply repeat exactly what they see, thus stifling creativity and individuality. Contrary to this expectation, however, research on the use and effects of modeling as a teaching strategy indicate that observers usually do not pattern their behavior after a single source, but instead they accommodate aspects of preferred models into a unique behavior pattern (Bandura, 1977b).

By observing modeled behavior, students can learn much about skills important for successful transitions. In fact, it can be argued that one of the most important skills a person can take into the workplace or into interactions with others in the community is the capacity to learn from watching what others are doing. So, for example, although specific job skills are important for a potential employee to possess (e.g., computer-related skills are important in many office settings), there is simply no way that every possible workplace skill can be predicted, more or less learned, before the employee enters the workforce. It is critical, therefore, that students be able to learn by watching others perform similar jobs.

Verbal Persuasion

Another means to promote positive efficacy expectations is through verbal persuasion. Bandura stated,

> In attempts to influence human behavior, verbal persuasion is widely used because of its ease and ready availability. People are led, through suggestion, into believing that they can cope successfully with what has overwhelmed them in the past. (1977a, p. 198)

Indeed, most people can think of a time when they were cajoled or persuaded to attempt an activity at which they had previously had limited success.

Bandura (1977a) noted that the use of verbal persuasion, in and of itself, leads to fairly weak efficacy expectations when compared to those arising from performance accomplishments. At various times, however, verbal persuasion can serve as an effective bridge to encourage a person to try something that, whether he or she successfully accomplishes the activity, can build stronger efficacy expectations based on performance mastery.

Again, Bandura (1977b) included self-instruction as an important form of verbal persuasion (see Chapter 8) as well as supportive, honest feedback. Deci and Chandler (1986) emphasized the importance of such feedback to develop perceptions of competence. They suggested that when students strive to be effective, they need to know how they are doing. Such feedback should be given in such a manner as to be noncontrolling. Feedback should be honest, but nonevaluative. That is, feedback should be focused on the performance (e.g., "The first four answers are correct, but the final answer is not complete"), rather than on the student, and negative feedback should not be given in a way that portrays the child as a failure (e.g., "You did an awful job on the last question on that paper"). As Deci and Chandler (1986) concluded, teachers need to convey to students a sense of trust and a readiness to provide the support needed for the child to succeed.

Emotional Arousal

The final mode of induction through which Bandura (1977a) proposed that positive efficacy expectations emerge is emotional arousal. He pointed out that stressful or anxiety-providing situations elicit emotional arousal, which, in turn, can have an impact on the emergence of positive self-efficacy. Highly emotional or stressful circumstances place an individual in a state of psychological arousal and often make successful performance more difficult. To combat this, students need to learn skills they can employ to succeed in stressful or anxiety-provoking circumstances. Certainly effective problem-solving, decision-making, and self-management skills can enable students to cope in stressful situations. However, in addition to skills that allow students to address a problem, it is important to teach students skills to relieve their anxiety or stress so that they can implement the problem-solving strategies.

Relaxation training is one means of providing students with disabilities with the skills they need to cope with stressful situations. Cautela and Groden (1978) used a number of standard relaxation strategies with youth with disabilities. Their training program taught students to sit comfortably, tighten and relax targeted and specific muscle groups, and engage in a series of breathing exercises, all shown to reduce body tension and stress. As illustrated in the following case study, these types of exercises can enable students to perform much better in stressful situations, including transition-related circumstances such as job interviews and meetings.

Alex was nervous as a long-tailed cat in a room full of rocking chairs! He had his first job interview with Alvin, Beaumont and Klein (ABK), the law firm for which he hoped to work when he graduated. They were looking for a clerk, and Alex knew that he would be a great candidate for the job. Now the problem was convincing the senior partner at ABK that he was the right person for the job. He knew from past experiences that he did not come across well when he was nervous...he tended to speak too softly and look away from the person with whom he was talking.

Fortunately, he had a way to deal with his nervousness, and he had practiced this with some pretend interviews at school. The way he could deal with his nervousness was to do some relaxation exercises that Ms. Crossland had taught him in class. In these exercises he closed his eyes and concentrated on tensing and relaxing muscles in different parts of his body. So, for example, first he would tense and relax his arm muscles, then his leg muscles, then his neck and shoulder muscles, and so on. When he first did this, it surprised him how much it relaxed him. Of course he had not really been nervous then. After they learned these relaxation techniques, he and other members of his class had learned some interviewing skills and conducted some practice interviews. He was not really nervous for those, so he did not use the relaxation strategy. However, as a final "test" for the interview skills, Ms. Crossland had set up interviews for each student with a vocational rehabilitation counselor. It was not a real job interview but just an interview to talk about what each student could do and what vocational rehabilitation might have to offer. Before he went to that interview, Alex had used his relaxation technique and found that he did feel more relaxed.

Now, however, was the big test. Alex certainly did not want to be sitting in the waiting room at ABK with his eyes closed, doing all of those muscle exercises. So, he had arrived a little early and was outside in his car. He closed his eyes and thought about all of his skills. He tensed his shoulder and neck muscles and relaxed them. Tensed and relaxed. Tensed and relaxed. Then he did the same with his arm muscles. All the while, Alex thought about the interviewing skills he had learned. When it was time to go into the lobby, Alex felt a lot less nervous than before. He still had some butterflies in his stomach, but he also knew that he was going to be able to convince the interviewer that he had a lot of the skills they were looking for in the job.

Goal Setting, Progress Feedback, and Self-Regulated Learning Strategies

In reality, implementation of many of the strategies identified in this book will result in increased self-efficacy and outcome expectations! As students become more effective problem solvers and decision makers and more able to regulate their own behavior and learning, they will also experience increased efficacy expectations. For example, Schunk (1992) examined the effect of the implementation of learning goals and progress feedback on student self-efficacy, and the author concluded that teaching students to set instructional goals and to approach school work within a goal-oriented framework improved student self-efficacy. Schunk stressed the importance of the type of feedback provided, suggesting that teachers provide both effort-related feedback (e.g., "You are really working hard on that task") and ability-related feedback (e.g., "I know you can do that task"). Strategies to teach goal-setting and goal-directed behavior are discussed in Chapter 9. Likewise, self-regulated learning strategies, such as self-instruction (Chapter 8), self-observation, and self-reinforcement (Chapter 7) strategies have been shown to improve student self-efficacy.

Teacher Expectations, Efficacy Expectations, and Achievement Attributions

One important factor influencing students' efficacy expectations are teachers' expectations of the students. Research has examined the effects of how teachers respond to different students on students' perceptions of control and efficacy and the relationship between teacher expectations and student expectations. Wigfield and Harold (1992) reviewed research on the latter and concluded that students' expectancies for themselves are strongly associated with teachers' expectations for them. As for the influence of teachers' responses to students on student perceptions, research by Weinstein (1985, 1989) and colleagues has shown that students perceive teachers as providing more negative feedback and directed instruction to low-achieving students. They also perceive teachers as providing more choice and messages of high expectations to high-achieving students. Just these interactions, in and of themselves, serve to shape students' efficacy expectations and achievement self-perceptions. Students who believe that teacher interactions with them are overly directive and consist of negative feedback or students who do not perceive themselves as having choice opportunities in the classroom will use their perceptions of teacher interactions to attribute such interactions to the fact that they must be low-achieving students.

Wigfield and Harold (1992) provided several suggestions for educational practice to counter the negative impact of teacher expectations and differential treatment on students' self-perceptions. First, although most teachers are quite aware that their beliefs about students influence their performance, they are typically not cognizant that they are treating children differently. Wigfield and Harold pointed out that student–teacher interactions occur so frequently and so rapidly that teachers cannot realistically process such interactions and may be unaware of the kinds of messages they are providing to different students. An additional problem is that it is neither preferable nor feasible to treat all students exactly the same because students vary considerably in what they need in order to succeed. Teachers should not necessarily strive to treat all students the same, but instead they should strive to make sure that they are not treating children differently based on their own beliefs or expectations. Wigfield and Harold suggested that, in addition to being aware that their expectancies can influence behavior, teachers should collaborate with colleagues, observe one another's interactions with students, and discuss ways in which their behavior might influence students' self-perceptions.

Wigfield and Harold (1992) also pointed out that part of the reason that teachers develop specific expectations about students is the emphasis in most classrooms on ability. They suggested that by focusing attention on student progress and mastery, instead of on comparative ability assessments, teachers can overcome the inherent biases and expectations built up by a constant emphasis on ability levels.

CONCLUSION

The role of teachers in promoting self-efficacy and outcome expectations is to provide students with experiences that lead them to believe that they have the capacity to act in situations that have an impact on their lives and that by doing so they will achieve positive outcomes. A recurring theme in this process is that students need to experience successes in their lives. This may be particularly important for students with disabilities in the transition process, who may have experienced too few successes in their lives, particularly in educational settings. In addition, teachers should examine their own expectations and biases and consider how these affect students on a day-to-day basis.

QUESTIONS FOR REVIEW

1. The belief that one can successfully execute a given behavior required to produce a specific outcome is called self-efficacy. Describe how this belief is important for self-determination.
2. Outcome expectations are an individual's probability assessments of the likelihood that a predicated outcome will occur. How do these differ from self-efficacy beliefs?
3. What effects do self-efficacy and outcome expectations have on human behavior?
4. Describe some of the important issues to keep in mind when using modeling as a teaching strategy.
5. How do stressful situations have an impact on performance? What can teachers do to help students cope with such situations?
6. How do teacher expectations affect students' psychological empowerment?
7. What other strategies are important to promote self-efficacy and positive outcome expectations?

REFERENCES

Bandura, A. (1977a). Self-efficacy: Toward a unifying theory of behavioral change. *Psychological Review, 84,* 191–215.
Bandura, A. (1977b). *Social learning theory.* Englewood Cliffs, NJ: Prentice Hall.
Bandura, A. (1982). Self-efficacy mechanism in human agency. *American Psychologist, 37,* 122–147.

Betz, N.E., & Hackett, G. (1986). Application of self-efficacy theory to understanding career choice behavior. *Journal of Social and Clinical Psychology, 4,* 270–289.

Butler, R. (1990). The effects of mastery and competitive conditions on self-assessment at different ages. *Child Development, 61,* 201–210.

Cautela, J.R., & Groden, J. (1978). *Relaxation: A comprehensive manual for adults, children, and children with special needs.* Champaign, IL: Research Press.

Deci, E.L., & Chandler, C.L. (1986). The importance of motivation for the future of the LD field. *Journal of Learning Disabilities, 19,* 587–594.

Doll, B., Sands, D.J., Wehmeyer, M.L., & Palmer, S. (1996). Promoting the development and acquisition of self-determined behavior. In D.J. Sands & M.L. Wehmeyer (Eds.), *Self-determination across the life span: Independence and choice for people with disabilities* (pp. 65–90). Baltimore: Paul H. Brookes Publishing Co.

Dweck, C.S., & Elliott, E.S. (1983). Achievement motivation. In E.M. Hetherington (Ed.) & P.H. Mussen (Series Ed.), *Handbook of child psychology: Vol. 3. Socialization, personality and social developments* (4th ed., pp. 643–691). New York: John Wiley & Sons.

Eccles, J., Midgeley, C., & Adler, T.F. (1984). Age-related changes in the school environment: Effects on achievement motivation. In J.H. Nicholls (Ed.), *The development of achievement motivation* (pp. 57–90). Greenwich, CT: JAI Press.

Frey, K.S., & Ruble, D.N. (1987). What children say about classroom performance: Sex and grade differences in perceived competence. *Child Development, 58,* 1066–1078.

Ghatala, E.S. (1986). Strategy-monitoring training enables young learners to select effective strategies. *Educational Psychologist, 21,* 43–54.

Hackett, G., & Betz, N.E. (1992). Self-efficacy perceptions and the career-related choices of college students. In D.H. Schunk & J.L. Meece (Eds.), *Student perceptions in the classroom* (pp. 229–246). Hillsdale, NJ: Lawrence Erlbaum Associates.

Higgins, E.T. (1989). Continuities and discontinuities in self-regulatory and self-evaluative processes: A developmental theory relating self and affect. *Journal of Personality, 57,* 407–444.

Lent, R.W., & Hackett, G. (1987). Career self-efficacy: Empirical status and future directions. *Journal of Vocational Behavior, 30,* 347–382.

Nelson-Le Gall, S., Kratzer, L., Jones, E., & DeCooke, P. (1990). Children's self-assessment of performance and task-related help seeking. *Journal of Experimental Child Psychology, 49,* 800–814.

Nicholls, J.G. (1978). The development of the concepts of effort and ability, perceptions of academic attainment, and the understanding that difficult tasks require more ability. *Child Development, 49,* 800–814.

Niles, S.G., & Sowa, C.J. (1992). Mapping the nomological network of career self-efficacy. *The Career Development Quarterly, 41,* 13–21.

Rholes, W.S., & Ruble, D.N. (1984). Children's understanding of dispositional characteristics of others. *Child Development, 55,* 550–560.

Ruble, D.N., Boggiano, A.K., Feldman, N.S., & Loebl, J.M. (1980). A developmental analysis of the role of social comparison in self-evaluation. *Developmental Psychology, 16,* 105–115.

Schunk, D.H. (1989). Self-efficacy and cognitive achievement: Implications for students with learning problems. *Journal of Learning Disabilities, 22,* 14–23.

Schunk, D.H. (1992). Self-regulation of self-efficacy and attributions in academic settings. In D.H. Schunk & B.J. Zimmerman (Eds.), *Self-regulation of learning and performance* (pp. 75–99). Hilldale, NJ: Lawrence Erlbaum Associates.

Stowitscheck, J.J., Ghezzi, P.M., & Safely, K.N. (1987). "I'd rather do it myself": Self-evaluation and correction of handwriting. *Education and Treatment of Children, 10,* 209–224.

Wehmeyer, M.L. (1994). Perceptions of self-determination and psychological empowerment of adolescents with mental retardation. *Education and Training in Mental Retardation and Developmental Disabilities, 29,* 9–21.

Weinstein, R.S. (1985). Student mediation of classroom expectancy effects. In J.B. Dusek (Ed.), *Teacher expectancies* (pp. 329–350). Hillsdale, NJ: Lawrence Erlbaum Associates.

Weinstein, R.S. (1989). Perceptions of classroom processes and student motivation: Children's views of self-fulfilling prophecies. In C. Ames & R. Ames (Eds.), *Research on motivation in education* (Vol. 3, pp. 187–221). San Diego: Academic Press.

Wigfield, A., & Harold, R.D. (1992). Teacher beliefs and children's achievement self-perceptions: A developmental perspective. In D.H. Schunk & J.L. Meece (Eds.), *Student perceptions in the classroom* (pp. 95–121). Hillsdale, NJ: Lawrence Erlbaum Associates.

SECTION VI

Summary and Conclusions

CHAPTER 16

Promoting
Self-Determined
Behavior Through
the Transition Process

After reading this chapter, you will be able to

1. Discuss the way in which a focus on self-determination affects all aspects of the transition services process

2. Implement transition assessment activities focused on self-determination

3. Implement transition-planning and decision-making activities focused on self-determination

4. Identify and implement student-directed transition strategies and procedures

5. Discuss the importance of self-determination to the success of the transition process

KEY TERMS

1. Curriculum
2. Instruction
3. Student-directed learning
4. Transition assessment
5. Transition planning
6. Transition program evaluation

The purpose of this text is to provide teachers and teachers-in-training information about strategies, methods, and materials they can use to promote self-determined behavior for students with disabilities in the transition process. The book operationalizes a definitional framework of self-determination as an educational outcome (described in Chapter 1) and is part instruction guide and part curriculum, in that curriculum refers to *what* is taught in a student's educational program (Sands, Adams, & Stout, 1995) and instruction refers to *how* a student is taught. In Chapters 1–3, we provided a comprehensive overview of self-determination as an educational and transition outcome, described the historical antecedents to the self-determination movement, and discussed the link between self-determination and transition. Chapters 4–15 addressed specific strategies, methods, and materials that educators can use to teach component elements of self-determined behavior.

It is our contention that too many students with disabilities lack the opportunity to learn and utilize self-determination skills as part of the curriculum and that the transition period is a particularly important time to address these skill areas. It is critical to focus attention on skills development in this area. There is, however, an inherent tension when calling for increased skills development for students with disabilities to become self-determined. This is because focusing exclusively on students' skills deficits suggests that all problems with self-determination experienced by people with disabilities are rooted in the individual. It should be clear, however, that we do not subscribe to this theory and in many ways agree that the most important steps that can be taken to promote self-determination do not involve increasing students' skill levels, but instead focus on changing the ways in which instruction is provided and the educational program is conducted. Throughout the text we have stressed ways teachers can both teach students the skills they will need to take advantage of opportunities in their lives and to address limitations and barriers in systems that contribute to less positive self-determination outcomes.

Napoleon Bonaparte is reported to have said that ability is of little use without opportunity, and it is certainly the case that what many people with disabilities need to become self-determined is simply more opportunities to do so. Williams (1989) spoke for many people with disabilities when he said that self-determination is "just another word for freedom....another word for describing a life filled with rising expectations, dignity, responsibility, and opportunity...another word for having the chance to live the American Dream" (p. 16).

Thus, it is critically important to increase the number of opportunities people with disabilities have to assume control in their lives. Likewise, it is equally true that opportunity is of little use without ability! For example, the Americans with Disabilities Act (ADA) of 1990 (PL 101-336) provides protection from discrimination based on disability to *qualified* applicants for jobs. Individuals who are not qualified to work in a specific job, who lack the ability to perform job tasks, will not benefit from ADA protections. As suggested in the chapter on teaching self-regulation skills (see Chapter 7), both capacity and opportunity must be enhanced for students in transition programs.

Unfortunately, too many students with disabilities leave school unprepared to take advantage of the growing number of opportunities available to them. Also, they frequently lack the skills they need to succeed. It is the function of education in our society to provide students with these skills, and it is the focal point of transition services to enable students to become as self-sufficient and independent as possible. As such, it is important that the skills students need to acquire to become self-determined become part of the transition curriculum and that strategies to promote this outcome become part of transition instruction.

The Individuals with Disabilities Education Act (IDEA) of 1990 (PL 101-476) and its amendments specifically define transition services (see Chapter 3) but do not describe the transition curriculum or the type of instruction that will lead to the outcomes described in the law. This determination is left to the members of the individualized education program (IEP) team. The following section examines the implications that a self-determination focus will have for curriculum and instruction in transition services, including the areas of transition assessment, transition planning and decision making, transition program implementation, and program evaluation.

ASSESSMENT IN TRANSITION SERVICES

Salvia and Ysseldyke (1981) identified five specific reasons for conducting assessment in education: 1) screening, 2) placement, 3) instructional planning, 4) pupil evaluation, and 5) program evaluation. Assessment in transition services is typically not performed for either screening or placement purposes but rather to aid in instructional planning, student evaluation, and program evaluation. Clark (1996) suggested that it is important that transition assessment include multiple approaches to assessment, including the use of standardized tests, interviews, direct observation, and criterion-referenced assessment. Clark identified a number of areas in which standardized assessments are available for use in transition services planning and evaluation, including

- Academic achievement tests
- Adaptive behavior scales
- Aptitude tests
- Interest inventories
- Learning style inventories
- Personality scales
- Prevocational/employability scales
- Quality of life scales
- Social skills inventories

- Transition knowledge and skills inventories
- Vocational skills assessments

Although many of these instruments are not specific to transition, they can provide information on a wide range of student strengths, limitations, knowledge, skills, interests, and preferences; and thus they enable transition planners to move forward with a comprehensive picture of the student. Clark (1996) also listed the types of informal assessment from which transition-related decisions can be made, including

- Adaptive, behavioral, or functional skills inventories or checklists
- Applied technology and vocational education prerequisite skills assessments
- Curriculum-based assessments
- Environmental assessments
- Observational reports from teachers, employers, and parents or guardians
- Personal futures planning activities and procedures
- Rating scales of employability, independent living, and personal-social skills
- Situational assessments in home, community, and work settings
- Situational or observational learning styles assessments
- Social histories
- Structured interviews with parents or guardians, advocates, and peers
- Structured interviews with students

Again, these assessment procedures enable planners to form a complete picture of student needs, interests, and abilities by gathering input from multiple sources. In addition to using these traditional components of transition assessment (e.g., standardized and informal assessment procedures), transition programs also need to include assessments that identify student strengths and limitations in self-determination skills areas and that incorporate student self-report measures and student self-evaluation procedures into the assessment process.

As was suggested in Chapter 3, the IDEA transition services process should begin with student needs, taking into account student interests and preferences. The logical first step in the transition assessment process, therefore, is to identify student interests and preferences. The most straightforward means of assessing student preferences is to interview the student and his or her friends or family members. For students who cannot easily articulate their preferences, Chapter 5 presented several strategies to identify the preferences of students with limited verbal skills. It is necessary to sample a student's interests and preferences often, in large measure because these preferences change over time (as do the preferences of almost all people)!

Once student interests and preferences in transition areas are established, assessment should focus on identifying student skill areas, or strengths, and areas of instructional needs. Accomplishing this in relation to self-determination will involve a combination of assessment activities. As was discussed in Chapter 13, this needs to be accomplished within the context of an empowerment evaluation framework, in which assessment activities are "designed to help people help themselves and improve their programs using a form of self-evaluation and reflection" (Fetterman, 1996, p. 5). Transition assessment then becomes a collaborative effort, combining the input of the student and other significant stakeholders.

Teachers involved in the transition assessment process should focus more on issues of student instructional and curricular needs in self-determination and use procedures to better enable students with disabilities to participate in the transition-planning process. Several chapters in this text provide direction for this effort. First, students need to acquire effective self-regulation skills, as discussed in Chapter 7. Self-monitoring and self-evaluation strategies are typically designed and implemented to assist students to monitor classroom behavior, social skills, or academic work (Smith & Nelson, 1997). One outcome of such an activity is that students begin to learn more about themselves, how they respond in specific situations, what they like and dislike, and how they can meet their unique educational and learning needs. If students are to participate effectively in the transition assessment process, and to achieve self-selected transition goals, they will need to be able to evaluate their needs, interests, and abilities. In addition, students should learn how to select feasible and achievable goals, base actions on these goals, and strive toward achieving them. Like other critical transition skills, these skills need to be systematically assessed and taught.

Assessing Self-Determination Needs

Determining instructional and curricular needs in the area of self-determination involves a combination of standardized and informal procedures incorporating input from multiple sources, including the student, his or her family, professionals, and others. Informal procedures are similar to those described previously by Clark (1996). We suggest that teachers utilize a few standardized measures of self-determination and specific component elements that could be used to identify instructional and curricular needs. Some of these are tied directly to instructional curricula. For example, the self-determination curriculum titled, *Steps to Self-Determination* (Field & Hoffman, 1996), described in Chapter 13, provides several criterion-referenced assessment instruments, including a student self-report measure. Likewise, students involved in the *Next S.T.E.P.* curriculum (Halpern et al., 1995), discussed in Chapter 12, complete the Transition Skills Inventory, a 72-item rating instrument assessing how well the student is doing in four transition areas: 1) personal life, 2) jobs, 3) education and training, and 4) living on one's own. The student's self-evaluation of these areas is combined with similar evaluations by his or her teacher and a family member to form a basis for future transition-planning activities. Students are encouraged to discuss differences of opinion between the teacher or family member evaluations and their own self-evaluation and to resolve these discrepancies either before or during the transition-planning meeting.

The ChoiceMaker materials described in Chapter 12, which are designed to promote student involvement in educational planning and decision making, include an assessment component that can be used to identify student self-determination needs. The ChoiceMaker Self-Determination Transition Assessment (Martin & Huber Marshall, 1996) is tied to the ChoiceMaker curriculum and provides teachers an opportunity to rate student skills and student opportunities to perform such skills in areas such as choosing goals and taking action.

Another instrument to assess student self-determination is The Arc's Self-Determination Scale (Wehmeyer & Kelchner, 1995b). This scale is a 72-item self-report measure that provides data on each of the four essential characteristics of self-determination (described in Chapter 1) as well as overall self-determination. The first section measures student autonomy, including the student's independence and the degree to which he or she acts on the basis of personal beliefs, values, interests, and abilities. The second section measures student self-regulation and is composed of two subdomains: 1) interpersonal cognitive problem solving and 2) goal setting and task performance. The third section of the scale is an indicator of psychological empowerment, and the final section measures student self-realization.

The Arc's Self-Determination Scale was normed with 500 students with and without cognitive disabilities in rural, urban, and suburban school districts in five states. The scale has been used to conduct research into the relationship between self-determination and positive adult outcomes (Wehmeyer & Schwartz, 1997) and quality-of-life variables (Wehmeyer & Schwartz, in press). The scale's primary purpose, however, is to enable students with cognitive disabilities to self-assess strengths and limitations in the area of self-determination and to provide students and teachers a tool with which they can jointly determine goals and instructional programming to promote self-determination.

Another measure of self-determination is the AIR Self-Determination Scale (Wolman, Campeau, DuBois, Mithaug, & Stolarski, 1994). This instrument measures individual capacity for and opportunity to practice self-determination. Educator, student, and parent forms of the scale are available, and the results of each can be used to develop a profile of a student's level of self-determination, identify areas of strength and areas needing improvement, identify educational goals and objectives, and develop strategies to build student capacity and increase students' opportunities to become self-determined.

All of the previously mentioned assessments measure global self-determination. Many instruments are available, however, that measure individual essential characteristics or component elements of self-determined behavior. For example, the Autonomous Functioning Checklist (Sigafoos, Feinstein, Damond, & Reiss, 1988; AFC) is a parent-completed checklist designed to measure the behavioral autonomy of adolescents. The scale has 78 items and is subdivided into four subscales: self and family care, management, recreational activity, and social and vocational activity. Lewis and Taymans (1992) used the AFC to examine the autonomous functioning of adolescents with learning disabilities. Although the scale was designed as a parent-report measure, it can easily be used as a self-report indicator for students with disabilities, simply by changing the tense of the questions from second-person to first-person (e.g., from "My son or daughter does..." to "I do..."). Wehmeyer and Kelchner (1995a) adapted the parent-report version to a self-report version to examine the autonomy of adults with mental retardation.

When assessing students' psychological empowerment and self-realization, it may be particularly important to identify self-report measures of constructs such as locus of control, self-efficacy, or self-awareness. Although probably underutilized in educational settings, a number of such scales have been used with adolescents and adults with disabilities. For example, the most frequently used locus of control scale, the Adult Version of the Nowicki-Strickland Internal-External Scale (ANS-IE; Nowicki & Duke, 1974) has been used and validated with students and adults with mental retardation and learning disabilities (Fincham & Barling, 1978; Hallahan, Gajar, Cohen, & Tarver, 1978; Rogers & Saklofske, 1985; Swanson, 1980, 1981; Wehmeyer, 1993a, 1993b, 1994a, 1994b).

Assessment Into Practice

The outcome of assessment in transition services should be the identification of students' transition interests, preferences, abilities, instructional needs, and necessary supports. This information will be used to identify transition-related goals and objectives, identify potential instructional environments and transition-related placement options (e.g., to what job sites might students gain access as part of transition programming), and identify or design instructional strategies to achieve transition goals and objectives. In too many situations, the student's involvement in assessment ends when he or she leaves the testing environment or turns in the assessment protocol. However, not only should students become involved in interpreting assessment outcomes but also in identifying and selecting goals, objectives, instructional environments, and teaching strategies. As was described in detail in Chapter 9, students can learn to set goals and to regulate their behavior based on these goals. The transition assessment process provides the information students and teachers need to set transition goals and objectives. Thus, transition assessment with an emphasis on self-determination will result in goals and objectives that are both teacher and student generated.

TRANSITION PLANNING AND DECISON MAKING

The impact of a self-determination focus on transition planning and decision making is significant (Browning, Dunn, & Brown, 1993; Halloran, 1993; Halpern, 1994; Johnson & Rusch, 1993). As is clearly the intent of the student involvement mandates in IDEA, and as was discussed in Chapters 3 and 12, students need to be involved in all aspects of transition planning and decision making (Wehmeyer & Ward, 1995). This involvement is particularly important because effective transition planning and services coordination have been validated as critical to positive transition outcomes (Kohler, 1993). As Wehman (1992) explained, "without coordinated efforts in planning for individual students, there is a high likelihood of duplication or interruptions in service provision flow" (p. 99). We might add that without student involvement in planning efforts, it is highly likely that service delivery will not match students' needs, interests, and preferences.

Kohler, DeStafno, Wermuth, Grayson, and McGinty (1994) identified several key elements of exemplary transition programs in implementing systematic, interdisciplinary transition planning, including

- Parent involvement in planning
- Transition team includes student, parents, school personnel, and adult services system providers
- Individualized planning and plans
- Objectives and activities of individualized transition plan (ITP) reflected on IEP
- Identified vocational, residential, and social outcomes
- Written transition plans
- Students made aware of agencies and services
- Interdisciplinary team approach for treatment planning and process
- Transition counseling

Kohler's (1993) findings from examining these effective programs and research cited throughout this text indicate that students need to be equal partners in the transition planning and decision-making process, instead of just recipients of services. The question then becomes how best to involve students. Chapter 12 introduced numerous programs designed to involve students with disabilities in their transition-planning process. Even without a specific program, however, steps can be taken to ensure that students are actively involved. Wehman (1994) identified the following five basic steps to formulating and implementing individualized transition planning. Each of these steps is examined in detail next to show how students can be involved along the way.

Step 1: Organize ITP teams for all transition-age students.
- Identify all students who are of transition age;
- Identify school personnel;
- Identify adult services and agency personnel.
Step 2: Hold initial ITP meetings as part of annual IEP meetings.
- Schedule meeting;
- Conduct meeting;

- Develop the ITP.

Step 3: Implement the ITP through secondary school and adult service provision.

- Operate according to guidelines defined in local interagency agreements.
- Use a transdisciplinary and cross-agency approach.

Step 4: Update the ITP annually during the IEP meetings and implement quarterly follow-up procedure.

- Phase out involvement of school personnel while increasing involvement of adult service personnel;
- Contact persons responsible for completion of ITP goals to monitor progress.

Step 5: Hold an exit meeting.

- Ensure most appropriate employment outcome;
- Ensure most appropriate recreation outcome;
- Ensure most appropriate community living outcome; and
- Ensure referrals to all appropriate adult agencies and support services. (Wehman, 1992, p. 100)

Organize ITP teams for all transition-age students. It is the local education agency's responsibility to organize the transition planning meeting. It is beneficial, however, for all participants if students have significant and meaningful input into this process, not the least because this increases the possibility that students will feel a sense of "ownership" over the process. For example, *Whose Future Is it Anyway?*, a student-directed transition planning program described in Chapter 12, teaches students to identify who in their school district is responsible for setting up transition-planning meetings, and it encourages students to approach that person and volunteer to take some responsibility for that process by

1. Helping to decide when their meetings will be held
2. Helping to decide where their meetings will be held
3. Helping to decide who will be at their meetings
4. Assisting in setting up for their meetings
5. Assisting in notifying meeting participants of time/place of meetings

Hold initial ITP meetings as part of annual IEP meetings. IDEA mandates that a statement of needed transition services be included in the IEP of each student of transition age. Some state regulations require that school districts hold transition planning meetings that are separate from the regularly scheduled IEP meeting and that findings from this meeting be included in the IEP. Other states require that transition planning occur at the regularly scheduled IEP meeting. In either case, students with disabilities can and should play a significant role at the meeting. Several programs and instructional strategies to enable students to participate in their transition planning meeting focus on teaching students to chair the meeting. For example (as was described in Chapters 11 and 12), the *ChoiceMaker Self-Directed IEP* program prepares students to assume responsibility for 11 tasks in their role as IEP chairpeople. Students learn to

1. Begin meeting by stating purpose
2. Introduce everyone
3. Review past goals and performance
4. Ask for others' feedback
5. State your school and transition goals
6. Ask questions if you do not understand
7. Deal with differences in opinion
8. State what support you'll need
9. Summarize your goals
10. Close meeting by thanking everyone
11. Work on IEP goals all year!

Other programs and instructional strategies focus on enabling students to participate in the meeting as an equal member of the interdisciplinary team. Whatever the role students eventually assume, be it chair or team member, students need to learn the skills that enable them to identify their preferences and make choices based on those preferences (see Chapter 5); set goals based on their needs, interests, and preferences (see Chapter 9); weigh options and consequences to reach decisions (see Chapter 6); and use assertiveness, self-advocacy, and effective teamwork skills (see Chapters 10 and 11).

The transition planning process provides an ideal setting in which students can 1) learn and practice self-determination skills such as goal setting, decision making, or self-advocacy; 2) generalize previously learned self-determination skills to another setting; and 3) take greater control over their lives, thus fostering positive self-efficacy and perceptions of control. Unfortunately, far too many IEP or transition meetings are viewed only as bureaucratic requirements, scheduled for the convenience of professionals, which become, essentially, a vehicle by which predetermined, professional-generated goals and programs are rubber stamped. Involving students in this type of a meeting will, no doubt, have opposite effects to those listed previously. Promoting student involvement in transition planning may first require systemic and significant changes in the transition planning process itself.

Implement the ITP through secondary school and adult services provision. Once the assessment process has been completed, and decisions regarding goals and instructional strategies reached, it is time to get down to the business of providing instruction in transition! This includes active student involvement in instruction and program implementation, described in detail in the next section.

Update the ITP annually during the IEP meetings and implement quarterly follow-up procedure; hold an exit meeting. The last two steps to effective transition planning identified by Wehman (1992) involve holding regularly scheduled follow-up and subsequent annual meetings and an exit meeting. Regular follow-up meetings provide the opportunity to both ensure that the transition program is being implemented properly, to identify additional people who need to be involved, and to enable students to report on progress. Students who have tracked progress on transition goals and objectives through some of the self-evaluation and self-monitoring strategies identified in Chapter 7 can use the follow-up meeting as a chance to generalize these skills.

In summary, a self-determination focus in transition planning involves active student involvement in educational planning and decision making and enables students to become equal partners in IEP and transition meetings. In many cases, however, there will need to be a significant change in the manner in which such meetings are conducted. Students can, and should, learn how to become more effective decision makers and problem solvers, how to communicate and negotiate more effectively, how to identify and assert their interests and preferences, and how to set and evaluate goals. By so doing, they will be able to play a key role in transition planning.

TRANSITION PROGRAM IMPLEMENTATION

Transition assessment and planning is conducted for one primary reason—the subsequent implementation of a student's transition program. It is just as important to involve students in the day-to-day instructional activities related to the attainment of transition goals and objectives as it is to involve them in the planning of these goals and objectives. As Agran suggested

> A fundamental shift in focus is occurring in special education. Rather than continue to rely on an instructional model in which the teacher is given full responsibility for *when, what, why, where* and *how* a student will learn, we are beginning to realize that there may be marked advantages in making the student more actively involved in educational decision-making, *as well as in the delivery of instruction itself* [italics added for emphasis]. (1997, p. 3)

A focus on self-determination does indeed change the when, what, why, where, and how of transition program implementation, as discussed in this section. The question of how a self-determination focus affects what to include in the transition program has been addressed in the sections related to transition assessment and planning. As we have suggested, a self-determination focus implies that 1) student skill needs related to self-determination are addressed by instruction and curriculum, and 2) students become active participants in transition assessment and planning. Likewise, this focus will affect when, where, and why students learn, and will particularly influence how they learn.

A self-determination focus changes the why of transition program service delivery in several ways. Kohn (1993) suggested that one of the most frequently overlooked aspects of the educational process is the need to involve students in talking about why they are learning. Students who are involved in transition-related activities need to understand that such programming is implemented to enable them to become more successful young people. If students see transition-related activities in that light, as opposed to viewing them as just more school-work imposed on them by others, they are more likely to assume responsibility for their own learning. Such an understanding emerges only from efforts to implement transition programs that are genuinely based on student interests and abilities and that have actively involved students in the planning and design of the program. A self-determination focus, in a sense, tells a student that the reason their transition program is in place is to assist them to achieve their dreams, goals, and aspirations.

Just as student involvement in transition planning typically necessitates changing the way meetings are conducted, so too involving students in program implementation will necessitate changes in the way instruction is delivered. Students should be provided more opportunities to choose when and where they work on transition-related activities. As an example of how to do this, Brown, Appel, Corsi, and Wenig (1993) identified seven ways to infuse choices into day-to-day instructional activities:

1.   Students can choose within an activity.
2.   Students can choose between two or more activities.
3.   Students can decide when to do an activity.
4.   Students can select the person(s) with whom to participate in an activity.
5.   Students can decide where to do an activity.
6.   Students can refuse to participate in a planned activity.
7.   Students can choose to end an activity at a self-selected time.

Students can participate in many decisions regarding when and where they learn transition-related skills. Indeed, because transition services must be provided in an outcome-oriented manner, it is important to ensure that students learn and/or generalize transition skills in environments in which they will employ such skills. Such environments will, by necessity, be determined based on student interests, abilities, and preferences. As such, work-related skills are better learned and rehearsed in work environments, leisure-related skills are better learned in the environment in which they will be used, and so forth.

Perhaps the most dramatic impact that a self-determination focus will have is on the how of transition program service delivery. Throughout this text we have described methods that place the learner in greater control of instructional activities, which have traditionally been activities assumed by teachers. These student-directed learning strategies include self-monitoring and self-reinforcement skills (see Chapter 7), self-instruction skills (see Chapter 8), goal-setting skills (see Chapter 9), choice-making skills (see Chapter 5), and decision-making and problem-solving skills (see Chapter 6).

Agran (1997) described student-directed learning strategies as "strategies to structure and facilitate [student] learning, independent of manipulation by other change agents (e.g., teachers, paraprofessionals, etc.)" (p. 4). Agran suggested five direct benefits to giving students the opportunity to direct and manage their own learning, noting that student-directed learning strategies

1. *Facilitate skills acquisition:* Considerable evidence, as presented throughout this text, illustrates that self-management strategies are effective ways to improve a broad range of academic and behavioral skills. So, first and foremost, student-directed learning strategies are effective ways to teach needed skills.
2. *Save teachers' time:* When students manage their own behavior and implement self-directed learning strategies, teachers are able to devote more time to teaching. Research confirms that teaching students to use self-management procedures reduces the amount of time used for the external management previously in place, which, in most cases, involves the teacher.
3. *Promote generalization:* Self-management strategies have been shown as effective means to promote generalization of skills across multiple environments. This is particularly important for students with more significant disabilities who frequently do not generalize skills learned in one environment to another.
4. *Promote cultural benefits of education:* Because the ultimate goal of our educational system is to create individuals who are self-reliant and independent, the use of self-management strategies moves us closer to that end and to the achievement of valued societal goals.

There would seem to be no better context in which to implement student-directed learning strategies than within the transition program delivery process. As was highlighted in Chapters 1 and 2, if we are to achieve the stated objectives of the transition process, educators must better enable students to become self-determined. Martin, Marshall, Maxson, and Jerman put this most succinctly:

> If students floated in life jackets for 12 years, would they be expected to swim if the jackets were suddenly jerked away? Probably not. The situation is similar for students receiving special education services. All too often these students are not taught how to self-manage their own lives before they are thrust into the cold water of post-school reality. (1993, p. 3)

TRANSITION PROGRAM EVALUATION

Kohler and colleagues (1994) found that one critical component of successful transition programs was the inclusion of program evaluation activities. The purposes for which program evaluation activities are implemented vary, from the desire to make periodic checks on progress to a need to formally summarize program achievements. This can occur from the molar (e.g., evaluation of an entire agency's program) to the molecular level (evaluating a single student's program outcomes). Particularly with the latter, a focus on self-determination will increase the need to involve students in evaluating the efficacy of their transition program, making design changes if necessary, and determining when (or if) to end interventions. Periodic checks of progress may identify the need to redesign the program or refocus instructional efforts to particularly problematic areas. Students can conduct these checks individually or in conjunction with their teacher, and they can work with the teacher to alter the program to continue to make progress. For example, students may determine that a specific task in a job is more problematic than had been predicted and suggest that more instructional time be devoted to that task.

In addition, students can assume more responsibility for determining when they have attained a specific outcome and need to move on to another goal or objective. Chapter 7 provided a number of student self-observation and self-monitoring strategies that might be put in place to enable students to identify when they have completed a goal. Students might graph progress on a specific activity and apprise the teacher when criterion mastery has been met on this activity. In the same manner that students are involved in assessment implemented to design instructional programs, they can likewise be involved in assessment activities implemented to evaluate the outcome of specific educational activities.

CONCLUSION

Since the passage of PL 94-142 (the Education for All Handicapped Children Act of 1975), considerable gains have been achieved in the degree to which students with disabilities learn the skills they need to become self-reliant, self-sufficient young people. However, transition follow-up and follow-along studies (see Chapter 3) have consistently documented the fact that students with disabilities leave school to face less positive outcomes than either desired or possible. This does not negate the efficacy of the many transition-related strategies that have been found to be effective over the years but instead suggests that more and different strategies need to be implemented if students are to ultimately succeed. We believe that focusing on self-determination as an educational and transition outcome is one such strategy.

As discussed in Chapter 3, Wehman (1993) identified issues of student choice and self-determination as one of the shortcomings of the original conceptualizations of transition and as one of the critical issues for transition in the next century. Returning to the questions posed at the beginning of Chapter 1 (What is the purpose of education?, What are the goals of education?), we concur with Halloran (1993) that one of the most important goals of education is to enable students to become self-determined—to be in control of their own lives and futures. Achieving this outcome will be as difficult and complex as, for example, the struggle to achieve employment and community integration for students with disabilities. We believe, however, that teachers have the tools they need to make this a reality. Teachers need to move independence and self-determination from being simply verbal constructs to actual real-life skills and activities that students practice throughout the day. With these experiences, students with disabilities will be more able to take control over and responsibility for their lives; become contributing, valuable members of communities; and experience a more positive quality of life.

REFERENCES

Agran, M. (1997). Teaching self-management. In M. Agran (Ed.), *Student directed learning: Teaching self-determination skills* (pp. 1–27). Pacific Grove, CA: Brooks/Cole.

Americans with Disabilities Act (ADA) of 1990, PL 101-336, 42 U.S.C §§ 201 *et seq.*

Brown, F., Appel, C., Corsi, L., & Wenig, B. (1993). Choice diversity for people with severe disabilities. *Education and Training in Mental Retardation, 28,* 318–326.

Browning, P., Dunn, C., & Brown, C. (1993). School to community transition for youth with disabilities. In R.C. Eaves & P.J. McLaughlin (Eds.), *Recent advances in special education and rehabilitation* (pp. 193–209). Boston: Andover Medical.

Clark, G.M. (1996). Transition planning assessment for secondary-level students with learning disabilities. In J.R. Patton & G. Blalock (Eds.), *Transition and students with learning disabilities: Facilitating the movement from school to adult life* (pp. 131–156). Austin, TX: PRO-ED.

Education for All Handicapped Children Act of 1975, PL 94-142, 20 U.S.C. §§ 1400 *et seq.*

Fetterman, D.M. (1996). Empowerment evaluation: An introduction to theory and practice. In D.M. Fetterman, S.J. Kaftarian, & A. Wandersman (Eds.), *Empowerment evaluation: Knowledge and tools for self-assessment and accountability* (pp. 3–46). Beverly Hills: Sage Publications.

Field, S., & Hoffman, A. (1996). *Steps to self-determination: A curriculum to help adolescents learn to achieve their goals.* Austin, TX: PRO-ED.

Fincham, F., & Barling, J. (1978). Locus of control and generosity in learning disabled, normal achieving and gifted children. *Child Development, 49,* 530–533.

Hallahan, D.P., Gajar, A.H., Cohen, S.B., & Tarver, S.G. (1978). Selective attention and locus of control in learning disabled and normal children. *Journal of Learning Disabilities, 11,* 47–52.

Halloran, W.D. (1993). Transition services requirement: Issues, implications, challenge. In R.C. Eaves & P.J. McLaughlin (Eds.), *Recent advances in special education and rehabilitation* (pp. 210–224). Boston: Andover Medical.

Halpern, A.S. (1994). The transition of youth with disabilities to adult life: A position statement of the Divisions on Career Development and Transition. *Career Development for Exceptional Individuals, 17,* 115–124.

Halpern, A.S., Herr, C.M., Wolf, N.K., Lawson, J.D., Doren, B., & Johnson, M.D. (1995). *NEXT S.T.E.P.: Student transition and educational planning. Teacher manual.* Eugene: University of Oregon.

Individuals with Disabilities Education Act (IDEA) of 1990, PL 101-476, 20 U.S.C. §§ 1400 *et seq.*

Johnson, J.R., & Rusch, F.R. (1993). Secondary special education and transition services: Identification and recommendations for future research and demonstration. *Career Development for Exceptional Individuals, 16,* 1–18.

Kohler, P. (1993). Best practices in transition: Substantiated or implied? *Career Development for Exceptional Individuals, 16,* 107–121.

Kohler, P.D., DeStafno, L., Wermuth, T.R., Grayson, T.E., & McGinty, S. (1994). An analysis of exemplary transition programs: How and why are they selected? *Career Development for Exceptional Individuals, 17,* 187–202.

Kohn, A. (1993). Choices for children: Why and how to let students decide. *Phi Delta Kappan, 75*(1), 8–20.

Lewis, K., & Taymans, J.M. (1992). An examination of autonomous functioning skills of adolescents with learning disabilities. *Career Development for Exceptional Individuals, 15,* 37–46.

Martin, J.E., & Huber Marshall, L.H. (1996). *ChoiceMaker self-determination transition assessment.* Longmont, CO: Sopris West.

Martin, J.E., Marshall, L.H., Maxson, L., & Jerman, P. (1993). *Self-directed IEP: Teacher's manual.* Colorado Springs: University of Colorado, Center for Educational Research.

Nowicki, S., & Duke, M.P. (1974). A locus of control scale for non-college as well as college adults. *Journal of Personality Assessment, 38,* 136–137.

Rogers, H., & Saklofske, D.H. (1985). Self-concepts, locus of control and performance expectations of learning disabled children. *Journal of Learning Disabilities, 18,* 273–278.

Salvia, J., & Ysseldyke, J.E. (1981). *Assessment in special and remedial education* (2nd ed.). Boston: Houghton Mifflin.

Sands, D.J., Adams, L., & Stout, D.M. (1995). A statewide exploration of the nature and use of curriculum in special education. *Exceptional Children, 62,* 68–83.

Sigafoos, A.D., Feinstein, C.B., Damond, M., & Reiss, D. (1988). The measurement of behavioral autonomy in adolescence: The Autonomous Functioning Checklist. In C.B. Feinstein, A. Esman, J. Looney, G. Orvin, J. Schimel, A. Schwartzberg, A. Sorsky, & M. Sugar (Eds.), *Adolescent psychiatry* (Vol. 15, pp. 432–462). Chicago: University of Chicago Press.

Smith, D.J., & Nelson, J.R. (1997). Goal setting, self-monitoring, and self-evaluation for students with disabilities. In M. Agran (Ed.), *Student directed learning: Teaching self-determination skills* (pp. 80–110). Pacific Grove, CA: Brooks/Cole.

Swanson, L. (1980). Cognitive style, locus of control, and school achievement in learning disabled females. *Journal of Clinical Psychology, 36,* 965–967.

Swanson, L. (1981). Locus of control and academic achievement in learning disabled children. *Journal of Social Psychology, 113,* 141–142.

Wehman, P. (1992). *Life beyond the classroom: Transition strategies for young people with disabilities.* Baltimore: Paul H. Brookes Publishing Co.

Wehman, P. (1993). Transition from school to adulthood for young people with disabilities: Critical issues and policies. In R.C. Eaves & P.J. McLaughlin (Eds.), *Recent advances in special education and rehabilitation* (pp. 178–192). Boston: Andover Medical.

Wehmeyer, M.L. (1993a). Factor structure and construct validity of a locus of control scale with individuals with mental retardation. *Educational and Psychological Measurement, 53,* 1055–1066.

Wehmeyer, M.L. (1993b). Gender differences in locus of control scores for students with learning disabilities. *Perceptual and Motor Skills, 77,* 359–366.

Wehmeyer, M.L. (1994a). Perceptions of self-determination and psychological empowerment of adolescents with mental retardation. *Education and Training in Mental Retardation and Developmental Disability, 29,* 9–21.

Wehmeyer, M.L. (1994b). Reliability and acquiescence in the measurement of locus of control with adults with mental retardation. *Psychological Reports, 75,* 527–537.

Wehmeyer, M.L., & Kelchner, K. (1995a). Measuring the autonomy of adolescents and adults with mental retardation: A self-report form of the Autonomous Functioning Checklist. *Career Development for Exceptional Individuals, 18*, 3–20.

Wehmeyer, M.L., & Kelchner, K. (1995b). *The Arc's self-determination scale.* Arlington, TX: The Arc National Headquarters.

Wehmeyer, M.L., & Schwartz, M. (1997). Self-determination and positive adult outcomes: A follow-up study of youth with mental retardation or learning disabilities. *Exceptional Children,* Vol. 63, pp. 245–255.

Wehmeyer, M.L., & Schwartz, M. (in press). The relationship between self-determination and quality of life for adults with mental retardation. *Education and Training in Mental Retardation and Developmental Disabilities.*

Wehmeyer, M.L., & Ward, M.J. (1995). The spirit of the IDEA mandate: Student involvement in transition planning. *Journal of the Association for Vocational Special Needs Education, 17,* 108–111.

Williams, R. R. (1989). Creating a new world of opportunity: Expanding choice and self-determination in lives of Americans with severe disability by 1992 and beyond. In R. Perske (Ed.), *Proceedings from the National Conference on Self-Determination* (pp. 16–17). Minneapolis: Institute on Community Integration.

Wolman, J.M., Campeau, P.L, DuBois, P.A., Mithaug, D.E., & Stolarski, V.S. (1994). *AIR self-determination scale and user guide.* Stanford, CA: American Institute on Research.

Index

Page numbers followed by "t" denote tables; those followed by "f" denote figures.